SHIFTING FRONTIERS IN FINANCIAL MARKETS

FINANCIAL AND MONETARY POLICY STUDIES

volume 12

SHIFTING FRONTIERS IN FINANCIAL MARKETS

Published by Martinus Nijhoff Publishers on behalf of
the Société Universitaire Européenne de Recherches Financières (SUERF)

For a list of the volumes in this series see final page of the volume.

SHIFTING FRONTIERS IN FINANCIAL MARKETS

Edited by

Donald E. Fair

with contributions from:

Marie-Christine Adam
Akbar Akhtar
Richard Aspinwall
Andrew Bain
Morten Balling
Didier Bruneel
Carlo Cottarelli
Franco Cotula
Michel Develle
André Farber
Charles Freedman
Wolfgang Gebauer
David Gilchrist

Charles Goodhart
Christopher Johnson
Jan Koning
Patrick Lawler
Robin Leigh-Pemberton
Mario Monti
Giovanni Battista Pittaluga
Jack Revell
Tadeusz Rybczynski
Hartmut Schmidt
Niels Thygesen
Pehr Wissén

1986 **MARTINUS NIJHOFF PUBLISHERS**
a member of the KLUWER ACADEMIC PUBLISHERS GROUP
DORDRECHT / BOSTON / LANCASTER

Distributors

for the United States and Canada: Kluwer Academic Publishers, 190 Old Derby Street, Hingham, MA 02043, USA
for the UK and Ireland: Kluwer Academic Publishers, MTP Press Limited, Falcon House, Queen Square, Lancaster LA1 1RN, UK
for all other countries: Kluwer Academic Publishers Group, Distribution Center, P.O. Box 322, 3300 AH Dordrecht, The Netherlands

Library of Congress Cataloging in Publication Data

```
Main entry under title:

Shifting frontiers in financial markets.

  (Financial and monetary policy studies ; 12)
  1. Capital market--Congresses.  2. Money market--
Congresses.  3. Finance--Congresses.  I. Fair, Donald E.
II. Series.
HG4523.S54 ▪1985        332        85-18821
ISBN 90-247-3225-5
```

HG
4523
S54
1986

ISBN 90-247-3225-5 (this volume)
ISBN 90-247-2605-0 (series)

Copyright

© 1986 by Martinus Nijhoff Publishers, Dordrecht.

PRINTED IN THE NETHERLANDS

CONTENTS

Preface IX

About the Editor and Authors XI

Part A
OPENING ADDRESSES 1

Chapter I
Introduction
by *Mario Monti* 3

Chapter II
Shifting Frontiers in Financial Markets: their Causes and Consequences
by *Robin Leigh-Pemberton* 9

Chapter III
What Monetary Targets in an Evolving Financial System? An Introductory Address
by *Niels Thygesen* 19

Chapter IV
Recent Changes in the Financial System: a Perspective on Benefits versus Costs
by *M. Akbar Akhtar* 31

Part B
CAUSES OF CHANGE AND INNOVATION IN THE MIX OF
FINANCIAL INSTRUMENTS 43

VI

Chapter V
Developments on the French Capital Markets in Recent Years
by *Didier Bruneel* 45

Chapter VI
Causes of Change and Innovation in the Mix of Financial Instruments: The New Emphasis on Small Company External Equity Financing and its Impact on Capital Market Structure
by *Hartmut Schmidt* 65

Chapter VII
The Birth of a New Market – The Case of the Swedish Money Market
by *Pehr Wissén* 79

Chapter VIII
Causes of Change and Innovation in the Mix of Financial Instruments: the UK Experience
by *Andrew D. Bain* 91

Chapter IX
Change and Innovation in Borrowing Patterns: Three American Cases
by *Patrick Lawler* 109

Part C
THE COST OF CAPITAL FUNDS AND THE FINANCING OF GROWTH 125

Chapter X
Real Rates and Capital Investment: a Fisher-Wicksell Perspective
by *Wolfgang Gebauer* 127

Chapter XI
A Few Insights into the Phenomenon of Real Interest Rates in the 1980s
by *Michel Develle* 141

Chapter XII
Interest Rates and Inflation: European v. US Evidence 1960–1984
by *Marie-Christine Adam* and *André Farber* 165

Part D
IMPLICATIONS FOR FINANCIAL INSTITUTIONS 181

Chapter XIII
Deposit Rate Discrimination: Effects on Bank Management and
Monetary Policy in Italy
by *Carlo Cottarelli, Franco Cotula* and *Giovanni Battista Pittaluga* 183

Chapter XIV
Deregulation: Implications for British Building Societies
by *David Gilchrist* 207

Chapter XV
Shifting Institutional Frontiers in Financial Markets in the United
States
by *Richard Aspinwall* 223

Chapter XVI
Implications of Information Technology for Financial Institutions
by *Jack Revell* 241

Chapter XVII
Shifting Financial Frontiers: Implications for Financial Institutions
by *Tadeusz M. Rybczynski* 257

Part E
IMPLICATIONS FOR MONETARY CONTROL AND THE
SUPERVISION OF FINANCIAL INSTITUTIONS 271

Chapter XVIII
Recent Developments in the Structure and Regulation of the Canadian Financial System
by *Charles Freedman* 273

VIII

Chapter XIX
Shifting Frontiers in Financial Markets and Adjustments of Supervisory Systems
by *Morten Balling* 287

Chapter XX
The Implications of Shifting Frontiers in Financial Markets for Monetary Control
by *Charles A.E. Goodhart* 303

Chapter XXI
Financial Innovation and Monetary Aggregate Targeting
by *Jan H. Koning* 329

Part F
REPORT ON THE COLLOQUIUM 343

Chapter XXII
General Report
by *Christopher Johnson* 345

PREFACE

The papers collected in this volume are those presented at the twelfth Colloquium arranged by the Société Universitaire Européenne de Recherches Financières (SUERF) which took place in Cambridge in March 1985.

The Society is supported by a large number of central banks, commercial banks and other financial and business institutions, by treasury officials and by academics and others interested in monetary and financial problems. Since its establishment in 1963 it has developed as a forum for the exchange of information, research results and ideas, valued by academics and practitioners in these fields, including central bank officials and civil servants responsible for formulating and applying monetary and financial policies.

A major activity of SUERF is to organise and conduct Colloquia on subjects of topical interest to members. The titles, places and dates of previous Colloquia for which volumes of the collected papers were published are noted on the last page of this volume. Volumes were not produced for Colloquia held at Tarragona, Spain in October 1970 under the title 'Monetary Policy and New Developments in Banking' and at Strasbourg, France in January 1972 under the title 'Aspects of European Monetary Union'.

In choosing 'The Shifting Frontiers in Financial Markets' as the subject for Cambridge, SUERF's Council sought to focus attention upon several issues that still seem unsettled and which involve at least four sets of problems: the causes of change and innovation in the mix of financial instruments; the role attributable to the cost of capital in financing growth; the implications of the changes for financial institutions; and the implications for monetary control and for supervision of financial institutions.

The Colloquium was attended by about 170 participants, representing a wide range of financial activities and academic teaching and research in the financial field.

The Chairman of the Colloquium as a whole was the President of

SUERF, Professor Mario Monti. After his introduction, opening addresses were given by Mr. Robin Leigh-Pemberton, Governor of the Bank of England, Professor Niels Thygesen, University of Copenhagen and Mr. M. Akbar Akhtar, Assistant Director of Research, Federal Reserve Bank of New York; these appear in Part A of this volume, Chapters I–IV. The contributed papers which follow had been distributed beforehand and were discussed in four separate Commissions meeting simultaneously. The themes of the Commissions were: 'Causes of Change and Innovation in the Mix of Financial Instruments', chaired by Mr. Martinez Mendez and Mr. Robert Piloy (Part B, Chapters V–IX); 'The Cost of Capital Funds and the Financing of Growth', chaired by Mr. Conrad Reuss and Professor J.R. Sargent (Part C, Chapters X–XII); 'Implications for Financial Institutions', chaired by Dr. Fritz Diwok and Mr. Warren McClam (Part D, Chapters XIII–XVII); and 'Implications for Monetary Control and the Supervision of Financial Institutions', chaired by Professor W. Eizenga and Dr. H.E. Scharrer (Part E, Chapters XVIII–XXI). The Colloquium reassembled for a final plenary session at which a report on the proceedings of the Commissions was given by Mr. Christopher Johnson, Group Economic Adviser, Lloyds Bank (Part E, Chapter XXII).

In some cases minor changes have been made to the papers before publication.

As on previous occasions the Colloquium was strongly supported by the local financial community. Generous contributions were made by the London clearing banks – Barclays, Lloyds, Midland, National Westminster, Williams & Glyn's and Coutts; by American banks in London – Bank of America, Citibank, First National of Chicago, Chemical Bank, Chase Manhattan, Mellon, Bankers Trust, Manufacturers Hanover, Bank of New York, American Express, Security Pacific, Seattle-First National, Texas Commerce, and First Wisconsin; by building societies – Halifax, Woolwich, Nationwide, and National Provincial; by the British Insurance Association; and by the Trustee Savings Bank Group. A warm welcome was extended at a reception given by the British Bankers' Association.

The Colloquium was highly successful both in the quality of the papers and discussions and in the opportunity it provided for contacts between experts from so many different countries and financial institutions. For this success thanks were given to Professor Hans Bosman, the Secretary-General of SUERF, to Miss Annelies Vugs, the Executive Secretary, together with her assistant Mrs. Tineke Kleine-Vromans, for their excellent organisation and ever-ready assistance and to the two British members of the Council of Management, Professor J.S.G. Wilson and Professor J.R. Sargent.

Donald E. Fair

ABOUT THE EDITOR AND AUTHORS

Editor: *Donald E. Fair*, Consultant, City University Business School, London; formerly Economic Adviser, The Royal Bank of Scotland Group

Marie-Christine Adam, Professor, Université Libre, Brussels

M. Akbar Akhtar, Assistant Director of Research, Federal Reserve Bank of New York

Richard Aspinwall, Vice President, Chase Manhattan Bank, New York

Andrew D. Bain, Group Economic Adviser, Midland Bank, London

Morten Balling, Professor, Graduate School of Business Administration, Aarhus

Didier Bruneel, Director des Etudes et Statistiques Monetaires, Banque de France

Carlo Cottarelli, Servizio Studi, Banca d'Italia

Franco Cotula, Servizio Studi, Banca d'Italia

Michel Develle, Chief Economist, Banque Paribas, Paris

André Farber, Professor, Université Libre, Brussels

Charles Freedman, Adviser, Bank of Canada

Wolfgang Gebauer, Assistant Professor, European University Institute, Florence

David Gilchrist, General Manager, Halifax Building Society, Halifax

Charles A.E. Goodhart, Chief Adviser Monetary Policy, Bank of England

Christopher Johnson, Group Economic Adviser, Lloyds Bank, London

Jan H. Koning, Head of Department of Financial Statistics, Netherlands' Central Bureau of Statistics

Patrick Lawler, Economist, Division of Research and Statistics, Board of Governors of the Federal Reserve System

Robin Leigh-Pemberton, Governor, Bank of England

Mario Monti, Professor, Universita Bocconi; Economic Adviser, Banca Commerciale Italiana

Giovanni Battista Pittaluga, Servizio Studi, Banca d'Italia

Jack Revell, Professor, Director Institute of European Finance, University College of North Wales, Bangor

Tadeusz M. Rybczynski, Economic Adviser, Lazard Brothers & Co., London

Hartmut Schmidt, Professor of Banking and Finance, University of Hamburg

Niels Thygesen, Professor of Economics, Institute of Economics, University of Copenhagen

Pehr Wissén, Assistant Vice President, Svenska Handelsbanken, Stockholm

Part A

OPENING ADDRESSES

Chapter I

INTRODUCTION

by *Mario Monti*

It is a great pleasure to open the eleventh SUERF Colloquium on 'SHIFT-ING FRONTIERS IN FINANCIAL MARKETS'. This opening plenary session is intended to provide an overview, a critical perception of the underlying themes, and some elements of anticipation of future trends, concerning the changes which have occurred and are occurring every day in financial markets.

It is well known that the policy issues in this area are far from being completely solved – and by policy I refer not only to supervisory and monetary policies, but also to micro-policies of individual institutions. But, in many cases, also the analytic issues are far from being clearly settled.

The objective of this Colloquium is to focus on the several issues that appear to be still unsettled. These involve at least four specific sets of problems:

1. the causes of change and innovation in the mix of financial instruments;
2. the role that, in the new environment, can be attributed to the cost of capital funds in the financing of growth;
3. the implications of these changes for financial institutions;
4. the implications for monetary control and for the supervision of financial institutions.

These four subtopics, actually, are those that the Council of Management has thought should be assigned to our four commissions.

A few remarks will be sufficient to highlight the issues that we expect to be addressed by each commission.

COMMISSION I: CAUSES OF CHANGE AND INNOVATION IN THE MIX OF FINANCIAL INSTRUMENTS

Changes in the mix of financial instruments used by borrowers and by

Fair, D.E., (ed.) Shifting Frontiers in Financial Markets.
© *1986, Martinus Nijhoff Publishers, Dordrecht/Boston/Lancaster. ISBN 90-247-3225-5.*
Printed in the Netherlands.

lenders may to some extent be due to the changing relative importance of traditional categories, such as equities against fixed interest stocks, short as against medium or long maturities, and (for any given maturity) instruments with variable as against fixed nominal rates of interest. But the mix has also been enlarged and enriched by innovations, such as indexed bonds, bonds issued at a deep discount, instruments of one type carrying an option to convert into another, and futures contracts, while leasing provides an alternative to borrowing. At the same time facilities for borrowing and lending in foreign as well as domestic currencies have been greatly expanded.

An important underlying question is: to what extent do the observed changes in the use of financial instruments reflect shifts in the preferences of lenders (e.g. indexed bonds may appeal particularly to small individual investors) or the preferences of borrowers (e.g. when future inflation is difficult to predict, corporations may prefer to borrow at variable rates which should to some extent fluctuate with it). An important stimulus for the innovations in financial instruments may have been the need to accommodate these shifts.

The influence of the public sector as a borrower, in terms not only of the amount but also of the types of debt instruments it supplies to financial markets will be an important consideration; how much 'crowding out' has there actually been? Another important question will be the extent to which differences in tax treatment of different financial instruments affect the preferences of those who issue and those who hold them, and may thus distort the flows of savings into investment with consequences for the efficiency of the process for the economy as a whole. A similar question arises in connection with official requirements concerning the liquidity of financial institutions and (to a lesser extent) their capital adequacy.

An important general issue is how far there has been a tendency towards a greater degree of intermediation of saving-investment flows through financial institutions as a result of changing borrowers' and lenders' preferences, and/or as a result of greater competition between the financial intermediaries themselves. To what extent has a greater degree of intermediation resulted in greater indebtedness of the corporate sector? What are the implications for sustainable growth?

The Commission will also wish to consider how permanent the changes and innovations discussed are likely to be. For example, will some prove unnecessary, should the uncertainties created by high and variable rates of inflation in recent years subside?

COMMISSION II: THE COST OF CAPITAL FUNDS AND THE FINANCING OF GROWTH

Although the various factors which lead to changes in the mix of financial instruments, and fall to Commission I, also contribute to changes in the level and pattern of interest rates, the latter provide a distinct perspective on the general topic for Commission II.

In the foreground there is likely to be the question: why have interest rates remained so high relative to the current rate of inflation? The assumption behind the question may need some examination; it can be argued that interest rates are not as high as they appear when account is taken of tax deductibility of interest payments, government subsidies, amortization rules applied for tax purposes (in the case of borrowers), and preferential tax treatment of certain types of interest income (in the case of lenders).

To the extent that the assumption stands, it may be asked whether the high level of interest rates is simply because of time lags; e.g. lenders are slow to reduce their expectations of future inflation in line with current experience, and in the meantime want to get some compensation for losses in the past from the negative real interest rates of the 1970s. When time lags such as these have run their course, what sort of changes in the level and pattern of interest rates are likely to result from changes which have occurred or are likely to occur in borrowers' and lenders' attitudes? Does the evidence support the conventional wisdom that government deficits have played a major role, and particularly those in the USA? Has the increased emphasis which most countries have given to monetary targets in the last decade resulted in interest rates being higher on average as well as more variable? To what extent has deregulation of financial markets helped to contain interest rates through greater competition? Or has it contributed to their high level?

A second major theme for Commission II should be the impact of interest rates on the cost of risk capital and the incentive to invest. It may be that fixed investment has become more interest-elastic than it used to be thought to be, because declining profitability has caused businesses to rely more on external finance and the existing factor-mix has steadily been shifting in a more capital-intensive direction; what is known about the impact of interest rates on investment decisions in the industrialised economies today? Have savings in general, and/or the supply of particular types of funds, also become more interest-elastic as a result of increasing financial sophistication among the general public and/or of increasing competition among financial institutions for their savings? To the extent that both savings and investment have become more interest-sensitive, the effect should be to reduce fluctuations in interest rates, and thus to improve the environment within which business planning has to be done.

The questions above can be considered within the domestic context of individual economies, but are nowadays complicated by the internationalisation of borrowing and lending flows. The consequences of this will require discussion, both from the standpoint of how each economy is affected by what happens abroad and from that of how its own interest rates affect others (e.g. LDCs).

COMMISSION III: IMPLICATIONS FOR FINANCIAL INSTITUTIONS

The role of financial institutions has traditionally comprised:
(a) providing facilities for making and collecting payment;
(b) providing loans of short or longer terms;
(c) acting as a repository for the public's liquidity and/or its long-term savings.

Involvement in each of these activities to a greater or smaller extent, and with differing emphases within them, has given rise to institutional frontiers within the financial system which in some countries (e.g. the USA and the UK in particular) are now beginning to crumble. How far will changes in the general economic environment, and in lenders' and borrowers' preferences between particular financial instruments, be likely to accelerate this process where it is happening and to spread it to countries where it has hardly begun? Are there other factors than these, arising from social and political influences in different countries, which may be of more importance either in accelerating the process or retarding it or in giving it a different shape and direction? How far one can envisage a gradual multilateralisation of financial institutions, which involves not merely breaking down old frontiers between them but also extending them to include in their normal activities such functions as cash management services, financial advice, portfolio management, stockbroking and forecasting of exchange rates and interest rates? To what extent do conflicts of interest arise within financial institutions when they are offering services of different kinds (e.g. one department may be lending to a business while another should be advising its clients to sell its shares)?

Another issue is the extent to which institutional frontiers are shifting not only within the financial system but also between financial and non-financial corporations (e.g. the development of deposit-taking and credit-granting by commercial or industrial companies).

Other types of change would fall to Commission III for discussion. A particularly important one would be the impact of technological changes affecting in particular the money-transmission system, and their consequences for the costs of maintaining chequing accounts. In addition it would be necessary to consider the implications for the way in which financial institutions price their services of the various technological changes which can be envisaged, as well as of more general factors such as the greater variability of interest rates and the changing mix of assets and liabilities.

COMMISSION IV: IMPLICATIONS FOR MONETARY CONTROL AND THE SUPERVISION OF FINANCIAL INSTITUTIONS

The developments discussed by Commissions I and II have probably been influenced by official requirements laid upon banks and other financial institutions for the purposes of maintaining their liquidity and/or capital adequacy. The discussion in Commission IV is likely to overlap with this to some extent but should be concerned less with the effects that official requirements have had than with the extent to which they continue to be appropriate and effective in circumstances which are changing in one way or another. If official requirements are ceasing to be appropriate and effective, how will supervisory authorities seek to adapt them? Will their attempts to do so influence the direction which is taken by financial innovation in the future? Must the net of official requirements be cast ever wider to prevent escape from it.

The question of monetary control by the authorities needs to be kept distinct from that of supervision, but similar issues arise. Experience with the targeting of monetary aggregates in a number of countries has raised the question 'what is money?', and focussed attention on the appropriate choice of the financial aggregate to be targeted. But the choice made is liable to invite shifts in the use of financial instruments away from those included in the target aggregate (e.g. towards bankers' acceptances not included in banks' balance sheets). In the face of such shifts enabling the monetary constraints to be circumvented, what are the monetary authorities to do? Can targets for the growth of the money supply make correct enough allowance for the changes in the velocity of circulation of money which may result from financial innovation? Are such changes predictable by the monetary authorities? They may well feel it to be easier in a shifting environment to target, or have regard to, several measures of the money supply (narrow, broad, some measure of domestic credit). But does this make their actions more, or less, effective in achieving the sort of control which will keep inflation to a reasonably low rate while fostering sustainable growth in the economy?

This morning we have the great privilege to have with us the Governor of the Bank of England, Mr. Robin Leigh-Pemberton. It would be improper for me to present the Governor. May I just say how honoured and grateful we are that he has agreed to be with us and to deliver the opening-address. Not only, Mr. Governor, you bring us the prestige and the flavour of that unique institution, the Bank of England, but you are also a uniquely qualified person to address our subject today, as you bear in your personality the most unusual combination of a distinguished background in commercial banking and of your present role of Governor of such a key central bank.

After the Governor's speech, this plenary session will continue with two other prominent speakers, who have been combining with great distinction academic scholarship and involvement in policymaking in their respective countries as well as at the international level: Prof. Niels Thygesen of the University of Copenhagen and Mr. Akbar Akhtar of the Federal Reserve Bank of New York.

Chapter II

SHIFTING FRONTIERS IN FINANCIAL MARKETS: THEIR CAUSES AND CONSEQUENCES

by *Robin Leigh-Pemberton*

INTRODUCTION

I should like to thank your President, Professor Mario Monti, for his kind words of introduction and to congratulate him on choosing a subject for this Colloquium that is not only apposite, but also of particular immediacy. Such a clear-sighted appreciation of the key issues of the day in financial affairs was to be expected from your President, for we have long admired him in this country as one of the foremost European experts on banks and banking. I am sure your Colloquium will be both thought-provoking and relevant, and I look forward with more than academic interest to learning your conclusions.

The title of the Colloquium encourages us to consider how the frontiers of financial markets may have shifted. But I wonder whether this goes far enough; indeed whether in many cases it is still possible to identify clear dividing lines between differing kinds of financial instrument, or differing kinds of financial intermediary. Is it true that recognizable frontiers within the financial system still exist?

RECENT HISTORY IN THE UK

The extent of innovation and change within the financial system, not only in this country but in several others during the last two decades, has been virtually unprecedented. The only possible comparison, for the UK at least, is perhaps with the structural change that occurred in the mid-19th century: then the development of commercial banking, particularly the joint stock banks and their expanding network of branches, the appearance of specialist mortgage lending institutions, more extensive marketing of insurance, and the shift from payment primarily by notes to transfers between bank accounts, all took place around the same time. For a century thereafter, the

Fair, D.E., (ed.) Shifting Frontiers in Financial Markets.
© *1986, Martinus Nijhoff Publishers, Dordrecht/Boston/Lancaster. ISBN 90-247-3225-5.*
Printed in the Netherlands.

basic structure of the financial system in this country remained broadly constant.

Despite improvements in communications and other relevant technologies the nature of the individual institutions, and the work of the people in them, changed little. Thackeray, if not Charles Dickens, would have had no difficulty in appreciating the nature of the work of a commercial banker, or stockbroker, or jobber, or insurance salesman.

This constancy of role began to change first in the wholesale money markets during the 1960s. The story of the growth of the eurocurrency market, and of its development in London, is well-known. Since then the tide of innovation has advanced further beyond wholesale money markets into both the retail deposit and capital markets. Let me turn first to the retail deposit market. Here the development of new technology, such as the automated teller machine, together with the increasing competition between building societies and banks, has led to a whole new range of services being offered to the public. Consequently, whereas there used to be relatively clear divisions between the characteristics of sight deposits, the clearing banks' seven day deposits, building society shares and deposits, and fixed longer term deposits, these distinctions are being progressively eroded. Instruments offered by building societies now cover virtually the whole spectrum of maturities, while the banks, in turn, are competing by offering near market rates on a range of deposits with varying forms of transactions facilities. Moreover, the building societies are hoping to extend their facilities further by issuing cheque cards and providing overdrafts, when allowed by prospective legislation.

Part of this greater competition for deposits has gone hand in hand with increased competition in lending. After the 'corset' constraint over bank operations was abolished in 1980, the banks moved into the mortgage market. In turn, the building societies have expanded their lending facilities to the personal sector. In face of such mutual encroachment on each other's business, the distinctions and frontiers between banks and building societies are becoming more blurred.

The pace of events appears even faster in our capital markets, where, as you know, there are to be radical changes in the method of trading after the abandonment of minimum commissions and the admission of corporate members to the Stock Exchange, in which both equity shares and bonds, including Government bonds, are traded. By their very nature many of these changes can hardly be made gradually: there is to be a 'big bang'. We, in the Central Bank, have a number of specific concerns about all this, in addition to our general concern for the good health and efficiency of the financial system. We wish to see as liquid a market as possible with adequate protection for investors; we are also anxious to ensure the continuing successful functioning of the market in gilt-edged stocks, and our ability to sell sufficient quantities of government debt to maintain sound monetary conditions. Another concern is that supervision should achieve its objectives without stifling the forces of continuing evolution in the capital markets.

DEVELOPMENTS ABROAD

While the recent pace of change in this country has had no parallel for some hundred years, it has been matched by similar kinds of change in many other countries, including the United States, Canada, South Africa, Japan and Australia. In the US, for example, the blurring of distinctions between banks and Savings and Loan institutions is very similar to developments in this country. Although payment of interest on demand deposits is still legally prohibited, sufficient loopholes have been found to make the distinctions between demand deposits and other short-term deposits somewhat fuzzy, again as in this country. Moreover, the development of many new financial instruments, and the markets on which they are traded, such as financial options and futures, have been pioneered there. Even so, there remain important barriers, often fixed by legislation (such as the Glass-Steagall and McFadden Acts), which constrain what the various financial intermediaries can and cannot do. The greater legislative involvement in the working of the financial system in the United States, and their preference for checks and balances, which, for example, results in many different supervisory bodies, both at the state and federal level, leads in some cases to a certain immobility, though this at times may be no bad thing. Innovation, however, then tends to be directed largely to the exploitation of legal loopholes, not always the best way forward. The difficulties of changing legislation when very strong vested interests have to be placated have been reinforced recently by a certain hesitation about the desirable extent and direction of change, partly associated with the difficulties experienced by a number of US banks over the past year or so.

Similarly, in Japan, the financial system has for some time been undergoing a process of gradual change, which has recently accelerated in response to both external and internal pressures. One particular aspect of change in Japan – the relaxation of exchange control at the end of 1980 – has had a major effect on international macro-economic developments within the last couple of years. Thus the ability of Japanese savings institutions to diversify a proportion of their assets abroad has combined with a sizeable interest rate differential in favour of the United States given rise to a portfolio outflow amounting in 1984 to almost $50 billion – almost half as much again as Japan's current account surplus – a large part of which has been invested in US bonds. Further change in Japan, both actual and in prospect, involves a gradual breaking down of the segmentation of financial institutions, the establishment of a more market-oriented interest rate structure, the introduction of new monetary instruments, the greater international use of the yen and freer access for foreign institutions to Japan's financial markets. Their system has underpinned a remarkable economic performance and I find understandable the wish of the Japanese authorities, in the face of the broad range of change which is in the air, and which conflicts with the hitherto highly regulated nature of Japan's financial markets, to seek to control its pace and avoid the dangers of monetary instability.

In comparison with this scene of rapid structural change in the US, UK and Japan, there is much less sign of fundamental change in most Continental European countries. There are no doubt a number of reasons, which will differ as between countries. In some respects, Germany, for example, may be ahead of the game which we are starting to play. All, or most, financial services are already available in German universal banks, so there may be less pressure for structural change there. The German financial system has already reached an advanced stage of integration but the variety of financial instruments available to German investors domestically is relatively limited. The reasons for the relatively slow pace of change in some other European countries may be rather different. In a few of these, government regulations, in the form, for example, of exchange controls and direct controls over the allowable business of the various intermediaries, may have had some restraining effect on innovation. I do not, however, have the time today to examine, in any depth, why the present pace of institutional change seems to be slower in most of Continental Europe than in the Anglo-Saxon countries, but it remains an intriguing question.

CAUSES OF STRUCTURAL CHANGE

What are the main explanations for the recent acceleration in structural change among the Anglo-Saxon countries? One reason why it may have been greater in the US and the UK is that the thrust of policy there has moved particularly towards a greater reliance on markets, which in turn has pointed towards deregulation. A second, more economic, factor distinguishing them from Germany, is the greater volatility and level of both interest rates and inflation in the last 25 years. Some of the changes in instruments, markets, and financial behaviour, have been primarily defensive, to allow financial intermediaries to protect both themselves, and in some cases their clients, against the worsening uncertainties and risks caused by such volatility. For example, the risks inherent in having a mismatched maturity or currency structure of assets and liabilities clearly increase with more volatile interest and exchange rates. This has led some financial intermediaries to make innovations enabling them to achieve a more closely matched book, and to shift risk to those who are more prepared to absorb it. These include a switch to variable rate lending, replacing fixed rate loans, and the development of instruments such as options, futures and swaps. There is also the development of a secondary market in such instruments as mortgages, and a recent more general trend towards making loans, especially in the international context, in a manner which enables them to be subsequently sold in a secondary market. All these are developments which better enable the individual intermediary to adjust its own liquidity and risk position through market operations.

While these developments are generally welcome and *may* help to reduce risk overall, some caveats should be mentioned. Although these developing markets do generally enable risk to be transferred from those who wish to hedge to those who are prepared to assume additional risk, the overall level of risk within the financial system is not *necessarily* reduced. Moreover, while these new developments allow intermediaries to reduce their exposure to certain kinds of risk, they may increase other kinds of risk, which, being less familiar and less well understood, may be more insidious. For example, the transformation of much lending on to a variable rate basis, while protecting the lending financial institution from unpredictable changes in interest rates, by the same token imposes unpredictable fluctuations in cash flow onto the borrowers. Borrowers' credit risk may thereby worsen. That this is no mere hypothetical possibility is demonstrated by the debt problem of certain LDCs.

Even though this kind of market innovation was essentially a reaction to worsening inflation and more volatile interest and exchange rates, I doubt whether the restoration of more stable prices and interest rates would restore the status quo ante. Some risks arising from the unpredictability of interest rates, equity prices and exchange rates will always remain with us, even if to a lesser extent than recently. There are also large set-up costs in founding a new market. Once those costs have been incurred, an established market is likely to continue to operate, even when the incentives that led to its foundation become less pressing. And once customers become used to the wider range of services, and better yields, available, they will not want to revert to the previous state.

Important though this essentially defensive response to worsening risk may have been, I do not regard it as the main factor underlying the recent structural changes; for many of the new initiatives have been undertaken by firms striving for a larger share of the market. The erosion of barriers between different classes of business induces new participants to seek to fight their way into markets which had hitherto been closed to them. One way of doing so is to offer a product which is, or could at least be described as, a new product. In the international bond market, for example, much ingenuity is currently being expended on innovative instruments. Furthermore, I would place a lot of weight on the extraordinary development of communications generally. These have brought about, during the last two decades, virtually a one-world integrated money and capital market encompassing the large multi-national banks, companies and sovereign country borrowers. The pressure of competition in these markets is now world-wide. Even beyond the effect on the international, offshore markets, themselves, this inevitably provides a spur to efficiency in each individual country's markets, except where blunted by exchange controls or other barriers. Perhaps the primary reason for change in our own capital markets is to provide a stimulus for competition. There is, I am confident, a great future for the City of London, but that future will depend, in this acutely competitive world, on our institutions and methods being as cost efficient as any in the world.

Similar competitive pressures in domestic markets are leading to the development of new technologies to extend more efficient, lower cost methods from large customers in wholesale markets to smaller customers in retail markets. Thus corporate treasurers of large companies can now be linked electronically to information on yields available on assets, both domestically and internationally; and can initiate financial transactions virtually instantaneously. But these kinds of electronic wizardry are not going to remain available only to the large customer. The electronic provision of information to the retail market, together with the possibility of initiating financial transfers at the point of sale, at work or at home, is already technically available. The costs and difficulties of extending such electronic banking to all will be considerable, and the process may well be protracted, but it will surely take place. May these developments imply a further proliferation of financial transactions remote from the reality of productive activity? How confident can we be that the direction of causality runs only from volatile financial markets to sophisticated innovation and not, at least in part, the other way?

ECONOMIES OF SCALE AND SCOPE?

I hope that this Colloquium will consider whether the factors that have led to the recent surge of innovation might also influence the pattern of economies of scale and scope within the financial system, and thus affect the size and structure of financial institutions. There are already many who believe that these new developments *are* changing the nature of the industry. Some believe that the future lies with the very big battalions, the huge conglomerates, able to offer their clients comprehensive financial services ranging from banking to access to all the main financial markets, at home or abroad. On this view the future financial system would comprise relatively few such giants, together with a fringe of small specialists confined to a particular locality or skill. There is a fear that medium sized institutions, whether building societies, banks or stockbrokers, are going to face a difficult future. I am not myself convinced that this is going to be the case. Some of the technological developments, for example home banking, may by their nature reduce, rather than increase, economies of scale, in this case by contracting the branch network needed. Again some forms of inter-firm linkages and associations may enable financial institutions to provide comprehensive services without having everything in-house. While there is now something of a fashion for financial intermediaries to take on an everwidening range of function, beyond their original field of specialisation, there remain certain advantages to maintaining some degree of specialisation. In particular, managers are ordinary mortals, and not supermen. One advantage of the specialist organisation is that its managers can more easily be fully appraised of the business and competent to direct it in every respect. As the scope and scale of financial conglomerates increase, especially if financial activities are combined with non-financial businesses of quite another kind, will the management have quite the same competence, insights and understanding of the business done by the various segments? It is widely recognised that the potential conflicts of interest in a financial conglomerate will require restriction on information flows between their constituent parts, and regulators may require dedication of capital to particular functions in free-standing subsidiaries. Under these circumstances one needs to think carefully about how much synergy remains to give the whole conglomerate advantages over the mere sum of its parts.

COMPETITIVE PRESSURES ON PROFITABILITY

I also wonder whether the structural changes now in process in this country may be leading some of those involved to anticipate opportunities for profit that might in practice not be realised. Indeed, the pressures of competition are already paring profit margins severely in some areas. For example, the operating margins being earned by building societies have shrunk recently to levels that are both historically low, and low in comparison with other institutions. Admittedly, the building societies operate in a special context: but are their circumstances, and the circumstances of the housing market more generally, such that one can view this development with equanimity?

Indeed competition is now quite generally holding down the profitability of financial intermediaries. In many ways such competitive pressures are healthy, providing the incentive for dynamism, efficiency, and innovation. Yet these come at a time when markets have been exhibiting considerable, perhaps unprecedented, volatility; so the riskiness of intermediation is raised. Moreover, the structural changes we are witnessing have so changed the nature of the game that the risks many are now facing are less familiar, and so, perhaps, more troublesome.

PRUDENTIAL IMPLICATIONS

Such circumstances make supervisors uneasy. The combination of greater competitive pressure, together with unfamiliar and perhaps more serious risk, enhances certain inherent dangers. Gilbert claimed that a policeman's lot was not a happy one, but he could just as well have been referring to a supervisor. The supervisor must try to balance an acceptance, even an encouragement, of competition, and with that innovation which leads business into new and unfamiliar territory, against the various risks of financial difficulties, whose eventuality may bring down obloquy upon his head. Indeed, there are those who believe that the incentive on the supervisor to avoid financial collapses is so strong that over-regulation will tend to ensue. I do not know how far that charge would stick in the United States, but I do not think that in this country the supervisory authorities have unduly delayed and prevented developments and innovation in recent years. Trying to get the right balance between safety on the one hand and experimental growth and development on the other is never easy.

There are other, somewhat similar, points of tension in a supervisor's life. If the supervised institution would voluntarily undertake every measure that the supervisor would wish, the supervisor would then be superfluous. Supervision is only intrusive when it requires institutions to do something that they do not presently accept the case for doing anyhow themselves. In that sense all effective external supervision represents an additional burden, and usually additional cost, at least in the short run, on the financial institutions being supervised. Faced with such an extra burden, the financial institutions are likely, understandably, to try to avoid it. I would not want to exaggerate this. In many ways, of course, there is a common interest between the supervised and the supervisors. Both are concerned to maintain the good reputation of the system. Both are concerned that fly-by-night operators should not take advantage of the good reputation of existing intermediaries to defraud the public. Moreover supervision, though on occasions resented by the supervised, may be willingly accepted in the broad as a necessary concomitant for other measures, such as deposit insurance, or Central Bank lender of last resort action, which, in the absence of supervision, would be prone to provide an incentive to banks to assume additional risk; that is the standard problem of moral hazard. Yet, despite this general coherence of interest, there must remain an inherent tension between supervisor and supervised. In seeking to avoid the extra burdens that supervisors impose upon them, the business, and the exposure to risk, of the supervised institutions may change. So the supervisors are led in turn to seek to extend their supervisory activities to cope with such consequential changes.

Let me take a case in point. Concern about increased risk, and profit margins being squeezed by stronger competition, have led the supervisory authorities in most countries to encourage banks to raise their capital ratios. The need for extra capital was, from the viewpoint of the banker, seen as an additional burden. It has recently led banks to try, among other things, to develop more of their business off-balance sheet. Thus there is a growing tendency for banks to transfer part of their loan books to separate financial vehicles. There is a saying: 'out of sight, out of mind'. Perhaps the institutions feel that this applies to operations off-balance sheet: but does it? In some cases the risk associated with the business is formally transferred away from the bank but in all cases the transactions in question depend on the reputation and standing of the financial intermediary initiating them; and the reputation of that financial intermediary continues to be at stake, even though the asset may not be on its books.

Some might view this tendency for supervision to generate attempts at avoidance, leading to more supervision, as an argument for abandoning supervision altogether. There are those who would take the same argument and develop it to argue for the establishment of general, and tight constraints, or indeed public ownership, over the whole system of financial intermediation. This is a field, however, where I believe that common sense and compromise which we sometimes like to think peculiarly British virtues will continue to pay dividends.

PERORATION

The speed at which institutional structures are currently changing presents us with a number of difficulties not only as supervisors but also as managers of the money supply. While the right answers to these problems are seldom easy to identify I am quite sure that it would be wrong to try to avoid difficult choices by stifling change. As the form which change takes will depend on policy and supervisory practices, the process becomes one of interactive give and take between the supervisors and the supervised. Change might be allowed to proceed more freely the greater the degree of self imposed prudential restraint exercised by the participants both in structuring their balance sheets and in their conduct of competition. I will be most interested in the conclusions of your deliberations on these particularly difficult questions. I am sure that you will contribute to the illumination of the way ahead for us all.

Chapter III

WHAT MONETARY TARGETS IN AN EVOLVING FINANCIAL SYSTEM? AN INTRODUCTORY ADDRESS

by *Niels Thygesen*

INTRODUCTION

The theme of this colloquium – 'Shifting Frontiers in Financial Markets' – is certainly appropriate to the mid-1980s. We have witnessed in the recent past in nearly all industrial countries a speed-up in the evolution of financial markets and institutions through an interaction of market forces and a political readiness to respond to them constructively, though sometimes with reluctance and delay. The general impression in North America, Japan and Western Europe is one of financial-market frontiers shifting or losing their traditional significance in a process of osmosis. Can the undoubted gain in the efficiency of financial markets be perceived to outweigh the complications involved for monetary policy?

The rapid financial evolution has a direct bearing on both dimensions of the problems facing the monetary authorities in a broad sense, i.e. including the supervisory agencies. Their twin task is to foster an efficient financial sector and to conduct monetary policy in order to achieve macro-economic objectives, in particular low inflation. To use the terms with which a major policy reform was introduced in the United Kingdom in the early 1970s the aim is to have competition *and* credit control. The two need not be in conflict, as indeed the formulation suggests, though concerned comments by policy-makers often imply a trade-off between them.

It is an important purpose of this colloquium not only to help us to understand what is happening in financial markets, but also to see the implications for the design of monetary policy; this theme is explicitly raised in Commission IV. I want to address myself to this topic in our introductory session without trying to enter into any analysis of the nature of the competitive process in financial markets. Others in this colloquium will have a clear comparative advantage – and a substantial absolute one – over an applied macroeconomist in taking up this difficult and wide-ranging subject, and a number of papers in the present volume focus on it.

Fair, D.E., (ed.) Shifting Frontiers in Financial Markets.
© *1986, Martinus Nijhoff Publishers, Dordrecht/Boston/Lancaster. ISBN 90-247-3225-5.*
Printed in the Netherlands.

Despite this restricted and somewhat biased agenda I approach my chosen subject with considerable humility. Academic economists interested in money and finance often suffer from an inferiority complex vis-à-vis both their colleagues in more rigorous disciplines of economics and men with first-hand knowledge of financial markets. The former tend to regard the analysis of monetary processes as vague and unrigorous – though that is hardly justified by much of the recent monetary literature – while the latter can quickly make an academic uncomfortably aware of a lack of familiarity with financial institutions and instruments. It is more than difficult to meet both of these types of criticism at the same time; to the monetary economist there is some choice between rigour and relevance.

As an illustration of the first type of inferiority complex which may also serve as a point of departure for a review of our main theme of the colloquium, permit me a short digression. As a graduate student in the United States I chose one term to follow a seminar by Professor Leontief, who pioneered the analysis of sectoral linkages in the real economy. He assigned to me, as topic for a seminar paper, the applicability of some of the tools and results of input-output analysis to financial stocks and flows. One essential assumption of that analysis is that there is no substitution in production; deliveries to a sector from other sectors are linked, through a structure of fixed coefficients to the output of the receiving sector. The analogy with the financial 'requirements' of the main real sectors seems far-fetched, to say the least, in the light of the experience of the recent past. It seemed less far-fetched in the early 1960s, at least to someone coming from continental Europe where quantitative methods of credit control were widely used, capital flows still severely restricted and the financial structure more rigid – and I embarked on a review of the concepts of input-output analysis. My efforts did not satisfy Professor Leontief who launched into a sharp attack on monetary economics for being too vague and *ad hoc*. 'You must at least *start* from the assumption of a stable structure to get anywhere', he admonished. I wonder how short his patience would be today where that starting assumption is almost replaced by its mirror image, viz. that we are faced with a continuum of financial assets and liabilities within which it becomes increasingly difficult to single out individual and well-defined categories. The title of our colloquium reflects that perspective.

Yet the search for empirical regularities in the financial structure in the spirit that Leontief has pioneered for the real flows of goods and services should not be completely put aside under the general impression that they have been made unrewarding by the shifting of frontiers. For the purposes of monetary policy we still need some strategic intermediate variables to aim for. They will be different from those we thought of ten years ago when targets for the monetary aggregates came into fashion, but they will still be useful as guides in policy-making and as signals to the public.

After reviewing the experience with these targets briefly in the light of shifts both in and between national financial markets, I shall consider three targets that are likely to retain importance in the design of monetary policy: the monetary base, the exchange rate, and total credit. These two quantities and one price are likely to retain sufficient distinctiveness and precision to make them useful intermediate targets even in a world of shifting financial frontiers.

NATIONAL AND INTERNATIONAL CAUSES OF UNSTABLE SHORT-RUN MONEY DEMAND

When monetary targets for the main aggregates were introduced in the mid-1970s in a number of industrial countries this move was based on the view that the long-run demand function for real balances by the public was relatively stable. SUERF has the distinction of having put together, in the papers from its 1977 colloquium one of the most readable accounts of the reasoning behind that overhaul of monetary policy, see Wadsworth and de Juvigny (1979). This basic premise remains undisputed, and the, on average, moderate growth rates of the main monetary aggregates have certainly been an essential prerequisite for the deceleration in inflation that we have seen, particularly since 1980.

However, the introduction of targets had more ambitious aims than just to apply downward pressure on the long-run inflation rate. In most countries it was expected that even in the short-run the target would prove controllable, and that, in particular, it would provide an anchor for exchange rate expectations and actual exchange rate movements in a world of flexible exchange rates – provided, of course, that the partner countries were pursuing roughly parallel policies.

Among academic economists and particularly those labelled monetarists there has always been considerably more doubt about the short-run properties of the relation between money and income than about the long-run one. Milton Friedman's early writings express that main point vividly by underlining the long and variable time lags linking changes in money to those in nominal income. The new classical economists make a distinction between anticipated and unanticipated changes in money which have rather similar practical implications. The view of both the older monetarists and the new classical economists is that there is no stable short-run linkage between the money stock and income; economic agents are not more or less continuous in their longer-run demand function.

In a recent comprehensive, but also somewhat depressing, survey of empirical work on the demand for money in the United States Robert Gordon (1984) lists several reasons for this unstable relationship. He notes that what we usually classify as a demand function for money is essentially a hodgepodge of several relationships between the main variables that enter the demand for money: output, prices, the rate of interest and the chosen concept of money, or, more technically, a reduced form for a complex model of the economy. These other relationships are (1) the supply function of money, relating the money stock to the instruments of the monetary authorities through the responses of the banking system, (2) the policy reaction function of the monetary authorities themselves, and (3) the inflationary mechanism in the goods and labour markets as demand changes relative to equilibrium levels for capacity utilization and employment (the non-accelerating rate of unemployment). In a similar spirit Goodhart (1984) introduces the concept of 'disequilibrium money', linking observed instability particularly to the supply behaviour, i.e. to the counterparts to the creation of money in the form of bank lending and public sector borrowing. Neither of these two studies emphasizes financial innovation as a principal reason for the observed instability of money demand, but obviously these aspects are the least tractable of all in terms of empirical research.

These and other surveys demonstrate that the role of both of the two main determinants of the readiness of economic agents to demand the financial assets traditionally covered by the term 'money' – nominal income and the opportunity cost of holding money instead of higher-yielding domestic assets – has changed significantly over the past decade or so. A rapidly increasing share of both narrow and broad definitions of money now bears a market-related yield; as strikingly illustrated by Akhtar (1983). Since this prevents differentials between rates quoted by deposit-taking institutions and in the markets for short-term financial instruments from fluctuating as much as they did when there was a dominant element of administered pricing in the deposit market, the sensitivity of money demand to changes in market interest rates has declined almost to the point of insignificance. In technical terms, as Akhtar notes, the LM-curve has become nearly vertical.

As regards the role of nominal income as a determinant of money demand, there has been an even more important change. Because of the rise in the share of monetary assets, even within a narrow definition of money, yielding a market-related return, the transactions and investment purposes for holding money have become less easily separable. This has a consequence not unfamiliar to economists from Cambridge: whatever measure of the money stock chosen, from M1 to private sector liquidity in a broad sense, the role of wealth has increased relative to that of income as a determinant of money demand. At the same time, some of the non-monetary components of financial wealth have varied far more in recent years than in earlier periods. As interest rates in the bond market fluctuate more widely, the value of fixed-interest securities shifts around; and as share markets react promptly to 'news' about inflation or the outlook for earnings by firms and to interest rate changes, wealth movements may become increasingly divorced from income trends. This point would no doubt be reinforced if we were able to include the changing valuation of physical assets, e.g. housing, in measured wealth. It is no longer, as early research from the 1960s showed, a matter of near-indifference whether we choose wealth or income as the level variable in the demand for money function. Money has become a truly financial asset with strong implications for the linkage to income.

Finally, a third factor tending to destabilize traditionally observed relations between money and income has an international origin. What is the true meaning of national money in a financially integrated world? Close substitutes for national money exist today in the Eurocurrency markets and, indeed, in other national financial markets. The frontiers of national states have lost much of their monetary significance.

The more academic contributions to the debate on the quantitative importance of substitution between financial assets have typically been unable to find significant evidence on outright currency substitution, i.e. shifts between assets included in the national definition of money in different countries. Liberalization of financial transactions has been less complete for bank deposits and other short-term instruments than for bonds; it can also be argued, that to an investor potentially interested in financial assets denominated in a foreign currency, bonds will normally be a superior alternative to money, because for foreign bonds the risks associated with changes in exchange rates and in interest rates will to some extent offset each other. Despite these caveats currency substitution, even between narrow definitions of money (M1), becomes increasingly plausible in a world where transactions balances are well remunerated and a large number of both financial and non-financial firms have the option and the incentive to shift these balances. In any case, as Cuddington (1983) has shown, outright currency substitution is not necessary for international destabilization of national money-demand functions. One can obtain qualitatively similar effects and policy implications by assuming that there is capital mobility in the traditional sense – between bonds denominated in domestic and in foreign currency – and that both these assets are substitutes for domestic money. We do have evidence of a significant role for foreign interest rates and for (some measure of) exchange rate expectations in a large number of studies of national money-demand functions. Though some of these results may be partly attributable to the reactions of domestic policy-makers to foreign interest rate movements, i.e. to supply rather than demand factors, there can be little doubt that shifts in the frontiers of currency domains are a further cause for reflection about the appropriateness of targeting on domestic monetary aggregates.

To summarize, the demand function for money has become sufficiently unstable to offer less guidance for policy-makers than was hoped when targets for the monetary aggregates were introduced in the mid-1970s. Frontiers between money and other financial assets, both domestic and foreign, have become harder to draw; there is also some evidence of substitution between different national monies. Changes in interest rate differentials between money and other financial assets, which used to provide a powerful handle for bringing developments in the money stock back to a targeted course, have become difficult to bring about, because 'marketization' – to use the term of Bingham (1985) – has made the yield on money move with other rates.

It is too early to dismiss monetary aggregates as intermediate targets. They are not as unreliable as has been made out, and they have been less unstable than in the first 5–8 years after introduction. But it is necessary to look at alternatives that are more robust in the face of financial evolution. I shall assume without adequate discussion that the option of doing away with intermediate targets altogether and aiming directly at ultimate objectives is unattractive for two reasons: (1) the information required for implementing it is not available, and (2) there is a value in intermediate targets both in conveying signals to the public and in making the monetary authorities more accountable than they would be in the absence of such targets. What intermediate targets are preferable?

THE MONETARY BASE

While the components of the traditional definitions of money, as one moves from the narrower to the broader and beyond into nonmonetary assets, have tended to become a continuum of assets where transition from one group to the other is becoming increasingly difficult to draw, there is at least one clearly monetary asset which is not easily substituted for others. It has a demand function of considerable stability. I am referring to currency in the hands of the private sector.

If one were to move to a target for a concept that includes currency as the major component – the monetary base or the narrower so-called central bank money stock – one would be moving further away from an intermediate target controllable by the monetary authorities though closer to one that had reliable links to nominal income. As Bryant (1980) has reminded us in his monumental study policy-makers always face this choice if they want to use the intermediate-target framework. Would a largely currency-based target imply an abdication of central bank responsibilities for monetary control?

There are solid theoretical arguments, advanced most recently in a survey by Fama (1983), that targeting on currency plus limited volumes of bank reserves would be enough to assure longer-run control of the price level and that with such a system of control one need not be concerned with the competitive process inside the financial sector, which produces shifting frontiers. More important, the experience of some countries that have relied on a monetary base approach or one closely related thereto suggests the same conclusion – if, obviously, other policies are roughly in place. One may point, in particular, to the German variant of the monetary base approach in which the Bundesbank targets on the central bank money stock. The latter concept is the sum of currency and required reserves (at constant reserve ratios). This particular formulation assures that external disturbances show up largely outside the target variable, viz. in excess reserves in the banking system. Some other countries, including the United Kingdom, have moved towards regarding the monetary base as a potentially informative and useful intermediate target, at least in the 'relaxed' sense described in the 1980 Green Paper, reprinted in Bank of England (1984). Adoption of such a target may imply a low level of ambition to influence money income over the short to medium term, but a realistic attitude to the central longer-run task of inflation control. It needs, however, reinforcement from other targets.

THE NOMINAL EXCHANGE RATE AS A TARGET

One of the most unsatisfactory recent features of the international financial system has been the increasing short-term volatility of exchange rates and the severe misalignments which have marked the relationship between the major floating currencies. Economists and some national authorities, notably in the United States, have been too ready to accept the view that the exchange rate is just a price quoted in financial markets which must be expected to move sharply in response to new information about the economies concerned. Some add as a consolation that it is not even as unstable as share prices or other sensitive indicators of financial market pressures. This is hardly a satisfactory standard, given the central role of the exchange rate not only as a price in financial markets, but as the relative price of goods. It has been an important disappointment of monetary targeting (and an indication that the real money demand was unstable) that these targets did not imply roughly stable nominal exchange rates; approximately parallel policies were apparently pursued in the main industrial countries over much of the period of targeting. As already argued in the previous section, a purely domestic orientation of monetary policy is not stabilizing, if international factors cause the money demand function to shift. To contain the impact of such shifts there has to be some explicit external orientation of policy which brings the exchange rate into focus.

It would take this paper too far to comment on the feasibility of exchange rate targets or target zones for the major exchange rates. Proposals of this kind may appear totally devoid of interest in the present state of volatile exchange markets and misalignments between the dollar and other currencies which turned out to be more persistent than expected. They could soon become topical, if the misalignments were substantially corrected through a market reaction and the major countries perceived a joint interest in preventing further cycles of medium-term misalignments; an external orientation of monetary policy would be an essential element in such a strategy. As notably McKinnon (1984) has argued, there would in such circumstances be a strong case for some jointly set monetary targets for the major industrial countries taken together, and for adjusting the national shares of this international target according to signals from the exchange market. If a currency is appreciating out of the target zone vis-à-vis one or more other currencies, the authorities of that country should allow its monetary target to be overshot, because appreciation is a sign that the demand for national money has risen. Conversely depreciation is a signal that a downward shift has occurred, and that the monetary authorities should let its domestic monetary target be undershot. Such a policy rule of conditional targeting would deal automatically with the effects of shifts in the frontiers between money and other financial assets denominated in different currencies.

Very approximately, this type of policy rule is meant to underpin the fixed-but-adjustable exchange rate regime of the European Monetary System. Within the EMS the participating currencies have already to some extent implemented the proposal made by McKinnon to allow exchange market pressures to be reflected in the way in which monetary targets are met. Such a procedure does not require direct interventions in exchange markets, if there are objections to that; domestic policy actions may serve as well. In this way an exchange rate objective can go hand in hand with a monetary base target, when the latter is appropriately defined to exclude the most volatile elements of external flows.

It used to be said, in the light of the difficulties of managing the final stages of the fixed-but-adjustable rate system which prevailed globally up to 1973, that it had become too risky to maintain exchange rate objectives in a world of high capital mobility; domestic monetary policy would have to become fully subordinated and targets for any monetary aggregate would not be attainable. Experiences of the late 1970s and early 1980s suggest that combining unconstrained flexibility of exchange rates with high capital mobility can be even more dangerous. Since any effective controls on capital flows could hardly be implemented, even if there were agreement among the main countries to do so, a high degree of financial integration and the implied shifts in financial frontiers have to be accepted as the starting point for any consideration of national monetary targets. This strongly suggests that the information contained in exchange market pressures be used systematically and symmetrically to modify the growth rate of the monetary base.

A TARGET FOR DOMESTIC CREDIT EXPANSION IN A BROAD SENSE?

If the combination of monetary base and exchange rate objectives outlined become feasible after the present misalignments have abated, there may still be a need for a further intermediate target, which is robust to financial evolution and designed to facilitate the monitoring of the current account.

It was recognized from the 1960s by the International Monetary Fund that under (largely) fixed exchange rates the appropriate domestic monetary target was one of domestic credit expansion, i.e. a target for the domestic sources of money creation corresponding to a normal monetary aggregate target such as M3. Targets for domestic credit expansion could be set so as to generate a capital inflow (or outflow) sufficient to compensate for current account imbalances. Such a policy would keep the sum of the autonomous items in the balance of payments – or their mirror image, changes in foreign exchange reserves – under control. A number of countries, including the United Kingdom, have at one time or another in periods of fixed rates adopted programmes of this kind.

Since the DCE approach is based on the notion of a stable demand function for the corresponding domestic measure of money, its usability as a target is directly linked to the usefulness of domestic monetary targets. Both fall by the wayside if the latter is unstable. Since that is the premise of the preceeding analysis, one would have to look at a broader notion of credit than purely the counterparts to money creation in a world of shifting financial frontiers.

A deficit in the current account must correspond to an imbalance between the increase in total credit extended to the domestic sector from other domestic sectors and from abroad over the readiness of the domestic sector to accumulate domestic and foreign assets. In this relationship the possible operational intermediate target – at least if one abstracts from direct control of borrowing abroad – is total domestic credit extended to domestic sectors, or total internal credit to use the terminology applied to this target when it was first introduced in 1974, see, inter alia, the survey on Italian monetary policy in Wadsworth and de Juvigny (1979). If the monetary authorities allow total internal credit to accumulate more rapidly than the domestic sector is prepared to accumulate foreign and domestic assets a deficit on current account will result. The important point is not whether the domestic credit extended has a monetary counterpart, i.e. whether it is extended by a bank in direct lending or in the purchase of securities, or it is raised in the financial markets outside the banking sector.

An aggregate target for total internal credit may be expected to be more closely related to current demand in the economy and be less forward-looking than a monetary aggregate or a monetary base target. It could usefully supplement intermediate targets for the monetary base and the exchange rate by facilitating the monitoring of the current account.

CONCLUSIONS

The aim of the present brief survey of monetary targets in an evolving financial system has been to review targets that were as robust as possible in the face of shifts in financial frontiers. The monetary base, heavily weighted with currency has its strong point in the absence of close substitutes and stable demand, though the authorities will have to watch the downward trend of demand for currency due to technological progress in the payments mechanism. The exchange rate has the advantage of being a precise objective and one that can hardly be left to move as unconstrained as it has done in the period of flexible exchange rates over the past decade. Contrary to opinions often expressed, objectives with respect to the base and the exchange rate are not in obvious conflict; on the contrary, they may be mutually reinforcing, provided some flexibility is left in the management of the monetary base. The overall flow of internal credit, whether it has a monetary counterpart or not, is seen as a useful complement to the first two intermediate targets in monitoring demand in the economy and the current account.

It may seem a serious omission to make no mention of interest rates either as targets or instruments. The interpretation of interest rates is notoriously difficult in periods where the inflation rate remains unstable, while differences in the tax treatment within a country or between countries will render comparisons of different interest rates hazardous. In short, the general level of interest rates (if that can be defined) is hardly a possible target; interest rates must be retained as the main instrument for achieving the intermediate targets mentioned above.

There is also a more institutional reason for not advocating interest rate targeting, even though that may sound appealing in a world of shifting financial frontiers. Monetary targets were introduced as a way of removing the political onus of taking direct responsibility for setting interest rates from policy-makers and central banks. By pursuing monetary targets the authorities could argue that interest rates had been left free to find whatever level was appropriate in the light of demand and supply in financial markets.

The present paper may sound like the position of the Radcliffe Committee of 1959. That report also stressed the vagueness of measured monetary aggregates and emphasized interest rates, liquidity in a broad sense and credit. But the Report was overly negative in its assessment of stability in the relationship between money and income, particularly if one thinks in terms of a narrow aggregate such as the monetary base. Some empirical regularities of the type sought by Leontief do persist. There is a case for both such a target and for an aggregate target for total internal credit. Needless to say, the Radcliffe Report assumed the continuation of fixed exchange rates and the need implied by that constraint for giving monetary policy some external orientation. That very much remains with us as a need, regardless of the exchange rate regime, as recent events in the exchange markets have demonstrated.

REFERENCES

1. Akhtar, M.A. (1983), Financial Innovations and Their Implications for Monetary Policy: An International Perspective, *BIS Economic Papers* No. 9, Bank for International Settlements, Basle.
2. Bank of England (1984), *The Development and Operation of Monetary Policy 1960–1983,* London.
3. Bingham, T.R.G. (1985, forthcoming), *Banking and Monetary Policy,* OECD, Paris.
4. Blundell-Wignall, A. *et al.* (1984), The Demand for Money and Velocity in Major OECD Countries, *OECD Working Papers* No. 13, Economics and Statistics Department, OECD, Paris.
5. Bryant, R. (1980), *Money and Monetary Policy in Interdependent Nations,* The Brookings Institution, Washington D.C.
6. Committee on the Working of the Monetary System (1959), (the *Radcliffe Report*), Cmnd. 827, HMSO, London.
7. Cuddington, J. (1983), Currency Substitution, Capital Mobility and Money Demand, *Journal of International Money and Finance.*
8. Fama, E. (1983), Financial Intermediation and Price Level Control, *Journal of Monetary Economics,* July.
9. Goodhart, C.A.E. (1984), Disequilibrium Money, Ch. X in *Monetary Theory and Practice: The UK Experience,* London.
10. Gordon, R.J. (1984), The Short-Run Demand for Money: A Reconsideration, *Journal of Money, Credit and Banking,* November.
11. Lamfalussy, A. (1984), Address to the American Economic Association Annual Meeting (December), forthcoming in *American Economic Review,* May.
12. McKinnon, R.I. (1984), An International Standard for Monetary Stabilization, *Policy Analyses in International Economics* No. 8, Institute for International Economics, Washington D.C.
13. Treasury and Civil Service Committee (1981), *Third Report on Monetary Policy,* Volume II, House of Commons, London.
14. Wadsworth, J.E. and F.L. de Juvigny (eds.) (1979), *New Approaches to Monetary Policy,* SUERF, Alphen aan de Rijn.

Chapter IV

RECENT CHANGES IN THE FINANCIAL SYSTEM:
A PERSPECTIVE ON BENEFITS VERSUS COSTS*

by *M. Akbar Akhtar*

It is a great pleasure and an honor for me to address this distinguished group of economists and experts on financial matters. My introductory remarks are intended to offer a broad overview of this Colloquium, not to deal with any particular aspect of the recent experience with financial deregulation and innovations. That important task is handled by others in many specialized papers scheduled for discussions here. In providing an introduction to the recent changes in the financial system, I have collected my thoughts in terms of the actual or perceived benefits and costs that arise from those changes.

Many (perhaps most) economists believe that financial changes over the last several years have greatly benefited society. Others argue that welfare gains have been a mixed blessing; a minority would probably go so far as to say that costs have outweighed their benefits. There is naturally no satisfactory resolution to this debate, considering the complexity of the issues as well as the judgmental nature of benefit and cost calculations. But it seems to me that a look at the presumed advantages and drawbacks might be helpful in providing a perspective on the debate. In what follows here I offer some preliminary thoughts on this subject.

SOME PROBLEMS OF THE BENEFIT-COST APPROACH

I begin by outlining some rather obvious difficulties in assessing the benefits and costs of financial changes. One such difficulty stems from a conflict between micro and macro optimality. This conflict is, of course, not new. In fact, it is part of an old controversy in political economy dating back at least as far as Adam Smith, who identified individual wealth with national wealth – increases and decreases in individual wealth lead to corresponding

---

* The views expressed are the author's and not those of the Federal Reserve.

Fair, D.E., (ed.) Shifting Frontiers in Financial Markets.
© *1986, Martinus Nijhoff Publishers, Dordrecht/Boston/Lancaster. ISBN 90-247-3225-5.*
Printed in the Netherlands.

increases and decreases in national wealth – and apparently believed that any restraints that impair an individual's ability to be wealthy must decrease national wealth. Among the early critics of this view were Bentham and Lord Lauderdale; their criticism launched the controversy on micro versus macro optimality. Actually, Smith's own comments on the evils of monopolies do not fit entirely with his identification of individual and national wealth.

In principle, the benefit-cost approach to financial changes seeks net gains for society as a whole. But it is difficult, if not impossible, to make welfare comparisons and to ascertain net gains through aggregation when benefits accrue to one group and costs to another. Perhaps even more importantly, standards for micro optimality differ considerably from those for macro optimality. Micro optimality is judged normally in terms of individual choices and efficiency in resource allocation. While relevant for macro optimality, unbounded consumer choices or efficiency in resource allocation are not necessarily consistent with the welfare of society as a whole. The national welfare demands fairness and equity in market competition. Moreover, macro optimality also seeks to achieve broader national goals by maintaining financial stability and efficient monetary control.

All this suggests that a given financial change or series of changes may benefit one group at the cost of another group, or of the whole society. Alternately, a financial change may be beneficial for the society as a whole but harmful for certain groups within it.

Let me illustrate these perhaps rather obvious points with two examples from recent experience. Deregulation of deposit rates and cash management practices have reduced the opportunity cost of holding deposits, thereby increasing the financial return to depositors. By encouraging incentives for savings, this presumably makes for a more efficient allocation of economic resources. Against this, banks have experienced a squeeze on earnings and lower profit margins, leading them to undertake certain defensive measures or other activities. These, in turn, have created certain supervisory concerns. Simultaneously, the same series of financial changes has added to monetary control problems by complicating the definition and measurement of money, and by making the demand for money more unpredictable and less sensitive to interest rates. Under these circumstances, *net gains* from the decontrol of deposit rates and cash management practices are difficult to determine.

A second example comes from the advent of electronic fund transfer payments. The evidence indicates strongly that, from the viewpoint of real resources, using electronic payments to replace checks would benefit society as a whole substantially. But this would entail a major cost for check users (both businesses and consumers) who now benefit from check float. In the United States, the unit cost per transaction is estimated to be around *minus 15 cents* for check users, compared with *plus 33 cents* for ACH (automated clearing house) users, and *plus 19 cents* for currency users. If the float transfer payments were to net themselves out, the unit cost per transaction would be substantially greater for check users than for ACH or cash users. This is obviously a case of 'market failure', but its solution would certainly limit individual choices and increase transaction costs for many consumers and businesses by reducing or eliminating check float.

Another major difficulty with the benefit-cost approach is that the benefits and costs associated with a given financial innovation must be assessed relative to the financial environment in which that innovation takes place. In general, a new financial instrument in a relatively less developed market would be viewed as providing substantial net gains if it either widens the spectrum of individual choices for wealth holding or increases the role of price competition. By contrast, net gains are less obvious in the case of a new financial instrument in a well-developed market that already offers a broad array of wealth-holding instruments and significant price competition.

This implies that welfare gains from financial innovations in various markets within a country may differ considerably. But even more importantly, a given innovation may yield markedly disparate net gains in different countries.

New financial instruments would be particularly welcome in a country with very limited individual or business choices for making payments, holding wealth, arranging loans, or hedging risk. In this case, the long-term benefits of new instruments are likely to outweigh their long-term costs by far. Net gains are not so easily reckoned in a country where there is a broad array of all types of financial instruments.

Viewed in this light, the recent experience with financial deregulation and innovation looks to me considerably less troublesome in some countries than in others. Notwithstanding the difficulties of broad generalizations, my personal view is that welfare gains stemming from the recent financial changes in France, Japan and, perhaps, Italy have been very substantial.

It is much more difficult, however, to make such a general, yet meaningful, statement about the benefits versus costs associated with the recent financial developments in the United Kingdom, the United States and Canada. On the whole, I think the recent experience in these countries would turn out to be beneficial eventually, but costs, at least during the transition, appear to be quite considerable.

A somewhat more meaningful perspective is possible by looking at particular innovations (or a particular type of innovation) in different countries. Take, for example, the case of deregulatory and other financial changes which are increasing consumer credit in various countries. The United States would not be well-advised at present to shift further resources into consumer credit, because household lending/borrowing facilities are already very highly developed – total consumer credit, excluding housing, is roughly equivalent to about 25 per cent of personal consumer expenditures, while net savings of the economy are only about 5–7 per cent of GNP. In France, by contrast, innovations increasing the flow of consumer loans may yield significant net benefits since household credit arrangements are rather undeveloped – total consumer credit is only about 3–4 per cent of personal consumer expenditures, whereas net savings of the economy are running around 8 per cent of GNP. The same may be true for Japan where consumer credit, excluding housing, ranges from 12–14 per cent of personal consumer spending, but net savings of the economy amounts to about 15 per cent of GNP.

One other complication in judging the benefits and costs of innovations is worth noting; this one results from the speed and extent of financial changes. Transition and adjustment problems are relatively modest when the pace of change is slow and its extent small. In this case, there is no significant distortion in the long-term benefits and costs of financial changes. But this cannot be said of a situation in which there are numerous fast-moving financial changes. Transition and adjustment problems created by those changes can be very substantial. And this can result in major, sometimes permanent, distortions in the long-term consequences of financial innovations.

Bearing these difficulties in mind, let me now turn to the major benefits and then to some important costs arising from recent financial deregulation and innovation.

MAJOR BENEFITS

It is widely believed that the latest wave of financial deregulation and innovation has generated several interrelated benefits.

1. Businesses and households now earn *higher returns* on their financial

asset holdings. Large corporations could do so since the early 1970s and even before. But small businesses and households generally did not have access to higher-yielding financial assets until the late 1970s. This situation has changed greatly in most industrial countries. Financial instruments with market-related interest rates (or at least with higher rates than before) are now available, to varying extents, for small denominations and short maturities in most countries; any list would certainly include Canada, the United Kingdom, the United States, Japan, France and Italy. Over time, this is likely to push up considerably the share of interest income in total personal income, which in turn could have significant consequences for consumer spending. This trend is already visible in some countries. In the United States, for example, interest income accounted for nearly 15 per cent of personal income in the second half of 1984, up from just about 10 per cent in 1978.

The movement toward higher-yielding financial instruments for large and small holders is now quite far advanced in the United States, the United Kingdom and Canada, and accordingly financial gains to households and businesses have been appreciable. The availability of higher-yielding financial assets for small investors has also served the interests of equity and fairness in the system since large holders could already earn high returns.

In many countries, the trend toward higher-yielding financial instruments has a long way to go. This is particularly true for household and small business holdings which remain subject to non-market and relatively low interest rates. In some cases, such as in Germany, this holds true despite the fact that deposit rates are not regulated by the authorities.

2. *Transactions costs* associated with holding, using or transferring financial assets have fallen in recent years.

(i) *For deposit instruments*, a variety of developments – cash management practices, new payments methods, the widespread use of interest-bearing instruments for transactions purposes and facilities for easy transfer between (or consolidation of) different types of accounts – has reduced transactions costs significantly in a number of countries, including Canada, the United Kingdom, the United States and Japan. The process of reduction in transactions costs of deposit instruments continues there as well as in other countries. The benefits of this process are spread fairly broadly across large and small depositors.

(ii) In the United States, transactions costs in *markets for bonds and equities* have also declined. Securities markets moved from fixed to negotiated commission rates in 1975. Since then competitive forces, along with advances in electronic communication and data processing technology, have led to substantially smaller underwriting fees for competitively bid bond issues and lower equity brokerage fees, especially for large trades. So far the benefits of negotiated commissions have gone principally to institutional investors with large transactions. The cost of securities transactions to small investors has actually risen considerably, mitigated only in part by the availability of discount brokers. A similar movement toward negotiated commission rates is now underway in the United Kingdom. The French authorities also plan to allow negotiated commissions on stock and bond transactions above a certain minimum. In addition to the official attempts to encourage competition in bond and equity markets, there is a more general trend toward internationalization and linking of these markets across national boundaries, which should lead to reduced transactions costs for securities in most (if not all) industrial countries. The area of international linkages in equity and bond markets may turn out to be the next frontier to undergo major changes over the next few years.

3. Financial deregulation and innovation have increased the ability of economic agents to *deal with risk*. The introduction of financial futures for foreign currency and interest rates, stock exchange futures and options on futures has facilitated hedging risk underlying commercial and financial activities. These markets are now being used extensively in the United States and, to a lesser extent, in the United Kingdom. In most other *domestic markets*, financial futures and options are not yet available to any significant extent. Of course, exchange market futures are widely available for most major currencies. Also widely available are variable rate lending/ borrowing instruments which shift the interest rate risk to borrowers from lenders.

4. Financial changes have enhanced *liquidity and financing* alternatives in the financial system.

(i) The decline in transactions costs and the advent of the futures markets, together with the deepening trend toward negotiability or marketability of financial assets, have all increased market liquidity. For an individual corporation or business, this widens the scope for conducting larger amount of business with given resources. More importantly, financial deregulation and innovations have expanded the supply of credit from traditional lenders, and the range of financing alternatives through new financial instruments which are frequently negotiable. Among these are floating-rate notes and bonds, zero-coupon bonds, variable-rate preferred stocks, euro-market borrowings, leveraged buyouts, and interest and currency swaps. The expansion in financing alternatives has swept across all major countries, although its extent is probably the greatest in the United States.

(ii) Deregulation and innovations have also increased financing or credit available to households. With the diminished profit margin, due to competition and/or removal of deposit rate ceilings, it is in the interest of banks and financial institutions to increase the supply of credit. At both the household and business levels, the expansion of credit supply appears to be fueled, in part, by the ability to pass along the interest rate risk to borrowers through variable-rate arrangements.

Taken together, these benefits have enhanced, to varying extents, the efficiency of financial arrangements in most industrial countries. This means better allocation of scarce resources, more price competition and consequently more output and higher standards of living, *ceteris paribus*.

SOME COSTS

On the negative side, a wide range of costs, actual or perceived, are associated with financial deregulation and innovation.

1. One such cost is reflected in *monetary control problems* stemming from various sources: greater difficulties in defining and measuring money; increased instability and/or unpredictability of the demand for money; and, more generally, greater uncertainty about the relationship between monetary variables and economic activity. These problems, which differ rather widely across countries, have been discussed and debated extensively in recent years. With that in mind, I have chosen not to dwell further on this subject.

2. Another generally recognized cost of financial deregulation and innovations is the *increased danger or risk to stability of the financial system*, i.e., the increased risk to its safety and soundness. Most discussions of this risk tend to be rather vague. However, several sources of financial instability can be identified.

(i) Decontrol or liberalization of deposit rates and the increased competition have lowered profit margins for deposit-taking institutions. To maintain profits (or perhaps to make any profits at all), financial institutions have expanded the volume of credit aggressively and, in the process, the quality of that credit has fallen. Both the lower profit margins and the lower credit quality, so the argument goes, increase the risk of financial instability. Some (e.g., A. Wojnilower) believe that there is a chronic excess demand for credit, so that in a deregulated environment there is presumably no end to credit expansion. And if the authorities are lax – either because the financial system is threatened by defaults or for other reasons – 'excessive competition' and lower credit quality are likely to ensue.

(ii) New payment systems have increased certain operational and settlement risks. For example, wire transfer networks in the United States transfer up to $500 billion a day, with an average transaction value of $2.5 million per transfer. In the current operations – both the Fed wire and the private sector's systems (CHIPS, Cash Wire, etc.) – many participants incur daylight overdrafts. Should a wire transfer participant fail (unexpectedly) to settle for funds while in a daylight overdraft position on a network, that single failure could lead to the systemic settlement failure of other participants on the same network. This credit risk facing all participants results from the interconnectedness among participants on a wire transfer network. And it can be reduced, of course, by controlling or eliminating daylight overdrafts.

(iii) Some new financing techniques or instruments seem to have generated financial risks of their own. One such technique is the so-called leveraged buyout, which has become very popular in the United States. But a firm heavily leveraged by debt finance has little ability to withstand external shocks. Another example of increased financial risk stems from the change in the ownership and trading of equities in the United States. At one time, most trading in equities was in the hands of individual investors; now more than half is done by institutional investors. Institutional investors now also own a larger share of equities. Yet another example of higher risk is the 'junk bond' – a high-yielding bond with a low credit rating (BB or lower) – which gained some popularity during the last few years. A recent study estimates that the default rate on junk bonds is 20 times higher than the default rate on all other corporate bonds.

(iv) By raising the amount of uninsured money or means of payments, recent financial changes have increased the danger to financial stability.

(v) Deregulation of interest rates and other financial changes have induced greater interest-rate volatility. That can lead to greater solvency risk for lending institutions.

3. Many analysts believe that the *rapid expansion of debt* associated with financial deregulation and innovations has damaging consequences for the real economy. Indeed, credit expansion over the last several years has been quite fast. In Japan and the United States, for example, since 1979/80 total debt-to-GNP ratio has expanded at more than twice the rate of the previous decade. In some other countries where such data are available, total debt relative to GNP also appears to be rising more rapidly than before. Moreover, the actual debt in most countries is probably understated because of credit lines and credit guarantees or commitments by banks and financial institutions, and because of enlarged balance sheets resulting from financial activities related to futures, options and swaps. In any case, several facets of the recent credit expansion are presumed to entail greater risks for the real economy.

(i) Some economists argue that the current fast pace of credit expansion is not consistent with a long-term national goal of price stability.

(ii) Others see problems with the fact that consumer debt has gone up so much in recent years. This further shift of resources toward consumer debt and spending, and so away from production, may not be desirable for some countries.

(iii) Strong growth of debt and increasing emphasis on debt financing is changing the debt/equity ratio for business, which tends to weaken its long-term viability and solvency.

(iv) During the recent credit expansion, short-term elements, especially in relation to the business sector, have become much more important, implying a greater risk to economic activity. In many countries, borrowing through short-term market instruments (e.g. commercial paper) and short-term bank loans accounted for a large proportion of business borrowings during the last few years. Over the first two years of the current recovery in the United States, for example, short-term borrowings by nonfinancial corporations were about 60 per cent up from around 35 per cent over comparable years in the expansions of the 1970s. That trend toward short-term borrowing has been deepened by the shortening maturity of long-term instruments. Moreover, floating rate market issues, and variable-rate loans and mortgages from financial institutions – all closely linked to short-term interest rates – represent a very substantial portion of total business and consumer debt. This broadly-based short-term orientation of debt may not be desirable because many nonfinancial activities are long-term in nature. This is definitely true for a considerable part of business activity. For the corporate sector, the short-term focus in business decisions is intensified by the fact that portfolio managers are increasingly being rated on short-term corporate performance, frequently on a quarterly basis. That kind of evaluation compels them to produce short-term results (sometimes through massaging of income statements) in businesses whose decisions are inherently long-term and entail short-term variability in earnings. All this could lead to increased business investment in short-term capital goods at the cost of long-term capital goods, which might not be desirable for the economy. In the United States, the trend toward short-term investment already appears underway; over the first two years of recovery, short-term business investment in producers' durable equipment accounted for around 50 per cent of the total, about 10 percentage points more than in 1978–79. It is, however, not clear whether the shift toward short-term investment relates to changes in the financial system, or to changes in the business tax code in 1981, or even to developments in office and communications technology.

4. Finally, many analysts perceive significant costs to possible further concentration of economic power, and the growing interdependence of financial activities and institutions. In addition, financial institutions' entry into new activities might also give rise to conflicts of interest. While these concerns are well founded, some of the perceived costs (e.g., those associated with concentration of economic power) seem to be overstated. Underlying these various concerns is the desire to have fair, equitable and open competition in the provision of financial services.

CONCLUDING REMARKS

Financial deregulation and innovation have enhanced the role of market forces and of the price mechanism, thereby improving economic efficiency. In some countries, however, they have also generated considerable costs – monetary control difficulties, risks to safety and soundness of the financial system along with some potential risks for the real sector. Still, in general the magnitude of these costs does not suggest a strong case for *complete or full scale reregulation*, as some analysts have argued recently. To be sure, 'excessive competition' in some areas of the financial marketplace together with 'excessive' credit expansion has led to additional risks, and market discipline does not seem to insure against those risks. But for now the risks do not appear widespread, although in a few cases, left unattended or unguided, they have the potential to cause serious damage. The challenging task for monetary and supervisory policies is to find ways and means to enhance safety and soundness of the financial system while guiding further financial changes in desirable directions.

Part B

CAUSES OF CHANGE AND INNOVATION IN THE MIX OF
FINANCIAL INSTRUMENTS

Chapter V

DEVELOPMENTS ON THE FRENCH CAPITAL MARKETS IN RECENT YEARS

by *Didier Bruneel**

This paper contains:
1. a review of the changes that have occurred on the French capital markets in recent years in the creation and the use of the different types of financial instruments,
2. a description of the factors that lay at the root of these developments,
3. an appreciation on the scope of the developments that have taken place and on the future prospects.

REVIEW OF THE CHANGES IN RECENT YEARS

The widespread adoption of variable interest rates

Bank lending and resources and interest rate variability
Banks greatly increased their medium and long-term lending at variable or reviewable rates. Most medium and a large part of long-term corporate lending is now in this form. More recently, the variable rate practice was extended to housing loans, though it remains marginal in this sector.

Meanwhile a higher proportion of bank resources has become more sensitive to interest rate fluctuations.

The noticeable decline in the share of the short-term and refinanceable medium-term loans, whose cost is traditionally linked to the banks' base rate, and the corresponding increase in predominantly fixed rate housing loans and exports credits explain that paradoxically the sensitivity of bank loans to customers (residents, in French francs) to interest rate fluctuations has been decreasing for the last ten years.

---

* This paper was written with the help of Mr J.M. Facq.

Fair, D.E., (ed.) Shifting Frontiers in Financial Markets.
© *1986, Martinus Nijhoff Publishers, Dordrecht/Boston/Lancaster. ISBN 90-247-3225-5.*
Printed in the Netherlands.

Table 1.

	1973	1983
	%	%
Bank loans to customers		
(Residents, in French francs)		
• Loans at regulated fixed rates or at unadjustable market rates	35.1	45.6
• Loans linked to the banks' base rate	64.9	54.4
• Total	100.0	100.0
Bank resources originating from customers		
– Customer deposits (residents, in French francs)		
• non-interest-bearing deposits	47.8	40.2
• deposits bearing interest at regulated rates	33.8	21.9
• deposits bearing interest at rates linked to the money		
market rate	15.6	24.7
– Bonds (in French francs)	3.0	13.2
• Total	100.0	100.0

The variable rate practice on the bond market

On the bond market, offerings at variable rates first appeared in 1979. The variability clause often refers to the fixed rate loan return.

Table 2.

	Issues on the bond market (in %)					
	1979	1980	1981	1982	1983	1984
Fixed rate issues	97.2	94.2	81.0	78.0	86.0	51.0
Variable rate issues	2.8	5.8	19.0	22.0	14.0	49.0
Total	100.0	100.0	100.0	100.0	100.0	100.0

Most variable rate issues are by banks.

The growth of long-term capital markets and the new financial products offered to savers

The bond market

Long confined to a marginal role among financial circuits, the bond market began a vigorous expansion from 1980 onwards.

Table 3.

Years	Gross issues		Issues net of redemptions		Issues net of redemptions and interest payments	
	Fr. fr. billion	GDP %	Fr. fr. billion	GDP %	Fr. fr. billion	GDP%
1977	49.42	2.62	38.49	2.04	14.71	0.78
1978	57.82	2.70	45.38	2.12	15.78	0.74
1979	65.48	2.68	49.92	2.04	15.27	0.63
1980	111.67	4.04	90.76	3.28	48.93	1.77
1981	106.85	3.44	81.13	2.61	23.72	0.76
1982	154.70	4.36	116.34	3.28	41.21	1.60
1983	193.65	4.65	148.29	3.79	50.27	1.28
1984	240.90	5.58	190.34	4.41	70.86	1.64

The growth of the market has been accompanied by a shortening of the average maturity of the new issues, from 15 to 12 years for public sector fixed rate issues, from 12 to 10 years for private sector fixed rate issues, while most variable rate issue maturities are of 8 years.

Meanwhile, on the secondary market, transactions have considerably increased, from Fr. fr. 63.2 billion in 1980 to Fr. fr. 409.7 billion in 1984. The total of French bonds, reckoned at their sale value on the Stock Exchange, rose from Fr. fr. 567.4 billion at the end of 1980 to Fr. fr. 1,231.5 billion at the end of 1984.

Products which amounted to new forms of loans were used on an increasing scale:

1. bonds carrying a warrant or a subscription voucher giving the bearer the right to subscribe, during a fixed period, for a second bond or share of the issuing body (bond carrying a bond or a share subscription voucher);

2. 'window' loans, carrying a facility for advance repayment either at the option of the holder, in which case the interest paid is the higher the longer the paper is held, or at the option of the issuer, in which case the yield to the holder is the higher the earlier the option is exercised;

3. 'twin' loans in the form either of a fixed rate issue coupled with a variable rate issue, or of a loan with a conventional fixed rate tranche and a 'window' tranche.

When the state makes new offerings, it often gives the choice between a fixed rate tranche and another tranche issued at a lower interest rate but giving the holder, at his option and after a two-year period, the possibility to exchange his paper against variable rate bonds according to the return rate of fixed rate state loans.

Moreover, in 1983, the Treasury was authorised to issue 'Treasury revolving bonds' with a six year maturity and giving the holder the option, after a three year period, of exchanging his paper against new revolving bonds which are then being issued. Interest is capitalized and paid exclusively at the final maturity date or, such being the case, at the time of the exchange. Revolving bond issues amounted to Fr. fr. 1.01 billion in 1983, against a total amount of state loans of Fr. fr. 51.01 billion. In 1984, they reached Fr. fr. 30.4 billion, i.e. 35.8 per cent of the total state issues on the bond market (Fr. fr. 84.9 billion).

Finally, among the new instruments offered to the investors on the bond market, the participating certificates (titres participatifs) should be mentioned. Created in 1983, they amount in fact to a mixed formula between a bond and a capital share.

Thanks to the participating certificates, the nationalized enterprises or the co-operatives can raise funds from the public. Such capital is like equity funds and represented by redeemable instruments only in case of liquidation of the company or if the issue contract stipulates it, at the company's initiative, after a 7 year minimum period.

The return paid to the holders is made up of a fixed part and of a variable one related to data reflecting the performance of the issuer's business (net profits, cash flow, turnover). In practice, such return is to remain between a floor and a ceiling. The holders of participating certificates are entitled to the same tax exemptions as other bond holders.

In 1983, five public sector corporations issued participating certificates for Fr. fr. 4.05 billion.

In 1984, the amount of participating certificates issued on the French market reached Fr. fr. 6.4 billion for banks and Fr. fr. 1.4 billion for non financial companies.

The share market

The appearance of new instruments of risk-capital-raising contributed to the revival of the share primary market in 1983[1]. The non-voting preference shares, among others, were a big success in the public. Reference should also be made to investment certificates – the share is split into a certificate giving the holder the financial rights attached to shares and a right of vote certificate which remains the property of the issuing firm – and the possibility given to firms to distribute shares as dividend payments.

As far as the ways in which savings are called upon to increase own or assimilated funds are concerned, the creation of participating certificates and of loans carrying share subscription vouchers should be mentioned here again (the issues of the latter instrument amounted to Fr. fr. 1.4 billion in 1983 and Fr. fr. 3.5 billion during the eleven months of 1984; for the first time, in October 1984, there was an offer of a loan issue with participating certificate subscription vouchers.

The appearance of short-term open-ended unit trusts (SICAV) and short-term mutual funds (FCP)

Created at the end of 1981 and at the beginning of 1982, the short-term mutual funds and short-term open-ended unit trusts are collective savings management undertakings which, in principle, specialize in investing the funds they collect in variable or fixed rate but short-dated bonds.

Such institutions allow subscribers to profit from the high returns offered on the bond market, and also from the tax exemptions granted under the so-called fiscal transparency regulation.

The liquidity of short-term mutual funds or open-ended unit trusts is very high: withdrawals can be asked by holders on the basis of a liquidation value reckoned daily for the short-term open-ended unit trusts or at least twice a month for the short-term mutual funds.

The channelling of investments by short-term open-ended unit trusts and short-term mutual funds toward variable rate bonds or bonds close to

Table 4.

	Net capital collected by short-term open-ended unit trusts and short-term mutual funds during the year	Net assets of short-term open-ended unit trusts and short-term mutual funds at the end of the year
	Billions of French francs	
1982	23.3	33.7
1983	53.4	96.2*
1984	85.–	196.3

* Of which French bonds and participating certificates: Fr. fr. 81.9 billion, i.e. 85.1 % of the total of net assets.
As a matter of interest: Total liquidity-residents M3R at the end of 1984: Fr. fr. 2,852.9 billion. Gross issues of French bonds and participating certificates on the domestic market in 1984: Fr. fr. 248.8 billion. Total of French bonds and participating certificates at their sale value on the Stock Exchange at the end of 1984 Fr. fr. 1,231.5 billion.

maturity was supposed to reduce the risks of capital loss. But, in fact, in numerous cases, those principles were transgressed and, availing themselves of the declining trend of long-term interest rates, the managers of such institutions looked out for capital gains by buying fixed rate bonds that had been recently issued. The authorities stepped in in order to control a development which could be seen as unsound and even dangerous for the smooth working of the bond market; they raised the proportion of assets that such short-term investing bodies may hold in the shape of Treasury bills and liquid items (see pp. 55–57).

Promoted by founding banks as substitutes for time deposits and liquid monetary assets, the short-term open-ended unit trust shares and mutual fund units were viewed as such by many holders, and especially by commercial firms. The high turnover of such shares and units shows that they are akin to monetary or near-monetary assets.

The new liquid products offered to savers

During the past two years, new types of liquid investments have been offered to savers with the specific aims to protect savings by low income households against inflation and to channel short-term savings towards business investment. These new products also have in common the fact that they are marketed whether by banks or non-banks.

Popular savings books (LEP)

From June 1982, an investment bearing a consumer price-indexed rate of interest was offered to the public. A bonus supplements the basic interest rate in order to preserve the purchasing power of deposits that remain stable for at least 6 months. Both basic interest and bonus are tax-free.

The savings books are available only to individuals with low taxable incomes, the criterion being that of the income-tax liability. There is a deposit ceiling (Fr. fr. 20,000).

The success of this new type of financial assets was swift.

Table 5. LEP balances (in billions of French francs)

End of 1982 : 7.7	End of 1983 : 30.1	End of 1984 : 43.–

Industrial development accounts (comptes pour le développement indus-triel CODEVI)

Created in October 1983, the industrial development accounts also bring tax-free interest. The sums deposited on each account and which can be withdrawn at sight cannot amount to more than Fr. fr. 10,000 per tax-payer; the spouse is also entitled to an industrial development account.

The deposits placed on the industrial development accounts are invested partly in bonds issued at market conditions by banks and in Deposit and Consignment Office special securities (securities for the industrial development). These securities are collectively managed and an agreement is concluded between the establishment which opens industrial development accounts and each of its customers in order to authorize the collective management.

Seventy-five per cent of the funds raised through industrial development accounts are finally earmarked for industrial loans at preferential rates and for the financing of a newly created public body, called the Industrial Modernization Fund; the remaining 25 per cent may be used as it likes by the establishment which raised the funds.

Following a reallocation of liquid assets, the industrial development account balances swiftly reached high levels.

Table 6. Industrial development account balances (in billions of French francs)

End of December 1983 : 43.–	End of December 1984 : 64.–

Business savings book (livret d'épargne entreprises)

Offered in August 1984, the business savings book is meant to facilitate the financing of business creations or take-overs. After a minimum 2 year initial saving period, the holder of such a savings book will be able to secure a loan at a favorable rate (8 or 7.5 per cent according to whether it will be a fixed or variable rate loan), the net return on the savings book being presently set at 4.5 per cent.

The amount and the maximum duration of loans vary according to the interest accrued on the book, after application of a 1.6 coefficient. The maturities of such loans varying from 2 to 15 years, they will be available to finance business creations and take-overs in all economic sectors, whatever the legal status of the company involved.

The new types of credit and venture capital promotion

While the real estate and equipment leasing mechanisms introduced during the 1960s continued to develop themselves, formulas which were new in France were initiated from 1978 onwards in order to associate credit institutions with the strengthening of the capital base of commercial firms. Moreover specific techniques aimed at channelling venture capital were devised.

Participating loans (prêts participatifs)

Inspired by the subordinated loan formula in the United States, the participating loan implies no lien on the assets of a company; the institution granting the loan is repaid in the event of the borrower's liquidation only after the claims of all the creditors have been met in full. Among the institutions that make participating loans, there is the Industrial Modernization Fund (see above) which uses to this aim the deposits raised under the industrial development account scheme.

While the bulk of claims on the banking and non-banking institutions reached Fr. fr. 3,227 billion at the end of June 1984, the outstanding 'participating loans' amounted to Fr. fr. 23 billion.

Venture capital promotion

In the early 1970s, industrialists and financial institutions associated to create venture capital firms in order to help small and medium sized companies using advanced technologies by bringing in capital, such participations being meant to be sold on the financial market once the firms have reached a sufficient development level. Several 'financial companies for innovation' were thus created during the recent period.

The appearance of venture mutual funds managed by banks or brokers should also be mentioned from 1983 onwards. These funds must invest at least 40 per cent of their assets in non-quoted companies. There is no withdrawal possibility before three years after the subscription. 37 venture mutual funds were in existence at the beginning of 1985.

Blurring of the distinction between 'banks' and 'non-banks'

The changes in the financing formulas and in the products offered to savers went together with a weakening of the differences between 'banks' and 'non-banks'. Banks resort more and more to the bond market, while the latter was previously mostly tapped by non-banking institutions. Similarly the services offered to their customers by non-banking institutions tend to be more and more similar to those made available by the banks.

The new banking law seals and enhances this state of things.

FACTORS BEHIND THE RECENT DEVELOPMENTS IN FINANCIAL TECHNIQUES, IN INSTRUMENTS OFFERED TO SAVERS AND IN FINANCING CIRCUIT STRUCTURES

In the French experience, financial innovations are often initiated by the public authorities or at least they are kept under their control or their guidance. However, spontaneous reactions from economic agents are not to be overlooked.

Changes in the behaviour of economic agents

Changes in the behaviour of economic agents in reaction to inflation and interest rate volatility

The level and the volatility of interest rates have greatly increased as a result of the worsened inflationary pressures and of the hardened foreign constraints which followed the two oil shocks. Economic and financial forecasts have become much more unreliable.

This conjunction certainly explains why variable or reviewable interest rates have become a general practice in bank loans and bond issues. For the latter, it moreover led to a shortening of maturities.

In France, the existence of interest rate variability clauses rather seemed to suit the needs of the banks, in a high rate environment. For this gives them the possibility to pass on to their customers a rise in their refinancing cost not only on recently granted credits, but also on the whole of their variable rate loan portfolios. As for companies, they are heavily indebted towards banks and an interest rate hike, resulting from variability clauses, would increase the average cost of their debt and thus make their financial liabilities all the heavier. A persistent trend to lower interest rates would obviously, in the French case, have a quite beneficial effect on the profit and loss accounts of companies.

On the French bond market, the fluctuations of the respective shares of the new fixed and variable rate issues show clearly how money lender's motives are predominant in this respect. When rates are expected to drop, fixed rate issues are obviously the most popular among subscribers and the share of variable rate loans in the new issues recedes; conversely, when the future trend of rates becomes more uncertain to the point where possibilities of a rise cannot be excluded, the proportion of variable or reviewable rate loans increases significantly as was the case in 1984 (see above, p. 46).

Changes in the behaviour of economic agents in response to regulations
1. Banks greatly increased their bond issuing activities on the bond market in order to grant credits outside ceilings, i.e. without compulsory reserves. For, under the ceiling system, the banks could deduct from their credits to customers the increase in their non-monetary liabilities (bonds, shares, etc.) from the beginning of the financial year. This increase was defined as the difference between the increases, on the liability side, of their own funds plus their bond issues on the domestic market and, on the assets side, of their security portfolios plus their fixed assets, leasing excluded.

The new system of monetary regulation for 1985, which does away with credit ceilings and introduces compulsory reserves at progressive rates on credits, takes up again most of the previous exemption system in favour of credits financed by banks on their net non-monetary liabilities.

Consequently, in 1985, in view of the prevailing regulations, banks will still have an incentive to issue bonds as well as participating certificates which are similar to own funds or, in the case of banks which are still in private hands, they will issue shares.

2. 'Short term' investment institutions – short-term open-ended unit trusts and mutual funds – were created by banks following the enactment of a more restrictive regulation of interest paid on time deposits and bank notes (bons de caisse). In September 1981 the thresholds (amount, time) above which the interest rates can be freely set in relation to the money market rate were raised.

Banks marketed the short-term mutual fund and open-ended unit trust shares as substitutes for time deposits, these substitutes being even said to be more advantageous from the profitability and liquidity points of view. The short-term collective investment institutions have moreover played the role of recipients as far as bank bond issues are concerned. However the formula met with such success that, in the autumn 1984, banks could with some reason fear dangerous competition for their short-term deposit and liquid savings raising activities.

Influence of public deficits and financing needs of the Treasury

The emergence of large budget deficits and the need to finance them as far as possible by non-monetary means led the state to introduce innovations as far as the nature of securities offered on the bond market and the issue techniques are concerned; the most original innovation being the creation of 'Treasury revolving bonds' (see above, pp. 46–48).

The new bond issues by public bodies on the domestic market covered an increasing share of their financing needs, themselves in significant progression; this share rose from 39 per cent in 1981 to 52.3 per cent in 1983, and can be estimated at 75.5 per cent for 1984. Meanwhile, issues made by public bodies made up about one third of the total of issues on the bond primary market from 1980 to 1983 and they should reach 40 per cent in 1984.

The growing presence of the government as a capital taker on the bond market has not yet resulted in the 'crowding out' of other sectors as far as quantity at least is concerned (following an implicit rule, government issues do not amount to more than a third of total issues). It obviously had a role in keeping bond interest rates at a high level, but it also made the market more dynamic by encouraging other issuers (financial institutions, companies) to diversify their borrowing techniques in order to make them more attractive to savers.

Action by public authorities

The behaviour of economic agents in response to regulations which were described above (pp. 54) was in fact only in part spontaneous: they were also deliberately encouraged or influenced by public authorities. Moreover, many innovations concerning savings instruments or financing circuits result from measures taken and implemented by public authorities.

Action taken by public authorities within the credit control policy

The reserve exemption system in favour of credits financed from bond issues and own funds net of fixed capital and securities does not only amount to a facility granted to banks and intended to introduce a practical element of flexibility in the credit control system, but also aims at stimulating an increase in bonds as stable liabilities and in funds owned by banks, such an increase being sought for by the authorities (while on the other hand they readily accept, not to say wish, that banks abstain from investing on the financial market).

The attitude of public authorities towards 'short-term' collective invest-ment institutions

A spontaneous creation by banks, short-term mutual funds and open-ended unit trusts could only develop with the agreement of the authorities which paid particular attention to get from these institutions the guarantee they would give the preference to the French bond market in their invest-ment policies.

Short-term open-ended unit trusts pledged before the Treasury to abide by a minimum ratio between those of their assets made up of securities quoted on a stock exchange, or waiting to be listed on such an exchange, dividends included, and the total of their assets. Every new short-term open-ended unit trust thus pledged to follow the 'code of good behaviour' proposed by public authorities. First set at 0.75, the minimum ratio of securities to be held by such trusts was recently lowered to 0.60 to counter speculative pressures on the bond market which could cause fear of the consequences of an interest rate trend reversal (the tendency had been toward lower rates since the end of 1981).

Taxation of household financial savings

Such taxation was changed in a way more and more favourable to bond holders.

Originally, according to the tax regime enforced in 1965, households could ask to come under a flat-rate withholding tax of 25 per cent for short-term investment interest payments as well as for bond coupons. The flat-rate withholding tax was raised from 25 per cent to $33^{1}/_{3}$ per cent in 1974, then to 40 per cent in 1978 and it presently amounts to 46 per cent and even 51 per cent for an anonymous investment[2]. On the other hand, French non-indexed bond coupons are only subject to a 26 per cent rate beyond a yearly tax-exempt amount which presently is set at Fr. fr. 5,000.– and which corresponds to an investment of slightly more than Fr. fr. 40,000.

The channelling of household savings towards the share market was encouraged by the Law of 13 July 1978 which allowed a certain amount invested in French shares to be deducted from taxable income. Then came the 1983 Budget which did away with this system and created a new formula of savings accounts in shares in which the net amounts of French shares bought each year may be deducted directly from the tax liabilities of individuals up to 25 per cent and with certain limits.

Specific measures aimed at encouraging long-term savings and channelling it toward corporate financing, to promote the backing up of technological innovation and of venture capital

A large part of the new products launched on the long-term capital market from 1983 onwards was created by the Law of 3rd January 1983 on the promotion of investment and the protection of savings. Among others, it made provision for bonds carrying a share subscription voucher, participating certificates, non-voting preference shares and investment certificates.

The Law of 3rd January 1983 also regulated the mutual venture funds.

Participating loans were created under the Law of 13 July 1978.

The Law of 8 July 1983 relative to industrial savings introduced the industrial development accounts (see p. 51). The Law of 8 July 1984 includes provisions about the taxation of venture capital and creates the business savings book (see p. 51).

Provisions concerning the activities and the structures of the banking system

Pursuant to and furthering a development already well started which tended to blur the differences between banks and 'non-banks' (see pp. 52–53) the Banking Law of 24 January 1984 widens the coverage of the banking regulations applying them to all credit institution networks while it takes care of their specificity; it also applies to certain companies which, in spite of the financial nature of their activities, were not until now bound by any special legal status (security portfolio managers acting on behalf of customers, money market brokers and 'financial companies' – compagnies financières – which control credit institutions).

Put into force on 24 July 1984, this Law also changed the institutions entrusted with the regulation and control of the banking system, the control function being reserved to the Banking Commission which has authority over all institutions coming under the Law, with the task not only of enforcing due respect for the rules of the banking profession, but also of examining the operating conditions and ensuring the quality of the financial structures.

It is stipulated that the new compulsory reserve system adopted on 16 November 1984 will be applied under particular conditions 'and at the earliest on 1 January 1986' to institutions which formerly did not come under the compulsory reserve system because of their non-bank character, such as savings banks, Crédit Foncier de France or Crédit National.

The influence of changes in the international financial environment

Among the factors at the origin of recent developments in France, mention should be made of the influence of practices followed on the international markets, in spite of the lines that divide domestic and international transactions within French banks as a result of exchange controls and in spite of the limited opening of the French capital markets to the outside world.

ASSESSMENT OF RECENT TRENDS AND THE OUTLOOK FOR THE FUTURE

The changes that have occurred in the savings system and in the lending circuits appear to have a particularly significant impact in four areas:
1. the lasting dynamism of the long-term capital markets;
2. the decompartmentalization of the capital markets;
3. the degree of bank intermediation and the ways in which that intermediation occurs;
4. the way in which monetary policy is implemented.

The lasting dynamism of the long-term capital markets

Since 'taking off' in 1980, the bond market has grown rapidly, though this now tends to be self-sustaining owing to the volume of redemptions and coupon payments. Seen thus, it is worth taking a look at the growth in the combined total of new issues, net of redemptions and coupons paid. The rising curve clearly shows that the French bond market has taken on a new dimension (cf. pp. 46–48).

Meanwhile, trading on the secondary market has intensified considerably, notably due to increasing activity by institutional investors, collective investment institutions especially.

Trends on the stock market have been less spectacular, though we may take encouragement from figures for share flotations by listed companies in 1983 and 1984 (cf. pp. 48–49).

The decompartmentalization of the capital markets

Not all the changes of recent years have favoured closer links between markets, though it does look as if those factors favouring intercommunicability between the capital markets are prevailing.

Decompartmentalization of the money market and the bond market

The tightening of regulations on interest-bearing term deposits in September 1981 tended to increase the segmentation for the different markets, by restricting the opportunities for arbitrage available to non-financial agents.

The 'short-term' open-ended unit trusts and mutual funds (respectively SICAVs and FCPs) were conceived as a response to this measure (cf. p. 54). However, the obligation to maintain a minimum ratio of 75 per cent of their investments in securities, and the barring of mutual funds from the money market, ran counter to the notion of free movement of capital between the different markets subject purely to considerations of yield and interest rates.

The lowering to 60 per cent of this minimum ratio of investments in securities, which was intended to curb the bond market's over-rapid expansion, may be regarded as a satisfactory move from the point of view of lowering the barriers between markets. What is more, the 'short-term' FCPs can enjoy money market rates de facto, by buying bonds through repurchase agreements.

Taken together, short-term SICAVs and FCPs can shunt substantial amounts between the money market and the bond market.

Innovations on the long-term capital markets: decompartmentalization of the bond market and the share market

The revolving Treasury bond answers the need for a wider range of available instruments, by introducing a medium-term security which can, if the holder so desires, be turned into a long-term one.

Two of the instruments created by the January 3, 1983 Act offer the possibility of bridging the gap between the bond market and the share market, namely:

1. bonds carrying share subscription warrants;
2. participating certificates, which amount to quasi-share capital for the issuer and represent a half-way house between a share and a bond for the purchaser.

Blurring the borderline between 'banks' and 'non-banks'

The new liquid savings instruments, e.g. the 'popular savings account' (L.E.P.) and the 'industrial development accounts' (CODEVI), which are available through all the different networks, are a good illustration of efforts to standardize instruments.

The January 24, 1984 Banking Act establishes a uniform set of rules applicable to all categories of financial institutions, notably with respect to deposit-taking and credit policy.

Bank intermediation

The expansion of the bond market has changed the face of the French banking system. Until 1980, the French economy was predominantly an 'overdraft economy', in which stocks and shares played only a minor role, while financial intermediaries, the distributors of credit and the creators of money, were virtually the sole links between lenders and borrowers.

Since that time, a fair dose of 'market economy' has been introduced into the financial system: part of the economy is financed directly on the bond market; above all a growing proportion of bank lending is financed on the bond market, at a market rate which is determined by the pattern of household demand for securities.

At any rate, in many cases still, deposit-taking and the allocation of credit in France are not yet determined by the play of market forces, as witnessed by the policy of selective credit controls, by the existence of lending at privileged rates and by the regulations imposed on interest-bearing deposits. Further, the changes now in progress, or in prospect, are either organized by the authorities or overseen by them. For example, bank-issued certificates of deposit are likely to be introduced shortly, as announced by the Ministry of Finance, while the possibility of establishing a bond futures market is also under discussion.

Monetary policy in practice

The changes that have occurred in the financial system create a need to redefine the monetary aggregates and ought to enhance the role of interest rates in the control of money stock trends.

Redefining the monetary aggregates

Redrawing the frontier between M2R and M3R. As pointed out earlier, the distinction between banks and non-banks is losing much of its relevance. The savings banks now offer their customers products identical to those offered by the banks, and there is no longer any difference in the behaviour of their respective clienteles. The authorities' efforts to harmonize the rules applicable to the different credit institutions and homogenize their deposit-taking operations merely serve to underscore the anachronism of classifying monetary assets according to whether they are managed by banks or by non-banks.

The importance attached to the M2R aggregate in determining monetary policy has therefore lost much of its theoretical justification. However, it is still justified on practical grounds, many years' experience having shown that M2R is a good proxy for M3R.

The blurring of the distinction between money and non-money. If we refer to the present behaviour of subscribers to short-term SICAVs and FCPs, what becomes plain is that the apparent fall in the demand for money represents no fundamental change in attitudes towards savings. Even so, the risk of capital depreciation can, as we have seen, materialize under quite definite circumstances. If SICAV shares and FCP units were included in the money stock, this reform might run into difficulties within a relatively short space of time.

Consequently, it is more or less out of the question to modify the monetary aggregates in the immediate future. The answer lies in taking into account the existence of FCPs and SICAVs pragmatically, and adjusting money stock targets to the behaviour of these instruments' users.

Enhancing the role of interest rates in controlling the money stock

Traditionally in France, the monetary authorities' preference for quantitative methods of controlling the expansion of the money stock flows from the fact that they are hindered in their freedom to manipulate interest rates by three factors:

1. the very important role played by external determinants (US, and still more so German, interest rates) in affecting French interest rate levels;

2. the high levels of French corporate indebtedness, which make French business highly sensitive to increases in their debt-service burden;

3. the heterogeneous nature of the French banking system (with some establishments being structural lenders, and others structural borrowers, on the money market), which implies very varying degrees of sensitivity to interest rate fluctuations from one establishment to another.

Falling inflation and a gradual return to equilibrium on the external account ought to give the authorities some measure of freedom of action where interest rates are concerned.

In the meantime, the structural weaknesses of the financial system are being attenuated.

1. The standardization of financial instruments is going hand-in-hand with an increasing similarity in the asset and liability structures of the

financial institutions, and the latter are now also becoming less hetero-geneous;

2. French companies are still debt-ridden, but the pattern of borrowing by the different economic agents is now tending towards that found in the other principal industrial countries. As the tables below show, corporate borrowing, which represented 5 per cent of GDP in 1980, will account for no more than 1.7 per cent in 1985, whereas the central government surplus, equivalent to 0.2 per cent of GDP in 1980, will have turned into a deficit equivalent to 3.2 per cent of GDP in 1985.

In this respect, the new system of compulsory reserves at progressive rates on credit, while still akin to a quantitative system, does contain certain favourable features. For instance, the contemporaneous reserve procedure re-establishes an ex ante relation between new lending and compulsory reserves, obliging the banks to link their lending closely to the cost of refinancing.

Similarly, arbitrage between control through quantities and control through price (i.e. interest rates) may be effected simply by tightening up or

Table 7.

| | Figures (as % of GDP) | | | | | |
	1980	1981	1982	1983	1984	1985
Corporate borrowing requirement	−5.4	−4.5	−5.3	−3.5	−2.7	−1.7
Central govt. borrowing requirement	+0.2	−1.8	−2.5	−3.3	−3.3	−3.2

Table 8.

| | Figures (as % of GDP) 1983 | | | |
	U.S.A.	U.K.	W. Germany	Japan
Corporate borrowing requirement	+0.7	+2.5	−2.9	−3.8
Central govt. borrowing requirement	−4.0	−3.2	−2.7	−2.9

These trends pave the way for a more active use of interest rates for purposes of money stock control.

easing the formula that is used to determine the level of compulsory reserves.

The French financial scene used traditionally to be distinguished by its profusion of regulations and its segmented markets and circuits. This situation is now in the throes of rapid and far-reaching change. Over the coming years, the developments that are now getting underway can be expected to gather added momentum, gradually bringing the financial structure of the French economy still more closely into line with that of the other leading industrial countries.

NOTES

1. Cash offerings by officially-listed companies, over the counter or on the secondary market, increased sharply in 1983, reaching Fr. fr. 10.8 billion, against about Fr. fr. 3–3.5 billion in the preceding years. Although of a lower scale, the results for 1984 are satisfactory (Fr. fr. 9.7 billion).

2. The interest paid on the first passbook accounts issued by the savings bank networks ('A passbooks') and by the Mutual Credit network ('blue passbooks') as well as on housing savings deposits, popular savings books, industrial savings accounts and business savings books remain tax-free.

Chapter VI

CAUSES OF CHANGE AND INNOVATION IN THE MIX OF
FINANCIAL INSTRUMENTS: THE NEW EMPHASIS ON SMALL
COMPANY EXTERNAL EQUITY FINANCING AND ITS IMPACT
ON CAPITAL MARKET STRUCTURE

by *Hartmut Schmidt*

FACTORS DETERMINING THE MIX OF FINANCIAL INSTRUMENTS

In the still challenging world of the seminal Modigliani-Miller model the mix of financial instruments is irrelevant, since there is no incentive to the issuing company to employ or to avoid any particular mix[1]. However, the irrelevance of the mix disappears as the assumptions creating that world of perfect financial markets are relaxed. Then a particular mix is desirable[2] if it

1. partitions the income stream of the company in a way that reduces tax exposure of both company and investors;

2. reduces payments to third parties by both company and investors or equivalents to such payments (e.g. direct and indirect costs of bankruptcy, costs of monitoring devices protecting bondholders or external shareholders, flotation costs, costs of countering present or anticipated regulatory or self-regulatory resistance, transaction and monitoring costs of investors);

3. takes advantage of differences in expectations among investors;

4. meets demands of investors hitherto unsatisfied, frequently because of regulatory restrictions.

Though the relative attractiveness of debt and equity is usually discussed in these terms, it appears tempting to explain the use of more than two classes of financial instruments and the emergence of innovative instruments by reference to these factors. The conclusion in most cases would be that a fairly broad set of complementing arrangements affecting a plurality of the above factors contributes to a successful innovation or to a re-balancing of the financial instruments mix. For instance, as it has long been held[3], an organized secondary market is required for the widespread acceptance of a new financial instrument; obviously, the lack of it imposes on investors transaction costs and monitoring costs that are high relative to established

Fair, D.E., (ed.) Shifting Frontiers in Financial Markets.
© *1986, Martinus Nijhoff Publishers, Dordrecht/Boston/Lancaster. ISBN 90-247-3225-5.*
Printed in the Netherlands.

instruments, and this disadvantage may well erode the relative benefits attained by the design of the new instrument.

Unfortunately, any attempt at a sufficiently detailed analysis of a variety of instruments would require more pages than allotted to this discussion paper. Thus, the paper will focus on only one particular type of financial instrument. It does not aim at an explanation of a shift in the mix that has occurred. It will rather try to suggest which complementing and mutually reinforcing arrangements may be suitable to facilitate a shift that is under way and that is widely believed to be most desirable: an increase in the external equity financing of small companies.

THE CASE FOR SMALL COMPANY EXTERNAL EQUITY FINANCING

In recent years increasing emphasis has been placed in various European countries on expanding small company external equity financing. This is witnessed by the extensive coverage of related topics by conferences, even at the level of the Commission of the European Communities[4], and in the financial press; in special tax measures such as the British business start-up and business expansion schemes; in the emergence of venture capital companies and other small firm investment companies at a surprisingly fast pace fostered, particularly in the Netherlands, by government guarantee and tax exemption schemes; and in the creation or reorganisation of special stock market segments for small company shares such as the unlisted securities market, the parallelmarkt, the aktiemarked III, the second marché, the new mercato ristretto and the terzo mercato[5].

The governmental and other official involvement in these and in related measures is motivated by the desire to create jobs, to assist in structural change and to promote innovation, growth and exports. Research on the job generation process in the United States, which pointed to the superior contribution of small firms in the creation of jobs[6], may have added to this. Since the cash-flow pattern of small growing firms is unsuitable for debt financing[7] and since funds from the retention of earnings tend to be insufficient or not yet available, the expansion of the small company sector of the economy requires a well functioning mechanism for small firm external equity financing.

However, a more gradual shift toward more small company external equity financing may have developed even without governmental involvement. As it has repeatedly been observed in competitive markets, services that have first been offered exclusively to wealthy consumers or larger companies will, if successful, later on become available to consumers and companies at large. For more than ten years there have been indications that the process of marketing corporate finance services (including primary and secondary market services) to medium-sized and small firms was slowly gaining momentum.

ON THE DESIGN OF A SMALL COMPANY CAPITAL RAISING MECHANISM

As pointed out in the first section, there are numerous factors to be taken into account in designing an attractive capital raising mechanism, and these factors do have implications extending clearly beyond what can be addressed by the purposeful organisation of financial markets as usually defined. Nevertheless, the design of the capital market seems to bear on the volume of small company external equity raising. Some aspects of this will be discussed below.

The sequence approach to small company capital raising

One view on the proper approach to small company capital raising holds that any public external equity financing should be preceded by an extended phase of private and preferably indirect capital raising. This view is firmly rooted in financial development and regulatory tradition.

Particularly in debt financing financial intermediaries have generally met the needs of small and medium-sized firms, and only large and established businesses have raised capital directly and publicly. As keen competition and growing sophistication lead financial institutions into assuming an expanded role in equity financing, intermediation appears to be the appropriate approach. This equity intermediation with an emphasis on smaller companies may be carried out either within existing institutions or by specialized venture capital and small business participation companies. Thus, a need for public capital raising by small companies does not seem to exist. Consequently, there is also no need for pertinent capital market arrangements.

This result is not at variance with regulatory tradition in European countries. From a regulatory point of view public equity financing of young and small firms appears undesirable. The protection of the investing public requires that companies offering shares publicly do need a certain threshold of quality and have attained a fair degree of stability. Moreover, the confidence in the financial system and the standing of established banks and brokers may be affected if these institutions would offer to the public securities of issuers that do not measure up to traditional minimum quality requirements and if these institutions, in due course, become associated with highly visible failures.

Therefore, a sequence approach seems to be appropriate. Small and high-risk companies, it is claimed, should turn to venture capital companies and other intermediaries providing equity capital and they should gradually establish an institutional shareholder base. Only later in their development, when their high-risk characteristics fade, they should be permitted to raise equity capital publicly.

The free-choice approach to small company capital raising

A second, less common view maintains that even a small and high-risk company should be free to choose whether to raise equity publicly or privately. This choice may well be relevant if small company equity raising is to be fostered. Of course, private financing may still be preferred to public equity financing because the placing of a minority interest with a venture capital company, a development company or with other institutional investors generally provides ready access to management experience. However, if a company looks strictly for capital, a number of reasons may lead it to publicly raise equity at an early date in its development.

First, in a private transaction the entrepreneur is selling non-marketable shares. Compared with equivalent marketable shares, this involves a discount which experts believe to amount to 20–50 per cent[8]. Thus, there is a strong incentive for a public flotation.

This discount probably is subject to economies of scale that result from the valuation process. In contrast to marketable securities, an established information and valuation process does not exist. If a share is marketable, there is a publicly available file with standardized information prepared or screened by identifiable investment bankers, accountants and lawyers and updated by annual and interim disclosure. Because of the more or less continuous nature of transaction opportunities, valuation work based on this material, and on incremental information to be obtained and analyzed can be used repeatedly. Repeated use of valuation work spreads the costs of valuation activities, and frequent transactions in the stocks so followed serve to recapture these costs. A potential buyer or seller may well simply rely on the competition of those who follow the stock[9]. In the case of non-marketable shares, however, a potential buyer is burdened with all the information and valuation efforts, which frequently involves several weeks of professional work. Obviously, a major part[10] of the discount for non-marketability reflects these efforts and the discount can be expected to decline with the size of the interest in the company that is to change hands. The second reason for raising equity publicly results from the problem of pricing shares in a private transaction. Since a market price is not available, the entrepreneur is likely to be convinced that the price granted is too low, even if he accounts for the lack-of-marketability discount. There is no way to prove that the entrepreneur is wrong. In addition, the overall discount may be enlarged by a lack of competition.

The overall discount is equivalent to a flotation cost component. It will be incurred again in later rounds of private equity financing. Of course, going public also requires substantial flotation costs, which include obvious major components such as professional fees, printing and advertising expenses and, less obvious, the opportunity cost of underpricing. However, contrary to private capital raising, discounts or underpricing will not be a factor in subsequent public share issues, since they will be based on the market price then prevailing. As these remarks suggest, a flotation cost advantage of public capital raising may or may not result. It would account for the first two reasons mentioned above.

A third reason are what could be labelled net continuing benefits of raising equity publicly. Obviously, any decision must look beyond initial or flotation costs and also reflect continuing costs and benefits. Shareholder servicing costs including continuing disclosure costs seem to be higher with going public, but there are benefits that may offset this disadvantage. First, being quoted implies that the company enjoys a higher degree of flexibility because of the marketability of the shares. This may become important in a variety of situations: shares and options are more useful as instruments to attract desirable executives and to motivate them; conflicts among major shareholders are likely to be less burdening because dissatisfied share-holders are not locked into a company, they can sell their shares without incurring a prohibitive discount; shares may be used as consideration in takeovers. Second, spreading shares widely among investors appears to be the only major route to at the same time attracting capital and maintaining a relatively high degree of independence. Contrary to other suppliers of capital, the investing public accepts equity instruments with reduced, contingent or even without voting rights. Since the desire for independence is a strong motive for establishing a company, entrepreneurs tend to place a high value on this advantage.

To sum up, given free choice it is likely that some companies will go public earlier than would be acceptable under a sequence approach regime. The notion that these companies would be too small to go public does not carry much weight. In recent years there have been various examples of successful flotations by companies with less than 30 employees and sales below ECU 4 m. Of course, as the above analysis suggests, not all companies of this size would think of going public, but the few that do are likely to have a concept and a management that give rise to expectations of superior growth and of future rounds of external equity financings.

Comparative assessment of the approaches

The fact that some companies do have an advantage under a regime following the free choice approach does not imply that the sequence approach should be disregarded. The objective of this paper is to explore which arrangements may facilitate the shift toward more small company external equity financing. The two approaches and their consequences for the design of a small company capital-raising mechanism will now be discussed in this regard. Three aspects are central to this assessment: valuation-contingent impediments, investor protection and possible damage to the standing of established banks and brokers.

Valuation-contingent impediments

An agreement to transfer any financial instrument or, more generally, any asset is extremely difficult to strike if the seller holds that the asset concerned is worth much more than the buyer is prepared to believe. This situation is most likely to occur in private financings that are considered under a sequence approach regime. As a result, since a mutually agreeable value cannot be established, small businesses frequently do not accept external equity finance even where it is available. This valuation-contingent impediment may be overcome in two ways, both of which aim at reducing the extent of possible valuation errors.

Under the sequence approach a financing may finally be achieved by varying the financial instrument to be transferred[11]. The impeding effect of the problem of estimating and valuing an enterprise's net income in the near and distant future, which must be tackled if ordinary shares or other instruments with full upside potential are involved, can be reduced or even avoided if an instrument is used that in some ways resembles debt. Such instruments are redeemable shares, shares sold under a repurchase agreement or shares sold under an agreement that grants a call option to the seller. However, this solution has serious consequences for the investment policy of venture capital companies, small business development companies and similar intermediaries. Since those mutilated equity instruments lack the full upside potential, the portfolios of these intermediaries are unlikely to generate returns sufficient to match losses resulting from complete failures (which certainly cannot be avoided by simply limiting the holding period e.g. by repurchase agreements with the issuers; the full downside potential remains). Any highly successful entrepreneurs will buy their shares back and, contrary to venture capital philosophy, unusual capital gains benefit the entrepreneur, whereas unusual losses are to be borne by the intermediary.

Consequently, the intermediaries will have to behave more or less like lenders and they must try to avoid high-risk companies. In other words, the sequence approach will fail at the very core of the objective of expanding small company external equity financing, since the highly risky young and innovative companies are not likely to obtain equity under a sequence approach regime though these small businesses hold out the promise of high growth. Their high risk cannot be sufficiently diversified away given the limitations of that regime.

Under a free-choice approach regime the valuation-contingent impediment can be overcome in a direct and rather effective way. Financing agreements are facilitated by the existence of unseasoned companies that have gone public and are quoted on the secondary market. The valuations which they enjoy in the market are a much more suitable and convincing point of reference for valuations of small private businesses than the quotations of established larger companies that qualify for a listing under sequence approach regimes. Consequently, equity instruments with full upside potential will be used in private financings, regime-related limitations to diversifications do not exist, and an environment conducive to true venture capital companies develops.

A contributive factor of a free choice system in addition to the availability of market valuations for small unseasoned firms is the ability of venture capital companies to sell to the investing public an interest in a business whenever the market conditions appear favourable. Venture capitalists are not locked into their investments for the extended period until the sequence approach regime minimum quality requirements for public flotation can be met. This enhances the flexibility of equity intermediaries and adds, as does the abatement of valuation-contingent impediments, to the volume and scope of equity intermediation.

The first part of the comparative assessment may be summed up by the following proposition: by generating public flotations of unseasoned companies a free-choice system, paradoxically, widens the scope and increases the volume of private external equity financing of small companies beyond what is likely to occur under a sequence approach regime, which relies solely on private equity raising.

Protection of the investing public and stock market access

As pointed out above, proponents of the sequence approach maintain that highly risky equity instruments of unseasoned companies are unfit for public flotation. By contrast, the free-choice approach does not advocate minimum quality requirements except for disclosure that must be sufficient for valuation; there are five reasons for this:

1. individual and institutional investors in today's securities markets and their advisers seem to be well aware of the risk and return characteristics of available instruments. Restrictions on flotations are unlikely to benefit any number of investors to speak of.

2. Diversification strategies now are widely followed by investors. The risk of a particular small company share may appear unacceptably high if one looks at it individually. Inspite of this, the share may well be desirable in a portfolio context. Restrictions solely based on risk characteristics of individual companies are misguided.

3. Even the average individual investor has ready access to a wide range of domestic and foreign high risk investment vehicles. As is obvious in the case of options, the invested amount frequently will be completely lost. Against this background any regulatory efforts to restrict the investment in small company shares appear discriminating.

4. The riskiness of small company shares is not artificially created. It reflects the innovativeness of the firm and other business characteristics. For employment and other economic reasons it is desirable to take advantage of the growth of independent small firms which assume this risk. This requires external equity financing. In contrast with former years of high employment, restrictions on small company equity financing are likely to carry a much higher economic cost.

5. Going public is one of the strongest and most visible elements of the capitalistic economy's incentive system. Under a sequence approach regime the founder of a company will only exceptionally enjoy the financial rewards and the public recognition of going public. By contrast, a free-choice system is likely to generate a highly visible succession of young and successful entrepreneurs. The example of these entrepreneurs going public will assure more than any other remedy that talent is

attracted into company formation. Restrictions on going public based on company age, size and risk will impede this process.

Against the background of this reasoning it seems difficult to justify minimum quality requirements for investor protection purposes. Particularly the last reason lends support to the previous section's result that a free-choice system can be expected to enlarge the scope and volume of small company external equity financing more than a sequence approach regime.

The principle of open primary markets is paralleled by the principle of open entry to secondary markets, which also flows from the free-choice approach. If there are not to be minimum requirements for access to the primary market, neither should subsequent trading of small company shares in the secondary market be prevented by obstructing entry requirements. However, this is not at all meant to suggest abolishing stock exchange listing requirements. It simply means that unseasoned companies should have access to some secondary market. In considering from time to time markets for small company equity instruments, exchanges may well decide, as the example of the New York Stock Exchange demonstrates, to continue to cater only to companies that meet elaborate and demanding requirements and to leave it up to other market organizers to offer secondary market services to lesser companies. In contrast, European exchanges recently have stepped up their efforts to serve smaller companies, partly with a view to countering or avoiding the competition of off-exchange market organizers[12] and partly in response to government prodding.

As a result, the notion has become widely accepted that a well organized secondary market consists of a hierarchy of market segments. The top segment, the traditional official market for established companies, is to be complemented by lower segments for smaller and unseasoned businesses. A cross section analysis[13] suggests that two kinds of lower segments have developed: wide open bottom level segments for truly unseasoned and other high risk businesses, and advanced level segments that aim at companies which have been in business for some years, have achieved profitability and want to signal their ability to meet a certain threshold of quality though they do not yet measure up to traditional listing requirements.

Because of these recent developments stock exchanges now welcome companies that were formerly considered too small, too young and too risky. However, this desirable new trend does not seem to extend down to the bottom level segments, which are still met with opposition and the call for upgrading regulation. The controversy on quality control in secondary stock markets has been shifted to the bottom level.

Possible damage to the standing of established banks and brokers

Proponents of the sequence approach also maintain that the standing of established banks and brokers may suffer if these institutions would engage in the flotations of unseasoned company securities and become associated with highly visible failures. If a segmented market exists, any sponsors of an unseasoned company issue will certainly and ostensibly express their reservations as to the quality of the issue by having it assigned to a lower market segment. But even then subsequent poor performance will tarnish their reputation. Consequently, the free-choice approach simply may not work because small companies cannot find investment bankers to float their shares or, in other words, because flotation costs are prohibitive.

Only very exceptionally have established firms ventured to extend their investment banking services to unseasoned companies. Obviously, any damage to the reputation of a larger firm cannot be balanced by the very modest returns that flotations of unseasoned company shares generate. However, this does not hold for small securities firms, which try to establish themselves by virtue of superior judgement and luck in situations unacceptable to firms already in good repute. Not surprisingly, in several European countries firms from outside the mainstream of investment banking have floated small company shares. Of course, possibly all of these will sooner or later see their fledging reputation vanish and their investor clients disappear. If they are not replaced by an inflow of newly formed firms, investment banking services will not be available to small high-risk companies. Replacement will also be needed if any of these firms become established, since they then can attract more stable issuers and they will shed their unseasoned company investment banking activities.

If small company external equity financing is to be vigorously fostered, investment banking obviously is a key element. The working of the free-choice approach, which can be expected to stimulate public and private small company financing more effectively than the sequence approach, depends on the existence of competitive small investment banking firms and on the ease of entry to this securities business. Unfortunately, entry is severely restricted in a number of continental European countries. Moreover, according to the spotty evidence available, most European regulators will neither appreciate nor merely tolerate the 'investment bankers turnover process', the coming and going of small investment banking firms that is related to ill-fated flotations of unseasoned businesses and that has been observed in the United States[14]. However, the acceptance of this turnover process appears to be central to volume and scope of public and private small company equity raising.

SUMMARY AND CONCLUSION

The contribution of financial markets to a shift toward more small company external equity financing rests primarily on their ability to reduce payments to third parties by both issuer and investor or equivalents of these payments. The paper has focussed on arrangements conducive to such a reduction. These arrangements are mutually dependent. The much desired private equity financing of generally highly risky young innovative firms with considerable growth potential presupposes for its efficient and effective functioning public flotations and secondary market valuations of comparable unseasoned companies. A hierarchy of stock market segments based on graduated entry requirements is an appropriate way to provide the special secondary market services that unseasoned companies require. However, a tiered secondary market structure is of little account unless it is matched by a corresponding, but even more pronounced hierarchy in the primary market, a hierarchy of investment bankers. In turn, a high level of venture capital activity and of other equity intermediation is likely to foster an investment banking environment that is both competitive and geared to unseasoned companies.

NOTES

1. Franco Modigliani and Merton H. Miller, The Cost of Capital, Corporation Finance and the Theory of Investment, *American Economic Review*, Vol. 48, 1958, pp. 261–297.

2. For a brief survey of relevant literature see Richard Brealey and Stewart Myers, *Principles of Corporate Finance*, 2nd ed., New York: McGraw-Hill, 1984, pp. 369–403, and Thomas E. Copeland and J. Fred Weston, *Financial Theory and Corporate Policy, 2nd ed., Reading, Mass.: Addison-Wesley, 1983, pp. 440–459.*

3. *J.S.G. Wilson, Some Aspects of the Development of Capital Markets, Banca Nazionale del Lavoro*, No. 79, December 1966, p. 307, and, as a recent source, Gunter Dufey and Ian H. Giddy, The Evolution of Instruments and Techniques in International Financial Markets, *SUERF Series* 35 A, 1981, pp. 4, 18, 23, 31.

4. The most recent volumes on the Commission's Luxembourg Symposia are: John Michael Gibb, ed., *Venture Capital Markets for the Regeneration of Industry*, Amsterdam: North-Holland, 1984, and J.M. Gibb and Siegfried Neumann, eds., *The Needs of New Technology-Based Enterprises*, Luxembourg: Infobrief, 1983.

5. For a survey the reader is referred to Hartmut Schmidt, *Special Stock Market Segments for Small Company Shares: Capital Raising Mechanism and Exit Route for Investors in New Technology Based Firms*, Luxembourg: Office for Official Publications of the European Communities, 1984 (with contributions of E. Wymeersch, A. Young, H. Reuter, H.M. Domke and Ch. Herms).

6. For a comparative survey of this research see: *The State of Small Business*, a report of the

President transmitted to Congress, Washington: USGPO, 1983, pp. 61–88, and David Birch, The Contribution of Small Enterprise to Growth and Employment, in: Herbert Giersch, ed., *New Opportunities for Entrepreneurship,* Tübingen: J.C.B. Mohr, 1984, pp. 1–16.

7. This implies that debt financing would most likely give rise to expectations of non-trivial bankruptcy costs and to relatively high promised yields on debt instruments.

8. Wilson Committee, *Interim Report: The Financing of Small Firms,* London: HMSO, 1979, p. 14. Stanley C. Golder, Structuring and Pricing the Financing, in: Stanley E. Pratt and the editors of the Venture Capital Journal, eds., *How to Raise Venture Capital, A Guide to Locating Start-Up and Development Capital and Dealing with Venture Capitalists,* New York: Charles Scribner's Sons, 1982, p. 138 (25–50%). Occasionally such discounts may be readily observed, cf. Bolton Quits Making Markets in OTC Stocks, *Wall Street Journal,* December 27, 1982, p. 20.

9. For a more detailed discussion see H. Schmidt, op. cit., pp. 512–516.

10. Other parts reflect additional monitoring costs and additional execution and settlement costs.

11. The only alternative to this that the author has come across is to make the price ultimately to be paid for a regular share contingent on the development during two or three years after the transaction. In other words, the investor will receive for the amount paid to the entrepreneur an interest in the company increasing step by step during this period if the company fails to measure up to certain targets (or a decreasing interest if the company meets ambitious targets – on which the entrepreneur based his valuation).

12. The Unlisted Securities Market, *Bank of England Quarterly Bulletin,* Vol. 23, 1983, p. 230.

13. Cf. the tables appended, which are taken from H. Schmidt, op. cit., pp. XXXIX–XL.

14. David L. Cohen, Small Business Capital Formation, in: Board of Governors of the Federal Reserve System, ed., *Public Policy and Capital Formation,* Washington: Publication services, Board of Governors of the Federal Reserve System, 1981, p. 256. U.S. Securities and Exchange Commission and U.S. Small Business Administration, *The Role of Regional Broker-Dealers in the Capital Formation Process: Underwriting, Market-Making and Securities Research Activities,* Phase II report, August 1981, p. 26. Walter Holman and Allan Young, Small Business in the United States: Failures and Public Financing, *Strathclyde Convergencies Issues in Accountability,* No. 9, October 1983, p. 31.

Table 1. Core requirements for access to advanced level small company segments

Segment (country)	Minimum amount to be held by the public in mio of local currency	Minimum percentage of stock to be held by the public	Use of flotation methods that tend to avoid underpricing	Press advertisement of prospectus	Interim reports	Standard minimum age of company in years	Accessible only to public companies
Unlisted securities market (United Kingdom and Ireland)	not required	10%	rare	one or two box advertisements required	required	3	yes
Aktiemarked II (Denmark)	2.5	15%	required	one or two box ads. req.	voluntary	1	yes
Official parallelmarkt (Netherlands)	0.25	10%	no	box advertisement required	required	0	no
Geregelter Freiverkehr (Germany)	not required	not required	no	voluntary, prospectus not required	voluntary	1	yes
Official market (Luxembourg)	50	not required	no	voluntary	required	3	yes
Parketmarkt (Belgium)	not required	not required	no	voluntary	voluntary	5	yes
Second marché (France)	2–4[1]	10%	attempted	voluntary, prospectus not required	required	0	yes
Mercato ristretto (Italy)	200[3]	20%	no	full prospectus	voluntary	2[2]	yes
Official market (Greece)	25[3]	not applicable	no	voluntary	required	3[2]	yes
Recommended	ECU 1 mio	10%	incentive for use recommended	voluntary	required	3	yes

1. Tentative and preliminary.
2. Profits must have been reported for the latest two or three financial years respectively.
3. Calculated on the basis of related requirements.

Table 2. Core requirements for access to bottom level small company segments

Segment (country)	Minimum amount to be held by the public in mio of local currency	Minimum percentage of stock to be held by the public	Use of flotation methods that tend to avoid underpricing	Press advertisement of prospectus	Interim reports	Standard minimum age of company in years	Accessible only to public companies
Broker-dealer OTC (United Kingdom)	not required	not required	no	voluntary	voluntary	1	yes
Occasional bargains facility (Ireland)	not required	not required	not applicable	not applicable	voluntary	1	no
Aktiemarked III (Denmark)	1	15%	required	one or two box ads. req.	voluntary	1	yes
Non-official parallelmarkt (Netherlands)	not required	not required	no	voluntary, prospectus not required	voluntary	0	no
Ungeregelter Freiverkehr (Germany)	not required	not required	no	voluntary, prospectus not required	voluntary	0	yes
Off-exchange trading (Luxembourg)	not required	not required	no	voluntary	voluntary	0	yes
Ventes publiques (Belgium)	not required	not required	not applicable	not applicable	voluntary	0	yes
Marché hors cote (France)	not required	not required	no	voluntary, prospectus not required	voluntary	0	yes
Terzo mercato (Italy)	not required	not required	no	voluntary, prospectus not required	voluntary	0	yes
Recommended	not required	not required	incentive for use recommended	voluntary, prospectus not required	voluntary	0	no

Chapter VII

THE BIRTH OF A NEW MARKET – THE CASE OF THE SWEDISH MONEY MARKET

by *Pehr Wissén*

INTRODUCTION

The Swedish money market started on the third of March, 1980, when the first certificate of deposit was issued. The CDs were introduced to facilitate liability management for Swedish commercial banks and to give investors a liquid, fixed income investment opportunity. These goals were achieved. The most striking consequence of the introduction of CDs was, however, not that life was made easier for the banks (or the investors who bought the CDs), but rather that a money market was born. After four years this new market has had far-reaching consequences for the funding and short-term investment of banks, industrial firms, local authorities and government as well as for monetary policy.

The growth of the market has taken place in steps. The first step, the innovation which started the process, was the introduction of CDs. With the CDs a primary market for money market instruments was established. In the second step government T-bills were introduced. They were issued in such large quantities that they formed the basis for an active secondary market. After the T-bills, in the third step, the local authorities, industrial firms and finance companies started issuing commercial paper. Commercial paper was mostly sold on the primary market and was not subject to active trade in the secondary market.

After the introduction of these instruments the market expanded to longer maturities in a fourth step. T-bills with maturities up to 2 years were issued, and government bonds were actively traded in the market in a way which had not been common before.

The growth of the market also influenced the way in which monetary policy was conducted. The central bank started using open market operations to control the rate of interest, whereas monetary policy had preciously been conducted by changing administered interest rates. This change in monetary policy was the fifth step in the development of the market. The

Fair, D.E., (ed.) Shifting Frontiers in Financial Markets.
© *1986, Martinus Nijhoff Publishers, Dordrecht/Boston/Lancaster. ISBN 90-247-3225-5.*
Printed in the Netherlands.

sixth and most recent step is the introduction of a futures market. It is still in a very early phase, but represents a logical step in the development.

This development, which will be described in further detail below, was started by a financial innovation – the introduction of CDs. The motives for the innovation were rather limited, but the consequences were important.

Many countries have experienced a rapid development in their financial markets in the last decade[1]. There are important similarities in these experiences, which have led to attempts to generalize and construct a theory of financial innovation[2]. The theory identifies certain exogenous causes behind financial innovations. One example of such a list of exogenous causes is given by Silber (1983), and includes: inflation and its effects on (a) the level of interest rates, (b) the general price level and (c) tax effects, the volatility of interest rates, technology, legislative initiative and internationalization.

Most of these factors have been at work in Swedish money market development, and to the list could also, in the Swedish case, be added shifts in the sectoral distribution of financial savings.

The purpose of this paper is to present what may be called a case study of financial innovation. The Swedish experience is described with an aim to explaining why the different stages of development occurred. The main reason why I think this is an interesting example is that a rather limited innovation was the starting point for a long process (as described by the six steps above).

In the following section I discuss the introduction of the money market in Sweden. The reasons why the commercial banks introduced certificates of deposit are discussed, as well as some of the conditions which had to be satisfied in order for the market to start operating.

The rapid growth of the money market after the introduction of CDs was due to the large government budget deficit, as well as de-regulation in the capital markets. These are treated on pages 83–86.

The consequences of the development of the money market for monetary policy is discussed in a separate section, where I also address the question of whether the money market has led to crowding out of real investments – a suspicion which has been voiced in the Swedish debate.

Finally I summarize the main features of the process.

THE BIRTH OF THE SWEDISH MONEY MARKET

In order to get a perspective on the introduction of a money market in

Sweden, it is useful to go back to the 1960s[3]. In those days it was, at least in some respects, easy to handle the financial affairs of an industrial company. The rate of inflation was low and fairly constant, the exchange rates were fixed under the Bretton Woods agreement, interest rates did not vary much (a natural consequence of a constant rate of inflation) and Swedish industrial firms were investing most of their internally-generated funds in real capital. There was no need for great sophistication in financial affairs in industrial companies. Most firms did not have a separately staffed department responsible for borrowing and lending. In this period it was customary for an industrial firm to have a 'house bank' to turn to. The ties between the firm and the bank (usually one or, at most, two banks) were very strong.

During the 1970s the scenario changed. First, the Bretton Woods agreement broke down, which led to more frequent changes in the exchange rates. Second, following the oil price shock, inflation accelerated, which brought with it higher and more variable interest rates. On top of this, the competitiveness of Swedish industry was drastically decreased, which led to lower profits and a much lower rate of investments. Now it was much more difficult to manage the financial operations of a big multinational firm. The positions in various currencies had to be monitored, and the greater variability in interest rates gave strong incentives to plan the borrowing and lending of firms in accordance with the expected development of interest rates.

Perhaps firms could have solved these problems by relying even more on their banks than before, but they did not. Instead they started forming finance departments as a part of their staff organization to handle the firm's asset/liability management. This increased their sophistication and also made the firms less dependent on their 'house bank'. Thus, the competition in the capital markets increased. Firms started to shop around among banks to see where they could get the highest rate of interest on their short-term funds. Also, finance companies started to fund themselves by borrowing from the firms, which drove the short-term interest rates higher than they otherwise would have been.

The banks had to increase the interest they paid for large volumes of short-term funds. The bank short-term funding from industry took the form of prime rate deposits (in Swedish 'specialinlåning') which were either accounts with seven days notice or accounts with longer maturities (90 days was the most important among the longer maturities). Mostly, the interest paid was variable and tied to the official rate of discount. As is seen in Table 1 the volume of these prime rate deposits grew rapidly from 1975 up to 1982.

The terms of these accounts were often negotiated with each customer

Table 1. The volume of prime rate deposits in Swedish commercial banks (billions of Swedish crowns)

Year	Prime Rate Deposits, SEK billions
1976	17.6
1977	19.1
1978	28.0
1979	34.4
1980	39.1
1981	36.5
1982	44.7

Note: The figures refer to the month of May in the respective years.
Source: Nyberg, L. (1982).

separately. Thus, there was no market-determined, official price of short-term funds. Also, the funds were not perfectly liquid for the firms. A firm *could* cancel a special account before maturity, especially big firms could do this, but the account was less liquid than for example an investment in a T-bill in a well functioning money market. The accounts had disadvantages also for the banks. Since the accounts were part of a personal relationship with the customer, it was sometimes difficult to change the conditions. It was particularly difficult to lower the rate of interest paid. The interest rate on the accounts tended, for this reason, to be rigid. In practice, the interest rate was not changed more frequently than 3–5 times a year. This meant that the account was a rather inflexible way of funding a bank. In spite of this it was an important part of the banks' short-term funding.

When the certificates of deposit were introduced, in March 1980, the situation could thus be characterized by:

1. a growing degree of financial sophistication on the part of the industrial firms. This brought with it less and less dependence on a 'house bank'.

2. A growing liquidity among Swedish firms.

3. A growing dependence on the part of the banks on the prime rate accounts for their short-term funding.

In response to the need for a market in which the firms could place their liquidity and in response to the needs of the banks to have a more flexible means of funding themselves, certificates of deposit were introduced. They were constructed with fixed rates of interest and maturities ranging from 30 to 360 days. They are tradable on a secondary market where, initially, the banks themselves were the only market makers.

THE INTRODUCTION OF T-BILLS

The money market in Sweden would probably not have been very lively today if the development had stopped with the certificates of deposit[4]. The volume of CDs did grow rather rapidly, as seen in Table 2, but it is not clear that the volume of CDs was big enough to make the market function efficiently.

Table 2. The volume of CDs 1980–1983 (SEK billions)

1980	5.631
1981	7.364
1982	5.163
1983	14.839

Source: Sverige Officiella Statistik (1984).

There are economies of scale in the money market. If it does not reach a certain volume it will probably never be very active. There was a limited volume of CDs that could be issued, and therefore it was important that new categories of borrowers started funding themselves on the market.

In July 1982 the government started issuing treasury bills on the Swedish money market. The T-bills were constructed exactly like the CDs and were immediately accepted by the participants in the market. The volume of T-bills grew very rapidly and they soon became the most important instrument traded in the market. Figure 1 shows the volume of T-bills and CDs in the money market up until today.

At first the National Debt Office, which issues the treasury bills, issued them with maturities up to one year. The interest rate was set by the authorities and offered to the market. Later this was changed, so that the T-bills were issued with maturities up to two years, and the interest rate was determined by auction.

In order to understand why the government started issuing such large amounts of T-bills in 1982 one can look at Table 3, which shows the distribution of financial savings in various sectors of the economy in the years 1970 to 1983.

From Table 3 it can be seen that the government sector has had increasingly negative financial savings, and that industry has had first negative and then positive financial savings. The negative savings on the part of the government reflects the large government budget deficit.

The growing positive financial savings on the part of industry mainly

84

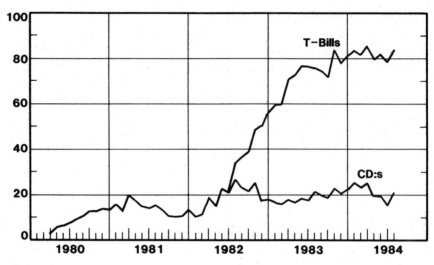

Figure 1. The volume of money market instruments issued in Sweden 1980–84 (SEK billion)

reflects the effects of the devaluation policy followed by Swedish government. In order to increase the competitiveness of industry the krona was devalued in 1982 by 16 per cent relative to a basket of foreign currencies. This led to booming profits in industry. It did not, however, lead to investments. Apparently the expectations of future profits were not bright enough to warrant an investment boom. The result was thus a large cash flow in industrial firms, which was, mainly, invested in short-term financial assets. In 1984 real investments in industry started increasing. Still the firms are very liquid and invest considerable amounts in short-term financial assets[5].

Table 3. Financial savings as per cent of GNP 1970–1983

	1970–74	1975–79	1980–83	1983
Government	0.6	− 2.4	− 8.3	− 8.4
Local authorities	− 0.9	− 0.3	0.0	− 0.1
Public insurance	4.4	3.9	3.0	2.6
Household	− 0.4	− 0.7	0.5	0.5
Industry	− 4.8	− 5.0	− 2.1	0.4
Financial firms	1.8	3.1	4.2	4.1
Current account	0.7	− 1.5	− 2.7	− 0.9

Source: Långtidsutredningen (1984), Swedish Ministry of Finance.

Thus, the government needed to borrow large amounts to cover the budget deficit and the industrial firms had a growing liquidity which they wanted to invest in short-term financial assets. At least two methods to transfer the funds from the firms to the government were discussed. The first was to initiate government-controlled funds with long-term bonds, where the firms could buy shares. This alternative was discussed seriously and the plans to start the funds were advanced when a second alternative was proposed. The second alternative was that the government should start issuing treasury bills which were to be sold to the firms and traded on the money market. The treasury bills were chosen and, in hindsight, this seems like the natural solution. It is interesting to notice, however, that at the time it was not the only solution under consideration.

The fact that the money market by 1982 had developed a lot was probably an important factor behind the choice the government made. In the period from 1980 to 1982, a trading system with Reuter screens had developed. The first non-bank dealer in money market instruments had been established. The spread between the bid and the ask price in the market was down from 25 points initially to 10 points. Without all this development in the market it is doubtful whether the government would have chosen T-bills. The introduction of the CDs and the subsequent learning period were thus important for the choice of T-bills on the part of government and hence for the rapid development which later took place.

After the introduction of the T-bills, the changes in the market came very fast. A brief list includes:

1. The introduction of T-bills with maturities between one and two years.
2. The issuing of T-bills by auction.
3. The issuing of government bonds at market interest rates. Earlier the government had issued bonds below market interest rates, and via a system of liquidity ratio requirements forced the banks and the insurance companies to buy and hold the bonds.
4. The removal of the liquidity ratio requirements for the commercial banks. The ratio requirements are still maintained for insurance companies.
5. The issuing of commercial paper by local authorities, finance companies and industrial firms. Recently this has expanded rapidly.
6. The use of open market operations by the central bank to control the level of interest rates.

This list is not exhaustive, but it clearly shows the trend towards market orientation. Once a sub-market on the capital market starts functioning like a market, it seems to become much harder to control the rest of the capital market with rules and regulations. Thus, the money market may have been the catalyst behind the above development.

CONSEQUENCES FOR MONETARY POLICY

The establishment of a money market had one obvious and important consequence for monetary policy: it enabled the central bank to conduct open market operations, which they started in a systematic way in spring 1984.

Before the spring of 1984 monetary policy, or rather interest rate policy, was conducted mainly by changing interest rates which were controlled by the central bank. A simple graph of demand and supply in the Swedish money market can illustrate[6].

Sweden has foreign exchange regulation, preventing free transfer of money out of the country. Partly for this reason the central bank has adopted a discount window policy, enabling the commercial banks to borrow (in principle) unlimited amounts at a given interest rate on a day-to-day basis, and to deposit unlimited amounts at another, lower, interest rate. The rate at which the banks can borrow unlimited amounts is called the ceiling rate in Figure 2, and the rate at which they can deposit unlimited amounts is called the floor rate. Figure 2 depicts the determination of the day-to-day interest rate, which in turn affects market rates on longer maturities.

It is obvious that the ceiling and the floor rates set an effective ceiling and an effective floor for the day-to-day interest rates. If the equilibrium rate was for example above the ceiling rate, someone could borrow unlimited amounts at the ceiling rate in the central bank and invest them at a higher rate. That represents a money machine and can never be an equilibrium. Hence the highest possible equilibrium interest rate must be the ceiling rate. A similar reasoning applies to the floor rate.

The demand curve is determined by the ceiling, the floor and in between these levels, by ordinary portfolio substitution. If the interest rate goes down, the opportunity cost of holding money decreases and the demand for money increases.

The supply of money consists of the supply from the central bank, which is interest-inelastic, and the supply of money coming from abroad. If the interest rate in Sweden increases, Swedish firms can take home payments from abroad earlier than they otherwise would have done. This increases

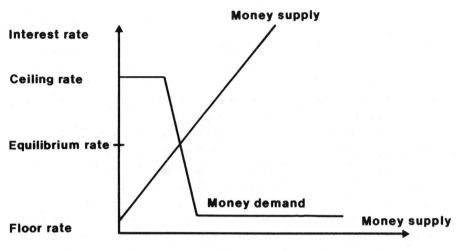

Figure 2. Interest rate determination in the Swedish money market.

the supply of money. They also have the possibility to borrow, for example, on the American money market, sell the dollars, buy kronor, invest the kronor on the Swedish money market and at the same time buy dollars on the forward market. This, of course, is pure interest rate arbitrage. It explains why the money supply schedule is upward sloping.

Before spring 1984, when the open market operations started, the central bank controlled the level of interest rates by holding down the money supply, and thereby keeping the commercial banks in the zone where they had to borrow over-night money at the ceiling rate. If the central bank wanted to change the level of interest rates they simply changed the ceiling rate, and the money market rates followed. This method has been used also after the spring of 1984. During the summer of 1984, for example, the ceiling rate was increased by 2 percentage points. Whenever the banks are borrowing at the ceiling rate this is, of course, the only way to affect interest rates. Apart from changes in the ceiling rate the central bank (before the use of auctions) tried to influence money market rates through the rates they set when they issued new T-bills.

Since the spring of 1984 the central bank appears to try to keep the system in the interval between the ceiling rate and the floor rate (see Figure 2). There, the central bank can easily change the market interest rate by buying or selling T-bills – that is by open market operations. This has also been tried with success. The advantage with open market operations is that it is a much more flexible instrument for monetary policy. It allows the central bank to interfere as often as is deemed necessary. It is an important consequence of the establishment of a money market.

A question which has been discussed is whether the establishment of the money market has led to any crowding out of real investments. After all, the money market offers high returns to a firm's short-term funds, which may be hard to obtain by investing in e.g. machinery. There have been no systematic studies of this question in Sweden. Most economists seem to agree that, so far, there are no signs of any crowding out, however. The reason that investments have been stagnant in Swedish industry is not that present interest rates are high, but rather that expectations of future profits are not bright enough. The money market has provided an alternative to investing in plant and equipment. Competition in the money market has, probably, pushed up short-term interest rates above what they would otherwise have been. This does not seem to have affected business investment in plant and machinery so far. It has merely siphoned money from industry to government. This does not exclude that crowding out could occur in the future, however.

CONCLUDING COMMENTS

A financial innovation could loosely be defined as a new way of solving problems in the financial markets. With such a broad definition of the term the Swedish financial market has witnessed a number of innovations in the past four years: certificates of deposit, treasury bills, commercial paper, forwards and even changes in monetary policy could all be regarded as financial innovations.

This paper has stressed the interdependence between these innovations. In my opinion the important innovation was the introduction of CDs. It was the starting point for the whole process which followed. The reason why it was important was that it led to the establishment of a new market. The introduction of CDs was followed by a period of learning. The investors learned how to calculate with fixed income securities, a dealing system was installed and dealer firms were established.

Thus the introduction of CDs was important not primarily because it achieved the goals of making liability management easier for the banks or that it gave the investors a better instrument for short-term investment. It was important because it created a new market.

NOTES

1. See e.g. Akhtar (1983) for a survey.
2. See e.g. Silber (1983) and, for a discussion of the issues, Bank of England (1983).
3. This section is largely based on Nyberg, L. (1982).
4. This section is largely based on Heikensten, L., Nyberg, L., Wissén, P. (1984).
5. The importance of changes in financial savings for the development of the financial market in the US is discussed by Friedman, B.M. (1980).
6. The graph is adopted from Englund P., et al. (1984).

REFERENCES

1. Akhtar, M.A. (1983), 'Financial Innovations and Their Implications for Monetary Policy: an International Perspective'. *BIS Economic Papers* No. 9. – December 1983, Basle.
2. Bank of England (1983), *Quarterly Bulletin*, September 1983 pp. 358–377, vol 23, No. 3.
3. Englund, P., Hörngren, L., and Viotti, S. (1985), 'A Short-term Model of the Swedish Money Market', *The Stockholm School of Economics, EFI Research Paper* 6293.
4. Friedman, B.M. (1980), 'Postwar Changes in the American Financial Markets', from Feldstein, M. ed.: *The American Economy in Transition*, National Bureau of Economic Research, The University of Chicago Press.
5. Heikensten, L., Nyberg, L., Wissén, P. (1984), 'Den svenska penningmarknaden – tillkomst och utveckling', *Företag och Samhälle, SNS Orientering Nr 1/84*.
6. Långtidsutredningen (1984), SOU 1984:4, Finansdepartementet. (The 1984 Medium Term Survey).
7. Nyberg, L. (1982), 'De svenska bankcertifikaten'. Expertbilaga till SOU 1982:53, Kreditpolitiken. Fakta, teorier och erfarenheter.
8. Silber, W.L. (1983), 'The Process of Financial Innovation', *American Economic Review*, papers and proceedings, May, 1983.
9. Sveriges officiella statistik (1984), 'Bankaktiebolagen, Fondkommissionärerna, Fondbörsen och VPC 1983', Bankinspektionen, Stockholm 1984.

Chapter VIII

CAUSES OF CHANGE AND INNOVATION IN THE MIX OF
FINANCIAL INSTRUMENTS: THE UK EXPERIENCE

by *Andrew D. Bain*

INTRODUCTION

The factors which influence the choice of financial instruments and pattern
of financing in an economy can be classified into three categories: structural, legislative, and market. (Hood, 1959). Structural factors are the most
fundamental and wide-ranging. They include the location of surplus and
deficit units in the economy; the needs and preferences – as regards the risk
and maturity characteristics of the instruments they hold – of the agents
concerned; the legal framework and social practices, e.g. regarding provision for retirement and maintenance in old age; and the economic and
political environment, reflected for instance in experience of past and fear
of future inflation, and in the actual and perceived risk characteristics of the
liabilities of deficit units and financial intermediaries. While none of these
structural factors is immutable most are regarded as permanent, or at least
persistent, features of a country's economic life, features which cannot be
changed quickly or tampered with by governments lightly.

Legislative factors are factors which can in principle be changed by the
legislature. The boundary between structural and legislative factors is
therefore not clear-cut; occasionally legislative changes alter the way in
which things get done – for example, wholesale abolition of the tax reliefs
attached to occupational pension schemes might well lead people in Britain
to adopt other means of providing for old age. But other legislative changes
– particularly changes in tax rates, and in other provisions of the tax law –
may well affect financial decisions at the margin, and so the pattern of
financing in the economy, without ranking as structural adjustments.

Market factors, the third category, also affect the range and relative costs
of the financial instruments available to savers and investors. In part these
reflect the stage of development of financial institutions and markets in the
economy – the choice between negotiable and non-negotiable financial
instruments often reflects market factors, and changes in the competitive

Fair, D.E., (ed.) Shifting Frontiers in Financial Markets.
© *1986, Martinus Nijhoff Publishers, Dordrecht/Boston/Lancaster. ISBN 90-247-3225-5.*
Printed in the Netherlands.

position of one group of institutions relative to others affect the costs of different financial instruments. In part they reflect cyclical influences and the policies of the monetary authorities, which affect both absolute and relative interest rates.

In this paper I shall examine the causes of three changes in financing practice in the UK which have occurred in recent years. First, the heavy reliance of industrial and commercial companies (ICC) on finance provided by the banks, to such an extent that considerable amounts have had to be refinanced by the Bank of England; secondly, the growth of finance leasing; and finally the addition of index-linked securities to the menu provided by the public sector.

COMPANY FINANCING AND 'OVERFUNDING' THE PUBLIC SECTOR BORROWING REQUIREMENT (PSBR)

The facts

Tables 1 to 3 detail three important changes in the pattern of company financing in the last 25 years. First (Table 1), there has been a movement away from the capital market as a major source of external funds, with the banks becoming the dominant source – in the decade from 1958–1967 the sums raised from the banks and the capital market were more or less equal; in the ten years from 1973–1982 the banks provided five times as much as the capital market. Secondly (Table 2), in recent years much of the growth in bank lending has taken the form of commercial bills accepted by the banks.

Table 1. UK industrial and commercial companies, selected sources and uses of funds (% of GDP at market prices)

	1958–62	1963–67	1968–72	1973–77	1978–82	1983
Sources						
Bank borrowing	1.07	1.29	2.23	2.71	2.23	0.48
Ordinary shares	0.71	0.30	0.44	0.52	0.46	0.57
Preference shares						
and debt	0.45	0.90	0.45	0.03	0.03	0.03
Uses						
Bank deposits	0.06	0.56	1.32	1.27	1.07	1.78
Other liquid assets	0.36	− 0.09	− 0.01	0.20	0.15	0.17

Sources: Bank of England *Statistical Abstract* No; 1 C.S.O. databank.

Table 2. UK industrial and commercial companies, bank borrowing (£m)

	1976	1977	1978	1979	1980	1981	1982	1983
Loans	2,430	2,242	2,407	3,454	5,806	4,298	4,093	2,114
Bills	253	234	− 13	527	534	1,549	2,480	− 667
Total	2,683	2,476	2,394	3,981	6,340	5,847	6,573	1,447

Source: Bank of England.

Table 3. Bank of England, Issue Department holdings of UK commercial bills etc. (end of period)

	£ million
1979	27
1980	430
1981	2,989
1982	7,703
1983	6,978
1984 Q3	9,275

Sources: Financial Statistics, June 1984 Table 27D; *Bank of England Quarterly Bulletin*, December 1984.

Thirdly (Table 3) a high proportion of the commercial bills outstanding are now held by the Bank of England – holdings within the monetary sector were reduced by some £ 3,000 million between the end of 1979 and the end of 1983.

The trend towards bank finance

The most significant change in the structure of UK ICC's external financing in the last 25 years has been the increased importance of bank finance in comparison with funds raised directly in the capital market. This has come about for three main reasons:

1. the effect of inflation on interest rates reduced new long-term bond issues to virtually zero for many years, from which a slow recovery is only now beginning to take place.
2. The low valuation ratio for ordinary shares, and the tax treatment of dividends in comparison with interest, have made new equity capital seem expensive to many companies.
3. Banks developed term lending and project finance facilities.

As a result ICC turned increasingly to the banks as their principal source of funds.

The effect of inflation on bond yields needs little elution here – the yields demanded by lenders must include an allowance for future inflation *plus* a risk premium to persuade bond-holders to retain their funds in nominal, rather than real, assets. For borrowers, however, the inflation risk is on the other side. Provided inflation remains high or, even better, rises, servicing and repaying long-term debt will not prove unduly burdensome. But if inflation should fall, long-term debt with fixed high servicing costs would prove very burdensome, particularly if competitors are able to fund themselves at lower rates. From the allowance for future inflation which could reasonably be built into the fixed interest rate the borrower therefore wants to *deduct* a risk premium to provide some protection against the possibility that inflation might fall. The effect is that yields on existing bonds rise to the level required to compensate bond-holders for their risk, but that new issues dry up because this level of yields is more than most potential new issuers are prepared to pay.

By comparison, variable-rate loans are attractive to borrowers because, although short-term interest rates are subject to influences other than inflation, by and large they do correlate well with the inflation rate. Borrowers may therefore reasonably hope that a decline in inflation will be reflected eventually in their cost of funds.

Nevertheless, variable-rate loans are not altogether satisfactory as a substitute for long-term fixed rate bonds. As a source of quasi-permanent finance they are inferior, because the term to maturity is usually much shorter, and because of the risk that the cost may rise sharply at an inconvenient time if a restrictive monetary policy is pursued. If, owing to the risks associated with inflation, bonds seemed unattractive as a source of finance companies might therefore have been expected to turn to the equity market as the preferred alternative source of finance, rather than to the banks.

They did not do so, presumably because equity funds seemed too expensive. First, the valuation ratio – the ratio of the market value of UK companies to the estimated replacement cost of their assets – has generally been low (Figure 1). New shares could only be sold at prices which allowed new shareholders a slice of the company's assets for less than their replacement cost. With a rights issue, any existing shareholders with sufficient spare cash to take up their rights could avoid diluting their interest in the company, but for those without sufficient cash dilution would be unavoidable. In these conditions company directors, who thought their company was

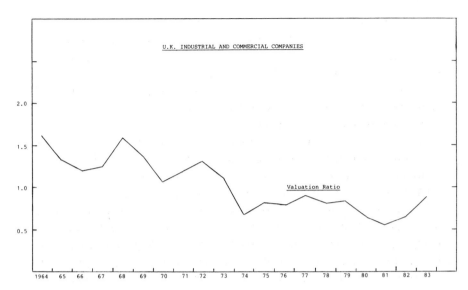

Figure 1. Source: Bank of England Quarterly Bulletin, September 1984.

undervalued by the market, were reluctant to raise new equity capital.

The fundamental cause, of course, was the low level of profitability of much of British industry. The real yield demanded by shareholders was not being earned by UK companies, so the market placed a lower value on companies' assets than their reproduction cost. Subsequent scrapping of out-dated capacity and improvements in efficiency (and profitability on capital employed) suggest that the market may well have been right. Nevertheless, at the time company directors often did not see it this way.

The tax system also seemed to discourage equity issues. Dividends have to be paid out of gross income, whereas interest is deductible as a charge before tax. This adds to the apparent servicing cost of equity capital. Until 1973, with the 'classical' system of corporation tax, dividends were in effect taxed twice – once as part of the company's profits, and again in the hands of the shareholders as their income. Since 1973, however, the 'imputation' system has been in force and while companies have still been required to pay advance corporation tax on dividend payments, this has been credited towards the shareholders' tax liability[1]. Nevertheless, so far as the company is concerned, the cash required to service debt is the gross interest less corporation tax (provided that the company has sufficient taxable profits) whereas that required for equity is the net dividend plus advance corporation tax. This has served to narrow the cost difference between debt and equity; indeed, for companies whose shares have high dividend yields the cost of servicing new equity capital often exceeds that of debt[2].

For balance sheet reasons growing companies do, of course, have to raise new equity capital if they cannot generate and retain sufficient profits to build their equity base from internal sources. But equity issues have not generally been seen as an attractive alternative to long-term debt. Instead, companies turned to the banks for their funds.

Banks responded to the demand for funds by improving the facilities they procided for ICC. Twenty-five years ago most bank lending in Britain took the form of overdrafts, technically repayable on demand though in practice continued virtually indefinitely in many cases. Banks also had a preference for the provision of working, rather than fixed capital, with the latter being financed from a company's permanent resources. Since that time project loans and medium-term lending have become commonplace, the former being particularly well-suited to individual investment projects from which the cash generated can be readily identified, and the latter giving to the borrower some of the assurance of the long-term loan for which it is a substitute.

Bank lending has generally been on variable-rate terms, matching in this respect the banks' own funding arrangements. That is not necessarily convenient for company borrowers. Nevertheless, for those companies which were prepared to use medium-term financing, and which could in principle have issued long-term loans if they had wanted, the banks have provided a superior alternative[3].

The trend towards finance can thus be seen to result from a combination of structural factors – inflation and low profitability – the tax treatment of debt and equity capital (a legislative factor) and market factors influencing the facilities provided by the banks.

The supply of bank loans

To meet this demand for loans banks would need either to increase their deposit and capital base sufficiently or to cut back on lending elsewhere. Lending to ICC is, of course, only one part of their sterling lending.

Superficially it may appear that the supply of deposits to the banks will be governed by the monetary targets chosen by the Government. No doubt this is correct, so far as it goes, but it begs the question of what determines the monetary targets. These ought to be influenced by the growth in the economy's demand for bank deposits. What the authorities have to guard against is undue *temporary deviations* from the trend increase in the permanent demand for money holdings – the permanent demand can safely be accomodated. It is necessary therefore to examine the factors influencing the demand for bank deposits.

In the UK the demand for bank deposits by the personal sector has been affected by pension arrangements, incentives for home ownership, and government competition in the market for liquid savings.

Pension arrangements in Britain represent a partnership between the public and private sector. The state provides a basic flat-rate pension, with a supplementary scheme linking pension rights to income for those not covered in other ways. But employers with approved occupational pension schemes may contract their employees out of the supplementary scheme, so that the income-related benefit is provided through private schemes. Contributions to such schemes are paid out of gross income by the employer or employee, and the investment income of the pension funds is also free of tax. Self-employed people can also now take advantage of similar arrangements run by life assurance offices. The schemes are much the most tax-effective method of saving for retirement.

Until the 1984 Budget saving through life assurance also benefited from tax relief (of 15 per cent of the premiums), though this is no longer available on new life policies. However saving through life offices is still encouraged by the arrangements for mortgage interest relief on house purchase. Tax relief on borrowing is maximised if, rather than repaying by instalments, the entire mortgage loan is repaid at maturity out of the proceeds of an endowment life policy.

The result of these arrangements has been a trend increase in the flow of saving through life assurance and pension funds (LAPF) (Table 4). How far the causes should be classified as structural and how far as legislative is a moot point. Any change in the balance between public and private pension provision could reasonably be regarded as a structural change, and features

Table 4. Personal sector saving 1958–1983 (as % of GDP)

	1958–62	1963–67	1968–72	1973–77	1978–82	1983
Saving through life assurance and pension funds	3.1	3.3	3.6	4.3	5.2	5.1
Saving through deposits etc.	3.2	4.1	5.2	5.9	6.6	5.3
(of which bank deposits)	(1.0)	(1.3)	(2.6)	(3.5)	(2.1)	(1.0)

of the tax system like mortgage interest relief seem firmly embedded. But it is possible that the extent of tax discrimination in favour of pension funds may be reduced, perhaps by providing some encouragement to other forms of saving.

Turning to personal saving in the form of deposits or closely competitive instruments (e.g. national savings), the most important factor is no doubt a structural need for liquidity – a desire to hold part of savings in a highly liquid form. The extent of such saving is of course influenced by the main factors which enter into models of personal saving as a whole – of key relevance here is the effect of inflation, which raises the personal saving ratio and more particularly the flow of funds into deposit-taking institutions. A decline in inflation has, of course, the opposite effect. It is no doubt inflation which accounts for the major movements in the share of GDP represented by personal sector liquid saving in Table 4.

Mortgage interest relief and other tax advantages enjoyed by owner-occupiers have also had a bearing on the banks' share within this total. The building societies, which specialise in lending for house purchase, have been put at an advantage (though this is a segment of the loans market in which the clearing banks are now more actively engaged). As regards competition for interest-bearing deposits, the building societies had until recently an arrangement for the payment of personal tax which made their deposits more attractive than bank deposits to tax-paying savers; and the Government has offered various forms of national savings instruments at interest rates which ensured that a significant part of personal liquidity flows direct to the public sector.

The result is that there has been a tendency for an increasing proportion of personal savings to be directed towards the LAPF and a diminishing proportion of the liquid element in saving has been attracted by the banks.

Neither the non-bank financial institutions nor the public sector have a strong preference for bank deposits. The building societies do, of course, hold up to 20 per cent of their assets in a liquid form, part of which is normally held as bank deposits or CDs, but only a small proportion of the deposit funds taken by building societies returns to the banking system in this way. LAPF normally hold under 5 per cent of their assets in liquid form, though this may rise *temporarily* if they are awaiting more favourable opportunities for long-term investment. The degree of centralisation in public sector finance ensures that this sector is not a major source of deposits.

ICCs themselves do, of course, hold a substantial volume of sterling bank deposits (about £25bn at the end of 1984); they may be expected to rise in line with ICC's liquidity needs, but not by enough to satisfy any abnormal demand for loans.

On the assets side of their balance sheets the banks have encountered a strong (and profitable) demand for loans from the personal sector, and demand from non-bank financial institutions (particularly for leasing, which is discussed below) as well as from companies. For many years space for this lending was found by reducing the proportion of their lending to the public sector, which had been well above the level which seemed necessary for portfolio management purposes. The scope for reductions in this sector of the asset portfolio is now limited.

The end result has been that in recent years the demand for bank loans has exceeded what the banks could supply, consistent with an acceptable rate of growth of bank deposits. Rather than attempt to curtail this demand by raising interest rates the authorities have chosen to refinance a substantial volume of bank lending (Issue Department holdings of commercial bills, see Table 3) thus taking the pressure off the banks' balance sheets.

Overfunding

The Bank of Engeland have been able to do this because the combination of the trend of company financing away from the capital market and the trend of the personal sector towards saving through LAPF has left LAPF with potentially surplus funds. By issuing gilt-edged stocks in excess of what was required to fund the PSBR the Bank have mopped up these surplus funds.

In effect the Bank (and Government) have engaged in financial intermediation between the long-term institutions and ICCs. This has been necessary because LAPF have a strong preference for long-term assets, refecting the long-term nature of their liabilities. Moreover, they have no tradition of holding variable-rate loan instruments, preferring either the certainty of a fixed rate of interest or the possibility of a higher return associated with property or shares. And, as noted earlier, their demand for bank deposits is low. The gilt-edged stocks sold to LAPF meet their preference for long-term assets, while the commercial bills bought by the Bank of England accord with the preference of ICCs.

This potential excess supply of funds directed towards long-term financial instruments, matched by excess demand for funds raised by issuing short-term financial instruments, reflects a 'structural imbalance' (Bain, 1982) in the financial system. This imbalance is not, in my judgment, something that can easily be corrected by market forces operating solely or mainly through a change in relative interest rates. Ideally the 'solution' would involve a fall in long-term yields relative to the cost of bank borrowing, so that borrowers reverted to the long-term market, without any change in the average cost of funds. However, for the reasons discussed below it seems to me unlikely that in the absence of overfunding, this is what would happen.

To bring the system into balance there has to be an increase in the demand for long-term funds (with a corresponding reduction in short-term financing) from borrowers or an increase in the supply of short-term funds (with a corresponding reduction in long-term saving) by savers. And since the structural imbalance is not merely transient (i.e. likely to reverse itself spontaneously within a comparitively short period such as a year) the change in the balance of demand or supply must be permanent.

Consider the suppliers of short-term savings first. A rise in short rates is unlikely to make companies hold more of their funds in liquid assets, since a very high proportion of their financial assets (other than trade investments) are already held in this form (Table 1). Higher short rates might tempt the LAPF to build up liquid assets *temporarily*, but since liquid assets do not satisfy their long-term investment objectives, they are unlikely to do so permanently. And while there would almost certainly be a change at the margin in personal liquid asset holdings, it is unrealistic to expect any substantial switch out of longer-term contractual saving.

It is in fact very likely that, rather than causing a reallocation of saving, higher short-rates would have quite a strong effect on expenditure, particularly stock-building by companies and house-building by persons. Higher rates for savers mean higher rates for borrowers, and both stock-building and house-building appear to be sensitive to financing costs. And there is a further difficulty: any switch to short-term saving would lead to more rapid growth of the monetary and liquidity aggregates. Although this would be warranted, and would justify the adoption of higher monetary targets, it is by no means certain that money and foreign exchange market traders would understand. There is a danger that more rapid monetary growth would merely feed fears of inflation, leading to an upward adjustment in long as well as short-term rates and to a weakening in the exchange value of the currency.

The alternative, that higher short-rates would drive domestic private borrowers into borrowing in the long-term market on the required scale seems equally unlikely. The personal sector has shown no interest at all in long-term fixed rate borrowing for many years. It is really appropriate only in the house mortgage market.

How far would short-rates have to rise or long-rates fall before demand
for fixed-rate mortgages revived? And much the same question can be
asked of industrial and commercial companies. In spite of lower long rates,
and Government hopes that the loan stock market would revive, there have
been few new issues of any size. That would probably change if long yields
fell *substantially,* but even if new issues of gilts were reduced that is
something which is unlikely to occur so long as inflation remains at or near
its current level.

There remains the question of what the LAPF would do with their funds
if the Government gave up overfunding. The answer is that they would
increase holdings of other long-term assets – UK equities, property and
overseas securities – and that (other things equal) the prices of the UK
assets (equities, property and gilts) would rise. Ordinary portfolio management considerations imply that a higher proportion of LAPF funds would
be invested overseas. Higher equity prices would, however, encourage
some companies to issue more equity and reduce their bank borrowing,
while higher gilts prices might stimulate some switching out of gilts into
liquid assets. How far this process would go depends on how well UK
financial markets are integrated with the rest of the world. It seems likely
that *substantial* increases in UK equity or gilts prices would discourage
further overseas investment in these assets, or lead to disinvestment, which
would tend to weaken the exchange rate, with further consequences for the
real economy.

It is clear that if the Bank of England were to abandon overfunding the
'market' solution would involve considerable effects on the course of
economic activity and prices. The structural factors (supported by current
legislation) are so strong that very large changes in interest rates would be
required; and the control regime is such that it would be difficult to avoid a
considerable rise in the average level of interest rates in conjunction with a
change in the interest rate structure. (It would be unusual for rising short-
term rates of interest to be associated with a strengthening of the gilt and
equity market.)

That is not to say that overfunding is an ideal solution. First, it is not
costless to the taxpayer. The gilts issued to the LAPF will generally bear a
higher coupon than the bills which the Government refinance, partly as a
result of the longer maturity and partly because of the premium on long-
term debt instruments demanded by the institutions. Secondly, it has led
the Bank of England to acquire a bill mountain, and by manipulating
interest rates artificially encouraged companies to issue bills rather than
take bank loans (Table 2). This may have led to some further shortening of

the maturity of companies' debt, and it has helped to create opportunities for 'round-tripping' in the money markets, with companies issuing bills at artificially low yields and depositing the proceeds with banks at a profit – which would be a harmless enough pastime if it did not distort the monetary aggregates, with implications for monetary policy and for sterling! Thirdly, it inflicts considerable transaction costs on the Bank of England, which typically purchases several hundred million pounds worth of bills each day, (sometimes running into thousands of bills). This burden is, however, self-imposed and could be greatly reduced if the Bank chose to purchase bills with a longer average maturity.

In the longer run it does seem unsatisfactory for the Government to have to compensate for a structural imbalance in this way. There are several possible solutions. The best, but not necessarily most practicable, would be to reduce inflation to the point that long-term fixed rates of interest fell sufficiently to attract borrowers to the long-term market.

The second, and indeed much the simplest, way for most of the imbalance to be removed would be for the Government to concentrate its own demand for funds on the long-term market. This would imply adopting a lower target for national savings – set recently at £3 bn per year – which competes strongly with deposit-taking institutions. National savings do, of course, appear to provide a cheap source of funds to the Government, but only because the interest on many forms of national savings is paid free of tax, which allows the Government to raise funds at a comparatively low gross rate. When the Government has had simultaneously to overfund because the growth of bank deposits would not support sufficient lending, such a high target for national savings seems unjustified.

A third possibility would be to educate LAPF and create a demand for long-term variable-rate financial instruments. These are not fundamentally ill-suited to pension funds since they provide some protection against inflation, although the interest margins over short-term funds would have to be adequate.

The final possibility would be to change the tax system in a number of ways. Removing the bias in favour of borrowing (particularly in a period of inflation), and some reduction in the tax incentives to saving through pension funds, are examples of how this might be done.

None of these structural and legislative changes seems likely to occur in the immediate future or on the scale required to eliminate the problem of structural imbalance. Until changes such as these do take place, overfunding remains the best available policy.

LEASING

A second major change in the finance of industry in Britain has been the growth of finance leasing. Leasing of items of equipment, particularly when they are to be used for periods much shorter than the equipment's life, is a long-established practice. 'Finance leasing', when it is intended that the plant or equipment will be used by the same firm throughout, has developed more recently, first because (until the accountancy profession caught up with the practice) it enabled companies to increase the assets they employed without disclosing the fact in their balance sheets, and later for tax reasons. Table 5 shows the growth of finance leasing in the UK since 1975[4].

In recent years many companies have experienced 'tax exhaustion'. A combination of generous stock relief (introduced to relieve companies of tax on illusory profits due to stock appreciation in a period of inflation) and 100 per cent first year capital allowances on plant and equipment meant that many companies had insufficient profits to use up all their allowances. But other companies, particularly banks and other financial companies, still had taxable profits, because their investment for their own purposes was less than the profits earned and stocks were not important in their business. They could, however, claim tax relief on equipment purchased but leased for use elsewhere in the economy. Even after passing on most of the benefit of tax relief to the lessees this remained profitable business. In practice the banks generally conducted this type of business through leasing subsidiaries, to which they lent the necessary funds, and whose activities could be consolidated with those of the parent bank for tax purposes.

The scale of this business can be regarded as a product mainly of legislative rather than structural factors. Although the conditions which make it

Table 5. Finance lessors' capital expenditure on assets for leasing out (£ m)

	1975	1976	1977	1978	1979	1980	1981	1982	1983
Manufacturing	122	165	239	482	596	772	826	819	870
Other industries	125	202	278	471	1,021	1,269	1,277	1,371	1,258
Unidentified	81	95	181	281	335	340	469	999	622
Total	328	462	698	1,234	1,952	2,381	2,572	3,189	2,750
% of GDP	0.31	0.36	0.48	0.73	0.99	1.03	1.01	1.15	0.91

necessary to relieve companies of tax on profits were partly structural – inflation and poor profitability – the legislation can easily be changed. Indeed, the 1984 Finance Act abolished stock relief and contained provisions to reduce the capital allowances over a 3-year period.

Companies' need for external finance is not likely to be greatly affected by these tax changes, but the form of that finance will change, probably reverting to bank lending. Finance leasing can, however, be expected to continue on a much reduced scale, being employed primarily by companies which, perhaps as a result of rapid growth, do not have sufficient taxable profits to absorb all the capital allowances available to them.

INDEX-LINKED SECURITIES

Index-linked securities, issued almost entirely by the Government, are now a feature of the British financial system. They have been introduced by stages. First, in 1975, index-linked national savings certificates were made available to pensioners, with a limited contractual savings arrangement for other people. Later the savings certificates were made available generally and index-linked gilts were issued in 1981. At the end of 1984 index-linked national savings of more than £5,000 million were outstanding – less than the peak of over £6,000 million in mid-1982 – and gilts with a nominal value of about £7,500 million were in issue.

The decision to issue index-linked national savings instruments was a response to pressure to provide some facility for small savers to preserve the real value of their savings at a time of rapid inflation. Other ways of holding wealth, such as property or equity shares, were quite unsuitable for these savers. Although initially the real rate of return was virtually zero the instruments were very popular when inflation was high, partly because of the real value certainty and partly because, especially after tax[5], the real return on other liquid financial instruments was negative. More recently, as inflation has fallen and the threat of a resurgence has diminished, index-linked savings have seemed less attractive and, although the yield on index-linked national savings has been increased, higher yields, both before and after tax, have been available on other instruments.

There were a number of motives behind the introduction of index-linked gilts. Probably most important was the Government's desire to have an instrument which it could employ for funding at times when the inflation outlook was uncertain and the demand for conventional gilts dried up: these conditions, even if only temporary, caused considerable difficulty for monetary control. But other reasons had also been advanced e.g. the value to pension funds of an asset whose real value was secure and the value to society at large of this improvement in the usage of financial instruments available.

Like demand for index-linked national savings, the demand for index-linked gilts has proved to be variable. Compared with other investments they have not performed very well, because real yields have risen in the market since they were first issued, inflation has been on a downward trend – thus benefiting the prices of conventional gilts – and the equity market has been strong. Nevertheless there have been periods when index-linked gilts were in demand, and their defensive qualities are likely to seem more prominent if the equity market turns down or if there are genuine fears (e.g. as a result of changing political conditions) that inflation might accelerate.

So far index-linked securities have made almost no impression in the private sector. Index-linked annuities are available, and a small amount of long-term housing finance has been provided on index-linked terms. But the concept is still unfamiliar and people view the issue of index-linked liabilities with considerable misgivings. These are not always well-founded – there is great confusion between risk exposure due to relative price changes and those due to a rise in the general price level – but where misgivings reflect an appreciation of the tax system they are fully justified. When tax relief is available on interest, borrowers gain in a period of inflation from the tax relief on that component of the interest which reflects of diminution in the real value of the capital outstanding.

In summary, index-linked securities exist mainly as a result of structural factors: the need for a secure means of holding wealth in a period of inflation. Their development has been hindered by legislative factors, in particular the failure to distinguish between the real and inflationary elements in interest payments. And market factors, in the form of the expected returns on other financial instruments, have also affected the pace of their development.

CONCLUDING REMARKS

In the last 25 years the most important structural factors affecting the financial system have been inflation and the growth of contractual saving. These have affected the pattern of company financing and the availability of funds in the capital of credit markets. Inflation also created the conditions which justified the introduction of index-linked securities, and contributed to the tax changes which led to the growth of finance leasing in the economy.

But while structural factors may often be the underlying cause of changes in the financial system, legislative factors – particularly tax legislation – have a crucial influence on their manifestation. Tax factors have a bearing on the choice between debt and equity issue, on the merits of leasing versus borrowing, and on the advantages and disadvantages of index-linked securities to both borrowers and lenders. The lack of indexation in the tax system, the failure to distinguish purely inflationary elements from real income flows, has had a distorting effect on the entire financial system.

This feature of the financial system is likely to remain with us for some time. Though now apparently under control, inflation has not yet been eliminated from the British economy, and even if it had, the memory and fear that it might re-emerge, will continue to influence financial decisions for many years.

Nevertheless, other important market factors are now at work. Deregulation and competitive forces are changing the face of the City, and the boundaries between financial institutions and between what were previously separate financial markets are breaking down. Disintermediation – in the form of a commercial paper market – may be beginning to take place and new financial products are being introduced. Competition for savings is becoming ever more intense. In the next decade it seems likely that it will be market factors which play the leading role in altering the pattern of financing in the UK.

NOTES

1. And can be reclaimed by non-taxpayers.

2. A proper comparison of long-run cost must, of course, take account of expected growth of dividends.

3. In some cases project loans, matching the cash profile of a project, may be superior in every respect to a conventional long-term loan. Moreover, many companies still prefer the flexibility and cheapness of the overdraft or line of credit, which they can hope to manipulate to their advantage to minimise the cost of funding or take advantage of temporary anomalies in the yield structure, rather than structured finance of any kind.

4. For comparison, fixed investment by ICCs averaged just under 6.5% of GDP in 1978–82.

5. The capital uplift on index-linked securities has been tax-free.

REFERENCES

1. Bain, A.D. (1982) 'Structural Imbalance in the UK Financial Markets', in *Bank of England Panel of Academic Consultants, Panel Paper* No.19.
2. Hood, W.C. (1959), *Financing Economic Activity in Canada,* Ottawa: Queen's Printer.

Chapter IX

CHANGE AND INNOVATION IN BORROWING PATTERNS: THREE AMERICAN CASES

by *Patrick Lawler**

As capital markets develop past the primitive stage, one of the early signs of progress is increasing standardization of debt securities. In order to make possible large, liquid markets, bonds must be sufficiently alike so that investors can switch back and forth between different issues without long study, so that prices can be expected to move together, and so that provisions designed to make bonds just right for one investor, do not make them unsuitable for most others. At a much grander level of size, sophistication, and computer software, though, there is room and interest for a proliferation of debt varieties to suit the needs of different groups of borrowers and lenders. Today, the large securities firms all have special working groups whose sole purpose is to design colorful new instruments like puttable bonds, extendible notes, bonds with warrants to purchase stock in other firms, and subordinated exchangeable variable rate notes.

Some of the new varieties have been directed primarily toward the repackaging of old varieties to give them a wide source of demand. Collateralized mortgage obligations have successfully increased demand for mortgages and mortgage pass-throughs by giving investors the option of buying only a part of the interest and principal payment stream so that the maturity may be more narrowly defined. Salomon Brothers' new CARS program will attempt to increase the liquidity of auto paper. Merrill Lynch has given improved access to the commercial paper market to savings and loan associations than thrifts are able to acquire for themselves by setting up subsidiaries to collateralize the paper.

Banks and S&Ls have also developed instruments for consumer borrowing to reduce the risks caused by interest rate movements. The adjustable rate mortgage in its many variations, captured the bulk of the new mortgage loan market last year, and variable rate consumer loans have become increasingly familiar.

* The views expressed in this paper do not necessarily reflect those of the Board of Governors of the Federal Reserve System or other members of its staff.

Fair, D.E., (ed.) Shifting Frontiers in Financial Markets.
© *1986, Martinus Nijhoff Publishers, Dordrecht/Boston/Lancaster. ISBN 90-247-3225-5.*
Printed in the Netherlands.

This paper will concentrate on just three of the recent credit market developments: two changes in the mix of new corporate borrowing and one important innovation in the government securities market.

THE SHIFT BY US CORPORATIONS TO SHORTER MATURITIES

Since the early 1960s, the proportion of long-term to total credit market debt of non financial corporate business has been falling fairly steadily, dropping from more than 70 per cent to less than 50 per cent. Although the decline is impressive, that statistic understates the shortening of corporate debt maturities because it doesn't take account of the even more dramatic decrease in maturities within the long-term category. New public issues by US corporations of straight debt (not convertible to equities) with maturities of 20 years or more have greatly diminished in recent years (Table 1, columns 1, 2, and 3), even in nominal terms. As a proportion of new issues of all maturities greater than one year, very long-term bonds held fairly steady at about five eighths through 1979, but last year were less than one eighth. Relative to GNP, the decline has been of similar proportion, but with slightly different timing.

Several factors are probably at work, but the most obvious possible

Table 1. Gross offerings of long-term debt (maturities of 20-year or more)

	US firms (billions of $) (1)	US firms (as a % of all maturities) (2)	US firms (as a % of GNP) (3)	US Treasury (as a % of GNP) (4)	All long-term (as a % of GNP) (5)
1974	15.3	59.9	1.07	.08	1.15
1975	16.7	53.1	1.08	.21	1.29
1976	16.4	63.6	.95	.18	1.13
1977	16.7	70.3	.87	.21	1.08
1978	12.3	63.2	.57	.28	.85
1979	14.9	59.9	.62	.33	.95
1980	18.2	48.2	.69	.29	.98
1981	11.8	34.4	.40	.51	.91
1982	10.5	25.8	.34	.33	.67
1983	11.7	30.0	.35	.88	1.23
1984	8.0	12.2	.22	.99	1.21

Sources: Federal Reserve Board, Securities and Exchange Commission, Commerce Dept.

explanations are based on the steepness of the yield curve, which has been pronounced throughout this economic expansion (Table 2). During 1983 and 1984, corporations had more than a 3 percentage point incentive to keep their borrowing in short-term markets. And, indeed, interest savings is the most commonly mentioned reason offered by corporations and underwriters for the reluctance to borrow long. Recently, the incentive has swelled to about 4 percentage points. In the past, the shape of the yield curve has been largely a cyclical phenomenon. While it has been quite steep over the 2¹/₃ years of the current business expansion, it was similarly steep in 1975, 1976, and 1977. Nevertheless, in the earlier cycle, as in most others, the yield curve was flattening during its third year; in the current cycle, the yield curve is still steepening – the difference between corporate bond and commercial paper yields widened by 177 basis points between September and February.

If the slope of the yield curve were based entirely on expectations of future short-term interest rates, then the yield curve's positive slope would be irrelevant, as any near-term cost savings would be expected to be offset by later interest rate rises, unless corporations are simply more optimistic than lenders. Recently, the total volume of credit market debt has been growing faster than GNP and, as long as the Federal budget deficits remain

Table 2. Difference between short- and long-term business interest rates (per cent)

	Recently offered A-utility bond yield	1-month, average quality commercial paper yield, bond-equivalent basis	Difference
1974	10.11	11.18	− 1.07
1975	10.57	6.75	3.82
1976	9.07	5.36	3.71
1977	8.56	5.74	2.82
1978	9.36	8.20	1.16
1979	10.67	11.70	− 1.03
1980	13.81	13.96	−.15
1981	16.63	17.16	−.53
1982	15.49	13.02	2.47
1983	12.73	9.51	3.22
1984	13.81	10.71	3.10
1985–Jan. and Feb.	12.77	8.73	4.04

Source: Federal Reserve Board.

very high, likely will continue to do so and to force up real interest rates in the process. Simulations with a primitive macro-model suggest that future increases in the structural or cyclically adjusted deficit may be expected to raise short-term real interest rates by as much as 1 to $1^1/_2$ percentage points over the next 5 years[1].

These are large increases, but not perhaps enough to justify the full disparity between short- and long-term rates in a period when inflation appears to have stabilized. Another major factor in determining the shape of the yield curve is uncertainty about future short-term rates. Unless lenders have only specific future cash needs that are fixed in nominal terms, long-term assets involve risks stemming from unanticipated decreases in the purchasing power of money and unanticipated increases in real rates which would present the lender with a capital loss if the security had to be liquidated before maturity. Thus, long-term lenders demand liquidity premia which increase in size with increases in the volatility of either inflation or real interest rates. But while the Treasury's borrowing strategy appears insensitive to the size of these premia, that of corporations need not be. While businesses might be willing to pay a higher premium (above expected future short-term rates) for long-term debt when real interest rate uncertainty increases, an increase in inflation uncertainty should have the opposite effect. So if both lenders and borrowers are risk averse, a rise in the yield curve slope caused by increased inflation uncertainty should reduce new issues of long-term relative to short-term debt, but if the yield curve becomes steeper because of greater real rate uncertainty, the distribution of debt securities over the maturity range might not be greatly affected.

A different, but not necessarily conflicting, explanation of the yield curve's slope is the recent growth of public debt. The implication of this view is that the US Treasury in its efforts to fund its huge deficits has simply pushed private corporations out of the long-term market. As Table 1, column 4 shows, the rise of long-term Treasury offerings as a per cent of GNP has risen even faster over the past decade than corporate offerings have fallen. This increase reflects more than the enormous increase in the deficit; it also reflects the Treasury's decision to lengthen the average maturity of its outstanding debt, which has now increased to 4 years 7 months from 2 years 5 monts, nine years ago. About a third of that increase has occurred in the past 2 years when long-term government issuance has been especially heavy. Thus, even though corporate long-term borrowing has fallen sharply, total long-term borrowing (Column 5) has risen to a high plateau during this period.

This flooding of the long-term new issue market is having increasingly obvious effects on the supply of outstanding long-term securities (Table 3). Looking at the stock of bonds with at least 15 years remaining to maturity – composed almost entirely of bonds with original maturities of 20 years or more – it appears that the US governments are about 2 years away from surpassing the supply of corporates after being about 30 per cent as large 2 years ago and less than 15 per cent as large 5 years ago, before the government's maturity lengthening has progressed very far. Relative to GNP, total taxable long-term debt outstanding is climbing rapidly after several years of stagnation and downward drift.

The argument that this surge of government debt has affected the yield curve is consistent with a segmented markets or preferred-habitat theory of term structure. There are some institutions, like life insurance companies and pension funds, that have a large portion of their liabilities that are fixed in nominal terms and highly predictable in the timing of the payments. These institutions actually prefer long-term assets, and as long as the total volume remains small, the yields on such securities will remain modest relative to short-term rates. But as the supply of long-term debt increases, it must be added to portfolios for which it is increasingly less well suited, forcing up long-term rates relative to short-term rates.

The preferred-habitat view also suggests that relative quantities of government and corporate long-term debt should affect their relative yields. Support for this theory is presented by the yield spread data between long-term private and Treasury securities (Table 4). Spreads are unusually narrow now, indicating that the Treasury yield curve has steepened more than the corporate curve. The narrowness of the spreads is remarkable

Table 3. Outstanding long-term debt (15 or more years to maturity)

End of	Publicly offered straight corporate bonds		US public debt held by private investors		Sum
	(Billions of $)	(% of GNP)	(Billions of $)	(% of GNP)	(% of GNP)
1979	170.5	6.71	24.7	.97	7.68
1980	179.9	6.41	31.4	1.12	7.53
1981	183.2	6.05	46.0	1.52	7.57
1982	180.9	5.76	55.6	1.77	7.53
1983	182.3	5.28	82.8	2.37	7.65
1984	180.0	4.74	116.5	3.07	7.81

Source: Federal Reserve Board, Salomon Brothers, Inc., US Treasury Dept.

considering that the only period during the past decade when they were comparably low came before October, 1979, when interest rate volatility was much lower. With more rate volatility now, the risk of substantially falling interest rates is larger, so the value of the much better call protection on Treasuries is also larger. One would, therefore, normally expect higher spreads in the absence of any relative supply effects[2].

Whatever the weights one might assign to the various explanations of the yield curve's steepness, other developments have reduced the dangers to firms of shortening maturities and have therefore augmented the effects of the steeper yield patterns. In the 1960s and 1970s, the possibility of a credit crunch in which firms would be unable to get funds at any reasonable price because of credit rationing has been greatly reduced by financial market deregulation. The evisceration of regulation Q – which often prevented depository institutions from paying market interest rates for retail deposits – the expansion of the commercial paper market to include 1,300 firms compared with only 700 nine years ago, and the increased willingness of banks to provide commitments to loan money at specified terms ($ 366 billion outstanding) and lines of credit without specified terms ($ 148 billion outstanding) have combined to substantially reduce the chances that a well established firm depending on short-term credit may find itself unable to

Table 4. Spreads between long-term corporate and government bond yields (per cent)

	Recently offered A-utility bond yield	20-year Treasury bond yield	Difference
1974	10.11	8.05	2.06
1975	10.57	8.19	2.38
1976	9.07	7.86	1.23
1977	8.56	7.67	.89
1978	9.36	8.48	.88
1979	10.67	9.33	1.34
1980	13.81	11.39	2.42
1981	16.63	13.72	2.91
1982	15.49	12.92	2.57
1983	12.73	11.35	1.38
1984	13.81	12.48	1.33
1985–Jan. and Feb.	12.77	11.64	1.13

Source: Federal Reserve Board.

roll over its debt when money is tight or if the firm's credit rating deterio-rates[3].

However, reliance on short-term borrowing does expose a business to the risk of cost increases after an unanticipated rise in real interest rates. This danger is likely to be more tractable, and even this risk can be hedged or capped by buying interest rate options or futures – strategies that were unavailable just a few years ago but are now supported by thriving markets. For example, a firm with a long-term need for future short-term borrowing can sell Treasury bond futures short. If yields rise, profits in the futures market will tend to offset higher than expected borrowing costs. Or, if the firm wants merely to limit the potential future interest costs, it can buy put options for Treasury bond futures as a sort of insurance contract. Of course, to the extent a corporation's borrowing rate varies independently of Treas-ury rates, these strategies are imperfect, but they may be good enough to induce firms to take greater advantage of relatively low short-term borrow-ing costs.

Finally, the interest rate risks assumed by nonfinancial firms are, especi-ally in the past year, overstated by failing to take account of increasing use of interest rate swaps which enable nonfinancial firms to borrow in short-term markets and swap those variable-rate liabilities for fixed-rate pay-ments to bondholders. These swaps, however, virtually never involve bonds with maturities as long as 15 or 20 years, so the picture of declining use of long-term debt given in Tabel 1 is not affected.

THE SHIFT BY US CORPORATIONS TO EUROBONDS

Last July, legislation was enacted that repealed the 30 per cent withholding tax on interest income paid to foreigners on US-issued bonds. Shortly thereafter, procedures were established by the Treasury Department mak-ing it possible for US firms to issue bearer bonds targeted to foreign investors without going through Netherlands Antilles financing subsidiaries with legally uncertain tax consequences. Subsequently, issuance of Euro-bonds by US corporations soared, but was tax repeal the reason, or even an important contributing factor?

From the outset, it seemed unlikely that repeal of the withholding tax would have any substantial effect on foreign demand for dollar-denomi-nated assets. Most short-term assets, including Treasury bills, were never subject to the levy, and the tax on bond interest had been effectively zero or close to it, for residents of many countries for some time[4]. For those in many other countries, the tax was creditable against their domestic taxes. Large investors who still faced a positive effective rate found a variety of ways to avoid the tax. They could, for example, set up an investment company in the Netherlands Antilles, which would be exempt by treaty, or they could buy US Treasury securities, hold them until a couple of days before the coupon date, sell them to a dealer, then buy them back after the coupon payment.

The effects of the repeal on foreign demand for Eurobonds issued by US corporations actually figured to be negative. For those few investors who had been affected by the withholding tax, its repeal made it attractive to sell the corporate Eurobonds and buy domestically issued, registered issues of US corporations or even the US Treasury – all of which offered higher yields. And for those investors who required bearer securities, the threat of a move by the Treasury into that market seemed likely to diminish the appeal of corporate Eurobonds. In the event, political considerations overcame any temptation for the Treasury to issue pure bearer bonds, and its "foreign-targeted" issues last fall were not successful.

If the withholding tax repeal were the cause of the surging volume of Eurobonds issued by US firms, it would have to be because it increased supply. Companies that had not issued Eurobonds before because of questions about the legality of the use of financing subsidiaries for tax avoidance or because of concern about the "limbo" status of the treaty between the US and the Netherlands Antilles, which had expired but was not cancelled, became able to issue bearer Eurobonds directly without risking future tax problems by using a foreign finance subsidiary. On the other hand, the same legislation that repealed the tax also removed an incentive to using these subsidiaries for bond issuance involving excess tax credits on foreign earnings. Perhaps most critically, however, any dash to Euromarkets was destined to be limited by the difficulty of less well known firms in gaining access to Euromarkets because Euro-investors have always relied greatly on name familiarity and much less on bond ratings.

The first seven months' experience provides little indication that withholding repeal brought new firms into the Euromarket. Tabel 5 shows the monthly average volume of bonds sold aboard by US firms in recent years and individual months since repeal. The upward jump last August is impressive, but, of the nearly $ 20 billion of new issues since the tax repeal, only $ 3.8 billion was issued directly by firms which had not previously issued bonds through foreign subsidiaries.

While new firms weren't pouring into the Eurobond market, however, the old firms obviously stepped up their Eurobond borrowing substantially.

For the most part, this was merely consistent with the dual stimulus of an increased need for funds as the expansion continued and declining interest rates. As the table shows, domestic issues of firms rated A or better (firms that could conceivably borrow abroad) also rose dramatically over this period, though not quite so fast.

Some other developments may have added special impetus to Eurobond volume. First, looking closely at the firms who did take advantage of the new rules to issue their first bonds in these markets, many had special borrowing needs or interests (which might have led them to set up foreign finance subsidiaries even if the rules had not been changed). Of the new firm volume, one-fourth was issued by banks, which were under regulatory pressure to increase their capital. The regulations allow notes issued with a promise to sell equity sufficient to pay off the principal at maturity, equity commitment or contract notes, to qualify as capital, and floating rate Eurodollar bonds with maturities of 10 to 12 years were seen by many banks to be the least painful way of raising the funds.

Table 5. Selected bond offerings by US corporations (monthly averages in millions of dollars)

	Eurodollar and foreign currency issues		Domestic issues rated A or higher
	Total	New firms only	
1977	94		1494
1978	94		1204
1979	239		1729
1980	342		2571
1981	515		2200
1982	1136		2431
1983	695		1950
1984–H1	1248		2066
1984–July	659		3815
Aug.	2386	810	5566
Sept.	3647	436	3436
Oct.	2497	472	6223
Nov.	3624	825	5050
Dec.	2260	579	3596
1985–Jan.	5085	725	3762

Source: Federal Reserve Board. *Note*: Data reflect gross proceeds rather than par value of original issue discount bonds; full face amount of offerings done on a partly paid basis included.

Another fourth of the new firm volume was issued by savings and loan associations. An innovation was largely responsible in these cases. Underwriters discovered that, while little known and financially shaky S&Ls could not issue standard Eurobonds, subsidiaries of the S&Ls could issue Eurobonds if the bonds were collateralized with US government or US government-guaranteed securities.

At least one new issue entered the Eurobond market, not to raise funds, but to take advantage of an arbitrage opportunity. Yield spreads between top quality US corporate Eurobonds and US Treasuries were so favorable in September and October that some firms found they could lock in a guaranteed profit by selling Eurobonds, paying the commissions, and buying Treasury securities with the proceeds. At the time, the firms were undoubtedly hoping to cancel both transactions from their balance sheets by a procedure called "in-substance defeasance", which involves setting up a trust to hold both the liability and the asset. However, the Financial Standards Accounting Board ruled against them, and this arbitrage technique has disappeared as firms are reluctant to add debt to their balance sheets for the sake of a small profit. Also contributing to the demise of this practice is a change in Japanese tax law. Most of the issues corporations hoped to defease were zero-coupon bonds, for which demand was very strong in Japan because taxes were not payable on interest until it was received at maturity. If the bonds were sold before that, no tax was due at all. However, the Japanese Tax Ministry has since scheduled a new withholding tax on zero-coupon bonds, and demand has contracted.

Another change in Japanese regulations stimulated a large volume of Eurobond issues by US companies in December and January but should now be coming to an end. The government opened the European bond markets to a much larger group of firms than had previously been eligible. A peculiarity of Japanese tax law and another in portfolio regulation have made it profitable for US firms to issue Euroyen bonds and swap the interest and principal payments. Japanese firms have an advantage borrowing in dollars because Japanese investors are restricted in the proportions of their assets they can invest in foreign securities, and Eurodollar bonds are foreign securities if issued by US firms, but not if issued by Japanese firms. US firms, however, have had an advantage borrowing in yen because Euroyen bonds issued by Japanese firms are subject, at least until April 1, to a withholding tax, while those issued by US firms are not.

Swaps of fixed rate for floating rate debt have also increased Eurobond volume. Less well known or lower rated US firms which want fixed rate debt have found they could get good terms by borrowing in short-term markets and swapping the payment stream with a better credit, usually a bank or other financial entity, which wants variable rate debt but can borrow cheaply in the Eurodollar bond market. In 1984, such swaps may have been on the order of $10 to $20 billion, and although the financial partner in the transaction was frequently a foreign bank, Eurobond issues of US banks and securities firms also were boosted.

The effects of all these supply factors on the volume of Eurobond offerings of US companies would have been limited without a simultaneous increase in the quantities demanded abroad. Investor interest has been fueled by relatively high inflation-adjusted yields; confidence in US economic and political stability increased purchases of US companies' Eurobonds has been a part of the swelling capital flow into the US. Underwriters have added further strength, at least temporarily, by their eagerness to gain market share and corresponding willingness to offer attractive deals to issuers and subsequently to hold large unsold inventories. The strength of demand has kept borrowing costs from bonds issued below alternative domestic borrowing costs despite high volume of both US and foreign issues. The cash needs of US firms have been growing in line with expanding capital expenditure programs, and Euromarkets, which have specialized in intermediate maturities of 4 to 7 years, have served well for companies that have nearly abandoned longer term markets, as discussed above. A few special factors, such as the opening of the European market, swaps, defeasance, higher bank capital standards, and innovative borrowing vehicles for S&Ls also have contributed, but the withholding tax repeal seems to have had only very minor effects.

US TREASURY STRIPS

Innovations in financial markets reflect sometimes the availability of technologies, sometimes the promulgations of new regulations, sometimes changed financial conditions – such as increased interest rate volatility or inflation, sometimes developments in portfolio management theory and practice, and sometimes the maturing and growth of markets which makes more specialization possible. The creation of STRIPS (Separate Trading of Registered Interest and Principal of Securities) has involved all of these over a period of several years.

Coupon securities are well-grounded in tradition and experience. Long-term bonds with regular interest payments evolved as a standard debt vehicle only in the nineteenth century but reflected long standing common

practice in more individualized loans[5]. The benefits, in many circumstances, of periodic interest payments over a single payment of principal
and accumulated interest payments at maturity have been fairly obvious.
The regular interest payments enforce a discipline on the borrower which
reminds him of the debt and requires the maintenance of a certain minimal
liquidity. The lender is reassured that the debt is not forgotten or repudi-
ated, and he is alterted to the existence of serious problems if the borrower
is unable to pay and has the right to try to salvage some of his capital by
forcing the sale of the borrower's assets. The interest payments also make it
easy for the lender to live off his capital by providing a steady income
stream without the necessity of making periodic sales. As designed in a
world without long run price trends, the income stream represented the
amount that the capital owner could spend without impairing future purchasing power.

The current case for a coupon payments on US government debt, however, is not strong. Despite its recent large deficits and ballooning debt, the
Treasury's credit status is unsurpassed. Furthermore, the existence of
inflation premia in long-term debt yields after 50 years of nearly unrelieved
growth in prices has destroyed the equality of interest payments and real
income. But until 1982, there were few signs of change in the government
securities market. Some coupon stripping, removing a bond corpus from its
semi-annual interests entitlements (with a scissors) for separate sale, occurred as early as the mid-1970s. As the primary motivation appeared to be
a desire to misrepresent earnings for tax or window-dressing purposes, both
the Treasury and the Federal Reserve actively discouraged the practice and
kept the volume of stripped securities quite modest[6].

In the meantime, a market was rapidly developing for corporate zero
coupon bonds. Increased interest rate volatility in the late 1970s had raised
the risks of mismatching the income streams of their assets with the payment streams required by their liabilities. The concept of duration was
resurrected, and immunization and dedication became common strategies
of insurance and pension fund managers.

Household demands were changing as well. Legislation broadening the
allowable use of individual retirement accounts (IRAs) was enacted in mid-
1981. These accounts provide for tax deferred accumulations of both interest and principal over long spans of time – perfect for zero coupon bonds.
Responding to these demand changes, US corporations over a 16-month
period starting in early 1981, raised over $2 billion from the sale of these
one-payment bonds[7].

By summer of 1982, the force of market demands, and a new tolerance by the Treasury and the Fed, made an acceleration in stripping inevitable. However, a just-passed tax law mandated the issuance of new Treasury securities in registered form only, and the supply of existing physically strippable issues was widely dispersed. Securities firms quickly developed a new security which gave owners rights to specific interest or principal payments of the registered securities which were placed in a trust. Given a variety of zoological acronyms (TIGRs, CATs, COUGARs, LIONs, GATORs, etc.) these are essentially zero-coupon Treasuries.

Firms found the sum of these zeros was often worth more than the whole bond, and the volume of stripped bonds surged, tripling in 1984 to an estimated $45 billion of original principal, representing over a third of privately held Treasuries with more than 10 years to maturity. Although some of the stripped bonds were nearer to maturity, most were 30 or, especially, 20-year issues. Stripping seemed clearly to have an effect on the Treasury yield curve as yields on the commonly stripped 20-year bonds fell relative to 10 and 30-year yields. Trading and market-making in the new zeros were greatly facilitated from the start by computer programs which created an implied yield curve for the zeros consistent with the current yield curve of the whole bonds.

The Treasury's STRIPS program is designed to facilitate stripping by allowing individual coupon payments to be separately registered, thus doing away the need for the menagerie issues and widening their market to include buyers who will only hold governments or who cannot hold derivative securities. Although stripping of the two issues thus far eligible amounted to only about $2 billion by the end of February, and a few wrinkles remain to be worked out, the prospects for STRIPS are very bright. It is easy to imagine a time, not far in the future, when a large volume of zero coupon Treasuries will exist for a host of maturity dates over the next 30 years. The extremely heavy Treasury financing schedule should make it possible to create a very liquid market in a very short time. Investors will use the STRIPS to "custom-make" bonds of any maturity and any interest rate they like by varying the proportions of the different STRIPS. Trading in STRIPS may outpace that in whole bonds before too long, and, with some helpful legislation, a few regulatory changes, and further improvements in transaction technology, Treasury bonds may become ancient history.

CONCLUDING COMMENTS

Each of the three cases considered in this paper involves changes in the preferences of both borrowers and lenders. Corporations are borrowing less in long-term markets not only because lenders are so overloaded with long-term government debt that they don't want much more long-term corporate debt and because heightened uncertainty about future inflation has raised liquidity premia, but also because firms have been able to reduce the risks of short-term borrowing for long-term needs. Similarly, US companies have borrowed more abroad partly because high interest rates have made dollar-denominated assets attractive, but also because they've had a greater desire to borrow in intermediate maturities which are well suited to Euromarkets. The Treasury's STRIPS program owes part of its likely success to increased demand stemming from IRAs and dedicated portfolios, but another part to its own burgeoning credit needs which have so expanded its debt market as to greatly increase the probable liquidity in individual coupon payment securities.

A continuing thread in these stories is the importance of large budget deficits, just as the main thread in explanation of financial market change a few years ago would have been inflation. Inflation has receded substantially, but variable rate securities remain, even thrive, because real interest rates remain unstable. If budget deficits should recede, that may calm the behavior of real rates, but the huge remaining size of outstanding government debt should affect bond markets for some time.

NOTES

1. These results use a model presented in Patrick J. Lawler, "Are Real Interest Rates Good Measures of Monetary Policy?", Federal Reserve Bank of Dallas, *Economic Review* (July 1982) pp. 1–12. The outcome depends on the extent to which monetary policy permits further decreases in the unemployment rate and, of course, the size of future deficits.

2. Empirical tests of the effects of the maturity structure of government debt on the term structure of yields have gotten mixed results; see Franco Modigliani and Richard Sutch, "Debt Management and the Term Structure of Interest Rates: An Empirical Analysis", *Journal of Political Economy*, (August 1967), pp. 569–89, and Richard W. Lang and Robert H. Rasche, "Debt-Management Policy and the Own Price Elasticity of Demand for Government Notes and Bonds", Federal Reserve Bank of St. Louis *Review*, (September 1977), pp. 8–22.

3. This is limited by restrictions in many credit agreements that cancel the arrangements if borrower's credit standing falls appreciably.

4. The withholding tax was generally reduced to zero under treaties with Austria, Denmark, Finland, West Germany, Greece, Hungary, Iceland, Ireland, Luxembourg, the Netherlands,

the Netherlands Antilles, Norway, Poland, Sweden, the U.S.S.R., and the United Kingdom. Reciprocal reductions in rate were provided under treaties with Belgium, Canada, Egypt, Morocco, and the Philipines (15 per cent), Jamaica and Malta (12.5 per cent), Korea (12 per cent), France, Japan, and Romania (10 per cent), and Switzerland (5 per cent).

5. Peter Mathias, *The First Industrial Nation,* Charles Scribers' Sons: New York, 1969, pp. 176–177.

6. James Laskey, "How Stripping Became Respectable," *Euromoney,* (December 1982), pp. 47–53.

7. Until May, 1982, corporations had a tax incentive of their own to issue these bonds; interest tax deductions could be computed in a way that permitted shifting some of the deductions forward.

Part C

THE COST OF CAPITAL FUNDS AND THE FINANCING OF GROWTH

Chapter X

REAL RATES AND CAPITAL INVESTMENT:
A FISHER-WICKSELL PERSPECTIVE

by *Wolfgang Gebauer*

INTRODUCTION

Recent statistics seem to reveal that real rates of interest have reached "extremely high levels" at all maturities; most figures cover roughly the first half of the 1980s and consist of deflated short-, medium-, and long-term interest rates for major OECD countries and, in the British case, of yields on indexed bonds, too.[1] Such factual information has stimulated increasing concern as regards the determinants and effects of (high) real interest rates.

Modern attempts to explain the phenomenon have reopened old controversies of interest rate theory.[2] The role of international capital flows and of national financial portfolio shifts is taken explicitly into account; on a purely domestic level, it is reductions in savings, increases in profitability, and restrictive monetary policy actions which are examined as causes of rising real rates.[3]

As regards the possible effects of (high) real interest rates, recent attention and (political) concern seem to be particularly pronounced. Practitioners are said to rely on real interest rates for investment decisions in financial assets as well as in physical capital.[4] Theoreticians consider real interest rates as a centrepiece of modern business cycle models and related savings and consumption decisions.[5] Open-economy macro-models and modern theories of exchange rate determination focus on real interest rate movements.[6] Politicians wonder whether they can influence real rates, by means of appropriate monetary action, to the benefit of investment decisions in order to rebuild and enlarge the economy's capital stock (and therefore, to stimulate total economic activity).

Given the importance of these current issues and problems centered around real rates of interest, it is puzzling to see how little attention has been paid to the basic, and pathbreaking, work of Irving Fisher himself, With a few exceptions,[7] current research work pays only cursory attention to Fisher's original work, and the concept of the real rate of interest is rarely

Fair, D.E., (ed.) Shifting Frontiers in Financial Markets.
© *1986, Martinus Nijhoff Publishers, Dordrecht/Boston/Lancaster. ISBN 90-247-3225-5.*
Printed in the Netherlands.

discussed, despite its theoretical and empirical complexity. Therefore, this paper attempts to place the above-mentioned modern discussion into the perspective of Fisher's interest rate theory. One specific purpose is to dispose of the "neutrality" issue in the present context. Thereafter, the alleged detrimental effects of high real rates of interest on (private) investment into physical capital equipment are questioned by an elaboration of old concepts of the rate of return on capital (Wicksell and Keynes). This leads ultimately to a Tobin-type argumentation and framework as regards analysis of financial incentives for capital investment. The distinction between deflated interest rates (real rates) and rates of return on physical capital (nominal or real) will be considered crucial for a proper macroeconomic understanding and interpretation of real interest rates.

FISHER'S THEORY OF REAL INTEREST RATES

Nature of Fisher's original formulation

All versions of Fisher's original formulation (for details see Appendix on pp. 139–140) express his desire to translate interest rates from one standard (unit of account) into another, according to his basic view that "the rate of interest is always relative to the standard in which it is expressed".[8] None of his formulae (Appendix, (1) to (3b)) determine an interest rate in any standard, whether in nominal or real terms. Fisher: "These rates are mutually connected, and our task has been merely to state the law of that connection. We have not attempted the bolder task of explaining the rates themselves".[9] Hence, the "law of connection" can be illustrated only if the rate of interest in one standard is already known (see graphical illustration in the Appendix).

Because of the assumption of perfect foresight, the original theorem in all its versions implies a prompt and complete adjustment of nominal interest rates to inflationary expectation. Whenever there is a change in expected inflation, the nominal interest rate reacts immediately and completely. Hence, in theory, expected real interest rates are constant: they are not influenced by (changes in) inflationary expectations ("neutrality", i.e. they are homogeneous of degree zero in prices). Fisher: "If men had perfect foresight, they would adjust the money interest rate so as exactly to counterbalance or offset the effect of changes in the price level, thus causing the real interest rate to remain unchanged at the normal rate".[10]

Revised formulation

Fisher's empirical results, put forward in 1930 (i.e. some three decades after his initial work on appreciation and interest in 1896), were clearly inconsistent with his original theorem, as the adjustment of nominal interest rates to inflation (and deflation) took place only partially and slowly. Fisher: "The adjustment is imperfect and irregular ... It requires the cumulative effect of a long rise to produce a definite advance in the interest rate ... The adjustment is very slow."[11] As a consequence of this slow and incomplete adjustment, real interest rates were found not to be constant, but to fluctuate in an "erratic" way, as Fisher put it. With reference to the theoretically required constancy of real rates, Fisher summarized: "What we actually find, however, is the reverse – a great unsteadiness in real interest when compared with money interest."[12] Real rates indeed fluctuated, in Fisher's calculations, to a far greater extent than nominal interest rates.

The inconsistency between Fisher's original theorem and his own evidence, which has recently been called – misleadingly so – "Fisher's Paradox",[13] provoked a series of further empirical investigations into the constancy issue of the real rate of interest. After some contradictory first results, the constancy hypothesis for expected real interest rates can be firmly rejected nowadays. There is overwhelming evidence that inflation, even if it is fully anticipated, has less than a unit effect on nominal interest rates, and therefore real interest rates do move, even in the long run. This has been shown for all kinds of expectation formation hypotheses and also across countries.[14] Hence, inflation (and inflationary expectations) are not "neutral" with respect to real rates of interest. And, therefore, the original Fisher theorem should finally and firmly be rejected, being inconsistent with the observed factual evidence.

This conclusion sounds radical and surprising. However, it has already been drawn half a century ago by Fisher himself. In response to the factual evidence which contradicted his theorem, Fisher concentrated on quantifying as precisely as possible the relation between nominal interest rates and observed inflation rates and the time lag involved. For this purpose, he calculated correlation coefficients to determine the closeness of link between nominal interest rates and distributed lags in inflation rates. The original assumption of perfect foresight together with the associated implication of perfect nominal interest adjustment was dropped. Specifically, Fisher tested the relationship between the present nominal interest rate i_t and the weighted average p of the distributed lags of inflation rates $\bar{p}_{t-1}$, i.e. $\bar{p} \rightarrow i$, with arithmetically declining weights w_l, i.e.

$$\bar{p} \to i, \ \bar{p} = \sum_{l=1}^{n} w_l \, p_{t-l} \, . \tag{1}$$

I call this relationship the "revised Fisher equation".

Fisher's results: lagged past inflation rates show a very close, positive correlation with current nominal interest rates, with the lags extending over two to three decades. These results explain and quantify, in an extreme way, the evidence found earlier that nominal interest rates do not adjust perfectly to inflation rates.

In a macroeconomic disequilibrium discussion, Fisher described this relationship in terms of the "transition period" of an economy from one state of equilibrium to another. In the "short term", i.e. for the duration of a transition period covering roughly a decade, it included an incomplete, slow, and cumulative adjustment of nominal interest rates to past rates of price change. Consequently, in such periods a (fairly considerable) variability in real interest rates is implied: real interest rates fluctuate inversely to the change in inflation rates. Since fairly long historical phases of price stability (rates of price change = zero) cannot be observed, we have in practice a series of transition periods following and overlapping one another, a sequence of (price) disequilibria such that we are in a permanent state of incomplete and lagged adjustment of nominal interest rates to observed rates of price change. Therefore, Fisher's revised equation is incompatible with the classical postulate of neutrality put forward in monetary theory: even in the longest of runs, (expected) real interest rates continue to be influenced, in fact, by (expected) price level changes and any monetary changes that lie behind.

The inverse relationship between inflation and real interest rates was "rediscovered", to be sure, some twenty years ago by Mundell [15] within the framework of Metzler's model. [16] Combining Keynes' theory of liquidity preference with a Pigou-type real balance effect, Mundell demonstrated that an inverse relationship between inflation and real interest rates holds even if we assume perfect foresight; this implied, of course, an attack against Fisher's original theorem. [17]

It should be mentioned that such an inverse relationship may be considered as an additional factor to explain the present level of ("high") real rates. Successful disinflation policy actions by authorities are, taken by themselves, a means of directly raising real rates. However, such effects could be compensated by adverse inflationary influences, brought about by recent innovation and deregulation in financial markets. For example, it may be argued that, due to a richer "menu" of loan facilities offered to a broader range of potential borrowers, loan-financed expenditures will be stimulated, causing – via inflationary pressures – a corresponding drop in real interest rates. This subject matter is taken up by other contributions in the present volume.

REAL RATES AND CAPITAL INVESTMENT

In an ideal theoretical world with perfect foresight, absence of risk and perfect competition, the rate of return on all assets will be the same. Hence, there will be equality between the real rate of return on physical capital assets and the real (deflated) interest rate on financial assets. To cite Sargent, for example: "Irving Fisher ... noted that in equilibrium the nominal rate of interest must equal the sum of the marginal rate of return from holding real capital and the expected proportionate change of prices. This condition follows from the fact that in a riskless world, holding period yields must be equal for all assets."[18] To be sure, Fisher has never "noted" this expressly. But we obviously are invited, by looking at the underlying assumptions of the original Fisher theorem, to visualize indeed the ideal world of, say, intertemporal price theory. Consequently, Sargent proceeds later on by explaining that "... The real rate of interest ... is the rate of return associated with holding real assets ...".[19] Given this equalization of real rates, it is only one little step further to arrive at the popular assumption that investment in real capital is influenced by a Fisher-type real rate of interest. This popular view, embodied in policy statements as well as in influential economic textbooks,[20] is most astonishing, since it:

1. ignores relevant classical contributions by Wicksell and Keynes as well as modern work by Brunner/Meltzer,[21] Malinvaud,[22] and Tobin;[23]
2. appears to be inconsistent with both Fisher's original and revised equations, despite intertemporal price theory.

The following argumentation attempts to substantiate these charges.

Wicksell, Keynes, Tobin, and the rate of return on physical capital

A major point in Wicksell's theoretical work is his attempt to overcome the "inextricable confusion" between the interest rate on money and on (physical) capital in the application of classical interest rate theory.[24] His proposal is to look at the relationship between the (nominal) interest rate on financial markets ("Darlehenszins") and a specific (nominal) rate of return on physical capital ("natèrlicher Kapitalzins"). The latter is a theoretical-physological construction, an equilibrium internal rate of return on capital investment expected by entrepreneurs. The relationship between the two interest rates is postulated to determine, via investment and production decisions, the movement of national price levels.[25]

By the very force of this idea, Wicksell indeed managed to overcome the aforementioned classical confusion – but only at the price of paving the way for another (neoclassical) one: the confusion between real rates in Fisher's sense of a deflated nominal magnitude and real rates in the sense of a (nominal or deflated) rate of return on "real", i.e. physical capital.[26] It took until Keynes' General Theory to overcome this defect, which had already been widespread. Keynes "marginal efficiency of capital" (MEC) is, except for its marginal specification, basically identical with Wicksell's natural rate;[27] and it is again the interplay with some interest rate on financial markets which is designed to govern theoretically the equilibrium stock of physical capital.[28]

This was Keynes' basis to attack Fisher's theorem explicitly, arguing that it is not any market rate of interest, but the MEC which will be directly affected by inflationary expectations.[29] In the framework of the General Theory, there is no positive financial incentive for capital investment if the nominal rate of interest increases pari passu with the marginal efficiency of capital; what is required is an increase of the MEC relative to the market rate of interest.

A well-known modern version of the contributions by Wicksell and Keynes is Tobin's proposal to analyse financial incentives for capital investment by comparing the internal rate of return on investment at its cost in the commodity markets R (which is equal to Fisher's rate of return over cost), with the financial cost of capital r_K, that is, the market rate of interest (nominal or real) at which investors discount the future returns from such investment. The marginal relationship

$$q = R/r_K \qquad (2)$$

is postulated to reflect incentives for rates of investment faster or slower than the trend growth of the economy ("normal growth"), an incentive which can be measured by the market valuation of existing capital goods relative to their replacement costs. Tobin is quite explicit as regards the intellectual heritage of this concept: "This inducement is essentially what ... Wicksell ascribed to a natural rate of interest higher than the market interest rate".[30] Central bank policy affects this q-relationship through a chain of asset substitutions, to be initiated by interest rate changes in the money market and transmitted via changes in interest rate structures. The linkage is loose, as perceived risks and uncertainties of current business earnings may change, together with varying estimates of future earnings.[31] It should be worthwhile to connect this conceptual framework of Tobin with recent innovative and deregulative innovations in financial markets: the supply of more, and more tailormade, opportunities to invest financially might play a role as disincentive for investment decisions into physical capital.

In the tradition of thought just sketched, it is obviously decisive to draw a clear dividing line between (nominal or real) rates of interest on financial markets and expected rates of return (nominal or real) on physical capital assets. For any analysis of financial incentives for capital investment, it is essential to see that the two percentage magnitudes are distinctly different. Therefore, Tobin's warning should be emphasized that "naive calculations of Fisherian real rates of interest are very unreliable indicators" of financial incentives for capital investment.[32] And indeed: it is hard to imagine any proposition more divorced from experience than the currently fashionable proposition that "marginal efficiency of capital and real interest rates are always equal to each other and constant".[33]

There remain, however, some points of real interest rate theory to be discussed; this is taken up in the following, final section.

Fisherian real rates and intertemporal price theory

To arrive at the Wicksell-Tobin view just sketched, it is not necessary to accept the underlying theoretical model or school of thought. Careful analysis of Fisher's real rate theory and a critical look at intertemporal price theory are yielding the same sort of conclusions.

If we take Fisher's original theorem, we have the implication of a constant real interest rate. However, in interest rate theory proper, the real rate of return (on physical assets) moves systematically with the opportunity to invest and with time preference. Hence, even if formally possible, the conceptual and factual equalization of a Fisher-type real interest rate with some rate of return on physical capital assets appears rather dubious. For the moment, we may "resolve" this issue formally: the original Fisher theorem does not exclude that the real rate of return on physical capital will move, according to its fundamental determinants just mentioned; but such movements are outside the scope and nature of the theorem.

If we take for granted that Fisher's original theorem is inconsistent with the evidence, and therefore concentrate on (what I called) a revised Fisher equation with imperfect foresight, variable time lags, and overlapping sequences of transition periods, then we definitely leave the ideal world of intertemporal price theory, moving closer to reality. Having left this ideal world, the conceptual and empirical equality between real rates of return on physical capital and real rates of interest on financial assets falls apart. As it falls apart, "neutrality" is removed to the far distance of some future, ideal, and practically unachievable equilibrium situation. Hence, all theoretical, empirical, and political considerations of an alleged importance of real rates of interest on financial assets for investment decisions into physical capital are without proper foundations. We should once again return to Fisher's assessment that the relation between interest rates and inflation is an important practical tool of financial market analysis: ". . . In view of almost universal lack of foresight, the relation has greater practical than theoretical importance . . . It is consequently of the utmost importance, in interpreting the rate of interest statistically, to ascertain in each case in which direction the monetary standard is moving, and to remember that the direction, in which the interest rate apparently moves, is generally precisely the opposite to that in which it really moves."[34]

In contrast to the arguments so far advanced, real interest rates and real rates of return on physical capital are treated as one and the same thing in most price-theoretic reasoning. This is due, as already mentioned, to the same set of ideal world assumptions which form the basis of Fisher's original theorem, too. Indeed, it can be shown that equality between the two real rates follows necessarily from individual optimization behaviour;[35] and Fisher's original theorem itself can be deduced from intertemporal price theory.[36] Nevertheless, there are some basic differences between intertemporal price theory and Fisher's theory of real interest rates which are, in conclusion, listed below. They demonstrate that intertemporal price theory cannot be used as a sort of microeconomic foundation for Fisher's real rate theory, be it original or revised.

First, real rates are basically variable in price theory, reflecting time preferences and opportunities to invest. In Fisher's original formulation, real rates are constant, reflecting neutrality with respect to inflationary expectations; fundamental determinants like time preference and opportunity to invest are not taken into account. If we choose Fischer's revised formulation, we get rid of real rate constancy, but we leave, in doing so, the ideal world of intertemporal price theory assumptions.

Second, real rates are, in intertemporal price theory, real phenomena,[37] as they "behave" like relative prices: their (long-run) equilibrium values are independent of the price level or the money stock (this reflects the "classical dichotomy" – there is no "money veil"). Real rates are, in other words, homogeneous of degree zero, or "neutral", with respect to prices and money, which of course implies absence of money illusion. Hence, we have at this point consistency with the original Fischer formulation, but not with the revised one (see above).

Third, the underlying direction of causality is different, if not reverse: in Fisher's formulations (both original and revised), real rates are analysed by investigating the effects of inflation or inflationary expectations on the nominal or market rate of interest. Rates of return on capital investment are, however, typically placed in an opposite causation scheme, running from a real rate relationship (see Wicksell-Tobin approach) via economic activity to price level movements.

SUMMARY

The paper attacks the present-day "conventional wisdom" of an inverse relationship between real rates of interest and investment activity. The criticism does not focus on existing calculations of real rates. Instead, Fisher's real rate theorem and basic conceptual ideas of Wicksell and Keynes on capital investment analysis are recalled and placed into perspective. It follows that the absolute level of (real) interest rates on financial assets is of no particular consequence by itself. In particular, it is irrelevant for investment decisions into real capital unless it is related to any useful (operational) rate of return on capital investment. The argument implies that the analysis and policy of financial incentives to capital investment should be conducted in frameworks like Tobin's q-theory of investment. Variable Fisherian real rates on financial assets are, taken by itself, a useful practical device for financial market analysis. Their equalisation with rates of return on capital investment may be justified in the ideal theoretical world of intertemporal price theory, but it is misleading for practical policy analysis.

NOTES

1. Blanchard and Summers (1984), p. 273 and tables 1–5.
2. For recent contributions, see Blanchard and Summers (1984), Campbell and Schiller (1984), Roley and Walsh (1984), and Andersen, Ando, and Enzler (1984).
3. See Blanchard and Summers (1984), pp. 287–315.
4. See e.g. Mullineaux and Protopapadakis (1984), and Tobin and Brainard (1977).
5. See e.g. Lucas (1975) and Barro (1980).

136

6. Dornbusch (1976), Frenkel (1979), and Mussa (1982).

7. Rutledge (1977), Gebauer (1982) and (1983), and Blanchard and Summers (1984).

8. Fisher (1930), p. 41.

9. Fisher (1896), p. 92. Fisher dealt with an explanation of interest rates in his interest theory proper on the assumption of a constant price level, i.e. equality of nominal and real interest rates.

10. Fisher (1930), pp. 414/15.

11. Ibid., pp. 411 and 416.

12. Ibid., p. 413.

13. Carmichael and Stebbing (1983).

14. Fried and Howitt (1983), and Mishkin (1984).

15. Mundell (1963), and later on Mundell (1971).

16. Metzler (1951).

17. For an elaboration of this point, see Gebauer (1982), pp. 194–202.

18. Sargent (1969), pp. 127/28.

19. Sargent (1972), p. 212.

20. See e.g. Dornbusch and Fischer (1981), p. 189, or Hirshleifer (1980), chapter 16.

21. Brunner (1971), Brunner/Meltzer (1972). I am referring here to their relative price p/P, which is conceptually equal to Tobin's q and which is, in equilibrium and multiplied with MEC, equal to Fisher's real rate.

22. Malinvaud (1983).

23. For references, see next section and footnote 30 below.

24. To quote: "Die Nationalökonomen werden nicht müde, ihren Schülern einzuschärfen, daß Geld und (Real-) Kapital nicht dieselbe Sache seien, Geldzins und Kapitalzins somit zwei verschiedene Dinge; sobald es aber zu den Anwendungen kommt, lassen sie fast ausnahmslos jene beiden Begriffe in eine 'unentwirrbare' Konfusion zusammenschmelzen, wie Mill sich ausdrückt – nebenbei bemerkt, am Anfang einer Auseinandersetzung, in der er selbst, trotz allem Bemühen, nur dazu gelangt ist, jene Konfusion zu verstärken". Wicksell (1898), Preface pp. iii/iv.

25. Ibid.

26. Wicksell often used "real" for deflated as well as physical magnitudes. On this point see the well-taken comments by Hayek (1929), p. 124. To be sure, Wicksell himself never used or applied Fisher's theorem explicitly.

27. And is, by the way, strictly identical with the (earlier developed) "rate of return over cost" by Fisher.

28. See Keynes (1936), pp. 135 and 139, and the Lerner-based interpretation by Tobin (1978), p. 423.

29. Keynes (1936), pp. 141/42.

30. Tobin (1982), p. 179. His q-theory of investment was introduced in Tobin and Brainard (1968) and has been further discussed and applied in Tobin and Brainard (1977), Tobin (1978), and Tobin (1982). Recent applied extensions to the structure-performance relationship and to the case of many physical capital goods are given by Smirlock, Gilligan, Marshall (1984) and Wildasin (1984), respectively.

31. For details, see Tobin (1978) and, more recently, Shiller, Campbell and Schoenholtz (1983).

32. Tobin (1978), p. 426.

33. Ibid.

34. Fisher (1930), pp. 43/44 and 494.

35. Gebauer (1982), pp. 178/82.
36. Hirshleifer (1980), p. 508; and Richter, Schlieper, Friedman (1978), pp. 135/37.
37. According to the classification of Patinkin (1965), p. 379.

REFERENCES

1. Anderson, R., A. Ando, J. Enzler, Interaction Between Fiscal and Monetary Policy and the Real Rate of Interest, *American Economic Review,* Papers and Proceedings, May 1984.
2. Barro, R.J., A Capital Market in an Equilibrium Business Cycle Model, *Econometrica,* vol. 48, 1980.
3. Benninga, S., A. Protopapadakis, Real and Nominal Interest Rates under Uncertainty: The Fisher Theorem and The Term Structure, *Journal of Political Economy,* October 1983.
4. Blanchard, O.J., L.H. Summers, Perspectives on High World Real Interest Rates, *Brookings Papers on Economic Activity,* 2:1984.
5. Brunner, K., A Survey of Selected Issues in Monetary Theory, *Schweizerische Zeitschrift für Volkswirtschaft und Statistik,* no. 1, 1971.
6. Brunner, K., A.H. Meltzer, A Monetarist Framework for Aggregative Analysis, in: *Proceedings of the First Konstanzer Seminar,* Berlin 1972.
7. Campbell, J.Y., R.J. Shiller, A Simple Account of Long-Term Interest Rates, *American Economic Review,* Papers and Proceedings, May 1984.
8. Dornbusch, R., Expectations and Exchange Rate Dynamics, *Journal of Political Economy,* vol. 84, 1976.
9. Dornbusch, R., S. Fisher, *Macroeconomics,* 2nd edition, New York: McGraw-Hill, 1981.
10. Fisher, I., *Appreciation and Interest,* New York, 1896.
11. Fisher, I., *The Theory of Interest,* New York, 1930.
12. Frenkel, J.A., On the Mark: A Theory of Floating Exchange Rates Based on Real Interest Differentials, *American Economic Review,* vol. 69, 1979.
13. Fried, J., P. Howitt, The Effects of Inflation on Real Interest Rates, *American Economic Review,* December 1983.
14. Friedman, M., A Theoretical Framework for Monetary Analysis, in: R.J. Gordon (ed.), *Milton Friedman's Monetary Framework,* Chicago, 1970.
15. Gebauer, W., *Realzins, Inflation und Kapitalzins: Eine Neuinterpretation des Fisher-Theorems,* Heidelberg: Springer-Verlag, 1982 (Studies in Contemporary Economics, vol. 1).
16. Gebauer, W., Inflation and Interest: The Fisher-Theorem Revisited, *EUI Working Paper* n. 72, Florence, December 1983.
17. Hafer, R.W., S.E. Hein, Monetary Policy and Short-Term Real Rates of Interest, *Federal Reserve Bank of St. Louis Review,* March 1982.
18. Hayek, F.A., *Geldtheorie und Konjunkturtheorie,* 1929; 2nd edition, Salzburg, 1976.
19. Hirshleifer, J., *Price Theory and Applications,* 2nd edition, Eaglewood Cliffs, 1980.
20. Huizinga, J., F.S. Mishkin, Inflation and Real Interest Rates on Assets with Different Risk Characteristics, *Journal of Finance,* July 1984.
21. Keynes, H., *The General Theory of Employment, Interest and Money,* London, 1936.
22. Kierzkowski, H., A Generalization of the Fisher Equation, *The Economic Record,* September 1979.

138

23. Lucas, R.E., An Equilibrium Model of the Business Cycle, *Journal of Political Economy*, 83, 1975.
24. Malinvaud, E., *Essays sur la théorie du chômage*, Paris 1983.
25. Metzler, L., Wealth, Saving, and the Rate of Interest, *Journal of Political Economy*, April 1951.
26. Mishkin, F.S., The Real Interest Rate: A Multi-Country Empirical Study, *Canadian Journal of Economics*, May 1984.
27. Mullineaux, D.J., A. Protopapadakis, Revealing Real Interest Rates: Let the Market Do It, Federal Reserve Bank of Philadelphia, *Business Review*, March/April 1984.
28. Mundell, R.A., Inflation and Real Interest, *Jouranl of Political Economy*, Juny 1963.
29. Mundell, R.A., *Monotary Theory*, Chicago, 1971.
30. Mussa, M., A Model of Exchange Rate Dynamics, *Journal of Political Economy*, vol. 90, 1982.
31. Patinkin, D., *Money, Interest, and Prices – An Intergration of Monitary and Value Theory*, 2nd edition, New York, 1965.
32. Richter, R., U. Schlieper, W. Friedman, *Makrooekonomik*, 3rd edition, Berlin, 1978.
33. Roley, V.V., C.E. Walsh, Unanticipated Money and Interest Rates, *American Economic Review*, Papers and Proceedings, May 1984.
34. Rutledge, J., Irving Fisher and Autoregressive Expectations, *American Economic Review*, February 1977.
35. Santoni, G.J., C.C. Stone, The Fed and the Real Rate of Interest, *Federal Reserve Bank of St. Louis Review*, December 1982.
36. Sargent, Th.J., Commodity Price Expectations and the Interest Rate, *Quarterly Journal of Economics*, February 1969.
37. Sargent, Th.J., Anticipated Inflation and the Nominal Rate of Interest, *Quarterly Journal of Economics*, May 1972.
38. Shiller, R.J., J.Y. Cambell, K.L. Schoenholtz, Forward Rates and Future Policy: Interpreting the Term Structure of Interest Rates, New Haven, June 1983 (*Cowles Foundation Discussion Paper* no. 667).
39. Smirlock, M., Th. Gilligan, W. Marshall, Tobin's q and the Structure-Performance Relationship, *American Economic Review*, December 1984.
40. Symons, J.S.V., Money and Real Interest Rate in the U.K., *The Manchester School of Economic and Social Studies*, 1983.
41. Tobin, J., Monotairy Policies and the Transmission Mechanisms, *Southern Economic Journal*, January 1978.
42. Tobin, J., Money and Finance in the Macroeconomic Process, *Journal of Money, Credit and Banking*, May 1982.
43. Tobin, J., W.C. Brainard, Pitfalls in Financial Model Building, *American Economic Review*, Papers and Proceedings, May 1968.
44. Tobin, J., W.C. Brainard, Asset Markets and the Cost of Capital, in: B. Balassa, R. Nelson (eds.) *Economic Progress, Private Values and Public Policy*, Amsterdam, 1977.
45. Wicksell, K., *Geldzins und Güterpreise*, Jena, 1898 (revised new edition, Aalen 1968).
46. Wildasin, D., The q Theory of Investment with many Capital Goods, *American Economic Review*, March 1984.

APPENDIX

ORIGINAL FISHER THEOREM

Assumptions characterizing financial market conditions: inflation rate is anticipated with perfect foresight; no money illusion; no risk; no transaction costs; no taxes.

Implicit formulation
(1) $(1 + i) = (1 + r^*)(1 + p^*)$.
Explicit complete formulation (discontinuous compounding of interest)
(2a) $i = r^* + p^* + r^* p^*$, or
(3a) $r^* = (i - p^*)/(1 + p^*)$.

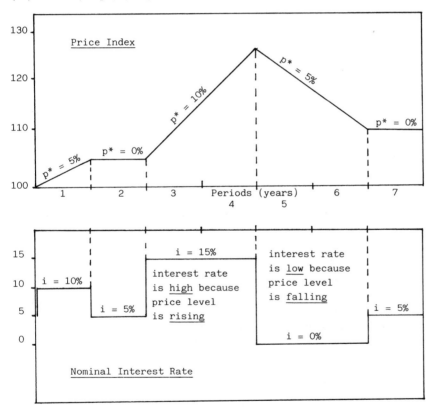

Theoretical, simplified relation between inflationary expectations p^* and nominal interest rate i assuming a constant expected real rate of interest of $r^* = 5\%$. *Source*: Fisher (1930), p. 412.

Explicit simplified formulation (continuous compounding)

(2b) $i = r^* + p^*$,

(3b) $r^* = i - p^*$.

i = nominal interest rate, $i \geqslant 0$;

r^* = expected real rate of interest, $r \geqslant 0$;

p^* = expected inflation rate, $|i| \geqslant |p^*|$.

Chapter XI

A FEW INSIGHTS INTO THE PHENOMENON OF REAL
INTEREST RATES IN THE 1980s

by *Michel Develle*

Now midway into the 1980s, the theories concerning the formation of short
and long term interest rates have been badly belied by reality. Can it not be
said that the impact of positive real interest rates on the pace of economic
activity has turned out to be one of the most disconcerting snags in neoclassical and Keynesian theory? Wasn't the Keynesian belief in their destructive effects on growth so strong that it was still widely held just a few
months ago that economic recovery was impossible in a western world beset
by excessive positive real interest rates? Has the American upswing and its
expansion to Europe really calmed all fears in this respect?

The differential between the inflation rate and the nominal interest rate,
already significant in 1982 in most of the major industrial countries, widened still further in 1984, particularly in the United States, despite the fact
that this country was the unequalled champion of economic growth last
year (GDP + 6.8 per cent)! Not only is the impact that real interest rate
levels have on the pace of economic activity a problem, but the reasons
behind the persistence of interest and inflation rate differentials, in a world
system suffering from intense disinflation similar to the one following the
"Korean boom", are also unclear. And apparently the popular proverb of
foreign exchange dealers that "a strong currency is recognizable by its weak
interest rates and vice-versa" is inappropriate to explain the current movements in foreign exchange rates, which are pushing the dollar ever higher
while at the same time plunging the Swiss franc, with its low return, into the
trough.

The phenomenon of real interest rates[1] is common to all the major
western economies, even if its intensity varies considerably from one
country to the next. We would in this report first like to trace how positive
real rate differentials emerged and consolidated and then examine these
events in the light of the major "classical" theories which are supposed to
explain the level of interest rates in terms of economic activity, inflation and
monetary policy. With their shortcomings in mind, we would in a second

Fair, D.E., (ed.) Shifting Frontiers in Financial Markets.
© *1986, Martinus Nijhoff Publishers, Dordrecht/Boston/Lancaster. ISBN 90-247-3225-5.*
Printed in the Netherlands.

part like to present several new explanations in a modest attempt to provide a few constructive ideas which could one day, after more investigation, become a new theory on the formation of interest rates in an industrial world characterized by disinflation, dissavings, a debt economy, flexible exchange rates and growing financial intermediation.

HISTORY

We will confine ourselves to examining the chronology of *real interest rates* – consumer price index adjusted nominal rates – in five major industrial countries (United States, Germany, Japan, United Kingdom and France). Figure 1 shows the changes which have occurred in their inflation, short and long term nominal interest and short and long term "real" rates.

In the United States

The premium on long term real rates has generally been positive, around 3 to 4 points over the long period, substantially less for the short term. In January 1985 it was close to 8 points. The first oil shock triggered a surge in inflation which failed to be offset by an equivalent rise in nominal rates. In 1974 and 1975 short and long term real rates were sharply negative, about 4 to 5 points. Long term rates regained their historic norm in 1976 and 1977 but the second oil shock only pushed the premium heavily into the negative again. Since 1980, the premium on real rates has gone from roughly −4 to +8, i.e. a change of 12 points in absolute value.

Though short term rates (Fed Funds) have fluctuated substantially under the effects of Federal Reserve policy (changes in the method of regulating the money supply and fight against inflation), long term real interest rates have in contrast risen steadily to attain twice, even three times, the historic norm observed since 1945. During the last five years (1980–1984) inflation has receded sharply – roughly divided by 3 – while economic expansion began to gain momentum in 1983, becoming even stronger in 1984 (GDP + 6.8 per cent) and the phoenix dollar (see Figure 2, p. 146) rose from its ashes to regain its value of early 1972 against the DM.

In Germany

The chronology here is not the same as for the United States. Allergic to inflation and systematically hostile to domestic and foreign deficits, Germany was the only country among the five which succeeded in preserving positive long term real rates throughout the entire period. Despite its monetary sagacity – inflation of less than 2 per cent at the end of 1984, sharp cutback in public sector borrowing requirements and current account surpluses – it did not, however, entirely avoid the "harsh law" of a rising real premium as from 1983 onwards. At the start of 1985, German long term real rates showed a premium of five points, historically extremely high for this country and which the weakness of the DM against the $ is unable to adequately explain. Likewise, short term real rates, negative in 1973 and 1975 and historically slightly positive, were at the beginning of 1985 nearly three points higher than inflation (inflation 2 per cent – long term rate close to 7 per cent) (see Figure 1).

In Japan

The disinflation of the Japanese economy over the last ten years (see Figure 1) has made for positive real rates, both for the short and long term, as nominal rates, traditionally moderate because of the country's capital market and government and corporate debt structures, varied only marginally during the 1972–1984 period. Long term real rates rose by nearly 17 points in absolute value between their low of 1974 (first oil shock) and the start of 1985, a record among the five countries in question. It should, moreover, not be forgotten that the Japanese economy is growing by 4 to 5 per cent, that its current account balance was in the black by $ 35.02 billion in 1984, that it successfully pruned its budget deficit during recent years and that the yen/dollar parity, in contrast to the DM, is not back to where it was thirteen years ago.

In the United Kingdom

The first oil shock and the laxist economic policies of the 1979–1980 period triggered two strong outbursts of inflation, which mechanically prompted sharply negative real rates (see Figure 1). Since 1980, as inflation cooled from 20 to 5 per cent in 1984, long and short term real rates turned highly positive. This did not, however, prevent economic growth, under the impulse of Tory government policy, nor did it stem the fall of the pound, wrongly considered as a "petromoney" by the exchange market.

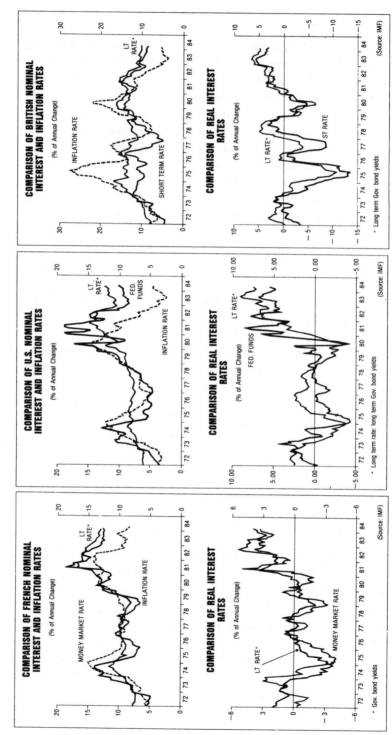

Figure 1. Review of inflation – interest rates in France, the United States, the United Kingdom, Germany and Japan.

Source: PARIBAS "Conjoncture".

145

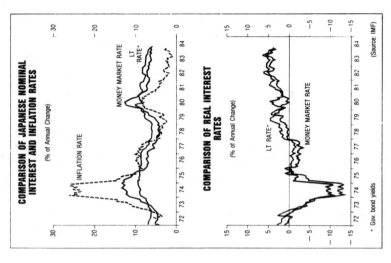

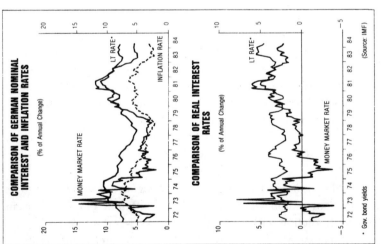

Figure 1. (Continued.)

146

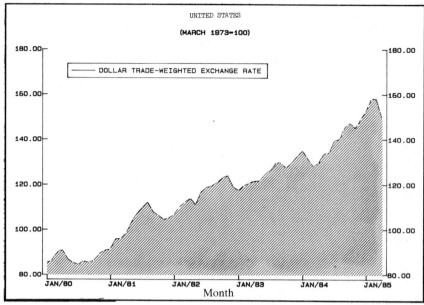

PARIBAS : Economic Research Dept.

Figure 2.

In France

France has not been left untouched by the phenomenon of real rates. Historically, the premium was small, around two points for long rates and practically nonexistent for the short term. At the end of 1984 it had attained close to five points. Though the two highly inflationist oil shocks brought on negative long and short term real rates, the trend has reversed since 1979. Real rates became positive in 1981 as inflation receded followed, though belatedly, by nominal interest rates (see Figure 1).

This detailed review demonstrates that *real rates have clearly tended to be on the rise*, a phenomenon which has resisted disinflation. (Table 1) Herein lies a first contradiction with the relationship between interest rate and activity levels as explained by theory. Graph profiles and premium levels vary from one country to the other, depending on their financial structures, control of inflation, foreign account positions, exchange rates and the results obtained in curbing public and private debts (corporation and households). In 1974, only German real interest rates were positive. In 1984, the premium, though variable from one country to the next, was positive everywhere and much higher than ten years ago.

What conclusions are to be drawn from such a phenomenon? Is it of a temporary or lasting nature? Are long and short term interest rates going to durably outpace the drift of the currency's domestic purchasing power? Obviously, capital markets, lenders and borrowers are the first to be concerned by the replies to these questions.

Before attempting to provide any answers, a preliminary comment should be made as to the relationship between *growth rates and real rates*. Long term real rates were positive in most industrial countries during the post-war expansion wave, the "Thirty Golden Years" so dear to the economist Fourastié, but were on the whole *below* growth rates in terms of GDP volume. What is new since 1980–1982 is the *excess* nature of the *premium* and not its existence.

Negative real interest rate periods corresponded to the exceptional situation created by the "inflation boom" of the 1970s and the impossibility to submit economies and their financial systems to a hike in nominal rates equal or exceeding that of the inflation rate. It, however, quickly became apparent that a reduction in the real money rate was only a makeshift attempt to gain a temporary improvement. In fact, in so far as the purchase of a long term claim implies opting for the future rather than for cash in hand, it seems normal to expect a positive real return in long range terms. If one wishes to finance investment by savings in a balanced growth economy, in other words one which is non-inflationist, positive real rates are apparently necessary, at least for long term vehicles. We now know that economic systems where the cost of money is zero have proved poor performers in the expansion race.

Nominal interest rates represent the opportunity cost of non-interest-bearing cash balances; they must thus be higher than inflation to help finance the future and reduce the preference of cash holders for liquidity. In

Table 1. Long term real rates* (annual average)

	1974	1980	1982	1984
United States	− 3.1	−2.1	+6.7	+8.–
Germany	+ 3.4	+3.–	+4.3	+5.6
Japan	−15.1	+1.2	+5.5	+4.6
United Kingdom	− 2.8	−5.8	+4.3	+5.7
France	− 3.2	−0.9	+3.7	+6.1

* Long term Government bond yields, deflated by average consumer price inflation.
Sources: IMF and OECD.

148

contrast, this raises the question of the value of the *critical gap*: the difference between the GDP growth rate in volume and real interest rates.

Does a real rate of interest which is durably higher than the growth rate in volume of GDP not strongly impede economic expansion? In other words, can an economic system grow in a durable way with a negative critical gap? The history of the American GDP growth rate in volume and real interest rates since 1949 shows that the GDP growth rate was on the average higher (see Figure 3) than the real rate of interest up until 1981. The critical gap was *positive* and its value was on the average around 0 to 3 points. In 1981 and 1982 the gap became highly negative (real rates outpaced the growth rate in volume of GDP), *strongly depressing US economic activity*. The American economy was then stimulated by the huge budget deficit and disinflation, which in 1983 and 1984 produced a strong upswing in GDP that helped to reduce the negative critical gap to around one point by 1984 (GDP growth rate: 6.8; long term real rates: 7–8) (see Figure 4).

A widening *negative critical gap* apparently has a powerful disinflationist effect and acts as a strong damper on the GDP growth rate. If the critical gap remains negative over a long period (real rates exceeding the economy's growth rate), it is to be feared that, once the effects of the budget stimulation have worn off, the growth rate will be depressed again by the weight of real rates. US prospects for 1985 seem to tally more or less with

Figure 3. U.S.A.: Real interest rate and GDP growth rate.

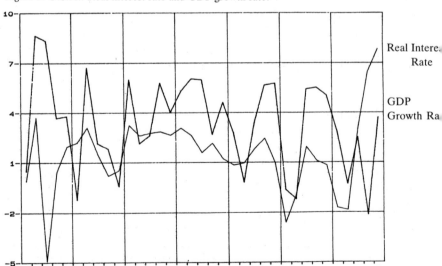

Figure 4. U.S.A.: Inflation rate-critical gap.

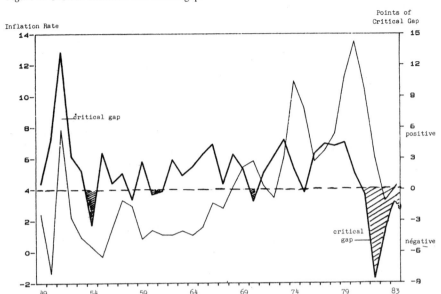

this idea. According to estimates, its GDP growth rate should be in the neighborhood of 3 to 4 per cent this year.

If real rates remain at their current level, the *negative critical gap*, "artificially" reduced in 1984, will begin to widen again (4–8) – we are speaking in terms of unchanged taxation. A further budgetary stimulation of the economy having become impossible, in light of the already enormous deficit, the *destructive* effect that the negative critical gap has on growth would show its full force. As the huge budget deficit and the Treasury's financing requirements will keep long term nominal interest rates high, the vicious circle of high real rates would then come back to where it had begun. The impact of real rates on growth would have simply been slowed in 1983 and 1984, in other words temporarily held at bay by the expanding budget deficit. The dead-end reached by supply-side economic theory would then be evident, notwithstanding the protests voiced by its proponents.

It should be added in the case of America that the constraint of real rates on growth was lessened by the capital inflows and the overseas borrowings of American banks and corporations attracted by the real yield of industrial and financial assets in the United States. Table 2 shows the share of foreign capital in the financing of American growth and its doping effect on the economy. The withdrawal, even of only a part, of this foreign capital and/or

Table 2. Share of foreign capital in financing American growth (in Bn US $)

	1981	1982	1983	1984[1]		
				Q1	Q2	Q3
Financing capacity in US:						
domestic (households + corporations)	515.7	517.4	537.8	573.6	575.2	570.0
net international savings	−5.8*	+6.6	+33.9	+77.7	+85.−	+119.4
Total	509.9	524.−	571.7	651.3	660.2	689.4
US financing requirements:						
gross investment	490.−	408.3	437.7	546.1	542.−	543.4
public sector deficit[2]	26.7	115.3	134.5	107.4	109.2	133.0
Statistical adjustment	−6.8	+0.4	−0.5	−2.2	+9.−	+13.0
Total	509.9	524.−	571.7	651.3	660.2	689.4
% of American financing requirements covered by net international savings	insig.	1.3	5.9	11.9	12.9	17.3

* 1981 was the last year when the American economy was a net capital exporter towards the rest of the world.

[1] On a yearly basis.

[2] This means the entire public sector and not just the Federal budget deficit. The budget surpluses of states and local governments have been included.

any change in the orientation of American banking and corporate flows, in the event of a drop in US economic activity – i.e. a decrease in the profitability of investments — or a loss of confidence in the face of the country's rising net debts (at the end of 1985 the United States will be a net debtor by $ 70 to 80 billion), will push nominal rates even higher. Inflation would then increase in the wake of a weaker dollar but the American economy would, no doubt, be asphyxiated within a few months by rise in the real premium, in other words by the widening negative gap.

Do the French and German situations comply with this reasoning?

In France, real interest rates between 1957 and 1980 remained substantially below the GDP growth rate in volume (see Figure 5). In contrast, since 1981 long term real interest rates have sharply outpaced this GDP growth rate. The negative effect that an excess real rate premium has on the growth rate thus apparently holds true. "The inflation rate and critical gap value" graph also seems to indicate that the appearance of a *negative critical gap* contributed strongly to the disinflation of the French system while at the same time holding GDP growth below its potential level (production growth rate plus growth of labor force and residual factors, including technical progress).

FRANCE

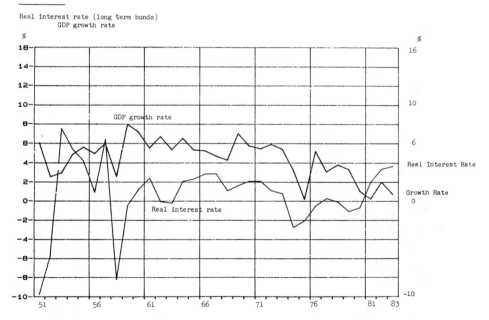

Figure 5.

152

The existence of a big budget deficit since 1982, not "financeable" by a drain on international savings (exchange controls and lack of confidence in the French franc) makes a neo-Keynesian type of growth support more difficult in France than it was in the United States. This explains why French growth remains modest, depressed as it is by the weight of real rates (highly negative critical gap in comparison to the French historic norm) (see Figure 6).

The phenomenon is less pronounced in Germany (see Figure 7). The GDP growth rate in volume remained on the whole close to long term real interest rates until 1980 when a gap began to form with the already de-scribed consequences on inflation and the growth rate. The existence of a substantial negative critical gap during the period, however, provides an explanation for two characteristics of the German economy: its slow growth rate compared to other European countries such as France until recently, and its extremely low inflation. It is also noteworthy that the German economic upswing of 1983–1984 brought the value of the negative critical gap down to −2.5 (GDP growth 2.5 − LT real rate 5) from the more than −4 it had been in 1982 (see Figure 8).

Under these circumstances, the phenomenon of long term real interest rates should apparently be examined in terms of the *critical gap* concept. A

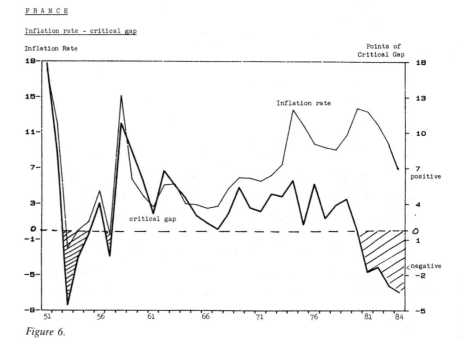

Figure 6.

GERMANY

Real interest rate (long term bonds)
    GDP growth rate

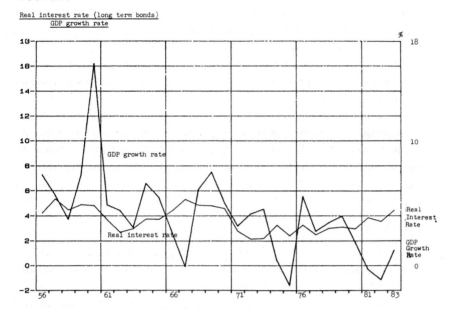

Figure 7.

GERMANY

Inflation rate - critical gap

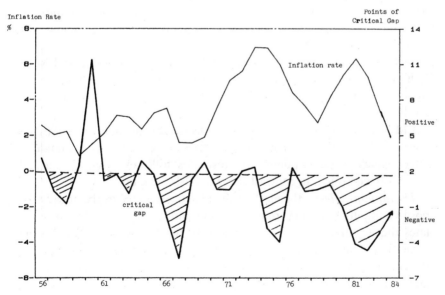

Figure 8.

negative critical gap between the GDP growth rate in volume and long term real interest rates seems to be a powerful disinflation factor at the same time that its acts as a sharp constraint on the growth rate, depending on the degree of budget support and the reflationary policy implemented. But in the long range, a wider budget deficit translates into a substantial public sector financing demand on the capital market which, as we shall see further on, prevents any drop in long term nominal rates. Disinflation continues under the impact of the negative critical gap whereas the premium on real rates remains high or even increases. The vicious circle of real rates is then in place. Is this observation, based on an analysis of recent trends, consistent with the economic theories on the formation of real rates?

Classical theories

Three major types of components should be singled out:

1. the negative influence of money supply fluctuations on the level of interest rates.

2. Business activity cycles which reduce or increase the amounts of monetary outstandings held for transaction purposes: changes in the liquidity effect according to the velocity with which money circulates.

3. The inflationist expectations effect discovered by Irvin Fisher in 1930.

A contemporary analysis of the conditions of interest rate formation in the five respective countries shows that these three "classical" relationships have only been imperfectly confirmed, especially as far as the phenomenon of real rates are concerned.

Keynes in his Treatise on Money spoke about the Gibson paradox, an 18th century English statistician whose works, in contrast to the quantitative theory, revealed the positive link between interest rates and price levels.

J.M. Keynes offered three explanations for this phenomenon. Any increase in the stock of money has three effects on interest rates: the liquidity effect, which decreases nominal interest rates, followed by the income and Fisher effects which, in contrast, tend to push them up.

The liquidity effect is the mark of an imbalance created by the negative or positive impulses coming from the central monetary authorities. It translates the negative influence – in line with the Keynesian theory on the formation of interest rates – that any changes in the money supply have on the general level of rates. A restrictive policy means higher interest rates and vice-versa. Lower interest rates, by stimulating economic activity, trigger an additional demand for credit – reducing the liquidity of the economy based on the constant velocity of the money in circulation, not always true in reality – which boosts interest rates in a stable money supply background.

The second effect, which comes simultaneously or follows on the heels of an upswing in the economic cycle is the *income effect*. It is a sign that economic cycles coincide more or less with interest rate cycles. The upswing prompts an increase in the distributed income within the economy, which gives greater momentum to the recovery and raises interest rates, unless the monetary authorities intervene. The increasing complexity of monetary and financial relations in modern economies, greater openness towards other countries coupled with flexible exchange rates, capital movements and the monetary levelling of central banks create a more or less pronounced lag between economic and interest rate cycles.

Lastly, *the Fisher effect,* no doubt the most important today in determining nominal interest rates, is based on inflationary expectations. Any increase in the supply of money, in conjunction with expanding economic activity, threatens to raise prices if the premium on real rates declines (see foregoing remarks on critical gap). Claim holders will in this event want a higher nominal return to forestall any loss in the value of their capital. They will try to obtain a *risk premium* based on their own inflationist expectations, thereby pushing up real interest rates. The disinflation, which began in 1975 but was countered by the second oil shock and President Carter's policy in the United States and came to be confirmed after 1980 in the major industrial countries, did not go hand in hand with an equivalent drop in nominal rates (see above graph). Under current circumstances, the Fisher effect seems to have come into doubt in favor of another explanation, based on the role played by the critical gap in a markedly disinflationist debt economy (dissavings).

OUTLINES OF A NEW APPROACH

A point of method should first be stressed as to the measure of real interest rates used so far in this report. The now commonly accepted definition of real interest rates is not too sturdy. An interest rate is an expected future; by comparing it to past price inflation – generally for the last twelve months – makes for a doubtful calculating method. It would be better if the issue or yield rate of a bond, of seven years for example, were compared to the inflation rate *expected* by purchasers over the same period. It might be added that inflation should preferably be measured more in terms of industrial and wholesale prices than consumer costs and that the taxation of corporate profits, particularly in the United States, should not be neglected. But even on this basis, real rates will still seem high in comparison to the historic norm; the industrial price trend is today in most countries below that of retail and consumer price indexes.

Nonetheless, it is by comparing these two factors – interest rates and expected inflation – that one can effectively apprehend real interest rates. The statistical approach of the phenomenon remains extremely fragile as the inflationist expectations of security buyers and sellers fluctuate with time. Some of the statistical research work done in Great Britain[2] and the United States[3] shows that the pace of expected inflation depends a great deal on *past and current*[4] price levels. The inflation forecasts commonly made by private and official organizations (OECD, IMF, domestic institutes, economists) do not usually exceed six months or one year. Financial operators do not thus know the premium (real rates) they should seek. The construction of a set of expected inflation rates for the next 3 – 5 years (averaged out over the period) would provide an element of appraisal, even if the problems and uncertainties raised by such an attempt are today discouraging the best efforts in this respect.

On the basis of this observation some people think that the current historically high level of real rates is essentially due to the fact that financial operators were *late* in taking world disinflation into account. Indeed, there is nothing today which justifies in the industrial economies an inflationary upswing as strong as that anticipated by the real interest rate differential. International prices, energy and commodities are on a downward bias, as demand has declined and stocks are abundant. Moreover, the persistent and active fight against inflation has led to a marked deceleration of unit labor costs in almost all of the big countries.

Inflationist expectations are, under these circumstances, excessive. In the United States many people thought that the strong economic upswing would in 1984 go hand in hand with higher inflation. The average forecast was that consumer prices would rise by 5 per cent for the year. They in fact increased by only around 4 per cent, though real rates did go higher again, a sign that the Fisher effect was not working. Apparently the mechanics of inflation have broken down under the weight of real rates and a negative critical gap between the GDP growth rate and long term real interest rates.

The slowdown in economic growth, under the constraint of real rates, and lacklustre investment spending since 1980, another victim of high real rates, have also undermined the working of the income effect in the world economy. Capital requirements should in fact have been smaller in 1984 than they were in 1974, a year when the premium on real rates was lower, even negative. The development of a technological innovations related investment cycle (Schumpeter wave) can perhaps be used to explain this apparent contradiction but it has, nonetheless, pushed up real rates in a background of worldwide dissavings.

The continued rise of the international standard of exchange – the dollar – against all currencies, gold, commodities and most other assets is a further sign of world disinflation. This should contribute strongly to curb the inflationist expectations of operators on the capital market. It is, however, patent that the phenomenon of real rates is persisting and is apparently even becoming deeply engrained in most of the major economies, threatening the lasting power of the expansion phase.

Link between public and private debts – real interest rates

The first cause of high real rates lies in the clash between the extremely high or still substantial budget deficits in the United States and the other countries under review and the disinflation engendered by prudent monetary policy. A rising real premium is in a debt economy the sign of a persistent imbalance between capital supply and demand. Debts have a considerable inertia effect in a system of real rates, which mechanically increases the debt service. The simulations made in France by INSEE show that the price inflation induced depreciation of debts between 1974 and 1983 offset 73 per cent of private corporate financing requirements. Today a large part of national wealth creation is being diverted to servicing the state debt. In Japan, the debt service represented the second most important item in the budget (18 per cent of the total) for 1984 and will take first place this year. In the United States, nearly 15 per cent of aggregate expenditures in the 1984–1985 budget are earmarked for this purpose. These deficits have become self-sustaining, as a substantial amount of new borrowings are being exclusively devoted to public debt repayments (see Table 3).

The deepening dissavings position of the state and public sector in general during the last ten years, despite the recent headways made by privatization, especially in the United Kingdom and Germany, has translated into wider public deficits and growing international and domestic public debts. (Table 4).

Mr. de Larosière has stressed that the Government debt – GNP ratio of the seven leading industrial countries had climbed from 22 per cent in 1974 to 41 per cent in 1983. In 1984, Japan's public debt represented 51 per cent of

Table 3. Public debt and national wealth creation in 1983

	France	United States	Japan	Germany	United Kingdom
Public debt service (in % of GNP)	1.7	2.8	2.7	3.1	4.2
Central Government financing requirements (in % of GNP)	4.1	5.5	4.8	3.2	3.8
Nominal GNP growth rate	10.9	5.7	4.1	4.5	7.1

Table 4. Central Government financing requirements* (in % of GNP)

	France	United States	Germany	United Kingdom	Japan
1973	+0.6	−0.4	−0.3	−6.5	−2.6
1983	−4.1	−5.5	−3.2	−3.8	−4.8

* Public sector financing requirements in the case of Germany and Great Britain.

GNP and 43 per cent in the United States, 41 per cent in Germany, 46 per cent in the United Kingdom and 25 per cent in France.

In the face of the huge financing requirements of the public sector and corporations undergoing restructuring, in response to the needs created by the new technological cycle, households, net contributors of resources, are no longer in a position to balance financial flows. As net suppliers of savings, in other words of capital, their savings rate has during the last ten years declined seriously in the major industrial countries, as their purchasing power shrank and inflation eroded the real value of their property and financial assets and then disinflation the nominal value. Lower leverage (disinflation) has indeed mechanically increased the debt burden of households. Between 1973 and 1983 the household savings rate fell from 17.3 to 14.6 per cent in France, from 8.6 to 4.9 per cent in the United States, from 14.2 to 12.7 per cent in Germany, and from 11 to 8.4 per cent in the United Kingdom. Japan was the only country which, for sociological and economic reasons, was able to avoid this dissavings process (its savings rate remaining stable around 20 per cent of disposable income). One would have expected that a rising real interest rate premium would boost corporate and household savings as invested capital was generating higher real returns. Supply-side economists in the United States thought so. Reality has so far proved them wrong. The "Gross savings in per cent of GDP" in Figure 9 shows how this dissavings phenomenon works out for the OECD, EEC and other countries, including Japan.

The imbalance prevailing between financing capacity and requirements in the industrial countries has only further perverted the mechanism governing the formation of real rates. The United States has become unable to finance its growth and budget deficit on the basis of its domestic savings resources. As it has the advantage of "minting international money" it has been able to drain an increasing portion of international savings. Though this has kept nominal rates in Europe and Japan high compared to their pace of economic activity (critical gap), it has been inadequate to push down US interest rates. The dominant position of America as a financial centre compared to the rest of the world is producing asymmetrical effects which are deforming rate structures, "manufacturing" high real rates in most economies. Germany and Japan, which have been able to maintain a net domestic financing capacity, have to some degree been advantaged by a more temperate system of real rates, held in check it is true by the constraint coming from the strong dollar exchange rate. France is in a similar situation, though for entirely different reasons related to its exchange controls (uncoupled domestic interest rates) and the pressure that the dollar is exerting on the DM, thereby indirectly supporting the "weak" currencies within the EMS (see "Financing capacity and interest rates" Figure 10).

The phenomenon of positive real interest rates thus seems in 1985 to be present simultaneously with dissavings, public sector debts, disinflation, mechanisms which are draining world savings towards the United States and the surge in new innovations (technology and restructuring of old industries). The effect that deregulation is having on the financial sector should also not be lost sight of. The rising cost of bank resources is impeding any drop in rates, regardless of the degree of inflation. The share of non-interest-bearing bank liabilities has decreased considerably in most of the industrial countries, to which should be added the difficulties raised by the need to rapidly reduce the cost of bank intermediation (low productivity of services).

A combination of two factors are needed to push the premium on real rates back to its historic level: reduction in public deficits, particularly in the United States, and decrease in corporate financing requirements. In Japan

160

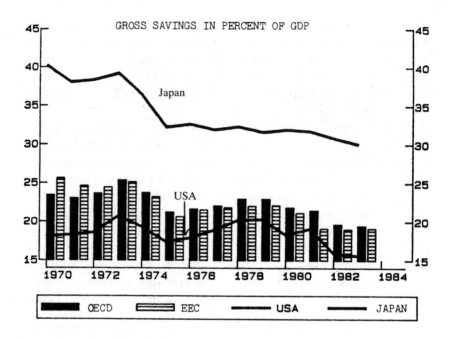

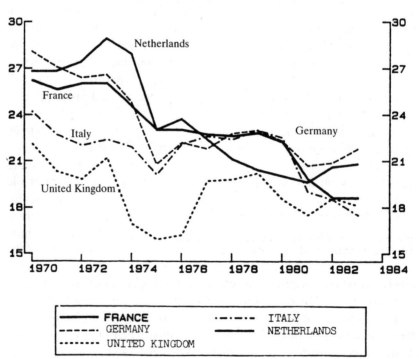

Figure 9.

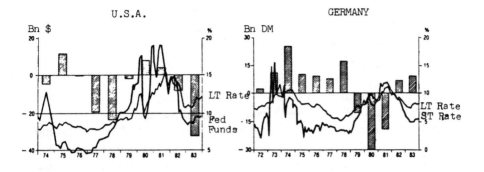

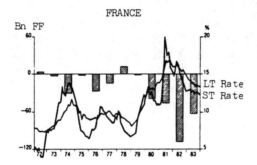

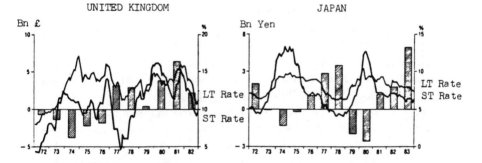

Figure 10. Financing capacity* and interest rates

* Claims and liabilities balance of all transactors
  (- = net financing requirements).

and Germany, the necessary budgetary moves have begun and their deficits in percentage of GDP are declining despite the debt burden. In France and the United Kingdom, the trend is still in a stabilization or deteriorating phase. As far as the United States is concerned, the problem is familiar enough. It is in the headlines of every economic newspaper. At this moment, we are sill waiting for the world's leading power to implement a tax reform that will help reduce its budget deficit and bring the premium on positive real rates down a notch or two.

On the private corporate front, financial structures have improved markedly (higher profit ploughbacks) in most of the five countries under consideration, which has ipso facto reduced their external financing requirements, a movement strengthened by currently low growth rates and investments in a strongly disinflationist background. But the modernization of industrial economies will require substantial capital. Can this take place when the real rate of return on investments is close to real rates and when the financing of public deficits tends to make the private sector less competitive on capital markets as its risks are higher and yields lower? If nothing else, the constraint of real rates threatens to divert capital towards the most speculative applications, to the detriment of heavy investments. Excessively positive real rates will thus perhaps have been the root cause of the "financialization" of the world economy and the instability of exchange rates induced by the wave of hot money ...

CONCLUSIONS

Growing capital market imbalances are pushing the debts of the industrial nations to levels which are incompatible with the targeted financial rebuilding and steady and persistent economic growth. In the United States, the aggregate domestic debt of the American economy (government-corporations-households, excluding the financial sector) at the end of 1983 stood at $5,245 billion ($6,200 billion including the debt of the financial sector). This represented 160 per cent of America's GNP in 1983 against 147 per cent in 1974 (for debts of $2,112.6 billion). According to the latest available figures dating from the summer of 1984, the debt has increased further to reach roughly $5,700 billion (see Table 5). On the same basis, Germany's aggregate debt at the end of 1983 amounted to $1,040 billion, i.e. 180 per cent of its GNP against 132 per cent in 1974. As for France, its non-financial sector liabilities at the end of 1983 totalled $630 billion, i.e. 140 per cent of its GNP against 135 per cent in 1974 ($389 billion). This growing public and private debt burden is closely and directly related to the phenomenon of persistently high real interest rates.

Real interest rates are not yielding to disinflation due to the high level of debts and insufficient savings, as the central monetary authorities have adopted a necessarily cautions attitude in an effort to prevent any re-

Table 5. US domestic debt (Bn $ – end of period)

	Federal debt* (held by the public)	Non-financial domestic sectors debt	Financial sector debt	Aggregate US debt
1972	437.3 (323.8)	1,754.6	310.2	2,064.8
1973	468.4 (343.–)	1,942.5	360.3	2,302.8
1974	486.2 (346.1)	2,112.6	399.4	2,512.–
1975	544.131 (396.906)	2,295.1	413.4	2,708.5
1976	631.866 (480.300)	2,532.6	435.9	2,968.5
1977	709.138 (551.843)	2,829.1	484.7	3,338.8
1978	780.425 (610.948)	3,200	559.3	3,777.4
1979	833.751 (644.589)	3,583.5	641.8	4,246.–
1980	914.317 (715.105)	3,926.1	705.1	4,652.–
1981	1,003.941 (794.434)	4,311.8	790.5	5,114.3
1982	1,146.987 (929.427)	4,709.2	859.8	5,569.9
1983	1,381.886 (1,141.770)	5,224.4	948.4	6,193.2
1984	1,576.7 (1,312.6)	5,937.6		

* fiscal years

surgence of inflation. The human cost (unemployment) of disinflation is too high to even think of having to go through only a part of the same ordeal again.

What can then be done? Monetary laxity would bring on high inflation and renewed growth which would, indeed, reduce the premium on real rates and thereby alleviate the burden now borne by the industrial countries. But satisfaction would be shortlived. The resulting imbalances and new inflationist expectations would be such that it would rapidly become necessary to suspend the engaged action.

A more reasonable solution would be to reform taxation and trim the

American deficit, while at the same time targeting a smaller growth rate in the United States, more in line with its domestic savings capacity. The resulting rise in the household savings rate could reduce the drain on international savings. The cutback in public deficits and the continued improvement in the corporate profit ploughback rate, obtained by scaling down household consumption in the other countries, would greatly contribute to rebalance world financial flows. At the end of this process could lie a lower real interest rate premium. One need not be Cassandra to wager that this will require much time and wisdom. The phenomenon of real rates is thus likely to persist. It is a threat to continued expansion and, therefore, undeniably represents an obstacle that the monetary authorities should make every effort to eliminate as rapidly as possible.

NOTES

1. Our remarks exclude taxation. The tax treatment of interest has a non-negligible impact which, however, needs to be appraised on a country by country basis. The United States is not the only one with an advantageous arrangement. European countries, with their system of allowances, also distort comparisons.

2. Holden and Peel worked out a set of quarterly one year inflationist expectations based on the forecasts of five English economic research groups.

3. Livingstone in the United States has been publishing 6 month forecast figures since 1947, obtained by the survey of American economists.

4. The Bank of England uses an estimate set of yearly inflation expectations.

Chapter XII

INTEREST RATES AND INFLATION:
EUROPEAN v. US EVIDENCE 1960–1984

by *Marie-Christine Adam and André Farber*

INTRODUCTION

The evolution of interest rates during the 1970s and the early 1980s posed considerable challenges to both market practitioners and academic researchers. While the high and variable interest rates that emerged following the breakdown of the Bretton Woods system seemed hardly avoidable in a world of sharp exchange rate readjustments and unprecedented levels of world inflation, the record of sustained volatility they exhibit more than a decade later attests to the radical transformation of the financial environment.

Accumulating evidence has in addition led many observers to question even the most basic relationships involving financial variables[1]. Purchasing power parity was found to have "collapsed" during the 1970s. Relatively high (low) interest rates were associated for several years with depreciating (appreciating) currencies thus questioning the wisdom traditional theories. Even the evolution of real interest rates has undergone, in most industrialized countries, puzzling modifications which appear to this date, unaccounted for by economic analysis.

Since these basic relationships form the core of most existing theoretical models of the financial sphere[2], a careful reappraisal of each of their components might constitute a useful first step into the understanding of the transformed financial environment of the 1980s.

In this paper we propose to examine the link between interest rates and inflation, as formalized in the so-called Fisher relation. To this end we will consider quarterly data series for the US and several European countries (UK, Germany, Belgium and the Netherlands) from 1960-I to 1984-III.

The aim of the research is twofold. First, to document the extent and the nature of the changes undergone by nominal and real interest rates during the period. To this end we will contrast trend and volatility in interest rate variables in the pre- and post-Bretton Woods era and investigate the impact

Fair, D.E., (ed.) Shifting Frontiers in Financial Markets.
© *1986, Martinus Nijhoff Publishers, Dordrecht/Boston/Lancaster. ISBN 90-247-3225-5.*
Printed in the Netherlands.

of the mid 1979 reorientation of American monetary policy. Second, since most studies of the Fisher relationship have been carried on the basis of US data, we will examine whether significant differences can be established from the empirical investigation of US vs European interest rates. Although the partial equilibrium nature of our enquiry obviously precludes an exhaustive treatment of the issue, it is clear that the belief (or lack of belief, depending on which side of the Atlantic one is based) in such behavioural asymmetries has played a central role in recent debates about US monetary policy prescriptions (see Von Furstenberg, 1983). Hardly any evidence has however been published to this date on this important issue attesting to the need for more complete comparative studies of the behaviour of interest rates.

The first section presents summary statistics on nominal and real interest rates and depicts the evolution of inflation rates in the five countries surveyed by our study. The second section presents the methodology of the model used to test the Fisher relationship (Fama and Gibbons, 1982) and comments on the results of the empirical investigation. The third section summarizes the conclusions of the study.

INTEREST RATES AND INFLATION: THE HISTORICAL DATA

The data base

The impact of inflation on short term interest rates is traditionally measured from Treasury bill (TB) rates since these "riskless" instruments avoid the distortions generated from variable but unobservable risk premia. In as far as possible we have followed this tradition. Annualized 3-month TB rates or rates on comparable 3 month Government certificates (end of period) were used for the US, the UK, Belgium and the Netherlands (source: OECD, Main Economic Indicators). Unfortunately no such series were available for Germany given the infrequent issue of comparable instruments. Considering the importance of this country, the 3 month interbank deposit rate (source: Morgan Guaranty Trust – World Financial Markets) was used alternatively although the available data series for this country starts only in 1967-IV. Nominal interest rates are hereafter summarized by the symbol R_t.

Annualized inflation rates (I_t) were computed from quarterly consumer price indices collected from the OECD Main Economic Indicators. Real interest rates (r_t) were obtained by subtracting the annualized inflation rates corresponding to each quarter (t, t+1)) from the end of period nominal interest rates (measured at time t).

Evolution of the series

Table 1 presents, for each country, the average value and the standard deviation of each of the series described above. To characterize the evolution of the series we calculated similar statistics over sub-periods delimited by the breakdown of the Bretton Woods system (fixed somewhat arbitrarily at 1971-III) and the mid-1979 reorientation of US monetary policy.

A first overview of the figures in Table 1 shows that in terms of historical trends, the global evolution of the variables was roughly similar across countries. Although starting from different absolute levels, nominal interest rates show a consistent upward trend over the three sub-periods. As a result, their average value over the last sub-period is 2.5 times greater than the corresponding value for the 1960s. Inflation rates exhibit a sharp increase in the immediate post Bretton Woods era (sub-period II) and a more or less marked decrease in the early 1980s. The UK presents the more contrasted pattern with a record upsurge of inflation (from an average of 4.5 per cent in period I to 13.27 per cent in period II) and a marked recovery over the last sub-period. It retains nonetheless, in absolute value, the highest average level of inflation in our sample. The US, Belgium and the Netherlands rise from average inflation rates in the range of 3 to 4 per cent in sub-period I to 7–8 per cent in sub-period II. During the early 1980s price increases are levelled out at around 7 per cent for the US and Belgium and fall down under 5 per cent for the Netherlands and Germany.

The contrasting trends in nominal rates and inflation lead to dramatic discontinuities in the evolution of ex post real interest rates. From an average level of 1 per cent in period I they drop to negative values[3] during the troubled 1970s as a result of the severe inflationary pressure. The subsequent deceleration in inflation combined with rising nominal interest rates leads however to their spectacular recovery in period III.

In contrast to historical average trends, changes in volatility throughout the period do not follow similar patterns across countries. There is certainly a common increase in the variability of practically all the statistical series during the post Bretton Woods era. However, the evolution of the dispersion parameters in Table 1 allows for significant differences in national experiences. US inflation as well as nominal and real interest rates exhibit persistently increasing volatility over time. Whereas the UK, Belgium and (within the more limited data sample) Germany seem to have reached a

Table 1. Mean value (and standard deviation) of interest rates and inflation, period: 1960-I/1984-III and sub-periods I (1960-I/1971-II), II (1971-III/1979-II) and III (1979-III/1984-III).

Countries	Nominal interest rates in sub-period:			Total sample	Inflation rates in sub-period:			Total sample	Real interest rates in sub-period:			Total sample
	I	II	III		I	II	III		I	II	III	
United States	4.20	6.18	11.09	6.28	2.87	7.53	6.79	5.22	1.33	-1.35	4.30	1.06
	(1.47)	(1.59)	(2.44)	(3.14)	(1.91)	(3.24)	(4.50)	(3.73)	(1.10)	(2.12)	(3.63)	(2.96)
United Kingdom	5.71	9.12	12.02	8.14	4.50	13.27	8.62	8.24	1.22	-4.14	3.40	-0.10
	(1.31)	(2.70)	(2.67)	(3.28)	(2.69)	(7.27)	(5.97)	(6.52)	(2.40)	(5.98)	(4.80)	(5.25)
Belgium	4.89	7.38	13.28	7.44	3.11	7.64	7.22	5.44	1.78	-0.25	6.05	1.99
	(1.48)	(2.54)	(2.19)	(3.77)	(2.12)	(3.69)	(2.25)	(3.50)	(2.27)	(3.57)	(3.13)	(3.69)
The Netherlands	3.77	5.79	8.17	5.34	4.13	7.16	4.86	5.27	-0.36	-1.37	3.31	0.07
	(1.68)	(2.79)	(2.56)	(2.83)	(5.37)	(3.52)	(2.24)	(4.48)	(5.29)	(4.39)	(1.70)	(4.79)
Germany*	—	6.37	8.62	7.14*	—	5.02	4.26	4.38*	—	1.35	4.36	2.76*
		(3.19)	(2.50)	(2.95)		(2.52)	(2.23)	(2.60)		(3.01)	(1.97)	(2.97)

* Money market rates were used for Germany instead of TBs. The available series starts in 1967-IV.

peak in variability during the second sub-period, inflation instability in the US worsens over the last sub-period, driving real interest rates to unprecedented levels of volatility: the standard deviation of the series triples from the 1960s to the early 1980s.

The UK highly erratic inflation record also has an obvious impact upon ex post real rate volatility: in spite of its observed dampening in period III, the real rate dispersion parameter reaches about twice its value in period I and remains significantly higher, in absolute terms, than the corresponding US parameter. The Belgian case presents a similar evolution in the three data series with relatively moderate increases and decreases in volatility during the second and third sub-periods. The rate of inflation in the Netherlands evolves quite differently; it exhibits an abnormally high level of variability during the first sub-period (due to atypical fluctuations in the

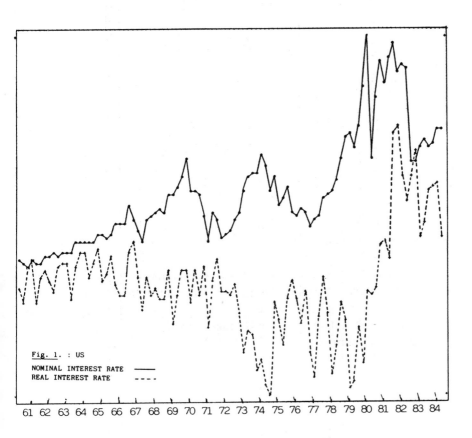

Fig. 1. : US
NOMINAL INTEREST RATE ———
REAL INTEREST RATE - - - -

61 62 63 64 65 66 67 68 69 70 71 72 73 74 75 76 77 78 79 80 81 82 83 84

Figure 1. Nominal and real interest rates in the U.S. (1960-II/1984-II).

170

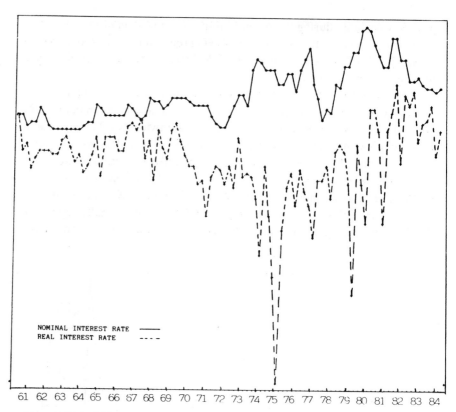

NOMINAL INTEREST RATE ——
REAL INTEREST RATE - - - -

61 62 63 64 65 66 67 68 69 70 71 72 73 74 75 76 77 78 79 80 81 82 83 84

Figure 2. United Kingdom.

CPI for the years 1960 and 1961). Since, as in the other European economies, inflation volatility decreases in the early 1980s the standard deviations
of inflation and real interest rates present a decreasing profile over time.

The detailed evolution of nominal and real interest rates over time can
also be appreciated from Figures 1 to 5 which illustrate the upward trend
and the increased volatility observed in nominal interest rates since 1973 as
well as the abrupt shifts in the average value of real interest rates over
different sub-periods.

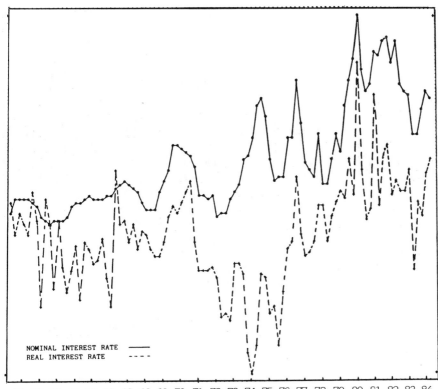

Figure 3. Belgium.

TESTING THE LINKS BETWEEN INTEREST RATES AND INFLATION

Fisher's (1930) celebrated decomposition of interest rates into an expected real return component and an expected inflation premium has given rise to countless applications in financial economics. Actual tests of the relationship were however hampered for many years by the unobservable character of its two main components. Fama's (1975) seminal work, integrating Fisher's relationship within the framework of the efficient market hypothesis opened the way for a new methodology of testing. Based on the assumptions that a) nominal interest rates fully incorporate rational market assessments of expected inflation and that b) expected real returns on US TB's are roughly constant over time, Fama's approach allows for the regression of ex post inflation rates on ex ante interest rates, thereby

172

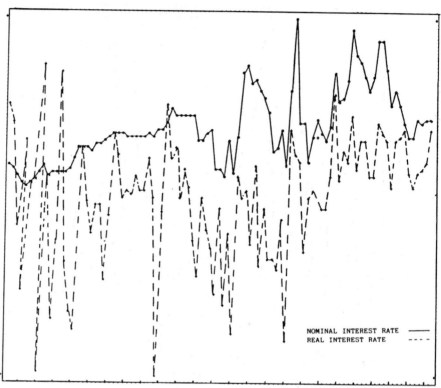

61 62 63 64 65 66 67 68 69 70 71 72 73 74 75 76 77 78 79 80 81 82 83 84

Figure 4. The Netherlands.

eliminating the need to resort to questionable proxies of anticipated inflation.

Later work, based on extended data series, led however Fama and
Gibbons (1982) to reject the assumption of constant real rates. While
retaining the efficient market approach they convincingly tested the joint
assumption that real rates follow a random walk, providing a successful test
of the Fisher relation for the US during the period 1953–1977.

Since, as illustrated in Figure 1, the early 1980s marked a considerable
evolution in ex post real US interest rates, the ability of Fama and Gibbons'
model to contend with more recent data is an open question. Tests of the
methodology based on European TB's are scarce in the literature. Accordingly very little is known on the adjustment of interest rates to inflation in
these economies.

Before presenting our results, we summarize hereafter the formal methodology of the tests by Fama and Gibbons (1982).

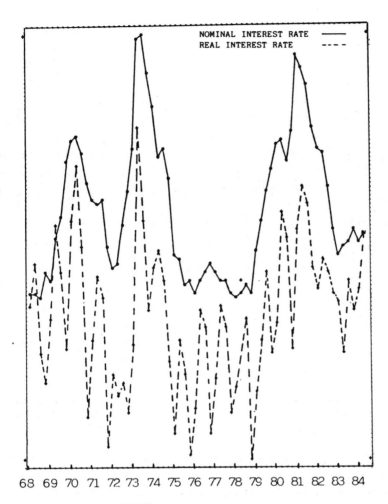

68 69 70 71 72 73 74 75 76 77 78 79 80 81 82 83 84

Figure 5. Germany (1966-I – 1984-II).

The theoretical model

The model is based on the following equations:

$$R_{t-1} = E_{t-1} r_t + E_{t-1} I_t \tag{1}$$

$$I_t = E_{t-1} I_t + \eta_t \tag{2}$$

$$E_{t-1} r_t = E_{t-2} r_{t-1} + a_{t-1} \tag{3}$$

where

R_{t-1} denotes the nominal interest rate for period t (fixed at t-1),
$E_{t-1} r_t$ is the equilibrium expected real interest rate for period t,
$E_{t-1} I_t$ is the expected rate of inflation for period t,
η_t denotes unanticipated inflation in period t,
a_t is the change in the anticipated real interest rate in period t.

Equation (1) gives Fisher's expression of the nominal interest rate as the sum of the expected real rate of return and the expected inflation rate. Equation (2) breaks the realized rate of inflation into an anticipated component $E_{t-1} I_t$ and an unanticipated element η_t. Under rational expectations, η_t is a white noise. The assumption that the equilibrium expected real rate behaves as a random walk is integrated in equation (3): changes in the expected real rate a_t are also a white noise.

Subtracting (2) from (1) and denoting by r_t the real interest rate realized in period t leads to:

$$r_t = E_{t-1} r_t - \eta_t \tag{4}$$

Equation (4) expresses the real interest rate realized in period t as the difference between the expected real rate (a random walk) and the unanticipated inflation rate (a white noise). The test of the model consists then in: 1) extracting the evolution of the expected real rate from the observed real rate series and 2) checking whether the residual unanticipated inflation component is a white noise.

The estimation methodology follows Ansley's (1980) approach. It is based on the observation that the first difference in equation (4):

$$r_t - r_{t-1} = a_{t-1} - \eta_t + \eta_{t+1} \tag{5}$$

can be expressed as the difference between a white noise and a first order moving average process (MA1):

$$r_t - r_{t-1} = \mu_t + \theta\,\mu_{t-1} \tag{6}$$

The parameters $\hat{\theta}$ and $\hat{\sigma}_\mu^2$ of this MA1 can then be estimated using a Box and Jenkins procedure. From the first step, the estimated variances of the variables a_t and η_t can be obtained as:

$$\hat{\sigma}_\eta^2 = \hat{\theta}\,\hat{\sigma}_\mu^2 \tag{7}$$

$$\hat{\sigma}_a^2 = \left(\frac{1+\hat{\theta}^2}{\hat{\theta}} - 2\right)\hat{\sigma}_\eta^2 \tag{8}$$

In addition, knowledge of the estimated values of μ_t allows us to express the expected real rate of interest as:

$$\hat{E}_{t-1}\, r_t = r_t - \hat{\theta}\, \hat{\mu}_{t-1} \tag{9}$$

From this second step, the expected and unexpected inflation rates can be respectively computed as:

$$\hat{E}_{t-1}\, I_t = R_{t-1} - \hat{E}_{t-1}\, r_t \tag{10}$$

$$\hat{\eta}_t = I_t - \hat{E}_{t-1}\, I_t \tag{11}$$

The empirical test of the model developed above will thus be based on the following regression:

$$I_t = \alpha_t + b\, R_t + \eta_t$$

Ideally, convincing results should satisfy the following requirements:
1. The estimated coefficient of the nominal interest rate variable ($\hat{b}$) should be close to its theoretical value of 1.0.
2. The residuals of the regression should be non correlated (i.e. the residual intertemporal autocorrelations $\varrho_{t-1}, \varrho_{t-2}, \ldots, \varrho_{t-i}$ should be close to zero).
3. Since the traditional measure of goodness of fit, i.e. the R^2 is difficult to interpret within the framework of a moving intercept regression, the overall performance should be appreciated on the basis of the residual standard deviation $\sigma\,(\eta)$. If nominal interest rates are good predictors of inflation, ex ante interest rates should absorb a substantial proportion of the variation in ex post inflation rates and the "unexplained" residual variance should be small.

Results of the empirical investigation

Table 2 presents the results[4] of the moving intercept regressions of ex-post inflation rates on ex ante nominal interest rates for the five countries considered in this study. The period of estimation extends from 1960-II to 1984-III except for Germany where the data base starts in 1967-IV. To provide a comparison, regressions were also run on the basis of the constant real rate hypothesis as originally developed by Fama (1975). The results of these tests are presented in Appendix 1.

In addition to the parameters discussed above ($\hat{b}$, $\sigma\,(\eta)$, ϱ_{t-i}) the last columns in Table 2 present the estimated value of the moving average parameter $\hat{\theta}$. As can be seen from equation (7), θ represents the ratio of the variance of the signal a_{t-1} to the variance of the unexpected inflation term η_t. Intuitively it can therefore provide an indication of the relative importance of the variability in unexpected inflation and expected real returns.

Table 2. Regressions of ex post inflation rates on ex ante nominal interest rates with a moving intercept 1960-I/1984-II*

Dependent variable: I_t	Coefficient of R_t: $\hat{b}$ (standard deviation)	Residual standard deviation $\sigma(\hat{\eta})$	Residual autocorrelations				$\hat{\theta}$
			ϱ_{t-1}	ϱ_{t-2}	ϱ_{t-3}	ϱ_{t-4}	
United States	.807 (.142)	1.27	.08	−.30	.12	.26	.471
⎡Fama-Gibbons⎤ ⎣(1953–1977)⎦	⎡.93⎤ ⎣(.197)⎦	[1.58]	[.01	−.04	.06	.15]	[.78]
United Kingdom	.996 (.249)	3.83	.11	−.09	−.13	.20	.728
Belgium	.235 (.134)	1.90	−.02	−.04	.06	.03	.620
The Netherlands	.161 (.179)	4.10	−.03	−.18	−.09	.40	.876
Germany	.342 (.110)	2.60	.14	−.39	.08	.56	.898

* The period of estimation for Germany is 1967-IV/1984-III.

The results presented in Table 2 suggest that for two of the countries considered above, the US and the UK, the model provides a reasonable approximation. The estimated coefficients of the nominal interest rate are not statistically different from their hypothesized value of 1.0 and the residual autocorrelations are relatively small. The UK coefficient (.996) is actually very close to the mark, but the US regressions present a more satisfactory adjustment in terms of the residual variance. It can also be noted that for both countries the moving intercept model performs clearly better than the constant real rate model (see Appendix 1). Comparing our results to Fama and Gibbons' evidence for the period 1953–1977 suggests however that the inclusion of more recent data leads to a relative deterioration of the regression: although the residual variance decreases, the lower value of $\hat{b}$ and the higher residual autocorrelations in the 1960–1984 regressions indicate a less satisfactory adjustment.

An interesting difference can also be observed in the estimated value of the parameter θ which drops from .78 to .47 in the US regressions, suggesting that over the last years the variability in expected real returns has increased relatively to that of the unexpected inflation term. This result seems consistent with the evidence presented in section 1 since it can be interpreted in terms of the incorporation, in ex ante expectations, of the marked increase in ex post real interest rate volatility.

The regressions for Belgium, the Netherlands and Germany present very different characteristics. The estimated coefficients of nominal interest rates are conspiciously low and significantly different from their theoretical value. In addition, substantial residual autocorrelations appear in the Netherlands and German regressions. These results as well as the evidence presented in Appendix 1 suggest that neither the constant real rate model nor the moving intercept version provide a satisfactory explanation of the experience of these countries. Since our experiments constitute tests of joint assumptions about the behaviour of real rates and the efficiency of financial markets it is impossible to determine the exact sources of failure.

Several factors could in principle be incriminated. European economies tend to be smaller and more open. Their financial markets can be more heavily regulated and/or may tend to reflect the impact of active exchange rate policies. It is also well known that in the smaller countries such as Belgium and the Netherlands, the pricing of TBs does not follow from a pure market process comparable to that of the US or the UK bond markets. However, whether and how these factors affect the relationship between interest rates and inflation is not a question that can be settled at this stage. To this end, further research is needed, based on models more specifically tailored to contend with market imperfections and to assess the impact of contrasting exchange rate and monetary policy programs.

What the results do suggest however, is that in as far as the asymmetry issue is concerned, there are indeed grounds to suspect that interest rate adjustments differ across the Atlantic: except for the UK, conceptually if not geographically closer to the US, nominal interest rates in European economies appear as very poor predictors of inflation.

CONCLUSION

In this study, we analyzed the empirical evidence on interest rates and inflation in the US and in a group of European countries for the period 1960–1984. The statistical analysis of quarterly data series suggests that in terms of overall average trends, the evolution of nominal interest rates, inflation rates and ex post real rates was roughly similar across countries.

While nominal interest rates exhibit a continuous upward trend over the whole period, inflation rates follow a broken evolution with sharp accelerations during the post Bretton Woods era and more or less moderate decreases during the last sub-period. As a result, significant discontinuities appear in ex post real interest rates trends. After a marked depression during the 1970s they display a spectacular recovery in the early 1980s and reach unprecedented high averages.

Changes in the observed volatility of interest rates and inflation did however not follow similar patterns across countries. Except for the general increase in variability following the breakdown of the international monetary system, significant differences appear in national experiences.

The uneven evolution of ex post real rates and their increased volatility show that financial market practitioners had to contend with significant alterations of the financial environment. Investment decisions are however based on expectations which are not necessarily reflected in ex post historical data. Accordingly, we tried to approach this issue using Fisher's celebrated decomposition of nominal interest rates into expected inflation and expected real returns. Following Fama and Gibbons we tested Fisher's relationship under the joint assumption that financial markets are efficient and that ex ante real interest rates follow a random walk. Our results show an obvious dichotomy within the sample of countries: while the model provides a reasonable approximation of the UK and the US experience, the results for the Netherlands, Belgium and Germany lead to a rejection of the joint assumption and tend to support the view that there are asymmetries in interest rate adjustments. However, whether and how these differences can be justified is an open question for further research.

APPENDIX

TESTS OF THE CONSTANT REAL INTEREST RATE VERSION (FAMA, 1975)

The constant real interest rate version of the model is based on the following regression:

$$I_t = a + b\,R_t + \eta_t$$

Testing this equation for the five countries under study leads to the following results:

	â	b̂	R^2	ϱ_1	ϱ_2	ϱ_3	ϱ_4	$\sigma\,(\eta)$
US	.42	.764	.414	.79	.60	.64	.60	2.87
	(.647)	(.093)						
UK	−1.53	1.200	.365	.48	.34	.28	.44	5.22
	(1.41)	(.161)						
Belgium	1.94	.466	.246	.54	.48	.50	.44	3.09
	(.692)	(.083)						
The Netherlands	3.32	.354	.050	.12	−.04	.02	.43	4.48
	(.965)	(.161)						
Germany	2.07	.342	.133	.58	.38	.57	.23	2.59
	(.831)	(.108)						

NOTES

1. See Frenkel (1981), (1983), Mishkin (1982).

2. As they do, for instance, in the currently most popular model of exchange rate determination, the asset market approach, developed by Frenkel and Johnson (1981).

3. The German real rate is an exception since it exhibits a positive value in period II. However, since this rate was calculated from a money market instrument instead of a TB, its absolute level cannot be compared to the other rates presented in Table 1.

4. The estimation was carried on the basis of a program written by G. Melard (Department of Statistics – University of Brussels) to whom we are deeply indebted. See also Khoury and Melard (1985).

REFERENCES

1. Ansley, C.F. (1980), "Signal Extraction in Finite Series and the Estimation of Stochastic Regression Coefficients", *Proceedings of the American Statistical Association.*
2. Fama, E.F. (1975), "Short Term Interest Rates as Predictors of Inflation", *American Economic Review* 65, June.
3. Fama, E.F. and Gibbons, M.R. (1982), "Inflation, Real Returns and Capital Investment", *Journal of Monetary Economics* no 9.
4. Fisher, I. (1930), *The Theory of Interest,* New York, reprinted by A.M. Kelley, 1965.
5. Frenkel, J.A. (1981), "The Collapse of Purchasing Power Parities during the 1970s", *European Economic Review* 16, 1 May.
6. Frenkel, J.A. (1983), "Turbulence in the Foreign Exchange Markets and Macroeconomic Policies", Chapter 1 in *Exchange Rate and Trade Instability,* D. Bigman and T. Taya eds., Ballinger Publishing Co., Cambridge-Massachusetts.
7. Frenkel, J.A. and Johnson, H.G. (1978) eds., *The Economics of Exchange Rates,* Addison Wesley Publishing Cy., Reading, Massachusetts.
8. Khoury, N.T. and Melard, G. (1985), "The Relationship Between the Canadian Treasury Bill Rate and Expected Inflation in Canada and in the US", forthcoming in *The Canadian Journal of Administrative Sciences.*

9. Mishkin, F.S. (1982), "Are Real Interest Rates Equal Across Countries? An Empirical Investigation of International Parity Conditions", *NBER Working Paper no 1048,* December.
10. Von Furstenberg, G.M. (1983), "Changes in US Interest Rates and their Effects on European Interest and Exchange Rates", Chapter 11 in *Exchange Rate and Trade Instability,* D. Bigman and T. Taya eds., Ballinger Publishing Co., Cambridge, Massachusetts.

Part D

IMPLICATIONS FOR FINANCIAL INSTITUTIONS

Chapter XIII

DEPOSIT RATE DISCRIMINATION: EFFECTS ON BANK
MANAGEMENT AND MONETARY POLICY IN ITALY

by *Carlo Cottarelli, Franco Cotula and Giovani Battista Pittaluga*

INTRODUCTION AND MAIN CONCLUSIONS

In Italy, as in most industrial countries, the pace of financial innovation and
of structural change in financial markets has been particularly rapid in the
last few years and has considerably changed the traditional pattern of
financial flows within the economy.

While in other countries innovation has been led by financial intermediaries and deregulated banking systems, in Italy the process has caught the
banks in a weak position, unable to react effectively to the new sources of
competition for households' savings stemming from the development of a
deep and efficient market for Treasury bills and floating rate securities.

In Italy, bank deposits, including checking accounts, have always yielded
an interest rate, which has been responsive to monetary conditions –
although the 1936 Banking Law enabled the central bank to regulate the
rates on bank assets and liabilities, the Bank of Italy has never used this
faculty. Thus the loss of market share suffered by the banking system has
not been due to ceilings imposed directly on deposite rates by the authorities; rather it has been caused by: the favourable tax treatment of
Treasury securities; the burden imposed on banks by the reserve requirement; and also, in our opinion, the absence of any significant discrimination
between the conditions offered by banks on different kinds of deposit
(Cotula, 1984).

In this paper we consider to what extent rate discrimination between
demand deposits held for transactions purposes and savings deposits could
be an effective tool to increase the efficiency of the banking system and
whether it would affect monetary control in Italy. In the section on developments in the structure of bankdeposits, we review the main developments
in deposit rate management in Italy in the last thirty years, pointing out the
progressive elimination of rate and maturity discrimination between checking and savings accounts, the prevalence of forms of rate discrimination

Fair, D.E., (ed.) Shifting Frontiers in Financial Markets.
© *1986, Martinus Nijhoff Publishers, Dordrecht/Boston/Lancaster. ISBN 90-247-3225-5.*
Printed in the Netherlands.

based on subjective factors and, finally, the loss of competitiveness of bank deposits vis-à-vis the new assets available to households. A reaction of the banking system to these developments appears inevitable; however, as argued in the second section of our paper, an indiscriminate increase in the responsiveness of bank deposit rates to changes in money market rates, as a result of a reduction in the burden of the reserve requirement, could jeopardize the effectiveness of monetary control. On the other hand, in the third section, on the effects of deposit rate discrimination, it is shown that differentiating interest rates by the motive underlying the demand for deposits and by the costs incurred in deposit management can enhance the efficiency and competitiveness of banks without necessarily endangering the authorities' stabilization objectives. In this perspective we consider the role that could be played by the new certificates of deposit, introduced in 1983, which take advantage of a more favourable reserve treatment. If these CDs come to be held on a sufficient scale, they may help to speed up the adjustment of loan rates, thus reinforcing the impact on private spending of open market operations, without necessarily hampering monetary base and money supply control, in view of the higher interest rate elasticity and lower liquidity of this component of bank liabilities.

DEVELOPMENTS IN THE STRUCTURE OF BANK DEPOSITS

The small number of financial assets available, the lack of large institutional investors, the fiscal discrimination against shares and the inefficiency of the capital market coupled with high and variable rates of inflation helped – especially until the second half of the 1970s – to sustain Italian households' propensity for liquidity and, in particular, for bank deposits (Figure 1).

Against this background of high demand for bank liabilities, the absence of legal restrictions on deposit rates allowed the banks to compete for deposits and to differentiate the conditions offered to customers according to the cost and the nature of the service supplied.

During the 1950s and early 1960s, the rates offered on savings accounts were substantially higher than those on checking accounts. This rate differentiation, ratified by cartel agreements among banks, implied a correspondence between the technical forms of deposits and the motives underlying the demand for them. This behaviour, encouraged by the high degree of specialization of the different categories of banks, is consistent with a profit maximization model for banks that have a degree of monopoly power and exploit the different elasticities of demand for deposits held as cash

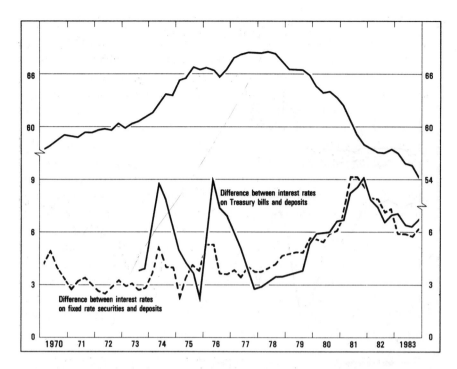

Figure 1. Bank deposits (as a percentage of total domestic financial assets)

balances and as investment (Appendix B).

During the 1960s, the increase in competition due to the gradual de-specialization of the Italian credit system and the tendency for banks' key objective to be size rather than profit maximization led to active competition for deposits: starting from the end of the 1950s the yield differential between long-term fixed rate securities and deposits gradually narrowed and banks attracted an increasing share of the private sector's financial savings, which they were able to invest in government and other securities. As a further effect of the increased competition for households' funds, banks were led to reduce and then eliminate the differentiation of interest rates based on the motives for demanding deposits. A form of competition thus developed in the deposit market hinging on the interest rates offered, the liquidity of deposits and, in the case of checking accounts, below cost charges for services.

As a consequence, there ceased to be a correspondence between technical forms and the motives underlying the demand for deposits. Checking accounts came to play a greater role as a store of value alongside that of a

186

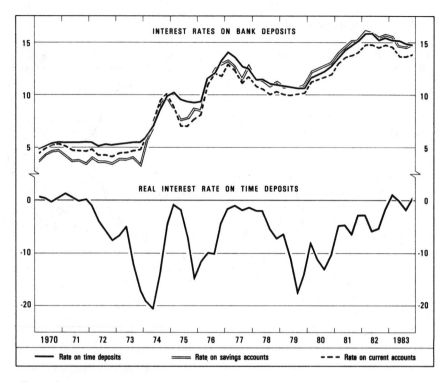

Figure 2.

means of payment; their share of total deposits was scarcely influenced by changes in the volume of transactions (Table 1). There continued to be forms of rate differentiation, but they were mainly based on deposit size and subjective factors, i.e. in favour of prime customers and those with more expertise (Table 2).

As a result of these developments, the share of time deposits in the total declined steadily until two years ago (Table 3). Checking deposits still account for a very large proportion of total deposits – around 55 per cent – and are considerably in excess of the means of payments needed for current transactions.

The disappearance of differentiated deposit remuneration has also had implications for monetary policy in recent years, by weakening the banking system's ability to react to changes in the interest rates controlled by the monetary authorities. When banks had to cope with competition from other instruments (primarily Treasury bills), they were unable to differentiate interest rates between checking and savings accounts, since their fund-

Table 1. Regressions results

Dependent variable	Independent variables	$\bar{R}^2$	SE
$(SD/TD)_t$	$.22 + .35\ (SD/TD)_{t-1} + .09\ (r_S - r_D) - .04\ \Delta GDP$ $(4.0)\quad (3.3)\qquad\qquad (4.3)\qquad\qquad (-1.4)$	.97	.006
$(SD/TD)_t$	$.19 + .40\ (SD/TD)_{t-1} + .09\ (r_S - r_D)$ $(3.7)\quad (3.8)\qquad\qquad (4.4)$	.97	.006

List of Symbols: SD = savings deposits
TD = total banks deposits
r_S = rate of interest on saving deposits
r_D = rate of interest on demand deposits
ΔGDP = changes of gross domestic product (logarithm)

raising policy in the 1960s and 1970s had resulted in the former containing substantial idle balances, the demand for which is related more to total wealth than to current transactions.

A second factor limiting banks' ability to react were the constraints imposed on the banking system. In recent years one way of making monetary policy effective has been by increasing the burden on deposits by raising the compulsory reserve coefficient, keeping the return on compulsory reserves unchanged in the face of high market rates and raising the tax on deposit interest relative to that on income earned from other financial assets[1]. This burden has been an impediment to increasing bank

Table 2. Interest rates by size of deposit

Years	Size of deposit*			
	0–24.9	25–249.99	250–499.99	5.000–300.000
1976	8.68	9.09	11.49	10.98
1977	9.81	10.64	13.05	12.31
1978	8.14	9.18	11.23	10.68
1979	7.85	9.03	10.62	10.30
1980	8.90	10.59	12.33	11.64
1981	9.79	12.64	14.70	13.21
1982	10.23	14.16	16.03	14.64
1983	10.45	13.73	15.22	14.33

* In billions of lire

Table 3. Composition of bank deposits (annual averages)

Year	Current accounts 1	Time deposits	
		1	2
1970	54.8	28.7	63.5
1971	60.1	25.1	63.0
1972	60.6	24.5	62.2
1973	61.3	23.2	60.1
1974	59.3	21.2	52.1
1975	52.4	21.4	45.0
1976	51.2	19.8	40.6
1977	51.0	16.6	33.9
1978	51.8	14.5	30.1
1979	53.5	13.1	28.1
1980	54.6	12.0	26.5
1981	54.8	11.2	24.9
1982	54.2	11.1	24.2
1983	53.5	11.3	24.3
1984	53.2	11.7	25.0

1. Percentage of total deposits (current accounts plus savings accounts)
2. Percentage of total savings accounts

deposit yields on the scale needed to counter the placing of government securities with the public and has encouraged a gradual reduction in the hyper-intermediation built up in the 1960s and 1970s.

While the ability of banks to react was declining for the reasons given above, the interest rate differential elasticity of the demand for deposits began to increase from the end of the 1970s (Cotula et al., 1984). The heavy losses of purchasing power incurred by deposits as a result of inflation, the wider ownership of short-term Treasury paper and the spread of information about interest rates causes economic agents to pay closer attention to the yields on financial assets. This development was particularly significant in the case of small and medium-sized agents, for whom bank deposits had previously been the only form of financial saving.

The increased interest rate differential elasticity of the demand for deposits coupled with banks' reduced ability to react to increases in the rates on government securities raised the *elasticity of the demand for money with respect to the rates on government securities*[2].

This development has permitted tighter control over the money supply and monetary base since a change in the yield on securities permits a larger volume of securities to be sold and a larger change in the monetary base (cf. section two, on the reaction of bank deposite rates to changes and Appendix A).

Furthermore, curtailing excess intermediation by the banks through a reduction in their securities portfolio tends to make the control of deposit growth more effective in influencing the expansion of bank lending to the private sector, a key variable in the transmission of monetary policy impulses in the short term. Since the abolition of the ceiling on bank lending in 1983, the ratio of lending in lire to deposits has actually started to rise again, reversing the downward trend of the previous fifteen years[3].

While the gradual reduction in banks' secondary liquidity enhances the effectiveness of monetary policy, the problem of whether the present constraints on banking can be kept at length must not be underrated. The very factors that have made monetary policy more effective in the short term – the high compulsory reserve coefficient and the fixed and low remuneration of the reserves themselves – could end up by weakening monetary control and increasing the uncertainty of the relations between monetary base and domestic final demand. After the mid-1970s the heavier compulsory reserve burden, together with higher taxes on bank deposit interest and the level of money market rates, caused the difference between the cost of deposits to banks and the net yield received by depositors to increase and fluctuate between 2.4 and 6.7 per cent. As pointed out in the literature (Gurley and Shaw, 1960), keeping banks at a persistent competitive disadvantage compared with other financial intermediaries tends to squeeze their rate of profit, promote a gradual reduction in their share of financial intermediation and distort the pattern of financial flows. An unforseen reduction in the proportion of financial assets subject to the reserve requirement may reduce the effectiveness of monetary base control (Tobin and Brainard, 1963), which is the main instrument of monetary policy action[4].

In any case it appears inevitable that stronger competition and greater efficiency in the financial markets will force the banking system to adopt a new fund-raising strategy. In particular, the development of an efficient market for government securities and the increasing attention to the (nominal and real) interest rates on different assets make it more difficult to sustain forms of price discrimination in the absence of clear differences between technical forms, maturities, liquidity, minimum denominations (in the case of certificates) and other features of fund-raising instruments.

THE REACTION OF BANK DEPOSIT RATES TO CHANGES IN THE TREASURY BILL RATE AND THE EFFECTIVENESS OF MONETARY POLICY

Changes in the responsiveness of deposit yields are of great importance for the management of monetary policy (see, for example, Cargill and Garcia (1982), Hadjimichalakis (1982) and Tobin (1983).

The consequences of the yield on bank deposits being more responsive to the rates controlled by the monetary authorities can easily be seen by considering the extreme case in which the banking system responds promptly and on a scale that leaves the rate differential unchanged. In this case the demand for money is completely inelastic with respect to the level of interest rates and the central bank is unable to control its supply: an attempt to reduce the money supply would only trigger a spiralling of the rates on securities and deposits. But if interest rates influence domestic demand (schematically, the cost of credit influences investment and the yield on financial assets expenditure on durable goods; cf. Appendix A), monetary policy can still influence the level of economic activity even if there is increased uncertainty about the effect on interest rates of a given change in monetary base. Indeed, the final effects of a given change in monetary base will be greater because the money market can only return to equilibrium through changes in income (and wealth).

Furthermore, if the private sector's expenditure is sensitive to the yield on all financial assets, greater responsiveness of deposit rates to the yields on securities entails a higher elasticity of aggregate demand with respect to the rate on securities. In this case the IS curve has a higher interest rate elasticity and this reinforces the effects of a given change in monetary base.

These conclusions are strengthened when account is also taken of the direct effects on the cost of credit. If more responsive bank deposit rates lead to faster and more flexible movements of lending rates, the rates controlled most directly by the central bank will influence domestic demand more rapidly. *Ceteris paribus*, the IS curve becomes more elastic and this amplifies the effects of open market interventions by reducing the movements in rates needed to obtain the desired restriction. If interest rates were the only channel for the transmission of monetary policy impulses designed to control aggregate demand, it would be of no importance whether achievement of a certain level of rates involved a greater or smaller quantity of money. The money supply might well be an important indicator for the monetary authorities, but it would not be an important variable in itself.

However, this hypothesis corresponds to a highly simplified view of the working of the economy. Actually, there are good reasons why, independently of interest rates, the quantity of bank money may be important for the control of domestic demand. Firstly, because the control of bank deposits regulates the supply of bank loans, and the more strictly the smaller banks' holdings of liquidity or securities. This is all the more important for the achievement of the final objectives if the short-term demand for credit is inelastic with respect to interest rates. In this case aggregate demand can be limited by the amount of credit available, which, in turn, is determined by the amount of deposits net of compulsory reserves.

On the other hand, the more deposit rates are responsive to movements in the rates on securities, the larger interest rate fluctuations will need to be to produce a given change in the money supply, and they may become incompatible with orderly conditions in the financial markets. Furthermore, if the higher level of interest rates, caused in part by the reaction of deposit rates (to those on securities), should persist, destabilizing pressures could develop arising from heavily indebted economic units; in particular, this could cause serious problems to the public sector with its huge debt both in absolute terms and in relation to GDP. It follows that there may be greater resistance to the very large fluctuations of interest rates required to maintain control of the monetary aggregates.

Nor, *a priori,* is it possible to exclude the direct effects (as opposed to those produced via interest rates) of the private sector's liquid assets on aggregate demand, especially when inflation is accelerating.

The conclusion that can be drawn is that an indiscriminate increase in the responsiveness of bank deposit rates may turn out to conflict with the monetary authorities' cyclical objectives. However, as will be shown in the next section, differentiating interest rates on the basis of the nature of the demand can enhance the efficiency and competitiveness of the banking system compared with other intermediaries, without, under certain conditions, diminishing the effectiveness of monetary policy.

THE EFFECTS OF DEPOSIT RATE DISCRIMINATION

Two aspects of liability management can be singled out:
1. a typical situation facing banks is that of having to cope with a sudden jump in the demand for loans. Since this demand is interest rate inelastic in the short term, banks that wish to maintain stable relations with their

customers must obtain extra deposits to meet the increased demand if they cannot realize securities. An important contribution to short-term flexibility can come from liability management in the narrow sense, i.e. from short or very-short-term borrowing at money market rates. The more a bank can cope with such tensions flexibly through a reduction in liquidity, the realization of securities or this form of liability management, the more cautious it is likely to be about changing the yields on its stock of deposits;

2. liability management also comprises the action banks take to achieve a balanced structure of total liabilities, in order to finance the growth in loans they expect.

In Italy the latter is still the most important form of liability management. Even the banks' certificates of deposit, which were encouraged by the measures of end-1982 (Carosio, 1983)[5], have more in common with "time deposits" than with money market instruments.

The preponderance of sight deposits in the total deposits of Italian banks is so great that there can be no doubt about the desirability of encouraging the growth of forms of fund-raising involving a time constraint. This was the aim of the above-mentioned decision to pay a higher return on the reserves corresponding to certificates of deposit. The incentive is rather small (a reduction ranging from 0.5 to 0.8 points in the cost of compulsory reserves per unit of deposits, depending on the average reserve coefficient), but when market interest rates are lower, the incentive for banks to improve the composition of their deposits is somewhat stronger.

The growth of banks' CDs has been small to date (cf. our first section). Their adoption on a larger scale has been discouraged by the very small minimum denomination (1 million lire) and by the impossibility for banks to differentiate the yield according to the denomination. On the one hand, these two factors have increased the risk that a return on CDs close to market rates might trigger a larger shift out of savings accounts (including those with very small deposits) towards this higher-yielding instrument and, on the other, they prevent account being taken of the different unit costs of administering CDs of very different denominations.

The lack of differentiation by denomination has also meant that the rule forbidding banks to repurchase their own certificates has had to be extended to the smallest denominations. The difficulty of creating a secondary market for very small CDs has reduced the liquidity of this instrument and thus discouraged its widespread use.

In the rest of this section we discuss the effects a clearer and more significant differentiation between bank deposits and, in particular, a

growth in certificates of deposit will have on:
1. the management of banks, and, above all,
2. the effectiveness of monetary policy.

The management of banks

By differentiating between deposits on the basis of whether they serve primarily as a *means of payment* or as *financial instruments* – a distinction that is reflected in different elasticities with respect to the interest rate on securities – banks can discriminate the yields they pay and thus improve their profitability (Appendix B)[6].

Compared with differentiation based on "subjective" factors, such as the extent of customers' economic information, that based on the motives for demanding deposits and the "objective" characteristics of the various technical forms of deposit (checking accounts, time deposits, negotiable certificates, etc.) might be more feasible, particularly after the development of efficient money markets and the ownership of short-term Treasury securities has become widespread (cf. our first section).

Differentiation according to the nature of deposits, enables banks to benefit from making the marginal costs of the various forms of deposit equal, including not only the *interest rates offered* but also the *costs of administration,* which vary with the form of deposit. Since those used as a means of payment in current transactions cost more to administer, banks would be led to take into account the implicit yield connected with the services provided by current accounts and to impose charges for these services in line with their production costs. Given the recent technological improvements in the recording and analysis of costs in the banking industry, different production costs are likely to become an important parameter for rate discrimination.

Furthermore, when the conditions on deposits are negotiated bilaterally with customers, administrative costs are higher and interest rates tend to be sticky downward. By contrast, rate differentiation based on objective factors would enable the conditions on deposits serving basically for transactions purposes to be predetermined in a clear and explicit manner for all customers, with account being taken of the difference in unit cost linked to deposit size. The rates paid on such deposits would change less often and would not follow short-term fluctuations in market rates. At the opposite extreme, since interest rates on negotiable CDs are linked to money market rates, they would come into line with these without delay at the moment of issue, even in a period of falling rates.

It also needs to be remembered that the yields on the assets that can be acquired with the various types of deposit are different. When liabilities consist mainly of sight deposits, banks have less control over their business. By reducing the uncertainty about the maturity of their funds, and lengthening it, banks can hold a smaller proportion of liquidity and expand the share of higher-yielding assets. At the same time by paying more attention to the composition of their deposits they can improve their maturity matching and thus reduce the risk of illiquidity.

Furthermore, at least initially, the banks are likely to be able, in view of the present structure of deposits, to reduce the volatility of their funds (cf. Appendix B) by increasing their ability to vary interest rates rapidly on the deposits with the greatest elasticity with respect to interest rate differentials.

The effectiveness of monetary policy

As regards the *impact on the effectiveness of monetary policy*, it must first be stated that changes in the remuneration of the various types of deposit causes changes in the liability structure owing to funds shifting, both between the various types of deposit and from other assets, with an increase in the component with the greatest interest rate elasticity. These changes lead to a greater (weighted) *elasticity of the demand for deposits.*

In the new equilibrium configuration following the differentiation of deposits not only will the proportion of deposits with the highest interest rate elasticity have increased but bank rates will also be more responsive to changes in those controlled by the monetary authorities as explained in point 1 above.

It is uncertain which of these two effects will predominate in the new equilibrium configuration (cf. Appendix B), so that it is uncertain whether differentiation reduces the ability of the monetary authorities to control the money supply with a given change in the interest rates they control[7]. If the "spiral" effect on rates should predominate over the regulation of the quantity of bank deposits, there would be a reduction in the ability of the monetary authorities to influence – with a given change in the rates they control – the *supply of credit* and hence the debt-financed part of domestic demand and, in particular, the forms of lending least sensitive to the level of interest rates. Conversely, the effectiveness of changes in the monetary base in influencing the *demand for credit* is enhanced because the responsiveness of *bank interest rates*, and especially lending rates, increases. This conclusion is strengthened if one considers that the issue of money market instruments by banks presumably implies changes in how lending rates are determined causing them to reach the equilibrium level faster after shocks in the money market. Indeed, if the rate on such instruments is closely linked to that on government securities it will appear, as far as the behaviour of banks is concerned, as an exogenous variable and, at the same time, as the marginal cost level corresponding to the equilibrium condition of the banking firm.

To assess the costs and benefits for the effectiveness of monetary policy in the new equilibrium configuration, account must be taken of a number of factors not considered in the analysis of Appendix B. A shift in the composition of total bank deposits towards more time deposits and certificates of deposit of the present type reduces the liquidity of the private sector's financial assets – and all the more so the longer the constraint. This both promotes more orderly money market conditions and increases the possibility of attenuating the effects of sudden fluctuations in the propensity to spend as a result of changed expectations or other shocks that alter the public's behaviour.

Moreover, the measures to make the public's behaviour in the markets for financial saving more selective and rational – by extending the habit of balancing the yields, liquidity and risk of the various instruments for the investment of financial wealth – together with those to increase the transparency of the conditions banks offer on their different fund-raising instruments create the prerequisites for the development of competition.

A complete analysis of the effects on monetary policy of deposit differentiation would also have to look at the question of whether it involves more or less uncertainty in the relationships between instruments and final objectives, but this is beyond the scope of this paper. It can nonetheless be noted that both the "spiral" of interest rates and the uncertain quantitative relationship between the cost of credit and domestic demand (which would become the principal channel of monetary policy transmission) tend to make the effect of a given change in monetary base less predictable.

Besides assessing the various effects of bank deposit differentiation on the effectiveness of monetary policy in the new equilibrium situation, it is also important to consider what will happen in the *transition phase*, especially in a country like Italy, where bank deposits are still largely undifferentiated.

Until the shift in the composition of deposits towards those with a higher interest rate elasticity is completed, the differentiation of yields will probably reduce the central bank's ability to control the money stock and the supply of credit in the short run. Since the demand for credit has a low interest elasticity in the short term and firms' expenditure can be influenced faster and more accurately by controlling the "availability" of credit, the effectiveness of monetary policy is somewhat reduced. Consequently, the manner and the timing of the transition phase are important.

Of course, the longer the banking system has to wait to supply liquid assets with lower opportunity costs, the more business it will lose to intermediaries with lower charges and the greater the incentive will be to create instruments that are designed to circumvent the compulsory reserve requirement and which may involve high risks.

The conflicting aims of reducing the charges borne by banks, in order to diminish their competitive handicap with respect to other intermediaries, and not undermining, even in the short term, the effectiveness of monetary policy can be reconciled, on the one hand, by promoting more transparent and efficient markets (thus raising the interest rate elasticity of deposits) and, on the other, by gradually making selective reductions in the charges mentioned above in order to ensure that the differentiation of the yields on the various types of deposit is implemented gradually.

NOTES

1. Econometric estimates have shown that the effect on the demand for deposits of changes in the interest rates paid on government securities would be reduced by about one third if the yield on compulsory reserves were linked to that on government securities instead of being fixed at 5.5 per cent as at present.

2. By contrast, in other countries, and especially the US, financial innovation and changes in regulations have led to bank rates being more flexible in recent years. The different starting points need to be noted, however: in the US the rates on the various categories of bank deposits were subject to limits that had become penalizing with the rise in the rate of inflation. In Italy, after the second World War the central bank has never exercised its faculty to limit banks' deposit rates and banks have competed actively for increased deposits through rate variations. Present developments are thus tending to reduce the differences between the markets for deposits in the two institutional contexts.

3. The steady reduction in the secondary liquidity held by the Italian banking system over the last three years, as a result of the fall in bank intermediation, will tend to increase the importance of the effects of credit availability.

The behaviour of the lending in lire to deposits ratio and the rise in the share of short-term Treasury securities in total bank assets are important factors in explaining why banks still do not feel the need to develop forms of liability management in order to finance loan expansion (Goodhart, 1984, ch. 5).

4. As far as the burden of reserves is concerned, there are still substantial differences between banks; since the marginal compulsory reserve coefficient has only been uniform since 1975, the ratio of reserves to deposits varies widely within the banking system, ranging from 14.0 to 19.5 per cent.

5. The decree issued by the Treasury Minister on 28 December 1982 fixed a higher return on the proportion of compulsory reserves corresponding to the ratio of CDs to total deposits.

6. Rate differentiation does not imply a zero yield on current accounts; on this point see, for example, Rondelli (1981).

7. There are two reasons why this is so:

1. when there are changes in the exogenous interest rate, compared with the situation of no interest rate differentiation, banks lose fewer deposits from the highest elasticity component by differentiating, while they lose more from the least elastic component; 2. the effect is also ambiguous for the highest elasticity component on its own (and mutatis mutandis for the least elastic) since, while the rate on this component is changed more than before, there is a larger outflow of deposits for a given change in the differential because the size of this component has increased as a result of differentiation.

REFERENCES

1. Cargill, T.F. and Garcia, G.G. (1982), *Financial Deregulation and Monetary Control*, Hoover Institution Press, Stanford, California.
2. Carosio, G. (1983), I certificati di deposito bancari: le prospettive dopo la nuova regolamentazione della riserva obbligatoria, *Banca d'Italia, "Supplemento al Bollettino"*, May.
3. Cotula, F. (1984), Financial Innovation and Monetary Control in Italy, *"BNL – Quarterly Review"*, Sept.
4. Cotula, F., Galli, G., Lecaldano, E., Sannucci, V. and Zautzik, E.A. (1984), Una stima delle funzioni di domanda di attività finanziarie, *Banca d'Italia, "Ricerche quantitative per la politica economica"*.
5. Goodhart, C. (1984), *"Monetary Theory and Practice. The U.K. Experience"*, Macmillan Press, London.
6. Gurley, J.G. and Shaw, E.S. (1960), *"Money in a Theory of Finance"*, Washington.
7. Hadjimichalakis, M.G. (1982), *"Monetary Policy and Modern Money Markets"*, Lexington Books, Toronto.
8. Klein, M.A. (1971), A Theory of the Banking Firm, *"Journal of Money, Credit and Banking"*, May.
9. Monti, M. (1971), A Theoretical Model of Bank Behavior and Its Implications for Monetary Policy, *"L'Industria"*, n. 2.
10. Pierce, J. (1984), Did Financial Innovation Hurt the Great Monetarist Experiment?, *"American Economic Review – Papers and Proceedings"*, May.
11. Rondelli, L. (1981), Alcuni aspetti dell'evoluzione aziende di credito italiana, "Bancaria", Nov.
12. Rondelli, L. (1983), Le tendenze all'innovazione nel sistema finanziario: prospettive e problemi per le banche italiane, *"Bancaria"*, Dec.
13. Silber, W. (1978), Commercial Bank Liability Management, *Federal Reserve Bank of New York*, June.
14. Suzuki, Y. (1983), Interest Rate Decontrol, Financial Innovation and the Effectiveness of Monetary Policy, *"Bank of Japan Monetary and Economic Studies"*, June.
15. Tobin, J. (1983), Financial Structure and Monetary Rules, *"Kredit und Kapital"*, n. 2.
16. Tobin, J. and Brainard, W.C. (1963), Financial Intermediaries and the Effectiveness of Monetary Controls, *"American Economic Review"*, Papers and Proceedings, May.

APPENDIX A

The model used in this paper is for a closed economy with five economic agents (households, firms, banks, the central bank, and the state sector) operating in five markets (one market for real goods and four financial markets, namely those for bank deposits, bank loans, government securities, and monetary base) (see Table A.1).

In Table A.1, Equations a.1–a.4 describe the equilibrium of the real sector, where it is postulated that in every period supply adjusts to aggregate demand, which consists of consumption, investment, and current public expenditure (Eq. a.1), which is considered to be exogenous. Investment demand (Eq. a.2) and consumption demand (Eq. a.3) are expressed in a form used in many macroeconomic models: note that for the sake of simplicity it is assumed that for firms the relevant interest rate is the rate on bank loans, the sole type of financing to firms, and that consumption demand depends on the interest rate relevant to households (the yield on financial assets, the sole form in which wealth is held). Eq. a.4 defines the savings function, enabling us to express the real equilibrium as $S = I + G$; since in the model all income accrues to households, they are the only possible source of savings, savings which are then utilized by the state sector and by firms. Consequently the economy's entire stock of wealth (W) is held directly or indirectly by households; and it consists of the stock of capital (K) and the stock of public debt (DP).

The financial markets are described by the remaining equations[1]. These may be most profitably examined if they are grouped by economic agent. Given the simplifying assumptions made (a sole form of investment financing), the financial behaviour of forms is described by the balance–sheet constraint of this sector (Eq. a.5), which determines the demand for bank loans, negatively correlated with the cost of credit. The government borrowing requirement is met by the issue of bonds, assumed for simplicity's sake to have single-period maturity and to be re-negotiated from period to period. The government balance sheet (Eq. a.6) therefore determines the supply of bonds in the market.

The balance sheet of the central bank (Eq. a.7) determines the supply of monetary base. Purchases of bonds by the central bank (Eq. a.8) are considered to be exogenous and constitute the instrument of monetary policy contemplated by the model.

Given that the banks are required to hold a fixed percentage of reserves kD with the central bank (Eq. a.10), in the model their behaviour is described by the setting of the deposit rate (Eq. a.11) and of the loan rate

Table A.1

Real Sector

(a.1) $Y = I + C + \bar{G}$ Equilibrium in the market for goods

(a.2) $I = I(r_L, \bar{r}k)$ Investment demand

(a.3) $C = C(W, r_D, r)$ Consumption demand

(a.4) $S = Y - C$ Definition of saving

Financial Sector

Firms

(a.5) $L^d = \tilde{K}_{-1} + I$ Firms balance sheet (demand for loans)

Government

(a.6) $\bar{G} + DP_{-1} = B$ Government balance sheet (supply of bonds)

Central Bank

(a.7) $B^{bc} = R$ Central Bank balance sheet (supply of monetary base)

(a.8) $B^{bc} = \bar{B}^{bc}$ Demand for bonds by the Central Bank

Banking System

(a.9) $B^b = D - L - R^d$ Banking System balance sheet (demand for bonds by the banking system)

(a.10) $R^d = K^D$ Demand for bank reserves

(a.11) $r_D = g_D r$ Deposit rate (supply of deposits)

(a.12) $r_L = g_L r$ Loan rate (supply of loans)

Households

(a.13) $B^h + D^d = \bar{W}_{-1} + S$ Households balance sheet (demand for bonds by the household sector)

(a.14) $W = B^h + D^d$ Definition of financial wealth

(a.15) $D^d = D(r - r_D, Y, W)$ Demand for deposits

Equilibrium conditions

(a.16) $R = R^d$

(a.17) $D = D^d$

(a.18) $L = L^d$

List of variables

Endogenous variables

Y = Income

I = Investment

C = Consumption

S = Saving

r_L = Loan rate

r_D = Deposit rate

r = Bond rate

W = Financial wealth

L^d, L = Bank loans (demand and supply)

D^d, D = Bank deposits (demand and supply)

B^{bc}, B^h, B^b, B = Government bonds (demand by the purchasing sectors and supply)

R^d, R = Bank reserves (demand and supply)

Exogenous variables

$\bar{G}$ = Public expenditure

$\bar{B}^{bc}$ = Purchases of bonds by the Central Bank (instrument)

$\bar{r}_k$ = Yield on capital goods

$\bar{K}_{-1}$ = Capital stock at $t-1$

DP = Public debt at $t-1$

(Eq. a.12). The form of these functions is crucial to the working of the model, in that for any given value for the instruments of monetary policy, the real and financial behaviour of households and firms depends on those interest rates. The form of Eqs. a.11 and a.12 is general in the extreme, but it makes it easy to examine the effects of greater responsiveness of bank rates to the interest rate most directly affected by the monetary authorities. Bank rates are made a direct function of the yield on government bonds. The balance sheet constraint of the banks (Eq. a.9) residually determines their demand for bonds.

Eqs. a.13 and a.14 refer to households, which for any given level of consumption decisions distribute their wealth between government bonds and bank deposits according to their comparative yields and the need to finance current transactions. Not that from the households' balance sheet equation we can derive the equation

$$\Delta W = I + G = \Delta L + \Delta B \qquad (a.19)$$

which indicates that in conditions of equilibrium the desired change in the financial assets of the private sector is equal to the total change in liabilities ($\Delta L + \Delta B$), or what is known in Italy as total domestic credit.

Finally, Eqs. a.16, a.17 and a.18 give the equilibrium conditions in the markets for bank reserves (monetary base), for deposits, and for loans.

In this model, the monetary control of aggregate demand depends on the central bank's ability to control the level of interest rates (or a variable correlated to the level of interest rates). On the one hand, investment expenditure is affected by the interest rate on loans, while on the other hand consumer expenditure is affected directly by the yield on financial assets and indirectly by the lending rate, because of the effects of more costly credit on aggregate investment and wealth.

The central bank can influence the level of interest rates by open market operations. Nevertheless, the behaviour of the banking system in setting interest rates is crucial in determining the quantitative effects of the central bank's action on the other variables of the system. First, the greater responsiveness of r_L to r heightens the effect of open market operations on the demand for investment. Also, the different responsiveness of r_D to changes in r influences the effect of a given open market operation on the rate on the level of interest rates.

These relationships are readily demonstrable using the traditional IS-LM framework. The IS curve is produced by inserting Eqs. a.2, a.3, a.11, and a.12 into Eq. a.1:

$$Y = I\,(g_L r,\ \bar{r}_k) + C\,(W,\ g_D r,\ r) + \bar{G}; \qquad\qquad (a.20)$$

further, from Eq. a.19 it follows that

$$W = \bar{W}_{-1} + \bar{G} + I. \qquad\qquad (a.21)$$

By substitution of (a.21) into Eq. a.20 and expressing I as a function of r alone, we get:

$$Y = I(g_L r,\ \bar{r}_K) + C\,(\bar{W}_{-1} + I\,(g_L r,\ \bar{r}_K) + \bar{G},\ g_D r,\ r) + \bar{G}\ \text{(the IS curve).}\ (a.22)$$

The slope of this curve is given by

$$\frac{dY}{dr} = (\frac{dI}{dr_L} + \frac{dC}{dI}\frac{dI}{dr_L})\,g_L + \frac{dC}{dr_D}\,g_D + \frac{dC}{dr} < 0$$

It must be noted that the IS curve is more elastic as the responsiveness of bank rates to changes in r increases. As g_L increases, so does the effect of changes in r on investment expenditure $(\frac{dI}{dr_L})$ and consumer spending through wealth changes $(\frac{dC}{dI}\frac{dI}{dr_L})$;[2] as g_D increases, the effect on consumer spending increases.

The LM curve can be derived using Eqs. a.10., a.11, a.12, a.15, a.16, and a.21:

$$R = K\,D(r - g_D r,\ Y,\ \bar{W}_{-1} + I(g_L r,\ \bar{r}_K) + \bar{G})\ \text{(the LM curve),} \qquad (a.23)$$

whose slope is given by

$$\frac{dY}{dr} = \frac{dY}{dD}\,(-\frac{dD}{d(r - r_D)}\,(1 - g_D) - \frac{dD}{dI}\frac{dI}{dr_L}\,g_L)$$

The LM curve therefore proves to be the more rigid, the more responsive the interest rate on deposits r_D is to r (in that changes in r have less effect on the differential and on the demand for money) and the less responsive r_L is to r (in that changes in r have less effect on investment, wealth, and the demand for money).

In conclusion, in the schema set forth here, greater responsiveness of bank deposit rates makes the IS curve more elastic and the LM curve more rigid, amplifying the effect on income of given changes in the monetary base. Looking at the money market alone this greater effectiveness of changes in the monetary base results from the higher impact on the interest rate on Government securities of changes in the monetary base and in the supply of deposits, as implied by the following equation (derivable from Eq. a.23)[3]:

$$\frac{dR}{dr}\Big|_Y = k \left[\frac{dD}{d(r - r_D)} (1 - g_D) + \frac{dD}{dW} \frac{dI}{dr_L} g_L \right]$$
(a.24)

NOTES TO APPENDIX A

1. Note that each market is represented by a demand equation, a supply equation, and an equilibrium equation, except the bond market, whose equilibrium condition is redundant in that it is derivable from a linear combination of the other equations (Walras' Law). In the market for loans and deposits, supply is assumed to be infinitely elastic in correspondence to the rates set by the banking system.

2. The higher IS investment, the higher is the increase in households' wealth (eq. a.21); if consumption had been expressed as a function of income the derivative $\frac{dC}{dr_L}$ would have reflected the usual multiplier effect.

3. Of course, even if more extensive liability management brings about a reduction of $\frac{dR}{dr}\Big|_Y$, the derivative $\frac{dR}{dr}$, which can be derived from the solution of the entire model, may still increase, in that an increase in g_D also produces, as we have seen, greater elasticity of the IS; this is all the more likely, the greater is the elasticity of consumption demand with respect to r_D.

APPENDIX B

B.1 – As it was shown in Appendix A, the effects on monetary policy performance of innovations in the deposit rate determination process can be summarised by the effects on the derivative $\frac{dD}{dr}$.[1] This section considers how this derivative changes when the banking system moves towards deposit rate discrimination, based on the different interest elasticities of the various components of money demand.

To this purpose, the profit maximizing monopoly model[2] will be used and it will be shown that the effects of rate discrimination on $\frac{dD}{dr}$ are ambiguous.

B.2 – Consider the problem faced by a profit maximizing bank acting as a monopolist in the deposit and loan market:

$$\max_{r_L, r_D} \quad P = r_k R + r_L L + rT - r_d D$$

under the constraints:

$$D = D(r - r_D, \ldots) \qquad \text{demand for deposits} \qquad (b.1)$$
$$L = L(r_L, \ldots) \qquad \text{demand for loans} \qquad (b.2)$$

$$R + L + T = D \qquad \text{budget constraint} \qquad (b.3)$$
$$R = kD \qquad \text{demand for bank reserves} \qquad (b.4)$$

where D, L, T and R are, respectively, bank deposits, loans, bonds, and reserves (a fixed proportion k of deposits) and P is bank profits. The bank fixes r_D and r_L (the deposit and loan rates) given the exogenous rates r (bond rate) and r_k (yield on reserves).

The "first order conditions" of the problem are:

$$L + \frac{dL}{dr_L} r_L - r \frac{dL}{dr_L} = 0 \qquad (b.5)$$

$$D + \frac{dD}{dr_D} r_D - H \frac{dD}{dr_D} = 0 \qquad \text{where } H = (1 - k)r + kr_k \qquad (b.6)$$

or, in terms of demand elasticities:

$$r^L = \frac{\eta_L}{1 + \eta_L} \qquad \text{with} \qquad \eta_L = \frac{dL}{dr_L} \frac{r_L}{L} < 0 \qquad (b.7)$$

$$r_D = \frac{H\eta_D}{1 + \eta_D} \qquad \text{with} \qquad \eta_D = \frac{dD}{dr_D} \frac{r_D}{D} > 0 \qquad (b.8)$$

Given the object under discussion, it is more convenient to express r_D in terms of elasticity with respect to the rate differential[3]:

$$r_D = \frac{H\bar{\eta}_D + r}{1 + \bar{\eta}_D} \qquad \text{with} \qquad \bar{\eta}_D = \frac{dD}{d(r - r_D)} \frac{(r - r_D)}{D} < 0 \qquad (b.8')$$

Two properties of this model are relevant for the discrimination problem:

a) r_D increases with $|\bar{\eta}_D|$; in fact:

$$\frac{d\, r_D}{d\bar{\eta}_D} = \frac{H - r}{(1 + \bar{\eta}_D)^2} < 0$$

b) changes in r determine changes in r_D which are larger the larger $\bar{\eta}_D$ is:

$$\frac{d\, r_D}{dr} = \frac{1 + \bar{\eta}_D (1 - k)}{1 + \bar{\eta}_D} > 0^4 \qquad \text{and} \qquad (\frac{d\, r_D}{dr}) / (d\bar{\eta}_D) < 0$$

B.3 – Consider now a monopolist bank facing two demand curves for deposits:

$$DD = DD\,(r - r_{DD}, \ldots) \qquad \text{with} \qquad \bar{\eta}_{DD} = \frac{dDD}{d(r - r_{DD})} \frac{(r - r_{DD})}{DD} \qquad \text{(b.9)}$$

$$SD = SD\,(r - r_{SD}, \ldots) \qquad \text{with} \qquad \bar{\eta}_{SD} = \frac{d\,SD}{d(r - r_{SD})} \frac{(r - r_{SD})}{SD} \qquad \text{(b.10)}$$

and $|\bar{\eta}_{DD}| < |\bar{\eta}_{SD}|$

Assuming that the bank can discriminate between different demand elasticities (for example on the base of some time constraint), it can be shown that profit maximization implies that r_L is set as Eq. b.7, and that, similarly to Eq. b.8:

$$r_{DD} = \frac{\bar{\eta}_{DD}\,H + r}{1 + \bar{\eta}_{DD}} \qquad \text{(b.11)}$$

$$r_{SD} = \frac{\bar{\eta}_{SD}\,H + r}{1 + \bar{\eta}_{SD}} \qquad \text{(b.12)}$$

which imply $r_{DD} < r_{SD}$ and $\dfrac{d\,r_{DD}}{dr} < \dfrac{d\,r_{SD}}{dr}$.

B.4 – Suppose now that the monopolist bank facing two demand curves, Eq. b.9 and Eq. b.10, cannot discriminate; the problem is formally the same as in B.2 and therefore Eqs. b.7 and b.8 give the equilibrium rates. In particular, for the deposit rate, we obtain:

$$r_D{}^* = \frac{\bar{\eta}_D^*\,H + r}{1 + \bar{\eta}_D^*} \; 5 \qquad \text{and } r_{DD} = r_{SD} = r_D^* \text{ by assumption} \qquad \text{(b.13)}$$

Note that $\bar{\eta}_D^*$ is the overall demand elasticity of deposits to $(r - r^*)$ and it can be proved that:

$$\bar{\eta}_D^* = q_{DD}^* \,\bar{\eta}_{DD} + (1 - q_{SD}^*)\,\bar{\eta}_{SD} \qquad \text{with} \qquad q_{DD}^* = \frac{DD^*}{(SD^* + DD^*)} \qquad \text{(b.14)}$$

From Eq. b.14 it follows that $\eta_{DD} < \eta_D^* < \eta_{SD}$ and therefore that:

$$r_{DD} < r_D^* < r_{SD} \qquad \text{and} \qquad \frac{d\,r_{DD}}{dr} < \frac{d\,r_D^*}{dr} < \frac{d\,r_{SD}}{dr}$$

B.5 – What are the effects on profits and on the bank size of relaxing the "no-discrimination" constraint (i.e. a move from the solution in Eq. b.4 to the solution in Eq. b.3)? Given the profit maximizing hypothesis, profits must increase: the unconstrained solution to the profit maximization problem in Eq. b.3 must be superior to the constrained solution in Eq. b.4.

With respect to bank size, SD increases, but DD decreases (incidentally, this implies that the overall demand elasticity increases). Clearly, the net effect will depend on the form of the demand curves and, given the general form of Eqs. b.9 and b.10, it cannot be derived analytically.[6]

Assume, however, that DD is completely interest rigid; under this hypothesis it is necessary to modify the terms of the problem, given that no finite solution exists for a profit maximizing monopolist facing rigid demand curves. Therefore it must be assumed that r_{DD} is fixed exogenously as:

$r_{DD} = \hat{r}_{DD}$.

In the case of no discrimination this implies:

$r_D^* = r_{DD}^* = r_{SD}^* = \hat{r}_D$.

Under this hypothesis discrimination implies an increase in bank size (provided $\hat{r}^* < r_{SD}$).

B.6 – Under the hypothesis of Eq. b.5 the effects on (dD/dr) of a shift to discrimination can be assessed only with reference to the derivative (dSD/dr) (dDD/dr being equal to zero). If we consider a constant elasticity demand for SD (see note 4), the effects of a change in r on SD are given by:

$$\frac{d\, SD^*}{dr} = SD^* \frac{\bar{\eta}SD}{r - \hat{r}_D} \frac{d(r - \hat{r}_D)}{dr} < 0 \text{ under no discrimination and} \quad (b.15)$$

$$\frac{d\, SD}{dr} = SD \frac{\bar{\eta}SD}{r - r_{SD}} \frac{d(r - r_{SD})}{dr} < 0 \text{ under discrimination} \quad (b.16)$$

By comparing Eqs. b.15 and b.16, it is impossible to ascertain whether, due to discrimination, the derivative increases or not. Under discrimination, banks can contain the increase in the differential between the bond rate and the rate on SD $(\frac{d(r - r_{SD})}{dr} < \frac{d(r - \hat{r}_D)}{dr})$; however the proportional increase in the differential may turn out to be higher under discrimination (given that $r - r_{SD} < r - \hat{r}_D$) and, most of all, the responsiveness of deposits to the differential is higher under discrimination ($SD > SD^*$), so that the effect of given changes in the differential will be amplified[7]. Thus, discrimination implies a "once and for all" recovery of business by the banking system, but may make bank deposits more sensitive to changes in the bond yield.

Finally, if the hypothesis $(dDD/dr) = 0$ is relaxed, uncertainty on the overall effect on (dD/dr) of discrimination increases further: indeed, even if the banking system manages to contain the loss in SD, this effect may be overriden by the higher loss in DD that occurs when there is discrimination.

NOTES TO APPENDIX B

1. The condition of income exogeneity, recalled at the end of Appendix A, will be omitted here given the microeconomic nature of the problem under discussion.

2. Cf. M. Monti (1971) and M.A. Klein (1971).

3. The relation between η_D and $\bar{\eta}_D$ is given by $\bar{\eta}_D = -\eta_D \dfrac{(r - r_D)}{r_D}$ or, in terms of exogenous variables, $\bar{\eta}_D = \dfrac{1}{H} [\eta (H - r) - r]$. Note that Eq. b.8′ cannot be applied for values of r_k or k yielding $r_D = r$, because it has been derived from Eq. b.6 by dividing and multiplying by $r - r_D$, which excluded $r - r_D = 0$.

4. This expression could be negative if $\bar{\eta} (1 - k) > -1$, which is unlikely in the range in which the monopolist is in equilibrium (i.e., for $\bar{\eta}_D < -\dfrac{r}{H}$, as implied by Eq. b.8′.

5. Henceforth starred variables refer to equilibrium solutions of the problem of profit maximization under the constraint of no-discrimination; this case differs from the problem in Eq. b.2 in which there was only one demand curve for deposits.

6. Even if we assume constant-elasticity demand curves (i.e. $SD = A^{SD} (r - r_{SD})^{\bar{\eta}SD}$ and $DD = A^{DD} (r - r_{DD})^{\bar{\eta}DD}$) the system formed by the demand curves, by Eqs. b.13, and b.14, is a non-linear system that cannot be solved analytically to derive DD^* and SD^* as functions of the parameters of the model.

7. Again, due to non-linearities, it is impossible to derive analytically what is the net effect of these factors in the case of constant-elasticity demand curves. However, it must be appreciated that the net effect will in general depend on the shape of the demand curves and that it proves to be ambiguous unless empirical results are referred to.

Chapter XIV

DEREGULATION: IMPLICATIONS FOR BRITISH BUILDING SOCIETIES

by *David Gilchrist*

INTRODUCTION

This paper considers the present and likely future role of British building societies in the financial services industry. The main emphasis is on the medium-term implications of changes in the law governing building societies.

The paper begins with a description of British building societies. It then examines the changing nature of the demand for financial services and how building societies may adapt to meet new demands. The possible wider range of services is considered, as is the context within which these services might be offered (the concept of the "financial supermarket"). The major problem of possible conflicts of interest is examined, as are other implications for capital adequacy, constitution and management. Finally, the paper attempts to foresee the position of building societies in the financial services industry of the 1990s.

UK BUILDING SOCIETIES

Building societies are mutual organisations, owned by their investors and borrowers. The legislation within which they operate states that societies exist for the purpose of making loans to members out of the funds subscribed by members. The manner in which societies raise and lend money and the way in which surplus funds can be invested are closely controlled. The main control is over the assets of the societies: loans to members must be made on the security of freehold or leasehold estate in the United Kingdom.

There are 190 building societies in the United Kingdom. Total assets are approximately £100 billions. The variation in size of societies is considerable: the smallest have assets of under £1 million and only a few hundred

Fair, D.E., (ed.) Shifting Frontiers in Financial Markets.
© *1986, Martinus Nijhoff Publishers, Dordrecht/Boston/Lancaster. ISBN 90-247-3225-5.*
Printed in the Netherlands.

Table 1. UK building societies: key statistics

History

Year	No. of societies	No. of share investors 000's	No. of borrowers 000's	Amount advanced £m	Total assets £m
1900	2,286	585	–	–	60
1930	1,026	1,449	720	89	371
1950	819	2,256	1,508	270	1,256
1960	726	3,910	2,349	560	3,166
1970	481	10,265	3,655	1,954	10,819
1980	273	30,640	5,383	9,506	53,793
1983	206	37,713	5,928	19,357	85,868

members; the largest, the Halifax Building Society, has assets in excess of £ 20 billions and about 9 million members. There is a relatively high degree of concentration: the top five societies have 57 per cent of total assets and the top twenty societies 87 per cent of total assets.

Building societies are, in effect, very large savings banks. In total, they operate 6,700 branch offices (around half as many as the total number of UK clearing bank branches) and are the dominant holders of personal sector liquid savings. Over half of all adults in the UK hold building society savings accounts.

The building societies are also the major providers of loan finance for house purchase (the main form of tenure in the UK, with 62 per cent owner-occupation). 77 per cent of home loans outstanding are with building societies, compared with 15 per cent with banks.

POSSIBLE LEGISLATIVE CHANGES

As indicated above, building societies are large institutions. Legislation does, however, restrict their role and, in particular, strictly limits the range and scope of assets and the services they are able to offer. Following representations from the societies' trade association, the UK government issued a consultative document in July 1984[1]. This suggested that the main purpose of building societies should continue to be the provision of housing finance, but that some diversification of assets would be permitted. This would include the ability to lend on second mortgage, the provision of equity mortgages[2] and (for all but the smallest societies) unsecured lending, the ownership of land and property and equity investment in subsidiaries and associates. New asset powers would be strictly limited: at least 90 per cent of assets would remain in the form of loans on owner-occupied residential property.

The consultative document also proposed that societies should be allowed to offer new services, specifically money transmission, conveyancing, structural surveys, insurance broking and other services acting as agent for a third party.

The document proposed that societies should retain their mutual status, but that procedures should exist for the voluntary conversion of societies into companies (probably licensed deposit-takers) should their members so wish and should the Bank of England approve.

There are, as yet, no firm proposals for legislation but it is hoped that a Bill will be presented to Parliament in the 1985–86 session and that some new powers would become available early in 1987.

THE DEMAND FOR A WIDER RANGE OF SERVICES: PROVISION OF HOUSING

The main pressure for change is on the lending side of the societies' business, and particularly in housing development. Although this is less relevant in a banking context than other forms of diversification, it is worth looking at the demand for building societies to become more involved with the provision of housing.

The main reason for this growing demand lies in the rapid decline of the private rented housing sector in the UK. Privately-owned housing available for rent now accounts for only about 10 per cent of the total stock, much less than in most other Western countries. Until recently, housing demand which could not be met (mainly for financial reasons) through owner-occupation was satisfied by the provision of municipally-owned rented property. Capital expenditure in this sector has recently been reduced, real rents have increased and a proportion of the stock has been sold to tenants. A variety of systems, including assured tenancies[3], shared-ownership schemes[4], index-linked[5] and equity mortgages have been developed to try to meet the demands of those who cannot afford immediate access to owner-occupation. Building societies are frustrated by current legislation in their efforts to become involved in these new forms of tenure. A major objective of new legislation would be actively to encourage societies to finance – and provide – new forms of tenure.

Availability of affordable housing, with relatively easy access, would be a major contribution to labour mobility and to easing the burden of unemployment. A greater provision of rented property would help with this. Another requirement is to lower the costs and simplify the administrative process involved in moving house. Accordingly, both the building societies and government see merit in societies providing a wider range of housing-related services under one roof. These services might include estate agency, conveyancing, structural surveys and insurance broking.

THE DEMAND FOR A WIDER RANGE OF SERVICES: FINANCIAL SERVICES

While the major reasons for wider powers in the housing market are social, relating as they do to housing and mobility problems, the motives for seeking changes in financial markets are quite different. Customers of building societies, who now number over 25 million, want a wider range of financial services to be provided by the societies. In particular, there are demands for an extension of money transmission services: cash, cheques, guarantee cards, credit cards, standing orders, direct debits and foreign currency. Most of the evidence for these wider demands comes from societies' own market research. However, an independent report was issued by the National Consumer Council in December 1983[6]. This indicated that while most people were satisfied with the service they received from their bank, half of all respondents would like their building society to offer a cheque book service, 39 per cent favoured standing orders, 32 per cent cash dispensers, 28 per cent personal loans, 26 per cent travellers' cheques and 20 per cent overdrafts.

However, even an independent survey may overstate the actual demand for a new range of services from a building society, were these to be offered. Banks' personal account customers were shown to resent bank charges. There may be a belief that building societies could avoid imposing such charges for low-balance account holders. This belief is probably mistaken: societies wishing to offer money transmission services, especially paper-based services, would face very high entry costs and many years would elapse before they achieved the economies of scale of the major clearing banks. Some societies might wish to start by subsidising such accounts, but they would not be able to afford to do so for long and still compete effectively in other market sectors. The public demand may not just be for a building society money transmission service, but for a wider challenge to the major clearers' control of this market. It is likely that there would also be public support for a personal banking service provided by one or more of the major retailers.

The demand for a wider range of lending facilities is one which building societies recognise and are likely to wish to meet. Initially, there are two main areas of demand. Firstly, building society customers often wish to borrow for housing-related purposes but not to do this with the dwelling itself as security. Usually this is because they are buying for the first time and the house-purchase loan is at or near 100 per cent of the valuation of the dwelling. Further finance is then required for carpets, furniture, fittings, consumer durables and the like. Such finance is available – from retailers, banks and hire-purchase companies – but customers feel that the total transaction would be simplified, and the cost perhaps lowered, if building societies could supply both secured long-term and unsecured shorter-term loans.

The second main extension of lending would be to provide second mortgages: that is, to take a second or subsequent charge on a property which is already in mortgage to a building society or other lender. The objective here would be to offer the borrower – who often feels tied to his main lender for all housing-related loans – the ability to seek finance elsewhere. This would be of benefit to borrowers when the main lender was short of funds for improvement loans or was perhaps charging an excessive rate of interest for such loans. Building society second mortgages would not compete with all other forms of second mortgage. The consultative document indicates that a building society second mortgage would have to be fully secured, whereas other lenders on second mortgage can offer loans which are only partially secured. However, the greater security would be reflected in a lower interest rate from the building society, and this, coupled

Table 2. Role in savings market

Personal sector liquid assets, mid-1984

Institution	£m	%
Building societies	83,630	50
Banks	57,144	34
National savings/savings banks	26,058	16
Other	435	–
	167,267	100

with societies' efficient loan application and administration systems, should generate a strong demand for loans for housing and other purposes.

There are also indications of a customer desire for a wider range of savings and investment services. Within current legislation, building societies have already responded to a widening range of investor requirements, as wealth has increased and personal investors have developed more sophisticated requirements. Thus the single main form of savings account of twenty years ago has been expanded into a range of accounts, offering different terms, conditions and interest rates to meet the varying needs of the investor. However, societies have not been able to meet a demand for risk investments (as part of a complete personal portfolio) nor have they been able to compete with pension funds or insurance companies in providing a long-term savings facility, mainly because they cannot invest directly in assets whose value is maintained or enhanced in real terms.

Government proposals for new legislation affecting the liabilities side of building society operations are very limited: there is a strong emphasis on maintaining the reputation of *all* society investments for protecting at least their nominal capital value. This would seem to rule out the possibility of a

Table 3. Role in housing market

Share of total net advances, building societies and banks

	Building societies %	Banks including TSB %
1973	69	11
1975	74	2
1980	77	8
1981	65	25
1982	58	36
1983	75	25

Shares of mortgage balances outstanding, building societies and banks

	Building societies %	Banks including TSB %
1973	77	6
1975	76	5
1980	81	6
1981	79	9
1982	75	14
1983	75	16

managed fund or investment trust type of operation. However if, as seems likely, societies are to be permitted to offer equity mortgages, it would seem logical to link these to equity investments – in effect a "residential property unit trust" in which the capital value of the original investment was not necessarily protected.

WAYS OF MEETING THE DEMAND FOR NEW SERVICES

The major strenghts of the building societies lie in their customer base and branch network. There are also some advantages of goodwill and reputation.

Societies would therefore wish to make the best use of their branch networks, staff and systems and might want to limit the marketing of some new services (for example, loans) to their existing borrowers or investors until they gained more experience. There are a number of ways in which societies could provide new services:

1. by straightforward diversification of their own operations,

2. by purchasing a controlling or partial shareholding in a subsidiary or associated company which would provide the service,

3. by establishing an agency service, using building society premises to offer the products and services of an outside company,

4. by joint operations involving a number of societies (group services),

5. by linking with another institution (for example, a bank) to provide additional services tied in with those of the building society.

Under present legislation, only the last of these is permitted, which is why most of the recent banking-type innovations by building societies have been joint ventures of this kind. It is probable that the larger societies will direct their attention to other methods of diversification, once these become possible.

The choice between developing new services "in house" and acquiring a specialist institution will be dictated by a number of factors. In-house development would be appropriate where relevant skills already exist in the organisation. These might be said to be present in respect of lending, but consumer lending (unsecured or on second mortgage) requires specialist skills which would probably have to be boosted by external recruitment, and by considerable re-training at the operational level. A more rapid route to providing the wider range of services desired might be to acquire a specialist institution. However, diversification through company acquisition is high risk, and often fails to generate a profitable and integrated operation. The management skills necessary to control such subsidiaries – to run, in effect, a holding company, are not currently present in building societies and are unlikely to be easily acquired. Moreover, the authorities are likely to prefer the slow extension of diverse activities arising from generic growth rather than rapid diversification through subsidiary operations. Two other arguments weigh against the subsidiary approach: firstly that building society managements, unskilled in this field, could choose acquisitions unwisely, or perhaps assume that currently unprofitable companies could be "turned round" as subsidiaries; secondly that the authorities would be most reluctant to allow the controlling society to let its subsidiary succeed or fail on its own merits. The consultative document says:

> "A financial institution of the standing of a building society would take on certain moral obligations towards a subsidiary to which it had lent its good name, over and above those required by the law of limited liability ... Any losses made by the subsidiary ... would potentially be those of the parent building society."

The extension of services through an agency operation (that is, entirely off-balance sheet) would be attractive to many societies. The advantages to such societies would lie in the wider provision of services under one roof, the more effective use of high street premises and the income generated from fees and commissions. However, the benefits of complete integration of administration and cross-selling would not be present, and the 'products' sold would have to carry a high reputation independent of that of the building society which acted as agent.

It seems probable, therefore, that the large societies will limit their agency activities, preferring to offer a wider range of services directly. The agency route may, however, be attractive to medium-sized societies and it may even be that a society would choose to start by acting as an agent for another institution, then go on either to acquire it (say, an insurance broker) or even be acquired by it (say, an overseas-based bank).

Joint operations, involving a number of societies, are difficult to arrange under current legislation but many societies would find such operations an attractive proposition. The recent Bankers' Clearing House paper on the future of the clearing system[7] suggests that groups of institutions might wish to join together to generate a sufficient volume of activity to become members of one or more of the clearing companies. Such a development is likely to be attractive to societies once legislation is enacted to allow societies to hold shares in other companies.

MULTILATERALISATION AND THE "FINANCIAL SUPERMARKET"

In its consultative document on new legislation, The Building Societies Association says:

> "...increasingly, customers are looking for convenience and institutions able to offer a package of financial services are at a substantial advantage over those able to offer only a limited range of services."

The Government's green paper acknowledges this (paragraph 1.10):

> "Major structural changes are now taking place in the financial services sector. Although these have not directly involved building societies, they will have a significant effect on the commercial environment in which they operate. Building societies will probably need to respond too to a trend towards "one stop" centres for financial and investment services."

Trends in retailing, and in financial institutions overseas, suggest the possibility of a "financial supermarket" approach. The technology is available to support such a development. It is worth examing whether building societies, once they are given new powers, should seek to become "one-stop" financial centres.

The success of one-stop shopping in the retail trade would seem to argue in favour of this. However, this success has been achieved by improvements in product packaging and transport, by new retailing techniques, by extension of shopping hours and by the wider availability of private transport. Very largely, one-stop shopping has come to dominate the convenience sector[8] of the retail trade, but not the comparison sector[9]. Convenience in collecting bulky and heavy goods, combined with keen price competition, have led to the growth of supermarkets and hypermarkets. In other sectors, where fashion dominates, or where occasional, high-value purchases are made – in particular where the retailing part of the distribution chain contributes significant added value – specialist retailers remain dominant.

Financial service institutions provide a mixture of "convenience" and "comparison" products. The clearing banks' cheque accounts are largely seen as a convenience service: there may be some shopping around by potential new customers, but most existing customers remain loyal to their bank, despite short-term competitive disadvantages. However, this loyalty will not necessarily extend to the other services provided by the bank: customers may seek to invest money elsewhere if the bank's deposit rates are unattractive, and will not be persuaded by "group brand loyalty" (as is often the case with multiple chain retailers) to buy other non-banking services from their bank. A distinction must also be drawn between packaged consumer goods which need no specialist explanation or advice, and financial services which require skilled human intervention in the selling process. There is as yet no evidence that printed literature, or even computer-based or video systems, can relieve branch staff of this advisory task. Even if this could be achieved, and if branch staff simply had to "activate" the sale, the complexities of administration would be considerable. Evidence from British Crown Post Offices, which handle a range of several hundred types of transaction, suggests that even where staff are offering minimal or no advice, and certainly carrying out little "selling", the quality of service on the main line of business is severely diminished by the attempt to cover a wide range of activities.

De-regulation for building societies will also present them with a choice between vertical and horizontal integration. Horizontal integration would certainly imply the provision of a wider range of financial services under one roof. Many societies might prefer the vertical route, in particular the provision of housing on which their loans are advanced. De-regulation is likely to result in different responses by different societies: those which choose to concentrate on the development of housing-related activities will have less scope for the provision of additional financial services.

The above arguments suggest that building societies will move cautiously towards extending their range of services, and that few will opt for the wide-ranging financial supermarket concept. There will be an attempt to develop new services, and to attach to these the "group brand loyalty" which adheres to the society's existing products and services. (This is an approach used by some of the largest and most successful non-food retailers: it requires cautious diversification into new areas, with close attention to the quality of the new service and with a willingness to retract if quality or sales targets are not achieved.)

COMPETITION AND PROBLEMS OF CONFLICT OF INTEREST

The Government consultative document states (paragraph 1.10) that:

> "... competition ensures the best service to investors. But the Government is also determined to ensure fair competition."

Later, referring to the provision of integrated house buying services, the document repeats that Government wishes to increase the range of choice open to consumers, but says (paragraph 4.05):

"The question is how to avoid possible conflicts of interest."

Diversification necessarily implies that building societies will offer new competition to existing providers of financial and housing-related services. Professional and other groups responding to the Government document have pointed out some of the hazards of allowing this new competition. Government, after allowing for professional self-interest, will doubtless take these views into account in framing new legislation.

The concerns which have been expressed concentrate on unfair competition and conflict of interest, often confusing the two. There is an important distinction. The fear of unfair competition, which relates mainly to the lending side of building society business, arises because other professions see dangers of "inertia selling" or "cross-subsidisation" by societies. Because of the importance of the mortgage loan, and because it is still possible (although unlikely) that mortgage funds will be rationed and the building society dominant in the transaction, other businesses see ample scope for societies to be able to persuade borrowers to accept conveyancing, estate agency, insurance or other services from the main lender. Even if the lender was not in this dominant position, there are fears that an additional service would be offered and priced below its true cost, with the lender compensating for this by increasing the general mortgage interest rate. This would in theory continue until such time as most of the specialist competition had been driven out of business, then charges would be increased to generate monopoly profits.

Building societies take the view that as competition increases in the provision of all financial services, as consumer knowledge expands and as it becomes increasingly important to ensure that any new service is profitable, there will be few dangers of unfair competition of the type envisaged above. Current fair trading legislation prevents any element of conditionality in the provision of services (for example, the granting of a mortgage being conditional on accepting the society's conveyancing service). Consumer choice does, however, depend on adequate consumer information. Professions which restrict the availability of such information (for example, solicitors, who only recently have begun limited advertising) will probably have to take additional steps to ensure that the quality and price of their service is brought to the attention of house buyers and sellers.

While societies might wish to avoid long-term cross-subsidisation, there will be new services where genuine economies of scale or integration will be possible, and it will be important for societies to be able to demonstrate that these economies are the real reason for the lower price of the service.

Cross-subsidisation can also take another form. If a society buys a subsidiary company to carry out a new operation, then regards itself as morally obliged to subsidise losses incurred by this company, the subsidiary is in effect competing unfairly with other businesses which do not have this "parental" protection. It is likely that the authorities would regard this kind of subsidisation as perfectly justifiable and desirable, if only on a temporary basis.

Problems of conflict of interest are different from those of unfair competition. The concern here is that as the range of services offered by any financial institution expands, there are dangers that the quality of advice and guidance are unduly influenced by the desire to sell some other service. So, for example, a building society acting as agent for a house seller would have a duty to obtain the best possible price; as a lender to the purchaser of the same property its duty would point in the opposite direction. Conflicts of interest of this kind can be avoided either by trying to prevent institutions engaging in activities which could come into conflict (a near-impossible task: the *basic* functions of a building society – raising funds from savers and lending to borrowers – represent a conflict of interest) or by ensuring that consumers are aware of the diverse activities carried out by the institution and of the potential conflicts which could arise. An "adversarial" approach to the provision of services may well avoid conflicts of interest, but the costs of adopting this approach probably outweigh those which will occasionally arise when multiple services are provided by one supplier. The answer lies not in regulation but in maximum consumer information and awareness.

IMPLICATIONS FOR FINANCIAL MANAGEMENT: CAPITAL ADEQUACY

The Government's consultative document points to the importance of a stronger capital base in relation to new activities. Effectively, the document makes three points:

1. new assets and activities would tend to imply greater risks.

2. The capital base has to be adequate to cover conceivable losses, especially since depositors still expect to receive their investments back "a pound for a pound".

3. Since there is no equity base and no possibility of raising additional capital from shareholders, the only source of increased reserves is from realised profits, but the mutual basis on which societies operate limits the scope for any rapid increase in profits.

For all these reasons the authorities will wish to control both the extent of diversification into new assets and activities, and the speed with which societies undertake new ventures.

Currently, building society regulations require societies to hold reserves according to a sliding scale, ranging from a minimum ratio of 2.5 per cent of assets for the smallest societies to 1.3 per cent for the largest. Actual reserve ratios are higher, averaging over 4 per cent at the end of 1983. However, this average is considerably lower than that achieved by US savings and loan associations, or by UK banks. The UK authorities' approach to the banks is not to prescribe precise numerical guidelines (apart from the minima in the Schedules to the Banking Act 1979) but for the Bank of England to judge a mixture of quantitative and qualitative factors in assessing capital adequacy. More specifically, a weighting system is used in assessing the riskiness of different types of asset. This involves the Bank in taking a view of three types of risk: credit risk (is the asset realisable at full value on the due date), investment risk (risk of depreciation) and forced sale risk (untimely sales in a narrow market). The Bank has, in fact, published its classification of assets and risk weights (BEQB September 1980). Building societies would not necessarily expect their own capital adequacy regulations to be precisely modelled on those for the banks, but the long and wide supervisory experience of the Bank will no doubt exert an influence on the views of the Treasury and Registrar.

The main implication must be that questions of capital adequacy (the quantifiable element) combined with those of management ability (the qualitative element) are likely to place fairly severe restrictions on any society that wishes to diversify rapidly, and especially into higher-risk areas such as property development or unsecured lending.

IMPLICATIONS FOR GENERAL MANAGEMENT AND CONSTITUTION

The Government's consultative document would place on building society boards of directors a series of duties, designed (as at present) to protect the interests of investors. However, these would inevitably be more wide-ranging and onerous with the potential diversification of societies. At the same time the document recognises some pressure from members of societies to have a more effective voice in the election of directors to society boards. These two themes are in opposition. Building society boards already consist mainly of non-executive directors (many societies have no executive directors at all) and despite efforts by leading societies to attract non-executive directors with the requisite skills and judgment, this can sometimes be difficult. Societies will have to stress that the value of attracting such skills to the board – particularly during a period of transition – outweighs the temporary appeal of a candidate claiming member or pressure-group backing.

Societies' managements will also have to be strengthened in order to undertake new activities. Experience gained by savings and loan associations in the United States suggests that new skills are best acquired by recruiting specialist staff, rather than by trying to re-train existing senior management. Existing management will also have to be able to exercise control over any new specialists. The clear implication of this is that there will be some element of competition among societies for generalists and specialists with the appropriate qualifications and track-record.

The main question in respect of building societies' mutual constitutions is how long this can survive in a competitive financial market place. The mutual constitution does not emphasise profit maximisation, does not impose the financial disciplines as on a company – where performance affects share price – and does not allow the board quickly to raise additional capital if reserves prove inadequate. At present, the Government thinks that these disadvantages are not sufficient to require societies to convert to company status. However, new legislation will provide a mechanism for conversion, if the members want this. The motivation for such a change would most probably arise from a desire to diversify rapidly into new areas requiring substantial additional capital. Since the general theme of this paper is that rapid and fundamental diversification are unlikely, conversions to company status will probably be rare until the mid-1990s. Exceptions to this might include some medium-sized societies with attractive branch networks. The members of such societies could be persuaded (by means of a distribution of reserves) to agree to a conversion to company status, and the former society could then be bought by another institution (perhaps an overseas-based bank) which wanted to expand its retail deposit and lending base. Provided that the interests of the borrowers could be safeguarded in such a conversion, the process could be seen as desirable and economically efficient.

BUILDING SOCIETIES IN THE FINANCIAL MARKETPLACE OF THE 1990s

Building societies will continue to specialise. Their activities will still be dominated by mortgage lending and savings and investment services. New forms of mortgage will be developed, and the range of investment products extended. The largest societies will extend their money transmission services, using the latest technology and avoiding, as far as is possible, paper-based systems. Most of the medium-sized and larger societies will offer unsecured loans (initially to their existing borrowers) and second mortgages. Most will offer an insurance broking service.

Beyond this, developments will depend on the objectives, policies and plans of individual societies. Deregulation and new competitive pressures imply different reactions by different societies. Some will choose to offer a range of housing-related services; others will not – perhaps stressing the value of an independently-provided legal or estate agency service. Some will venture into property development, either for sale or rent; others will not, or will limit such activities to "social" developments in areas of housing stress. Finally, some will opt for company status while others will remain mutual. Building societies will become more diverse in their functions, but their continued heavy dependence on personal savings and mortgage lending will ensure that they remain a clearly identified and specialised part of the financial services industry.

NOTES

1. The Government's consultative document is entitled *"Building Societies: A New Framework"*, Command 9316, HMSO £4.85.

2. Equity mortgages are loans on which the lender receives all (or part) of the appreciation in the value of the property. In return, the borrower's monthly payments will be lower throughout the whole term of the loan – not just initially, as with an index-linked or other low-start mortgage.

3. Assured tenancies were introduced in the Housing Act 1980. The property to be rented has to be newly-built, and the landlord has to be a Government-approved body. In return, the landlord is freed from normal rent control and security of tenure restrictions.

4. Shared ownership is a tenure involving part-ownership and part-tenancy. The occupier takes out a mortgage for a proportion of the value of the property (normally 25 per cent or 50 per cent) and pays rent – usually to a housing association – on the non-owned proportion. There is an option to purchase further shares in the property at later dates, but the cost of these will be based on market values at that time. The concept of buying additional shares until 100 per cent ownership is achieved is called "staircasing".

5. Index-linked mortgages attempt to re-create conditions of zero inflation in the loan arrangement. Interest is charged at a low "real" rate, and initial monthly payments are therefore low in relation to the debt. However, the debt and the monthly payment are increased each year according to the rise in the chosen inflation index (likely to be the UK retail price index). If household income increases in line with retail price inflation, the mortgage payment will remain a constant proportion of income throughout the term of the loan.

6. National Consumer Council: *"Banking Services and the Consumer"*, December 1983.

7. Bankers' Clearing House: *"Payment Clearing Systems: A Review of Organisation, Membership and Control"*, December 1984.

8. The term "convenience shopping" is generally used to relate to goods where convenience of access and transport is more important than quality or external image – essentially basic foodstuffs and household goods, non-fashion clothing, etc.

9. "Comparison" shopping covers those goods where quality, price, fashion etc are important and the purchaser wants to be able to compare the offerings of different retailers, usually in a town centre "High Street" shopping environment.

Chapter XV

SHIFTING INSTITUTIONAL FRONTIERS IN FINANCIAL MARKETS IN THE UNITED STATES

by *Richard Aspinwall*

INTRODUCTION

The traditional compartmentalization of financial markets in the United States is eroding. Whereas in the past classes of institutions tended to be associated with specific classes of services, with relatively little overlap, a widespread shift of approach to customers and to financial services is now in progress. It is unlikely, however, that this reorientation will result in a small number of large, highly diverse financial entities dealing with all kinds of customers in virtually every section of the United States.

The pace of financial change has reflected two kinds of forces. First, so-called exogenous forces have included economic discontinuities (including high and unusually volatile interest rates); declining costs of new applications of technology; and differing effects of financial regulation on various classes of institutions. Second, these exogenous forces in turn have spurred changes within markets for financial services. These include new competition to exploit the handicaps of existing suppliers; a greater incidence of explicit pricing of services, in many cases supplanting implicit returns; utilization of cost-saving innovations in service configuration and delivery; changes in asset and liability portfolio preferences; and strengthening of product lines in order to sustain existing customer relationships.

The balance of this paper will expand on these propositions. The emphasis is on why changes have taken place and how forces for change are likely to affect the financial services industry in the United States.

THE RECORD OF CHANGE

Framework

A financial system may be described along four lines: (1) classes of

Fair, D.E., (ed.) Shifting Frontiers in Financial Markets.
© *1986, Martinus Nijhoff Publishers, Dordrecht/Boston/Lancaster. ISBN 90-247-3225-5.*
Printed in the Netherlands.

services, (2) institutions supplying services, (3) users of services, and (4) delivery modes. The components of such a framework are detailed in Table 1.

The so-called 'financial services revolution' in the US has taken a number of courses within this framework. First, there have been changes in the balance sheet positions of users and suppliers of services. These changes have included a reorientation by institutions to assets and liabilities having different risk characteristics within markets already being served, shifts into new markets, changing supply costs, and changing customer demands.

1. Approximately 80 per cent of retail time and savings deposits at banks and other depository institutions are in deregulated accounts offering current-market rates. Of this, $ 400 billion (25 per cent) are in short-dated money market deposit accounts. In addition, something over one-third of transaction deposits (i.e., those in NOW accounts) currently carry an explicit interest return.

2. Savings and loan associations (S&Ls) have placed greater emphasis on adjustable rate mortgages (ARMs) in order to provide greater rate sensitivity in asset holdings. As much as 70 per cent of new home mortgage loan extensions during the past two years have been in this form (although this percentage was closer to 50 per cent in early 1985). Typically, however, such loans have limits on the size of rate adjustments – e.g., 5 per cent over the lifetime of the loan and 2 per cent in any one year. Moreover, new lending powers in business and consumer sectors have not produced much asset growth because of strong competition from other entities. Finally, the rate sensitivity of liabilities has also continued to increase. On balance, S&Ls seem to be relatively little better off in their interest rate sensitivity than they were three years ago.

3. Corporate issues of fixed rate bonds with maturities greater than 10 years have declined sharply[1].

4. Major US international banks with one half or more of profits generated from offshore markets are increasing the priority accorded to domestic income generation. Efforts have included holding company acquisitions of nonbank financial concerns (such as consumer and commercial lending), remote solicitation of deposit and credit services using telephone and mail, and greater emphasis on new services in investment banking.

Second, the use of balance sheet positions also permits calculations of changes in market shares among institutions. Such calculations are highly imprecise, however, since all components of the relevant market must be included and data rarely conform to market reality. In any event, over the

Table 1. Components of a financial system

A. Classes of finance-related services
1. Transactions
   a. Funds transfers
   b. Financial instrument purchases and sales
   c. Foreign exchange
   d. Nonfinancial asset purchases and sales

2. Investment instruments (saving)
   a. Fixed income
   b. Equities
   c. Commingled funds
   d. Futures and options
   e. Pension claims

3. Financing (borrowing)
   a. Credit
   b. Commitments and credit lines
   c. Futures and options
   d. Equity

4. Insurance
   a. Life
   b. Property & casualty
   c. Fidelity
   d. Credit protection
   e. Market valuation

5. Securities underwriting and distribution

6. Fiduciary
   a. Investment management
   b. Pension
   c. Trust
   d. Agency
   e. Safekeeping
   f. Advice

B. Institutions supplying financial services
1. Commercial banks
2. Thrift institutions (savings & loan associations, savings banks, and credit unions)
3. Other financial institutions (often called 'nondepository' – such as insurance companies, pension funds, investment banks and brokers, mutual fund sponsors, and finance companies)
4. Private nonfinancial entities
5. Governments

C. Users of financial services
1. Individuals
2. Nonfinancial business
3. Financial entities
4. Governments

D. Modes for delivering financial services
1. Offices (or branches)
2. Automated teller machines
3. Point-of-sale facilities
4. Organized exchanges and clearing facilities
5. Telephone
6. Mail
7. Computer

---

past decaue there have been pronounced shifts reflected in standard institutional data[2].

1. Money market mutual funds rose sharply between 1978 and 1982, largely as a result of binding ceilings on depository institutions. At year end 1984 such funds accounted for $170 billion, or almost 8 per cent of household deposit-type assets.

2. The share of thrift institutions in household deposits has declined somewhat, reflecting the effects of the money market mutual funds and also strong bank promotion efforts on newly authorized consumer deposits.

3. The share of life insurance as a discretionary household investment has fallen, reflecting the growing separation of life insurance per se from savings.

4. The share of private and government pensions has risen strongly, reflecting the proliferation of pension programs.

5. There has been a strong shift in the household sector away from direct equity investment into commingled pool accounts, in part attributable to aggressive marketing by fund sponsors and also to new tax sheltering opportunities for individuals.

6. Banks have packaged substantial amounts of business loans for resale to investors (including S&Ls). In addition, banks have encouraged use of nonbank credit resources (e.g., commercial paper) by providing off-balance-sheet backup lines. Between 1978 and 1983, standby letters of credit rose from $26 billion to $120 billion – three times faster than the growth rate of business loan holdings at banks.

7. Finance affiliates of retail and manufacturing entities have captured a sizable (though variable) share of consumer credit[3].

A third component consists of changes in delivery techniques. Here the evidence is even more fragmentary.

1. The number of automated teller machines (ATMs) now in operation in the United States approximates 50,000, which represents a five-fold increase since 1978. About one third of eligible consumer customers utilize ATMs, although incidence among users varies widely. The proportion of use has not changed much in the past three years. ATMs have supplanted other forms of transacting, but the extent is uncertain. Charges for ATM usage apparently do not yet differ much from charges for other forms of delivery of comparable services.

2. Other new transactions services, such as debit cards (point-of-sale), home terminals, and telephone transfers, have attained relatively small volume.

3. Discount brokers (many owned by bank holding companies and others serving banks) now account for about 9 per cent of revenues from retail stock transactions (where the number of shares traded is less than 900)[4]. In the wholesale area, discount penetration is negligible since commission rates are much more subject to negotiation.

A fourth manifestation of transition consists of so-called headline events – i.e., mergers, acquisitions, and prospective new business ventures. Virtually every class of institution has engaged in large numbers of such undertakings (often with more promotional effort than accomplishment).

The extent of cross-sector acquisition activity is reflected in Tables 2 and

Table 2. Major entrants into securities brokerage through acquisition, 1981–1984

Acquiring institution	Acquired brokerage firm	Year
American Express Co.	Shearson Loeb Rhoades, Inc.	1981
Phibro Corporation	Salomon Brothers	1981
Prudential Insurance Co.	Bache Halsey Stuart Shields, Inc.	1981
Sears, Roebuck & Co.	Dean Witter Reynolds	1981
Empire of America, FSA	William M. Cadden & Company, Inc.	1982
First Union National Bank	Salem Securities, Inc.	1982
John Hancock Insurance Co.	Tucker Anthony & R.L. Day, Inc.	1982
Kemper Group	Bateman Eichler, Hill Richards, Inc.	1982
Kemper Group	Blunt, Ellis & Loewi	1982
Kemper Group	Prescott, Ball & Turben, Inc.	1982
Travelers Insurance	Securities Settlement Corporation	1982
Union Planters National Bank	Brenner Steed & Associates, Inc.	1982
Bank America Corporation	Charles Schwab & Co., Inc.	1983
Chase Manhattan Corporation	Rose & Company Investment Brokers, Inc.	1983
First Union National Bank	Dis-Com Securities, Inc.	1983
Security Pacific National Bank	Commission Discount Corporation	1983
Security Pacific National Bank	Kahn & Company	1983
Security Pacific National Bank	Kenneth Kass & Company	1983
United Jersey Banks	Richard Blackman & Company, Inc.	1983
American Express Co.	Lehman Brothers Kuhn Loeb, Inc.	1984
Chemical New York Corporation	Brown & Company Securities Corp.	1984
Equitable Life Assurance	Donaldson, Lufkin & Jenrette	1984
Kemper Group	Burton J. Vincent & Chesley & Co.	1984
Northern Trust Corporation	Jerome Hickey & Associates	1984

Source: Steven D. Felgran, 'Bank Entry into Securities Brokerage: Competitive and Legal Aspects', *New England Economic Review,* Federal Reserve Bank of Boston, November/ December 1984; and *Federal Reserve Bulletin*, various issues.

Table 3. Major cross-industry ownership of FDIC-insured commercial banks in the United States

Date acquired or opened	Bank or trust company	Parent
1923	Amalgamated Bank, NY	Amalgamated Clothing & Textile Workers Union, NY
1941	Macy's Bank, NY	R.H. Macy & Co., Inc., NY
1952	Beneficial National Bank, DE	Beneficial Corporation, DE
1958	Eastern Heights State Bank, MN	Minnesota Mining and Manufacturing Co., MN
1968	Capital Guardian Trust Co., CA	The Capital Group Inc., CA
1969	Investors Bank and Trust, MA	Eaton Vance Corporation, MA
1970	Savings Bank Trust Co., WA	Shearson/American Express, NY
1979	Chicago Title & Trust Co., IL	Lincoln National Corp., IN
1979	IDS Trust Co., MN	American Express, NY
1981	Associates National Bank, CA	Gulf & Western Corp., NY
1981	Valley National Bank, CA	Household International, IL
1981	Boston Safe Deposit & Trust Co., MA	Shearson/American Express, NY
1981	First Deposit National Bank, NH	Capital Holding Corp., KY
1982	Colonial National Bank, DE	Teachers Services Organization, PA
1982	Wellington Trust Co., MA	Wellington Management Co., MA
1982	Avco National Bank, CA	Avco Corp., CT
1982	Dreyfus Consumer Bank, NJ	Dreyfus Corp., NY
1983	Marsh & McLennan Trust Co., MA	Marsh & McLennan Inc., NY
1983	Western Family Bank, N.A., CA	McMahan Valley Stores, CA
1983	J&W Seligman Trust Co., NY	J&W Seligman & Co., NY
1983	Beneficial National Bank, DE	Beneficial Corp., DE
1983	First National Bank, DE	Commercial Credit Corp., MD
1983	Fidelity Bank & Trust Co., NH	Fidelity Management & Research Co., MA
1983	J.C. Penney National Bank, DE	J.C. Penney Co., Inc., NY
1983	Prudential Bank & Trust Co., GA	Prudential-Bache Securities, Inc., NY
1983	Trust Management Bank, MA	Rollert & Sullivan Inc., MA
1983	International Central Bank & Trust Co., CA	Continental Corp., NY
1984	The Massachusetts Cos., Inc., MA	Travelers Corp., CT
1984	E.F. Hutton Bank, DE	E.F. Hutton Group, Inc., NY
1984	American Investment Bank, UT	Leucadia National Corp., NY
1984	Merrill Lynch Bank & Trust Co., NJ	Merrill Lynch & Co., NY
1984	Advest Bank, CT	Advest Group, Inc. CT
1984	First National Bank of Wilmington, DE	Commercial Credit Corp., MD
1985	Greenwood Trust Co., DE	Sears Roebuck & Co., IL

Sources: *Banking Expansion Reporter*, July 16, 1984, and *American Banker*, April 16, 1985.

3. The former summarizes acquisitions by nonbank firms (primarily insurance companies) of investment banking/brokerage concerns between 1981 and 1984. Acquisitions of small discount brokers during the period by banks and bank holding companies are also included in the table. Table 3 shows ownership of banks by major nonbank entities (although, unfortunately, not ownership of bank-like savings and loan associations by nonfinancial corporations).

Taken together, these show an enhanced stake in 'new' financial service positions by financial entities and by nonfinancial firms as well. The broadened range of services directly offered by new combined entities has clearly involved 'banking' services. This is reflected in Table 4, where, in addition, the disparities in activities between commercial banks on the one hand and nonbanks (including thrifts) on the other are quite evident. Indeed, a unitary S&L holding company may engage in virtually all functions from steel processing to check processing.

Finally, changes in regulations also provide a sense of momentum that is often misleading. Generally speaking, regulatory changes follow, rather than lead, changes in market practices. Successful avoidance of old regulations is usually a prerequisite to the promulgation of new (and more liberalized) ones. The experiences with deposit ceilings and the interstate positioning of banks and their holding company affiliates are prominent examples.

Changing supplier costs

The increasing proportion of bank deposits explicitly paying close to market rates combined with rapidly rising operating costs (e.g., occupancy and labor costs rose 13 per cent per annum from 1978 to 1983) have constituted a strong incentive to banks to streamline delivery procedures. This has entailed greater recourse to new applications of technology. Over the past two decades, technology costs have fallen sharply[5]. In fact, the alterations in processing and delivery that are now under way threaten to demolish the grounds on which past empirical studies have based conclusions that there are limited economies of scale in banking and, indeed, diseconomies in the larger size categories. Moreover, virtually no analysis has been done on scope economies[6].

In the past as in the present, however, the main impediment to greater technical efficiency is the resistance of consumers. This resistance has reflected a lack of familiarity with new processes and – in the past – the widespread availability of 'old-style' services that were free of explicit

Table 4. Comparison of products and powers of selected financial and nonfinancial institutions

	National Bank	State Bank California	Bank Holding Company	Federal Savings Bank/ Savings & Loan	Unitary Thrift Holding Company	Merrill Lynch	Dreyfus	Prudential-Bache	Sears	American Express
Demand deposit	Yes	Yes	Yes	Yes	Yes	Yes	Yes	Yes	Yes	No
Savings deposit	Yes	Yes	Yes	Yes	Yes	Yes	Yes	Yes	Yes	No
Certificate of deposit	Yes	Yes	Yes	Yes	Yes	Yes	Yes	Yes	Yes	Yes
Transaction account (NOW/ATS, etc.)	Yes	Yes	Yes	Yes	Yes	Yes	Yes	Yes	Yes	Yes
Federal insurance	Yes	Yes	Yes	Yes	Yes	Yes	No	Yes	Yes	No
Commercial loans	Yes	Yes	Yes	Yes	Yes	Yes	Yes	Yes	Yes	Yes
Consumer loans	Yes	Yes	Yes	Yes	Yes	Yes	Yes	Yes	Yes	No
Residential mortgages	Yes	Yes	Yes	Yes	Yes	Yes	Yes	Yes	Yes	Yes
Commercial mortgages	Yes	Yes	Yes	Yes	Yes	Yes	Yes	Yes	Yes	No
Margin loans	Yes	Yes	Yes	No	Yes	Yes	Yes	No	Yes	Yes
Credit cards	Yes	Yes	Yes	Yes	Yes	Yes	Yes	Yes	Yes	Yes
Credit related insurance agent	Yes	Yes	Yes	Yes	Yes	Yes	No	Yes	Yes	Yes
General insurance agent	No	No	No	Yes	Yes	Yes	No	Yes	Yes	Yes
Insurance underwriter	No	No	No	No	Yes	Yes	No	Yes	Yes	Yes
Stock brokerage	No	No	Yes	Yes	Yes	Yes	No	Yes	Yes	Yes
Discount stock broker	Yes	No	Yes	Yes	Yes	No	No	Yes	No	No
Investment advisor	Yes	Yes	Yes	Yes	Yes	Yes	Yes	Yes	Yes	Yes
Investment in corporate securities	No	Yes	Yes	Yes	Yes	Yes	Yes	Yes	Yes	Yes
Organization/Operation of mutual fund	No	Yes	Yes	Yes	Yes	Yes	Yes	Yes	Yes	Yes
Real estate broker	No	No	No	No	Yes	Yes	No	No	Yes	Yes
Real estate developer	No	Yes	No	Yes	Yes	Yes	No	Yes	Yes	Yes
Real estate appraisal for others	No	Yes	Yes	Yes	Yes	No	No	No	Yes	No
Data processing for others	No	Yes	Yes	Yes	Yes	No	No	No	Yes	No
Travel agency	No	No	No	No	Yes	Yes	No	No	No	Yes
Leasing personal property	Yes	Yes	Yes	Yes	Yes	No	No	No	No	No
Retail sales	No	No	No	No	Yes	No	No	No	Yes	Yes
Manufacturing	No	No	No	No	Yes	No	No	No	No	No

Note: Original footnotes have been deleted for brevity of presentation.

Source: 'Comparison of Products and Powers of Selected Financial and Nonfinancial Institutions', Committee on Banking, Finance and Urban Affairs,

charge. Such services constituted implicit returns in deposit markets where explicit price competition was severely constrained. Service charges on transactions deposits have risen sharply in recent years – from an average of $0.81 per $100 of deposits in 1978 to $1.50 in 1983. Nevertheless, new levels of charges apparently are not yet high enough to generate pronounced changes in users' delivery preferences. Technical capability still leads market feasibility by a fairly wide margin.

Regulatory avoidance through innovation

Innovative steps in product development have enabled depository institutions to circumvent regulatory restrictions. The old deposit ceilings were avoided successfully through use of retail repurchase agreements, deposit premiums, and loans to depositors in order to achieve minimum denominations. Location (i.e., branching) restrictions have eroded through greater reliance on the telephone, mail, marketing offices, nonbank affiliates within a holding company, and the sharing of ATMs. Finally, securities-related services (such as mutual funds) that banking institutions cannot provide directly have been obtained from other sources, such as brokerage and investment management firms.

Remaining regulatory constraints

Nevertheless, regulation continues to impose second-best avoidance requirements on most depository institutions (if not on other financial institutions). Within each of the classes of major regulation (pricing, service line, and location), significant constraints remain.

For banks, these cover commingled investment services, securities underwriting, general insurance underwriting, forms of interstate expansion (including impediments to bank/thrift combinations), a few remaining restrictions on deposit terms, and the imposition of non-interest-bearing required reserves by the Federal Reserve. For nonbanks (chiefly insurance and investment entities) seeking access to banking markets, obstacles are considerably less impressive. First, comparable products (deposit-like instruments, credit) need not be offered through banks per se. The money market mutual fund is only one example. Second, the offering of these services through nonbank offices avoids the locational restrictions to which banks themselves are subject. Third, for specific purposes such as deposit insurance and direct access to funds clearing, nonbanks have acquired or established thrift or limited-purpose bank subsidiaries. The latter, called 'nonbank banks', avoid the restrictions of the Bank Holding Company Act by relinquishing either the demand deposit or commercial lending power. These restrictions include what are permissible activities within the holding company (i.e., 'closely related to banking . . .') and constraints on interstate locations of bank offices.

Effects of pressures on capital

Capital positions have been under severe pressure from a number of sources. First, unanticipated inflation eroded the real value of capital, since loan spreads were too thin to compensate lenders adequately for the reduced purchasing power of their net monetary assets. Second, institutions with short-funded asset positions were punished by rising interest rates. Third, disinflation and (in sectors such as energy) slow growth have contributed to severe credit problems in both domestic and offshore lending-problems that are likely to take some years to resolve. Finally, investments in new delivery technology have absorbed sizable amounts of capital. At the same time, regulators have increased bank capital requirements (a step not taken as yet with respect to thrift institutions).

Adjustments to capital pressures have taken at least three forms: (1) the origination of loans for pass-through to investors; (2) greater priority to fee-generating services (in lieu of position spreads), including deposit service charges and fees on credit-related activity; and (3) greater sharing of operating facilities. These have tended to erode the distinctiveness of depository institutions as suppliers of intermediation services.

Common elements of past change

This review suggests several common features of changes in financial services activity in the United States. Perhaps having the broadest future implications, commodity attributes of financial services are increasing. By this is meant less differentiating contributed by factors such as widespread office locations and the provision of advice, occasional special services, and backup (or contingency) support. Increasingly, financial services are regarded by users as elements of information storage and processing – covering funds transfers, securities safekeeping and transactions, credit and deposits, and even standby services such as lines of credit. In virtually every instance, the enhanced service standardization represents an evolution to a mass consumer market of services originally offered at the wholesale level to large corporate customers.

The emergence of greater reliance on automated and highly technical investment by which to offer these services has sometimes been regarded as a serious threat to smaller market participants. So far, however, sharing and vendor processing – not exclusion – have evolved. Networks of ATM terminals, discount broker services, and an increasing role for independent processing firms are all examples of the ability of smaller suppliers of financial services to achieve access to systems requiring large investment. In addition, access to systems required for other (nonfinancial) purposes has encouraged 'do-it-yourself' financial functions by nonfinancial entities. For example, large multinational corporations engage as intermediaries in borrowing and lending on a global basis, funds transfers have become highly automated, and sizable amounts of insurance risk management and investment management has been shifted in-house.

THE COURSE OF FUTURE CHANGE

Three major forces must be incorporated explicitly into views of the future: (1) the role of the economic environment; (2) the acceptability to users (as well as feasibility to suppliers) of alterations to delivery terms; and (3) the interaction of these with political forces.

The economic environment

Probably the chief uncertainty facing various classes of institutions is the sensitivity of income originating from major business operations to the various economic environments. In essence, it is a question similar to strategies of portfolio diversification. Specialized institutions often find it difficult to make short-run shifts in business strategies to correct unsatisfactory earnings performance arising from adverse economic circumstances. Relatively extreme interest rate environments will affect major classes of financial services in widely differing ways. The cases summarized below are polar assumptions, not forecasts.

Under an extended low-rate environment, the traditional maturity intermediation in which retail entities (banks and thrifts) engage would be more profitable by far than spreads earned by larger entities engaged chiefly in wholesale credit intermediation. Since retail business will be increasingly attractive, stronger efforts to penetrate retail asset and deposit markets are likely to be undertaken by the wholesale entities. At the same time, the penalty for balance sheet mismatching and 'guessing wrong' on interest rates will be much less severe.

In the low-rate environment, protection (rather than subsidization) would become a major issue. In the jousting for turf and income share, political sentiment and support have often been inversely related to size. This consideration would have a constraining effect on the ability of larger 'outside' entities to enter local retail markets and could lead to reregulation. Reregulation approaches in retail markets could involve deposit pricing (perhaps tied to market securities rates), restrictions on remote delivery outside 'home' states, and slower liberalization of product powers.

The term structure of interest rates in the high case would, of course, be negatively sloped (as was the case during the high-rate period of 1979-1981), rate levels would average close to (if not above) peaks earlier in this decade, and rate volatility also would presumably be high.

Under the high-rate environment, maturity intermediation would be markedly unprofitable, and rates charged to borrowers would be closely tied to lenders' funding costs. As a result, interest rate risk would be shifted to borrowers, and credit risk would rise. Sectors such as residential housing, where borrowers' cash flow is relatively fixed in the short run, would face painful problems.

In an environment of high interest rates, mismatched (chiefly thrift) intermediaries would be under serious earnings pressure, chiefly reflecting the effects of sluggish responses in asset earning yields. Slow growth in major asset markets would exacerbate this pressure.

In the high-rate case, threatened retail-oriented institutions would have three general alternatives: first, greater emphasis on lines of business relatively less vulnerable to high-rate circumstances; second, buy-outs from large 'outside' entities that view distressed retail business as attractive; third, propping-up by government infusions of capital. In the high-rate environment money center banks with high portfolio concentrations in short-term credit to larger borrowers (both domestic and international) would enjoy relatively better earnings positions.

Finally, the neat distinction between high and low interest rate environments has avoided an obvious pitfall – something in between. That is, the economic environment is ambiguous with respect to the financial structure. The experience of government 'make-do' policies with thrifts during their current difficulties (which are tied considerably to asset quality problems) suggests that preservation of the status quo has considerable political support. New programs of government capital infusions, selective mergers, insurance, and intermediation may be expected for entities where serious strains develop.

Delivery terms

In most interest rate environments, suppliers of transaction services will be under pressure to reorient delivery. Adjustments to the higher explicit interest payments on retail deposit accounts are likely to center on further rises of service fees and reductions in the costs of providing traditional services. Pricing changes are likely to lead to increased consumer acceptance of reorientation of the services themselves. Check truncation (widely practiced by credit unions) and greater reliance on debit cards are examples of this process.

A major complication in prospects for changes in delivery systems is that, for a time, many institutions will in effect be maintaining dual delivery systems. In the case of banks, for example, traditional delivery services such as those available through branch offices cannot be radically altered before there is evidence that consumers are accepting new alternatives. But the new alternatives cannot be tested effectively without substantial commitment. Moreover, even after the branches have been supplanted by other delivery modes (such as broader card usage, ATMs, and home terminals), there is an operational lag before major realignment of branch systems can be accomplished.

Another uncertain longer run consequence of the explicit pricing tendency is that with a reduced physical presence required for the delivery of services, the composition of the relevant competitive market facing a given institution will change. New competitors will have access to markets previously foreclosed because of branching constraints or the substantial costs of physical investment. A primary remaining tie to location will be access to cash. There are already signs, however, that high-traffic retailers (such as grocery stores) will play an increasing role in providing cash services under operating arrangements with banks and thrifts. Allowing for some displacement of current inefficient procedures in virtually any economic scenario, transaction balances seem likely to continue to be the core on which depository institutions will offer their services and nondepository entities will seek entry. The pace of the shift away from paper and away from lobby-intensive service orientation reduces the obstacles facing those nonbank entities seeking to look (and act) like banks.

Political considerations

For some years the separation of banking and commerce has been an article of faith in the United States. This separation largely reflected a desire to avoid three conditions – concentration of resources, conflicts of interest and abuses of power, and perception of increased risk to a banking subsidiary by virtue of such tie.

In the near term, the greatest structural (and political) uncertainty entails the resolution of efforts by a number of banks to expand geographically. Because legislation authorizing full entry by out-of-state banks has been enacted in only a handful of states, interstate banking activity has concentrated on other approaches. Nonbank banks and regional interstate compacts have been the most dominant. As noted, the former is loophole exploitation. Under the Bank Holding Company Act, regulatory limitations on a bank holding company are predicated on the operation by the bank subsidiary of *both* commercial lending and demand deposits. Previous to 1984, the elimination of one of these (usually the former) has provided the means for bank acquisitions by entities that would not otherwise be eligible to do so (see Table 3). After the first general-service nonbank bank was approved by the Federal Reserve for a commercial bank holding company (in 1984), over 300 applications for charters for such banks were filed. Relatively few have received final regulatory approval and have opened for business. Strong political opposition and adverse federal review make proliferation of nonbank banks unlikely.

The regional compact is an effort on the part of various state legislatures to enable bank holding companies in one state to acquire (or be acquired by) banks in adjacent or other nearby states to the exclusion of distant (usually major money center) banks. The compact approach has been attacked as an unconstitutional restraint of interstate commerce, and the matter is now before the Supreme Court.

Regulatory treatment of banking risk constitutes the foremost current issue in banking regulation. The perceived objective of reforms in regulatory practices is more careful and conservative banking management. This has been sought heretofore through greater disclosure and higher capital requirements. More recently, at least one regulatory agency has embarked on greater publicity in instances of perceived internal mismanagement. A connected issue relates to reform of deposit insurance. It is recognized that a deposit insurance premium assessed without cognizance of differences among institutions in risk encourages the assumption of risks. While a major difficulty with a risk-related premium lies in the imprecision with which risk factors can be quantified, the estimation problem is also inherent in the current flat-premium structure as well.

Nonbank entities may offer almost every line of financial services. Thus, the question is not the ability of these entities to avoid regulatory obstacles, but rather their ability to capitalize on new entry under current circumstances. The ability of commercial banks to achieve a reciprocal liberalization of their operating powers is hindered by four factors. First, expanded powers are linked politically with extended geographic reach, the latter being a highly sensitive issue of local (rather than national) politics and small versus large banks. Second, regulators are highly jealous of their turf. Expanded operating powers suggest shifts in regulatory jurisdiction or – at the very least – additions of regulatory oversight. Third, there is a pronounced political sentiment which can be termed as anti-bigness. That is, there is strong opposition to operating authorization which would point to amalgamation of large financial entities. A fourth aspect of resistance relates to the perceived potential for conflicts and abuses. The expanding variety of services offered by financial entities generally has created new concerns about the potential for conflicts of interest. While this prospect cannot be ignored, there have been a number of reform steps over the past 50 years to discourage improper behavior and to provide for corrective action. These include broader disclosure, restrictions on inter-affiliate transactions involving banks under the Federal Reserve Act, anti-tie-in stipulations, prohibitions against interlocks, and enhanced regulatory powers to stop unsound or abusive practices. Finally, there is considerable uncertainty over the capability of banks to manage competently new lines of business[7]. This concern is complicated by the inability of regulators to measure riskiness, either ex-ante or ex-post.

In this light, the generators of change are likely to evolve from two primary sources: the banks themselves, in the innovation of services or delivery which avoid regulatory restrictions; or broad economic events which so weaken classes of suppliers that expanded powers for other entities are (short of direct government intervention) necessary to sustain service availability.

SUMMARY

The greatest uncertainty in the future configuration of US financial services markets lies with the services themselves and the methods of their distribution, rather than the institutional organization of these markets. While institutions obviously are not immune from the effects of changes in services or their delivery, there is no apparent correlation between these major changes and the ability of most institutions to adjust. Such adaptiveness need not entail a look-alike institutional configuration.

It seems unlikely there will be widespread institutional homogenization in the US. This expectation rests on four main propositions: (1) the lack of evidence that there are operating economies with increased size of firm; (2) the availability to smaller firms of sharing and joint ventures in those new efforts which require substantial capital investment; (3) continuing importance of nonprice attributes of service, including personal treatment and convenient access; and (4) the presumed absence of external shocks that threaten a specific sector on a virtually systemic basis – for example, the effects of high interest rates on maturity intermediating lenders.

Many services have tended to become more standardized. Consequently, new entrants to product markets will tend to emphasize better prices for specific services through more efficient delivery and a greater range of services for given customer classes. So far – except for the case of money market funds – there have not been pronounced innovations of intermediation services by new entrants that have constituted material incremental value to users as the service range is extended. Indeed, since many customers prefer several alternative sources of supply, this suggests resistence to one-stop packaging. This trait is true of both wholesale and retail markets.

The commitment of additional resources to support more diverse product configuration and delivery is likely to enhance pressures on regulatory constraints facing financial institutions. Near term, the nonbank bank vehicle offers a means for abrogating interstate banking restrictions and the ability of insurance and investment entities to acquire sizable banking footholds. The likelihood of reciprocal relaxation of barriers to bank positioning in insurance and investment banking will hinge on the ability of these nonbank firms to capture significant shares of markets where banks and thrifts have major stakes. On this count, without institutional dislocation or discontinuity (as in the past), some skepticism is warranted. A relatively gradual evolution of service terms will permit responses by institutions that result in relatively little change in market shares. On the basis of past experience, the principal source of uncertainty is the economic environment. Extreme economic conditions (whether high interest rates or low) would undoubtedly produce a considerably faster and broader pace of change.

NOTES

1. See Albert M. Wojnilower, *'Private Credit Demand, Supply, and Crunches – How Different are the 1980s?'* Paper presented to the annual meeting of the American Economic Association, Dallas, Texas, December 28, 1984.

2. For a detailed discussion of institutional patterns during the post-war era, see Benjamin M. Friedman, 'Financial Intermediation in the United States', in Richard C. Aspinwall and Robert A. Eisenbeis, eds., *Handbook for Banking Strategy* (New York: John Wiley & Sons, 1985).

3. See Harvey Rosenberg and Christine Pavel, 'Banking Services in Transition: The Effects of Nonbank Competitors', in Aspinwall and Eisenbeis, op. cit.

4. See Steven D. Felgran, 'Bank Entry into Securities Brokerage: Competitive and Legal Aspects', *New England Economic Review,* Federal Reserve Bank of Boston, November/December 1984.

5. See Chapter 2 in *Effects of Information Technology on Financial Services Systems* (Washington, DC: U.S. Congress, Office of Technology Assessment, OTA-CIT 202, September 1984).

6. For a review of banking costs see David Burras Humphrey, 'Costs and Scale Economies in Bank Intermediation', in Aspinwall and Eisenbeis, op. cit., and also 'The U.S. Payments System: Costs, Pricing, Competition, and Risk', *Monograph Series in Finance and Economics,* Salomon Brothers Center for the Study of Financial Institutions, Graduate School of Business Administration, New York University, Monograph 1984–1/2.

7. For a discussion of commercial bank entry into investment banking, see Samuel L. Hayes III, *'Commercial Banking Inroads into Investment Banking',* Working Paper, Harvard Business School, Division of Research, April 1984.

ACKNOWLEDGEMENT

The author gratefully acknowledges comments from Professor Robert Eisenbeis.

Chapter XVI

IMPLICATIONS OF INFORMATION TECHNOLOGY
FOR FINANCIAL INSTITUTIONS

by *Jack Revell*

BACKGROUND

There is one particular difficulty in analysing the impact of technology on the operations of financial institutions. When electronic methods were first applied some 20 years ago, they were used to solve problems that had arisen from the normal course of business. Gradually, however, the internal logic of technological development has begun to dictate the forms of the services offered by financial institutions. To begin with it was the problems that were susceptible to analysis, and technology was only a means of solving them. Later on the technology acquired to some extent a life of its own, and services came on offer largely because they were technically possible.

This factor has two consequences. In the first place it is very difficult at any stage of technological development to determine the relative importance of technology and other factors, such as inflation, the internationalisation of financial operations, or the growth of a mass market for financial services, in causing a particular change. The second consequence is the need for historical perspective and for the analysis of the impact of technology at each stage of its development. It is for these reasons that the paper starts with a brief outline of the stages in electronic technology, together with an analysis of the economics of the various services. This is followed by two main sections devoted respectively to payment services and to information and trading services.

TECHNOLOGY AND ECONOMIES OF SCALE

Stages in technological development

When technology was first applied to the operations of banks and other financial institutions, it took the form of large mainframe computers devoted to data processing. This use of new technology to maintain the

Fair, D.E., (ed.) Shifting Frontiers in Financial Markets.
© *1986, Martinus Nijhoff Publishers, Dordrecht/Boston/Lancaster. ISBN 90-247-3225-5.*
Printed in the Netherlands.

records of customers' accounts and for similar tasks was the answer to two problems besetting financial institutions in the 1960s. The first was the growth in the number of customers as affluence brought wider circles of the population into contact with financial institutions for the first time. The newly recruited customers tended to have small balances and to make frequent small transactions, a tendency that was intensified by the growth of 'salary accounts', into which the bulk of the population had their incomes paid, and the growing use of cheque guarantee cards; for insurance companies the spread of home and car ownership had much the same effect, while consumer credit brought similar problems to other institutions. The first problem was thus that the volume of paper to be handled had grown to such an extent that it would have been virtually impossible to continue with the old mixture of clerical labour and electrical accounting machines; there was just not enough labour available to financial institutions at a time of full employment.

Data processing computers provided some relief to this first problem and also to the second one, which was the constant rise in the ratio of operating (administrative) costs to the value of business handled (see Revell 1980). Because the paper still had to be handled several times before the figures were entered into the computer by hand, the relief was only partial. In some countries further progress has been made by entering details of all transactions at a terminal on the branch counter and sending these details by a telecommunications link to the computer centre without the further movement of paper. A somewhat similar use of computer technology is the automated clearing house, to which magnetic tapes of regular payments of income, mortgage payments, insurance premiums and so on are carried for exchange with other banks. The keys to increased productivity are the elimination of the movement of paper and the electronic recording of transaction details at the earliest possible stage, either at the branch counter or eventually by the customer himself without the intervention of the staff of the institution. So far progress towards these goals has been slow, although the technology to achieve them exists in a tried and tested form.

Computers are only part of the technology necessary to achieve greatly increased productivity; of equal importance are flexible telecommunications links between the place where the transaction is initiated and the computer centre. Up to the present time the norm for the computer processing of transaction details is the batch mode, in which the computer deals with a day's transactions at the end of the day and not as they occur. The communications from the branch to the computer centre are spasmodic, and the manual entering of transaction details in a form readable by the computer is not often in the branch. For some purposes (to be considered in the discussion of payments in the next main section) on-line working to the computer centre is essential; examples are automated teller machines (ATMs) in most countries and the answering of customers' balance enquiries. Almost everywhere this on-line working has been achieved by the use of telephone lines dedicated to the use of the financial institution and leased from the telecommunications authority; these lines have been a large element of fixed cost in the provision of the service. When a shared service is operated by several institutions, elaborate and expensive 'switch' computers add further to the fixed costs.

A new approach to on-line working is now possible. This is a network based on what are known as packet-switching principles. Unlike a normal telephone conversation or telex message, this does not require a continuous link between two points for the duration of the conversation or message; instead the system breaks each message into 'packets' of a standard length and routes them to the destination interleaved between messages from any other source. At the destination the full message is reconstituted from the packets; if the destination is off the line temporarily or during the night, messages can be stored for delivery as soon as possible. The messages sent on these networks can be originated either by an operator at a terminal or automatically by a computer or terminal. Between the network and the institution's own computer there is a 'gateway' mini-computer that translates the message into a form suitable for that particular model of computer, thus enabling all types of computer to communicate with each other.

Telecommunications links of this type are being established in many countries, often as public data networks open to all kinds of user. They have already had some influence on the development of electronic payment systems; the British public data network is being used by banks for their same-day interbank clearing system (CHAPS) and for the projected payment system at point of sale, and the London clearing banks recast their plans for these two services as soon as the public data system became available. Networks based on the same principles are often dedicated solely to traffic between institutions of a certain type or even to that of a single large institution. An early example was the international interbank telecommunications system SWIFT, which in its turn owed its origin to an attempt by European banks to counter the advantage derived by US banks from their private international telecommunications networks. Other international networks are operated by information providers (Reuter is an example) and computer companies.

These networks are able to carry out financial transactions of any type in a matter of seconds and are thus a complete substitute for leased lines. They have the further advantage that they can be used equally well for the internal traffic of a single institution and for traffic involving two or more institutions; they thus eliminate the need for computer 'switches' in inter-bank clearing, point-of-sale payment systems, and shared ATM systems. The effect of these flexible telecommunications networks is to transform what was mainly a fixed cost into a cost that varies with the volume of traffic.

The catchphrase of the present time is information technology, and the technical background for this consists of no more than the combination of computers and telecommunications links. The apparatus needed for a user's terminal is of the simplest kind. Even when the terminal is used solely for this purpose, it consists of no more than a full keyboard and a screen; this costs around £500. A micro-computer can be adapted to provide an interactive service by the addition of an acoustic coupler to link to a subscriber's telephone line. The screen can be that of the home television set, and the return communications to the information provider can come through a normal telephone link or a cable television channel, actuated by a key pad held in the hand.

Economies of scale

Economies of scale occur at many different levels in the application of technology to the operations of financial institutions. In the early days they came almost entirely from the cost, running into millions of pounds, of the large mainframe computers and the leased telephone lines necessary when on-line working was desired. There was no way of avoiding the economies of scale inherent in the large computers with the technology of the 1960s and 1970s, but from the beginning many institutions, particularly in Europe, avoided on-line working and much of the need for telecommunications links. They did this by using cash dispensers and even point-of-sale systems off line, recording transactions on magnetic tape that was transported to a computer terminal at the end of the day. This meant that the volume of transactions at a particular cash dispenser, supermarket or petrol station was no longer so crucial, but it enabled fraudulent use of plastic cards to go undetected for many hours.

One way of overcoming the handicap of economies of scale was by sharing facilities between several institutions, and by the present time this has developed to a great extent. Because it appeared to involve the suspension of competition in one aspect of business, this has attracted the attention of competition and cartel authorities in several countries, but they have generally recognised that banks have been driven into sharing because of the economies of scale and have imposed few conditions. If each institution continues to provide a particular service, for example automated teller machines, on its own, the service will be restricted to those locations at which the volume of transactions can justify the fixed costs of terminals and telecommunications, and the overall network available to customers of each institution will be much smaller than if there is sharing. The convenience of customers is thus a good competitive reason for sharing; since a significant number of people travel into foreign countries, the incentive to share extends beyond national boundaries.

In the course of time the economies of scale in computers and telecommunications have become far less important. Large mainframe computers are still needed to hold customers' account records, but the cost of computing power has fallen dramatically so that a mini-computer, costing perhaps £50,000, can today perform the same tasks as required a mainframe computer ten years ago. The impact of the flexible telecommunication networks has not yet been very great, but they will increasingly transform fixed costs into variable costs and enable electronic services to be extended to users with quite small volumes of traffic.

As fast as economies of scale disappear from their original positions, they reappear elsewhere. The services offered are becoming increasingly complex, and the customer is often given the choice of combining a number of services, sometimes involving another institution. The main economies of scale are now in the design of systems and in the marketing of the services. Once again, the answer lies in sharing, which often takes a particular form. Some institutions take the lead in designing systems and provide overall marketing for a branded service, which is then franchised to other institutions. The pioneers in this process were the credit card organisations Visa, MasterCard and Eurocheque. Holders of cards issued by banks all over the world under the name of the organisation can use them not only as charge cards, sometimes with extended credit, but also for obtaining local currency from ATMs in many different countries. Some individual banks are receiving considerable fee income from franchising cash management schemes and home banking systems.

PAYMENT SYSTEMS

Growth of electronic fund transfer systems

Although the term electronic fund transfers (EFT) is used to cover any use of electronic technology in payment services, it seems to have a connotation of payment services not supported by paper documents at any stage, of services performed largely by the customer himself without the help of the institution's staff. On this stricter definition of EFT it can be said with certainty that in no country can this yet be done in more than a few selected parts of the system. This is not really surprising because banks have used electronic technology in one area after another to reduce the costs of operating payment services; they may be on the brink of offering fully electronic systems, but they have not yet done so.

After converting their customer accounting to computers the banks in many countries began to develop automated clearing houses (ACHs) to handle the growing mass of regular payments. Even this service, which involves interbank payments for a large part of the traffic, is only now being fully automated as the ACHs begin to accept direct computer input from banks and their larger customers; for a long while the operation consisted of sorting the information on magnetic tapes that were physically transported to the clearing house from each bank. Such repetitive transactions were a large cost burden to banks, and even partial automation was a considerable relief. In some countries this process has been carried further by the automation of the clearing of large-value payments, with same-day settlement; CHIPS in New York and CHAPS in London are examples.

The next area for automation was the withdrawal of cash by personal customers, and this is the only customer delivery service that has so far been developed on a mass scale. To begin with, the machines were simple cash dispensers from which only a small fixed amount of banknotes could be withdrawn by inserting a plastic card; before long more elaborate machines called automated teller machines (ATMs) were used. The smallest difference between a cash dispenser and an ATM is that the customer has some choice over the amount to be withdrawn, but many ATMs tell the customer the balance on his account and enable him to deposit money and to order a chequebook; the most elaborate of all provide the facility of transferring amounts between accounts and of paying bills. Despite these extended facilities ATMs are used overwhelmingly for the withdrawal of cash, and it seems stupid to force customers who want only cash to wait around for somebody else to carry out complicated transactions when these extra facilities could be provided with a simple screen and keyboard at a cost of around 1 per cent of that of an ATM.

The attraction of ATMs is that they remove many customers from queues at bank counters and economise on staff time; as networks of these machines have been extended, they are already making some impact on costs and the need for staff. Their significance in the long run will turn out to be much greater than mere cost-saving. In the first place they are beginning to overcome the fear and ignorance of people about the use of electronic equipment, and already there is evidence that many customers prefer to use the machines even when there is no queue at the counter. The use of counter terminals by bank staff, at which the customer identifies himself and his account number by inserting a plastic card on his side of the counter, is also of considerable educational significance.

The long-run significance of ATMs lies also in the demonstration that, beyond a certain point, even the largest institutions have found it in their interest to share facilities with other institutions. Such sharing was a matter of course in many European countries, particularly among savings banks and co-operative banks, but it has begun to develop among commercial banks even in countries where the banks started by each developing its own network. It seems likely that within a few years many countries will have only one shared network, and that most others will have no more than two or three. This will greatly increase customer convenience because it will be possible to obtain cash anywhere in the country and increasingly to obtain local currency when abroad through arrangements between the networks; customers will not have to carry a multitude of plastic cards or need to memorise many different personal identification numbers.

This aspect of sharing is even more important with electronic payments at point of sale (usually referred to as EFTPOS or just POS) in supermarkets, department stores, petrol stations and other retail outlets, and it is doubtful whether any country could have more than one national network for this purpose. The reasons for sharing that arise from economies of scale are reinforced by the fact that retailers would be extremely reluctant to have more than one terminal at checkouts. One of the reasons for the slow development of EFTPOS has been the running dispute between banks and retailers, mainly over the share of costs to be borne by each of them. The dispute has hastened the development of EFTPOS in one way because banks fear that retailers will install their own systems (as one large retailer has done in Belgium).

One aspect of the sharing of electronic payment systems between financial institutions should be emphasised. Already the sharing of ATMs goes beyond institutions of the same kind and beyond the group that initiated the sharing. In some European countries commercial banks, savings banks, and co-operative banks have begun to combine their shared networks. In other countries the cartel or competition authority will insist that a shared network of ATMs and a POS system initiated by a group of dominant banks (such as the London clearing banks in the United Kingdom) should be thrown open to smaller competitors among commercial banks and to all banking institutions that wish to join. In some cases a complete outsider (usually a computer company) sets out to provide a shared service and invites all kinds of institution to join; this has happened in a projected ATM network in Britain called LINK, which was started by a computer company and has building societies, a small retail banking institution, the National Girobank and the Co-operative Bank as initial members. This factor is especially important because so many of the recent innovations in the form of accounts (money market funds and high-interest accounts, for example) have payment facilities of various kinds attached to them; when there are legal barriers to the offering of payment services by a non-banking institution, these can readily be overcome by employing a bank as an agent.

The real significance of the sharing of electronic payment networks lies in its effects on competition between large and small institutions of the same kind, between banking institutions of different kinds, and between banking institutions of all kinds and complete outsiders. Any kind of institution that is a member of a shared network can provide nearly as good a payment service for its customers as the largest bank can, and it seems certain that competition in banking will increase even further in the next few years. Small banks and near-banks, as well as non-banks, will have one considerable advantage in competing with those institutions that have hitherto dominated the payment mechanism, whether these are large commercial banks or savings banks: they are not saddled with the cost of maintaining large branch networks that have been rendered far less necessary by the automation of payments. As in the past, no doubt, the big battalions will win through in the end, but they will face a great deal of irritating guerrilla warfare from the smaller institutions in the meantime.

The last 'customer delivery system' for electronic payment services that figures in most discussion of the subject is home banking, in which the customer can initiate transactions of any kind (except the withdrawal of cash, although in some countries this can be delivered by the postman on the order of the bank) from his home. The first service provided in the United States consisted only of telephone instructions to bank staff, but the electronic services now being planned or in operation involve a screen (which may be on a personal computer or the television set) and a keyboard with full characters or just numerals. Many of the home banking services offered by banks have involved fairly heavy rentals for equipment, and progress has been slow. There is little doubt that eventually they will become a standard feature of the payment system, once the particular economics of this service have been realised.

With home banking there is no question of shared networks because the channels for communication are provided by the telephone or by cable television, and no institution can be debarred from participating. From the point of view of banks the service has the special advantage that all the investment, other than that involved in designing the system (which may well be franchised from another banking institution), is undertaken by others. For the bank customer, unless he is a fanatical devotee of information technology and home computers, the cost of renting the equipment and of telephone calls while he is connected to the bank computer may well seem prohibitive unless other services are provided to spread the cost. These other services are likely to be those standard on videotex systems, such as train, bus and air timetables, home shopping catalogues, and details of holidays. They are information services, particularly those interactive services in which the viewer can order the goods or services displayed on the screen. Home banking is thus on the borderline between payment services and the information and dealing services to be considered later, and many aspects of it can be left for a while.

Pricing

Electronic payment services are characterised by a very low marginal cost for each transaction and an average cost that declines as the volume of transactions increases. Viewing the matter in isolation it therefore seems sensible for banks to encourage customers to use the electronic services as fast as the necessary facilities can be provided. Although some of the costs of electronic services are fixed for the network as a whole, capacity can be increased by the addition of fairly small items of equipment, and average costs will fall below those of paper-based systems quite quickly. In this situation it will be to the advantage both of the bank and its customers to price electronic and paper services in such a way that the quickest transfer to the use of electronic services is achieved. The banks would thus price electronic payment services on a reasonable estimate of the volume of transactions that could be achieved rather than on present volumes and costs. Such 'incentive pricing' seems to be in the interest of both banks and customers, although in this country it is opposed by the consumer lobby and the Office of Fair Trading, which say that the consumer must always be given a fair choice between electronic and paper services.

Although the question appears to be relatively simple when viewed on its own, there are several other points to be brought into consideration. The first is that there is bound to be a long and uneasy transition period, probably lasting at least a decade, in which the electronic and paper systems will be existing side by side. It will probably be fairly easy to achieve 60 to 70 per cent penetration of electronic services within a few years, but there will remain a hard core of those who refuse to use them and certain types of transaction for which paper will continue to be used. The cost of payment services as a whole may not come down all that fast.

This consideration is reinforced by the fact that payment services remain labour-intensive, mainly because they still require a branch network, the extent of which plays a large part in determining the size of the total staff employed. The need for both branches and staff will decline during the transition period at a time when newcomers to payment services, unencumbered by a branch network, are offering strong competition. Although the size of staff can be trimmed over a short period by the suspension of recruitment and early retirement, many banks will be overmanned for a long while because of the difficulties and costs of discharging staff in mid-career. Some alleviation can be secured by retraining staff for ancillary services, particularly financial counselling; at a time when competition is also increasing in these services, this may not cope with the problem.

The last factor is one that was raised in my OECD report on electronic fund transfers (Revell 1983). It is the probable demise of the current account, coupled with a general increase in the cost of deposits. The argument can be summarised briefly. The high interest rates of an inflationary period have long caused customers to economise on current account balances, on which they receive a very low rate of interest or none at all, and to transfer excess balances to interest-bearing accounts, even for a short time. Banks have had to pay money market rates or rates close to them on an increasing proportion of their deposits, and in a recession it has not been possible to raise loan rates of interest to the same extent. The result has been a narrowing of the margin between total interest received and paid, a fact that is borne out for many countries by the 'Costs and Margins' statistics for the period 1978–82 given in Revell (1985).

So far the argument has depended on the high rates of interest caused by inflation, but the impact of EFT is already being felt. The ability to transfer balances from current accounts to other accounts at an ATM or by home banking would mean that people would begin to hold money in current accounts only for the short period necessary to carry out a transaction. Even before people have acquired this habit, some banks have begun to provide the service for them by 'sweeping' their accounts of excess balances at the end of each day. Banks will respond to this situation in one of two main ways: either they will unify all a customer's accounts into one interest-bearing account with full payment facilities or they will offer market rates of interest on current accounts. Some current accounts will probably remain, either because of unrepealed legal requirements or as a means of charging for payment services, a kind of compensating balance.

The corollary of the loss of 'free' or low-interest balances is that banks are having to face the prospect of charging realistically for payment services instead of subsidising them out of the interest margin. This is proving difficult, especially as 'free' or subsidised payment services have been a competitive weapon in recent years; some banks in Britain have recently moved further towards 'free' banking by removing the minimum balance requirement, and it will be interesting to see how long this response to fierce competition remains possible. To the extent that banks begin to move towards charging full or nearly full costs of payment services their interests will still be in using 'incentive pricing' to secure as quick a transfer to electronic methods as they deem desirable. The other factors that have been considered here show that the issue is much more complicated than appeared at first sight.

INFORMATION SERVICES AND DEALING

In the discussion on payment services the technical background to information technology has been described; to the extent that payment traffic is information, the other side of the picture, the impact of cheaper, speedier and more extensive information, has also been partly illuminated. It is now necessary to look briefly at those services in which payments are not the prime consideration, although we have already noted the tendency to combine payments with other services offered to retail customers.

Non-banking institutions

The impact of electronic technology on banks has not been restricted to payments, and by the same token the technology has also been used by other kinds of financial institution. All financial institutions have customer accounts, and these have nearly all been transferred to computers; the smallest institutions use computer bureaux or form consortia that run computer centres. The analysis of the payment mechanism has led us to think that many more institutions will be involved in payments through equal access to the telecommunications networks that are increasingly a feature of electronic payment systems. Information technology is thus enabling some other institutions to become more bank-like, providing strong competition to established banks in the process.

Many of the uses of information technology have nothing to do with account records or payments, but with disseminating information about the services of competing institutions; this is particularly so where many customers approach the institutions through brokers, as in insurance. The task of the broker is to find for his client the best service available to meet his particular needs, and for this up-to-date information is essential. There are already networks in operation giving details of all policies offered by companies and the necessary supporting information. These networks may be established co-operatively by the insurance companies themselves, but they may equally be organised by a computer firm, possibly in association with the telecommunications authority; the information may be fed into the network by the insurance companies themselves or it may be the responsibility of a specialist information provider.

Other examples of a similar kind could be given, but the main point is that speedy and up-to-date (even up-to-the-minute) information on financial matters and on factors influencing them has become a most important product in its own right. This information market is one in which organisations of all kinds, bank and non-bank, financial and non-financial, specialist providers of information and non-specialists, are in competition, with the telecommunications authorities taking a keen interest in the maximum use of their data networks and other facilities. Because many of the transactions that they handle have to be executed without delay, banks are deeply involved as information providers. They have several special advantages: they have long been a source of information for their customers, both corporate and retail, on a wide range of topics; even more important they are the only source for immediate information on the customer's cash position.

Banks have already begun to exploit their advantages as information providers, first for their corporate customers and more tentatively for households. The services concerned are called 'cash management' in corporate banking and 'home banking' for households. Although both of these titles conjure up pictures of instant manipulation of bank accounts, very few of them have yet reached this advanced stage; most of them provide information on the state of the customer's accounts at the end of the previous business day (throughout the country or throughout the world for large corporate customers) and access to general financial information without allowing him to take immediate action in response. The most sophisticated systems for multinational customers are much more complex; they provide information in the form of interest rate and exchange rate forecasts for a number of countries, demonstrate how a position may be hedged, carry out routine adjustments according to a set computer program, and enable the treasurer to effect important transactions immediately. These are still very rare.

Three important lessons can be derived from this brief description of financial information systems:

1. pressure soon arises for systems that started as conveyors of information to provide for payments and transfers as well,

2. banks and other financial institutions will largely be judged in the future on the convenience and sophistication of their information services,

3. these institutions are being drawn into a largely new market, in which they have certain advantages but in which they will meet strong competition from other information providers.

Treating home banking as the small-scale equivalent of cash management may not be entirely accurate, either historically or technically, but it underlines a particular view of the future information/payment system. This will consist of a vast number of terminals (screens and keyboards) in different locations, such as homes, offices, bank branches, public buildings, shops and so on. Certain of them (ATMs) will also disburse and receive cash, and those on shop counters will be specialised to payment use, but all the others will give access to a wide range of information services, with payments as a useful and necessary adjunct. All these terminals will be linked to a data network conveying traffic between the terminals and the computers of financial institutions and other information providers. This state of affairs is not so far off.

Organised markets

Information technology has been applied for some time to organised markets such as money markets, the foreign exchange market and securities markets, and it is already apparent that the whole nature of these markets will probably be altered as a consequence. As with payments, electronic technology was first applied to data processing. In several countries paper certificates of registration for securities have been abandoned in favour of computer registration. In many markets transactions are recorded by computer, and the accounting and settlement details are prepared automatically for participants. These are almost primitive applications of electronic technology, but recent developments carry things much further.

In money markets and the foreign exchange market the dealers are nearly all banks, served by a number of brokers. The first application of information technology was a one-way service of information on rates, brought up to date constantly by an information provider outside the banking system (Reuter, for example). Before long this was changed to an information and dealing service, with which banks could obtain quotations from a number of banks simultaneously and do business with one of them. The important features of this system are the following:

1. it calls into question the need for brokers,
2. it is an international market because a bank may contact other banks linked to the system throughout the world,
3. it demonstrates once again that the provision of price information leads very quickly to the development of a dealing system.

The present upheaval on the Stock Exchange in this country, with the provision of elaborate electronic systems for price information, has much the same implications, although in some respects they go even further. Some people are already querying whether dealing should not be added to the electronic information systems and suggesting that trading floors are an anachronism; since the main participants in the London market will be the broking arms of British and international banks, this may come about. One of the main features is the provision of simultaneous information on prices in London and New York, and already there is talk of a completely international stock market with 24-hour trading round the world and global markets in New York, London and Tokyo. Earlier the US National Commission on Electronic Fund Transfers (1977, pp. 186–90) reported a paper in which Paul A. Volcker (later the Chairman of the Board of Governors of the Federal Reserve System) discussed the desirability of money markets operating round the clock, with interest paid by the hour rather than by the day.

As a footnote, perhaps an author who lives in a rather more tranquil environment may raise the somewhat pathetic query whether the condition of the human race will be greatly benefited by people staying out of bed to conduct financial transactions and whether it is necessary to seek such speed and round-the-clock working just because it is technically possible.

REFERENCES

1. National Commission on Electronic Fund Transfers (1977), *International Payments Symposium* (Washington, DC: NCEFT).
2. Revell, J.R.S. (1980), *Costs and Margins in Banking: an International Survey* (Paris: OECD).
3. Revell, J.R.S. (1983), *Banking and Electronic Fund Transfers* (Paris: OECD).
4. Revell, J.R.S. (1985), *Costs and Margins in Banking: an International Survey: Statistical Supplement 1978–1982* (Paris: OECD).

Chapter XVII

SHIFTING FINANCIAL FRONTIERS: IMPLICATIONS FOR
FINANCIAL INSTITUTIONS

by *Tadeusz M. Rybczynski*

The financial industry has been and continues to be in a state of flux in all
developed countries. The implications of the changes which have been
taking place are widespread, profound and raise important issues not only
for those using the facilities of the industry and those concerned with its
efficient functioning but also for the members of the industry itself. It is this
last aspect I would like to examine in this paper and also endeavour to see
what the changes now under way mean to financial institutions, what
answers they may elicit and how these answers may alter the wider issues
now coming to the fore.

I propose to approach the task by, firstly, examining what has been
happening in the financial arena; secondly, discussing in a summary way
why these developments are occurring; and, finally, analysing the implications of the trends now gathering momentum from the point of view of the
industry but with reference to the consequences on the economy as a whole.

The shift in financial frontiers has been accelerating in the recent years
and although particularly marked in the US and the UK has not been
confined to these two countries. It has also covered all other developed
countries even though its impact and pace have been weaker elsewhere,
partly because of the different nature of financial systems in Europe and
Japan and partly because of the different phase of their development. My
paper concentrates on the situation in the UK, though I will also make
occasional and brief comments about the situation in other countries.

THE EXTERNAL AND INTERNAL FRONTIERS

The shift in financial frontiers has two different dimensions. The first,
which can be described as an external dimension relates to the extension of
the external frontiers within which the finance industry has been operating.
The extension of external frontiers in turn has two elements, that resulting

Fair, D.E., (ed.) Shifting Frontiers in Financial Markets.
© *1986, Martinus Nijhoff Publishers, Dordrecht/Boston/Lancaster. ISBN 90-247-3225-5.*
Printed in the Netherlands.

in an increase in the number of clients for the existing and new services offered by the industry but situated in a given area; and, secondly, that leading to the extension of the geographical area over which the services are made available.

The second dimension of the shift in financial frontiers can be described as the tendency for the removal and disappearance of internal frontiers between the activities undertaken by and confined to the institutions which have tended to specialise in providing them. Needless to say the weakening and indeed the breaking down of such internal barriers has occurred only wh. e they existed because of the formal or informal barriers created to separate different activities among different institutions, resulting in partial or full specialisation.

As I mentioned before, the degree of specialisation of the financial institutions differs between various countries, depending on the one hand on the regulatory framework, – which I will refer to later on – and, on the other, on the stage of development of the financial system. In this respect it is worth mentioning that until fairly recently the financial systems in the US and the UK tended to be characterised by the specialisation of financial institutions; the German, Austrian and Swiss systems have been and continue to be characterised by what can be described as a 'universal approach', – the system in Japan and other major countries in Europe sharing to varying degree the characteristics of both.

The 'internal barriers' dividing various financial activities are numerous, separating the broad field of activities as well as the narrower ones within them. Those relating to the former – broad areas of activities – correspond to the principal functions carried out by the financial systems and fall into three categories. They are, firstly, the provision and the management of the payments mechanism; secondly, the collection and the employment of savings; and, finally, the facilities for transferring current savings directly to their users as well as transferring past savings embodied in finance and real assets from existing owners to other owners.

The first type of activity can be said to cover deposit banking proper, involving current account and also time deposits, and is undertaken in principle by banks and the institutions undertaking the same function, such as the Giro institutions in Europe; the second comprises the collection of savings and is provided by non-bank financial intermediaries such as building societies, life insurance companies, hire purchase, and similar institutions; the third relates to what is described as investment banking, i.e. the underwriting of securities and fund management, and is undertaken by organisations which can be described as market intermediaries which, through the medium of financial markets and above all capital markets, bring together providers, collectors and managers of accumulated savings, (be it ultimate individuals, banks and non-bank financial intermediaries) and the users of such funds which, in addition to non-financial units – including government and public bodies – include banks and non-bank financial intermediaries.

THE SHIFT OF EXTERNAL FRONTIERS

The external shift in frontiers in the UK has involved, firstly, an increase in the number of clients availing themselves of the financial services offered by the industry and situated in the same geographical areas as previously covered; secondly, an expansion in the geographical areas over which they have been made available by the members of the financial industry; and, finally, the provision of entirely new services and 'products' by old and new members of the financial industry over the continuously expanding market.

The expansion in the number of clients is self-explanatory and needs no comment. There are numerous statistics showing that the number of people with bank accounts, with accounts in non-bank financial intermediaries such as the building societies and life assurance companies, and those using the services of capital markets and other financial markets has been and continues to increase. This increase has reflected an advance both in the number of customers within the areas where such services have been offered in the past as well as within the new geographical areas including those overseas.

Likewise there is voluminous information showing a large increase in the type of services and 'products' offered by the financial industry. They comprise new methods of money transmission, especially by industry in-cluding new 'cash management' accounts, as well as new types of facilities offered by non-bank financial intermediaries providing a large number of different 'deposit' accounts in different currencies and various types of savings contract linked to different types of financial and other assets, such as equity linked, real property linked, index linked and other types; and new types of marketable financial instruments handled by the capital markets such as convertibles, warrants in a number of different currencies including composite currencies such as SDRs, ECUs, etc.

While all the elements of the external shift in financial frontiers have been and continue to be important, those concerning the geographical expansion of the market have been particularly noticeable and commented upon, being described as the 'internationalisation' or 'globalisation' of finance.

The expansion in the size of the market (that is to say its deepening and widening), as covered by the finance industry in the UK, is reflected in an absolute and relative increase (i.e. in relation to GNP) in the financial assets held by the personal sector and by other sectors in the UK as well as in the rapid growth in turnover in the various financial markets for which statistics are collected. This development has not been special to the UK but has been shared by all developed and developing countries. It indicates that (as shown in the numerous works of R. Goldsmith) finance has been and continues to be one of the 'growth' industries – its rate of expansion exceeding comfortably that of the nominal GNP. The main reason for this is that an increase in per capita and total income leads to an accumulation of capital – financial and real – a process which increases the volume of financial (and real) assets and the use of financial channels through which new savings are placed and the transfer of previously accumulated savings to new users.

Probably for the UK the outward shift in financial frontiers has been greater and faster than in most other developed countries, with the exception of the US. This is so because the UK financial system has been in an advanced stage of development and because, as commented upon later on, the UK has re-established its role as one of the major international outward-looking financial centres forming an integral and pivotal part of the world financial system, involved not only in domestic financial affairs but also in overseas financial markets, international financial markets (i.e. 'Euro-markets') and acting as an entrepot centre.

WEAKENING AND/OR DISAPPEARANCE OF INTERNAL FRONTIERS

Accompanying the shift in the outward financial frontiers in the UK (and also in other industrial countries) has been a marked weakening and/or disappearance of internal financial barriers. In contrast to some other industrial countries, and above all the US, the internal frontiers or demarcation lines which existed in the UK after World War II and in the preceding years were not of a statutory kind but were essentially self-imposed and of an informal type, though backed by the powers of suasion of the Bank of England (the Central Bank), as well as some restraints embodied in statutory form and applying to some financial institutions such as building and friendly societies.

The weakening of internal financial frontiers in the UK has involved the entry of the predominantly specialised institutions operating mainly within one of three broad areas of finance mentioned before (i.e. banking and the payments system, the collection of savings by financial intermediaries, and the functions undertaken by market intermediaries and relating principally to capital markets) into the two other areas dominated by other, rather specialised financial institutions. In other words this has involved a move by banks into activities previously catered for by non-bank financial intermediaries and into those previously catered for by market intermediaries; a move by non-bank financial intermediaries into services offered by banks and also by market intermediaries; and a move by market intermediaries into services provided by non-bank financial intermediaries as well as by banks.

The increasing 'de-specialisation' or the weakening and disappearance of 'internal' frontiers has involved a trend towards conglomeration in the financial area. Until recently this trend has been confined to members of the industry, old and new entrants. While there were some attempts to enter the financial area by non-financial firms, such as a few retail chains setting up or indeed buying small banks to provide such service to their customers, by and large these were short-lived, ending in their disposal to existing financial firms in the industry. It is only very recently that substantial financial intermediary firms were acquired by non-financial firms. Whether or not this marks a decisive step in loosening the demarcation lines between financial and non-financial firms is discussed later on.

Of these three basic trends towards conglomeration the trend between institutions operating in the investment banking area and involving the absorption of market intermediaries and above all jobbers and brokers has been the most recent and has received the most attention. It has been most recent because it was forced on the industry by outside intervention designed to improve competition in this sector (the case brought by the Office of Fair Trading, an official body charged with ensuring that anti-competitive practices are removed – to abolish fixed commissions) and embraced wholeheartedly by the City authorities and The Stock Exchange as a means of strengthening and helping the City to maintain and increase its role as an international financial centre. At the heart of the change here has been the abolition of single capacity among members of The Stock Exchange (i.e. between jobbers and brokers) and the agreement that these market intermediaries could be owned by other firms (financial and non-financial).

As a result of these changes the (non-statutory) barriers to the involvement of banks and other financial intermediaries have disappeared following the relaxation of the informal ban operated by the Bank of England to the ownership of merchant banks by clearing banks some twenty years ago (when the Midland Bank was allowed to acquire Samuel Montagu).

This change in informal barriers and self-imposed demarcation lines has so far resulted in the disappearance of all the jobbing firms and virtually all large broking firms as independent units and the emergence (once full control is acquired and fixed commissions are formally abandoned) of new financial conglomerates undertaking the functions of the banking, financial and market intermediaries. As shown in Table 1 below, all clearing banks will be involved in these areas as well as the eight merchant banks, twelve foreign banks, four financial intermediaries and three market intermediaries. Likewise non-bank financial intermediaries such as the financial groups concentrating on the collection of savings by way of unit trust and similar bodies have been acquiring broking firms (market intermediaries) with some also acquiring interest in banks.

As mentioned before the disappearance of barriers between investment banking and the allied functions undertaken by market intermediaries by way of their virtual absorption by the banks and the non-bank financial intermediaries has been associated with the move by the banks into the area of the non-bank financial intermediaries and the tendency of the latter to move into the area dominated by the former. The move by the banks into the area dominated by the non-bank financial intermediaries has covered both the collection of savings and the employment of funds. As far as the collection of savings is concerned the large clearing banks have had an interest in acting in a fiduciary capacity as trustees. However, until the 1970s their involvement had tended to be entirely passive, acting as administrators and agents and, when buying, holding or selling capital market instruments for their clients. In the last fifteen years or so they have become very active in this field, creating large trust departments, creating open-ended trusts, and also expanding the types of activities undertaken by their merchant banking subsidiaries. On the fund-using side the large deposit banks, which until the early post-war years concentrated on the provision of short-term working capital for industry, extended their involvement in the provision of medium term finance to industry (competing with the Euro-bond markets dominated by market intermediaries), the provision of long-term and short-term credit to consumers and competing with specialised non-bank financial intermediaries, such as building societies in the case of the former and hire-purchase companies in the case of the latter.

On their part the non-bank financial intermediaries such as the building societies have been offering money transmission services and are now in the course of seeing a relaxation of the types of lending undertaken by them.

Table 1. Links of banks and non-bank financial intermediaries with market intermediaries

	Jobber	Broker	Market-maker in		Broker-dealers	Fund-managers	Merchant banks	Banker
			Gilts	Equities				
Clearing banks								
3	√	√	√	√	(?)	√	√	n.a.
1	–	–	√	√	?	√	√	n.a.
Merchant banks (members of the accepting houses committee)								
4	√	√	√	√	?	√	√	n.a.
1	√	–	–	–	?	√	√	n.a.
1	√	–	–	√	?	√	√	n.a.
1	–	√	–	–	?√	√	√	n.a.
Foreign banks								
5	–	√	√	√	√?	√	√	n.a.
1	–	√	√	–	√?	√	√	n.a.
4	–	–	√	√	–	–	–	n.a.
2	–	√	–	–	–	√	√	√
Financial intermediaries (savings-collecting institutions)								
1	–	√	–	–	–	–	–	√
2	–	√	–	–	–	–	–	√
1 (life assurance)	–	–	–	–	–	–	–	√
Market intermediaries								
2	–	√	–	–	–	–	–	?
1	√	√	–	–	–	–	–	√

FACTORS BEHIND THE WEAKENING OF INTERNAL BARRIERS

Economic factors

What were the factors responsible for the weakening and disappearance of the internal barriers between the various financial activities in the UK and those leading to the strong tendency towards conglomeration and changes in the size and character of the financial industry? Broadly speaking the factors behind this development fall into two groups. They are the fundamental economic factors and the regulatory framework. The former (fundamental economic factors) in turn include an increase in per capita and total income and technological advance within the industry. The latter (regulatory framework) cover the legal and institutional framework within which the industry operates.

The increase in per capita and total income (already referred to earlier when discussing the shift in external frontiers) bears also on the weakening and/or disappearance of the internal frontiers separating various activities. This development – which has made the financial industry a growth industry – has provided a stimulus and incentive to the management of the existing financial institutions to undertake activities offered by other institutions, provide new services and by doing so cross the previously well-delineated frontiers. It has also provided incentives for new firms to enter the industry.

Technological advance in the financial industry has had two results. The first has to do with a reduction in the real cost of providing services and reducing the margin between the cost of funds paid to the ultimate providers of savings, and the price paid by ultimate users. They arise as a result of new machinery and physical handling of old and new services. The second covers financial innovations which in turn comprise the development of new techniques and also new financial instruments which facilitate the reduction in the margin between the cost and price of funds by changing what may be described as a so-called 'kinked' opportunity curve reflecting a certain combination of risk, rewards and liquidity and other characteristics in a smoother curve.

That the application of technologically advanced machinery and above all computer and other types of labour-saving office machinery has reduced the real effective cost of financial services especially as regards money transmission is beyond doubt. This is also true of other services, such as the purchase and sale of foreign exchange and the transfer of financial assets.

Of the financial techniques which have been important in reducing the gap between the 'cost' and 'price' of funds, that of liability management has been most prominent. The technique replacing 'asset management' involves banks and similar non-bank financial intermediaries lending funds whenever there are attractive opportunities by raising funds by way of Certificates of Deposit (or similar instruments) mainly from other financial institutions subject only to capital ratio constraints rather than limiting such lending to the deposit liabilities in hand. Of other techniques which have come into prominence in the last few years those requiring mention are, firstly, the 'interest rates swap' and, secondly, the 'exchange rate swap'. They minimise risk and introduce an additional degree of flexibility to the behaviour of the financial institutions.

The new financial instruments which have appeared in the last fifteen years or so on the UK financial scene are numerous. They include those listed on the capital markets such as convertibles and warrants, and non-marketable instruments such as syndicated medium term loans, short-term instruments such as Certificates of Deposit, etc.

New financial instruments have enlarged the choice to the financial institutions of how to employ their funds and raise the funds as well as enhancing the scope of operations for market intermediaries when bringing together the users and the providers of funds.

Regulatory framework

While economic factors have been important in the weakening of internal barriers (as well as external frontiers) within which financial institutions in the UK have operated, the changes in the regulatory framework have been at least of equally great significance. Broadly speaking the UK, unlike the US, has not had and in principle still does not have a well-defined statutory legal and institutional framework regulating the scope and nature of the activities of various financial institutions. Although some specialised institutions such as friendly societies and building societies, and a few others, have been subject to special legislation guiding their activities, by and large banks, non-bank financial intermediaries and market intermediaries – apart from being subject to company legislation – have been subject only to the informal guide-lines issued by the Bank of England (the central bank) and to self-imposed rules and regulations such as those applicable to members of the (unified) Stock Exchange and to companies wishing to use their facilities.

The informal or eclectic approach of the UK authorities toward the financial industry has been reflected in the encouragement and support given to self-regulation as shown by the creation of the Council for the Securities Industry and moral suasion exercised by the Bank of England, regarded as the de facto supervisionary body covering all activities in the City, the financial centre of the UK. Until the mid-1960s the view of the authorities had been that it was desirable that the demarcation lines between the three broad functional areas previously mentioned, i.e. banks, savings-collecting by non-bank financial intermediaries and market intermediaries, should be maintained. The only exception to this rule was merchant banking which combined all these activities. However, the banking activities of merchant banks had been until recently – and for some still are – of a wholesale type and because of the emphasis on the acceptance business have been subject to special rules imposed by the Bank of England.

This division of labour emerged before World War I as a result of the different interests of the different financial institutions – large clearing banks concentrating as a result of their experience on the provision of working capital and the management of the payments system, non-bank financial intermediaries on the collection and the use of long-term savings, and issuing houses and other market intermediaries on helping the ultimate users of funds to raise them through the medium of capital markets.

In the last twenty years the official view appears, however, to have been changing gradually, favouring not only the removal of internal boundaries among the various activities but also trying to introduce certain safeguards to fund-providers, designed to strengthen the stability of the system as a whole. This change in attitude can be attributed to intensive competition across the rapidly broadening scene of financial services and geographic markets from other financial and also non-financial firms such as retail groups.

Reflecting this changing attitude has been the supporting attitude of the authorities in the 1960s towards the acquisition of hire-purchase and leasing companies by large clearing banks, the relaxation of the ban on banks acquiring the control of merchant banks, encouragement to foreign and other banks and other financial intermediaries to enter the field of retail and wholesale banking and savings-collecting business. However, accompanying this change in official views has been a growing emphasis on consumer protection and supervision. This has assumed the form of new rules regulating the way banks and other financial institutions operate, the introduction of a deposit protection scheme, relaxation of restrictions on building societies and, recently, the support for conglomeration of financial activities subject however to the quasi voluntary system of regulation.

The UK regulatory framework is now in a transitional phase. It is moving away from informal and self-imposed rules – backed, however, by the 'moral suasion' of the authorities – favouring specialisation but in no way restricting the geographic area of operation or indeed the supporting geographic concentration of certain activities, to giving encouragement to the conglomeration of financial activities and also the acquisition of financial firms by non-financial enterprises. This change in the attitude of the authorities has also been accompanied by a trend toward the introduction of formal direct and also indirect controls regulating the way various activities are carried out.

THE REGULATORY FRAMEWORK AND POLICY ISSUES

The present evolution of the regulatory framework in the UK with its implicit acceptance of a conglomerate approach raises the question of the way the authorities will deal with the three basic problems associated with the functioning of any financial system. They are stability of the system, consumer protection, and competition. Though analytically separate they are closely interconnected.

The problem of stability – arising from fractional banking, as distinct from 100 per cent cover banking – is to reconcile the need for risk-taking by financial intermediaries and indeed ultimate fund-providers with the need to contain risk-taking to the resources of risk-takers without impairing the ability of banks and non-bank financial institutions to meet their obligation to their depositors which, if not met, would result in financial panic and crisis. The approach which seems to characterise the UK approach is, firstly, to institute deposit insurance schemes for depositors, financed by flat premiums; secondly, to control capital and liquidity as well as subsidiary ratios of banks and financial intermediaries; thirdly, to require adequate public information.

To protect consumer and depositor from conflicts of interest especially in conglomerate units and to ensure that the risk attaching to various uses of funds and the rewards they are expected to earn are sufficiently known to fund-providers, the authorities are now in the course of reorganising the quasi-voluntary supervisory body and have created a new body, the Securities Investment Board (SIC). The SIC will receive statutory backing but its function will be to help evolve codes of conduct by members of the financial community and supervise them. Furthermore the authorities' aim appears to be that different activities should be carried out by separately capitalised subsidiaries acting at arm's-length – resembling in some ways the bank holding company approach adopted in the US.

Finally the UK authorities seem to be trying to generate sufficient competitive pressures by aiming to have a sufficient number of participants in various segments of the market. To this end they have been encouraging new firms, British and overseas, to enter the industry.

In brief, the now evolving regulatory framework in the UK appears to envisage that the problems of stability of the financial system, adequate competitive pressures and the protection of depositors and investors can be reconciled with a change in the structure of the industry involving a trend toward conglomerations (including conglomeration between financial and non-financial units) provided the members of the industry behave in a way increasingly regulated and monitored by bodies relying in the ultimate analysis on statutory procedures.

THE STRUCTURE OF THE INDUSTRY

How the structure of the financial industry, that is to say the number and size and distribution of firms, will be affected is not easy to assess. This is because of the continuing increase in the size of the market for financial products and services (outward shift in frontiers), because of changes in the degree of substitutability and complementarity between the various types of financial services, and because of changes in the unit costs of providing them as determined by technology and competitive pressures.

One important development important to both the authorities and the members of the industry is the trend towards the explicit pricing of various services and the tendency to 'unbundling' various groups of services. The 'unbundling' and separate pricing of services is likely to help delineate (disaggregated) markets for various financial products and services and consequently the efficiency with which the market allocates economic resources.

As in the non-financial area the probable outcome is the emergence in the UK of a few large financial conglomerates operating on a world scale surrounded by medium-size units operating on a larger or smaller scale in the selected segments of the market.

THE EVOLUTION OF THE FINANCIAL SYSTEM

The present change in the UK financial system should be looked at in the wider perspective of the evolution of the system accompanying the process of economic development. This subject has been examined by a number of serious students of the role of finance, among those deserving special mention are Gerscherkon and Goldsmith.

The former has argued that the financial system, and above all banks, can be and are used in the early process of industrialisation to channel savings towards the creation of fixed industrial capital with all the risks that involves. The latter has argued that all countries experiencing growth have one feature in common – the ratio of financial assets to GNP continues to increase.

My highly stylised version is that the financial system changes as economic advance continues, moving from a bank-orientated system to a market-orientated system and then to a strongly market-orientated system.

The bank-orientated system, characteristic of an early stage of economic growth, is associated with non-financial enterprises obtaining the bulk of external finance from banks and specialised institutions such as building societies, which are the principal institutions collecting savings and using them for productive purposes while also managing the payments transfer system. In such a system capital markets play a relatively modest role.

The market-orientated system, characteristic of advanced stages of economic growth, involves an increasing reliance of non-financial enterprises on external funds raised through capital markets from fund-providers; there being a fairly clear dividing line between banks, financial intermediaries and market intermediaries.

Finally, mature economies tend to have a strongly market-orientated financial system characterised by the dependence of non-financial enterprises on external funds raised in financial markets and also by financial institutions, banks and non-bank financial intermediaries, raising a significant part of the funds they employ in lending and otherwise also through the medium of financial markets. At this stage a financial system is characterised by 'securitisation' – to use the fashionable American phrase.

At the risk of great simplification one can say that the first stage of the evolution of the financial system is likely to be associated with a 'conglomerate' type of financial structure; the second with a specialised type of financial structure; and the third by a conglomerate type of financial structure surrounded by some specialised and quasi-specialised financial firms.

The UK as well as the US is now entering the third phase of the evolution of the financial system. Most of the countries of the continent of Europe are still moving into the second phase but might move into the third stage missing out part of phase two. And Japan is likewise moving almost directly from the first phase into the third stage of the evolution of the system.

Needless to say, this transformation of the financial system is as a result of the working of economic forces leading to a shift in the external frontiers and the disappearance of internal frontiers – as substitutability among financial products and services increases. Changes in the regulatory framework accompanying this transformation are in essence a response of the authorities to the working of economic forces. Such changes also take into account, if relevant, the impact of economies of scale, and the way inefficient units in the industry can and should move out without having a detrimental effect on the functioning of the market through the impact on confidence.

IMPLICATIONS FOR FINANCIAL INSTITUTIONS

If the stylised view of the evolution of the financial system is even approximately correct the choice facing the members of the UK financial community at present is to explore the opportunities of benefits offered by economies of scale in their operations in relation to the growth of the total market and to decide if conglomeration is likely to improve their competitive position or if they see the path of partial or full specialisation more attractive. This is the process now under way, but its final result will not be seen for some time to come.

Part E

IMPLICATIONS FOR MONETARY CONTROL AND THE
SUPERVISION OF FINANCIAL INSTITUTIONS

Chapter XVIII

RECENT DEVELOPMENTS IN THE STRUCTURE AND REGULATION OF THE CANADIAN FINANCIAL SYSTEM

by *Charles Freedman**

INTRODUCTION

In recent years there have been strong pressures for change in the financial systems of many countries. In some, the principal thrust has been one of removing controls on interest rates or quantitative restrictions on credit. In the case of Canada, the few interest rate controls that had existed had been removed much earlier, in the late 1960s, and therefore the distortions that surrounded the interaction of high market interest rates and controlled deposit or loan rates in many countries in the 1970s simply did not occur. The principal developments in Canada have been, first, the introduction and spread of new types of instruments and, second, the pressures by the various sectors of the financial industry to move into what had been each other's traditional territory. The former has had implications for the way in which monetary policy is implemented[1] but not for regulation. The latter has had no effect on monetary policy but may in the future have a significant effect on regulation and supervision. The focus of this paper is on the relationship between the structure of the financial industry and the type of regulation that is needed, with the emphasis on the ongoing Canadian experience.

In the next section of this paper I lay out the goals of regulatory policy in the financial structure. This is followed by a description of the Canadian financial structure and of the instruments of financial regulation used to achieve the desired goals in the context of this structure. I then discuss in some detail the sources of pressure for change in the Canadian financial system in the last few years and conclude by setting out the possible regulatory responses to these types of change.

---

* The views expressed in this paper are those of the author and no responsibility for them should be attributed to the Bank of Canada.

Fair, D.E., (ed.) Shifting Frontiers in Financial Markets.
© *1986, Martinus Nijhoff Publishers, Dordrecht/Boston/Lancaster. ISBN 90-247-3225-5.*
Printed in the Netherlands.

GOALS OF REGULATORY POLICY IN THE FINANCIAL SECTOR

In Figure 1 the ultimate goals of policy are presented in the left-hand column and the instruments potentially available to the authorities to achieve those goals are laid out in the right-hand column. In the centre column are listed what I call the intermediate goals, which are the means whereby the ultimate goals can be achieved but which are not instruments, in the sense that they are not the techniques used by the authorities to achieve their objectives. The solid lines connecting the items in the figure represent the positive links between the various elements in the scheme and the dashed lines represent unwanted side-effects that can result from the use of a given instrument. Note that most instruments impinge on more than one goal.

In most countries there appear to be three principal ultimate goals of regulatory policy in the financial sector.

1. Stability of financial system. The terms soundness and confidence are often used in this connection. This goal focusses on the need for the belief to be widespread that the financial system is sound if it is to function properly both as a payments system and as an efficient allocator of savings.

2. Protection of depositors. Normally the focus is on protecting unsophisticated savers against the possibility of loss resulting from financial institution failure.

3. Efficiency to be maintained at a high level. This includes both the classical static notions of efficiency and more dynamic notions. Included in the former are production at least possible cost and pricing to reflect costs. That is, the value of resources used in the 'production' and 'delivery' of financial instruments should be minimized, given the available technology. Also, the price charged for a financial product should reflect only the costs of production and delivery plus a normal profit. The more dynamic notions include the optimal introduction of new techniques of production and delivery.

In addition, in some countries attention is paid to two other goals which are of less importance.

4. The prevention of excessive accumulation of power. This is basically a political notion and not an economic notion.

5. Some measure of domestic control over the financial system.

I now turn to the intermediate targets which stand between the ultimate targets and the instruments used by the authorities to achieve the goals. The number in brackets refers to the relevant ultimate goal.

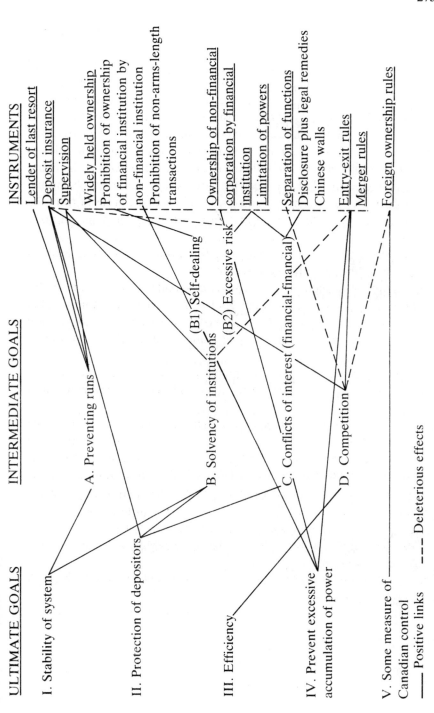

Figure 1. Goals and instruments in the regulation of financial institutions

A. Prevent runs (I.)

In order to ensure the stability of the financial system one would want to avoid or at least minimize the effects of runs on deposit-taking institutions. This is sometimes termed avoiding contagion effects, i.e. the spillover of concern from institution to institution as doubt is cast on the viability of all or a class of financial intermediaries.

B. Solvency of financial institutions (I., II.)

In addition to the concern about runs on the system as a whole there is also concern about the solvency of individual institutions. In part, this is related to the more basic concern about maintaining confidence in the system; in part it is related to the concern about protection of depositors. There are two elements which come under this heading:

(B1.) the prevention of self-dealing;

(B2.) the avoidance of 'excessively' risky investments.

While this intermediate target does not imply that no institution should ever be allowed to fail, it does suggest that, because of the importance of the financial system, there is a desire to avoid the kind of failures that would weaken depositor confidence in the stability of the system. If one or more financial institutions became insolvent because their investments were (ex ante) excessively risky, doubts might arise about the soundness of similar institutions[2]. Similarly, evidence of self-dealing will raise doubts about the safety of other institutions in the minds of depositors.

C. Avoidance of conflicts of interest (II.)

I use the term conflict of interest throughout to refer to financial-financial conflicts as opposed to issues of self-dealing. Most of these fall under the rubric of principal-agent conflicts. They can be harmful to the customer of the financial institution but unlike self-dealing will not endanger the solvency of the institution. Hence the concern regarding this type of activity derives mainly from the desire to protect the customer of the financial institution[3].

D. Competition (III.)

The goal of efficiency can be achieved by the maintenance of a reasonable degree of competition in various markets. Note that one should assess competition by markets (e.g. consumer loans, personal deposits, business loans) and not by classes of institution.

THE STRUCTURE OF THE CANADIAN FINANCIAL SYSTEM AND THE INSTRUMENTS OF REGULATORY POLICY IN CANADA

Historically, the Canadian financial system has been composed of a variety of different types of financial institutions which have had distinctive features, albeit with some considerable overlap of powers that has developed over the years. It is far from clear how much importance one can attribute to considerations of regulatory policy as a source of these separate industry groupings. What is clear is that over time these institutional differences have become an important element in the regulatory structure.

The principal regulated industry groupings have been (1) chartered banks, (2) trust and mortgage loan companies, (3) co-operative credit institutions, (4) life insurance companies, and (5) securities dealers. The chartered banks originally focussed on demand and short-term loans to businesses and on demand and short-term deposits. Over time they have become a significant force in the residential mortgage and consumer loan markets and make floating-rate term loans to business. They also issue deposits of longer duration, typically up to 5 years term. The trust companies initially specialized in the administration of trusts and estates and then developed an intermediation business in making mortgages and issuing matching longer-term deposits. In recent years they have expanded their interests to consumer and business lending and also issue demand deposits and short-term deposit instruments. Co-operative credit institutions began as suppliers of loan and deposit services to individual members but have now extended their clientele and make business loans. Life insurance companies have broadened their product from life insurance to term annuities, instruments that bear a very close resemblance to bank and trust company deposits. They also administer pension funds. The securities dealers' primary business was and continues to be underwriting, brokerage, market making and investment advice. More recently, securities dealers have offered customers credit balances that resemble deposits.

In addition to the inter-penetration of markets outlined above, banks have recently become involved in the discount brokerage business and co-operative credit institutions have established sister institutions in the trust and insurance industries. There has thus been a tendency over time for each industry grouping to try to enter into what had earlier been the preserve of other industries, typically while trying to protect its own area from increased competition. In the most recent period both the speed with which such developments are occuring and the intensity of the pressures for change have increased markedly.

An important additional development in the last few years has been the spread of the conglomerate movement to the financial sector. Owners of a financial institution in one industry have gained control of institutions in other financial industries and, in addition, non-financial firms have been purchasing financial firms. Thus, for example, some trust companies and life insurance companies have been brought under common ownership, in most cases closely held. This tendency has upset two long-standing traditions in the Canadian financial sector – first, that the ownership of financial institutions has commonly been widely held, and second, that financial institutions have largely been independent of major non-financial interests.

One final element of the Canadian financial structure worth noting is the divided governmental jurisdiction over the various institutions. Chartered banks come under federal law whereas trust companies and life insurance companies can be created under either federal or provincial law. The preponderance of legislation pertaining to co-operative credit institutions is provincial as is all securities legislation. The deposit insurance scheme also has both federal and provincial aspects.

With this background, one can turn back to Figure 1 and examine briefly the instruments that are potentially available to the authorities and those that have in fact been used in Canada to achieve the regulatory goals. The latter are underlined in the figure. Only the most important instruments are discussed in this section.

To prevent runs the principal instruments used are deposit insurance and the provision of lender of last resort facilities by the central bank. Deposit insurance also plays a crucial role in deposit protection and in permitting smaller institutions to compete effectively with the large ones. The existence of deposit insurance may also have the deleterious side-effect of encouraging riskier portfolios because of the weakening of depositor oversight. Although supervision may help prevent runs by assuring depositors that the authorities are paying attention to the portfolios of financial institutions, its primary function is to help maintain the solvency of individual institutions.

The principal means used in the past to avoid problems of self-dealing was the encouragement of widely-held ownership. In the case of the Canadian-owned chartered banks the law does not permit any individual, company, or associated group of individuals or companies to hold more than 10 per cent of the voting stock after the bank has been in existence for ten years. Mutual insurance companies are by definition widely-held. Furthermore until a few years ago virtually all the major federally chartered trust companies were widely held. As mentioned earlier there has been a significant movement to closely-held ownership in the last several years.

To prevent the abuse of financial-financial conflicts of interest the Canadian authorities have in the past relied upon a combination of limitations of powers, separation of functions, and the prohibition of ownership of non-financial business by financial institutions. Thus, for example, banks are not permitted to engage in trade or commerce or in the business of administering trusts. Nor are trust companies or banks allowed to engage in corporate underwriting.

SOURCES OF RECENT PRESSURES FOR CHANGE IN THE CANADIAN FINANCIAL SYSTEM

Most of the pressure in Canada for expansion of the powers of financial institutions in the recent period appears to be coming from the institutions themselves. As far as can be ascertained, with some minor exceptions, there has not been much in the way of complaints by customers as to services, nor any great demand for financial supermarkets. Furthermore, there is very little empirical evidence of economies of scope from bringing together functions under one roof. Indeed, components of the newly-emerging financial conglomerates do not appear as yet to have made advantageous use of their joint affiliation. Moreover, one can argue that any advantages that might accrue from financial supermarkets can be captured via networking[4].

What are the sources of the demands for additional powers by Canadian financial institutions, especially the trust industry and the life insurance industry? The pressures seem to have derived from a combination of circumstances, all of which have left the institutions concerned that they might not have the flexibility to cope with the situation that is expected to evolve over the next decade.

Focus first on the trust companies. In order to finance their rapidly increasing portfolio of mortgages over the 1970s, they developed into very efficient deposit takers. With their sizeable branch networks they are an important factor in the retail deposit market. The growth of mortgages[5], their principal asset, slowed markedly in the 1980s as the combination of declining inflation, higher real interest rates, and concerns about future high mortgage rates led households to repay their mortgages as quickly as possible. Furthermore, there was a widespread belief that, mainly for demographic reasons, residential construction would slow down in the 1980s and therefore that the mortgage lending business would not be a strong growth sector through the 1980s.

The concern felt by trust companies that the supply of their principal type of asset would be likely to grow relatively slowly over the next few years was further heightened by the consideration that the leading borrower over the coming period would be the government whose liabilities tend not to be intermediated to the same extent as household borrowing. Moreover, government bonds are not a profitable investment outlet for trust companies since the rates on their longer-term deposit instruments typically tend to be higher than those on government bonds of similar term.

Under these circumstances it is not surprising that trust companies have been increasing their penetration of the personal loan market and are seeking the right to make commercial loans more freely than has been the case in the past.

A further factor which has increased the desire of trust companies to move into the commercial loan area has been the shortening of term on their liabilities and the rapid growth of daily interest savings accounts, which have resulted in large part from the increase in interest rate volatility and the concomitant sharp rise in uncertainty as to future interest rate movements. These factors have also led trust companies to place much more emphasis on the need to match the term to maturity of their assets and of their liabilities. Since their traditional assets have been fixed-rate instruments, they have moved into new areas such as loans to corporations (via floating-rate debentures, for example) which enabled them to match the term of their floating-rate and very short-term liabilities. Having once entered this field they wish to be able to expand their involvement without the constraints that are currently placed on them by the regulations.

One might summarize the future situation as perceived by the trust companies as being one of continuing strong growth in retail deposits accompanied by considerable uncertainty as to the prospects for growth of their principal asset along with concerns about their ability to match the term of their assets and liabilities if they are not permitted a greater range of investment powers[6]. From a broader point of view, one can describe these developments by saying that these companies have made use of the economies of scope to extend their deposit taking from term instruments to savings deposits and to chequable deposits. Since their investment powers do not allow them to achieve similar economies of scope they are now potentially faced with 'excessive' liabilities and difficulties of matching.

One possible outcome under the circumstances could be that the share of the financial sector held by the trust industry gradually declines. This would involve their giving up the economies of scope and scale on the deposit side of their operation. Instead, their preference has been to develop or expand expertise in new asset areas. To justify this type of development, it might be argued: (1.) that there are economies to be exploited from lending to both mortgage borrowers and business borrowers (although these are not readily evident); (2.) that the banks have been permitted to take a considerable share of their specialized area, the residential mortgage business, and that it is only fair to allow them into the banks' specialized area, business lending; (3.) that with the slowing of mortgage growth they will have an underutilized senior management capability which it would be efficient to use in other directions. It should be noted that an alternative path open to trust companies would be conversion into a chartered bank but under current regulations this would require them to become widely held after ten years and to give up their estate, trust and agency business.

The motivation behind the desires of the insurance companies to expand their powers is similar. With the declining importance of whole life insurance they have been faced with a fall in their share of financial business. In addition, they, too, have faced a significant shortening of the term of liabilities desired by savers and have responded to this development by offering new kinds of annuities that are directly competitive with term deposits. However, thus far they do not appear to have had the same difficulty as trust companies in finding matching assets to cope with the shortening of term of their liabilities. The only potential economies that would appear to be pushing them in the direction of expanding their investment powers might be related to their agent delivery network (i.e. the desire to make wider use of their agents) and possibly to a less than fully utilized senior management. Since their requests to the federal government for an expansion of powers relate more to the right to purchase trust companies than to expansion of life insurance company powers it would appear that it is the ability of their senior management to extend their expertise into other industries that is dominant in their thinking. In any event, it is by no means certain that insurance agents could be effectively transformed into efficient marketers of a much wider variety of instruments than they sell at present.

The notion that insurance companies can make a profit out of purchasing trust companies relies on the existence of some form of synergy or, alternatively, underutilized management capacity. More generally, however, the gains from conglomeration are not self-evident. In the non-financial area there is little evidence that the wave of purchases by conglomerates in the 1970s led to cost reductions or profit increases. Indeed, the more recent trend has been to divestiture and a return by some companies to specialization in areas with which they are familiar. What seems to have happened was that management felt that they had the capacity to run other businesses more profitably than the current management of those businesses and were therefore willing to take over these other companies (sometimes at prices well in excess of stock market valuations) as a result of this perception. The recent reversal of some mergers and takeovers may indicate that conglomerates frequently encounter diseconomies of scale and problems of lack of knowledge and experience in areas which are far from the expertise of the management of the company doing the takeover.

In the case of financial conglomerates the expertise problem may not be as serious as that in non-financial conglomerates but there are potential costs in other directions, e.g. conflicts of interest and the potential for non-arms-length transactions and self-dealing. One additional factor that has been of significance in recent developments is the tendency for the newly-forming financial conglomerates to be wholly owned or controlled by non-financial businesses. This intensifies to a great extent the potential problems from a regulatory point of view because of the risk of self-dealing.

A final point worth noting is the role of emulation of foreign developments. With the pressure for change in the US and the UK financial systems it is not surprising that some spill-over effect has taken place in Canada. In part, it involves an increased awareness of potential changes; in part, a fear of missing out on new developments that might prove profitable, particularly during a period of technological innovation[7].

POSSIBLE REGULATORY RESPONSES TO PRESSURES FOR CHANGE

As discussed above and outlined in Figure 1, in the past the Canadian authorities have relied on deposit insurance and the lender of last resort facility to prevent runs, widespread ownership of financial institutions to minimize problems of self-dealing, supervision and a variety of limitations on types of permitted investments and lending powers to deal with the problems of excessively risky portfolios, separation of functions to cope with financial-financial conflicts of interest, merger rules to deal with efficiency and concentration of power concerns, and certain limitations on foreign ownership to maintain a degree of domestic control of the financial sector. Over the past twenty-five years an increased amount of attention has been devoted to efficiency concerns and the need to increase competition in various financial markets. In the main this was achieved by giving increased powers to the various financial institutions, a development which led to a considerable amount of penetration into each other's markets (e.g. personal loans, mortgage loans, deposit markets). In addition certain types of anti-competitive behaviour were made illegal (e.g. collusion among banks, cross ownerships of certain types) and interest rate ceilings on bank loans were removed. Also entry requirements for chartered banks were eased somewhat and the introduction of deposit insurance facilitated the ability of small institutions to compete with larger institutions for deposits.

For reasons discussed in the previous section there are pressures by some institutions for increased powers which would allow further penetration of each other's markets. More important, there has recently been a considerable extension of non-financial corporate ownership of financial institutions including common ownership of a number of institutions in different areas. These developments raise particular concerns of heightened problems in the areas of self-dealing and financial-financial conflicts of interest and possibly excessive riskiness of portfolios. The concerns about self-dealing are of particular importance because of their possible effects on system stability. On the other hand, the changes may increase competition in the financial system.

When one is evaluating the potential gains of implementing the various suggested changes in the financial system the goals of efficiency and system stability may at times be in conflict. In the earlier period the trade-off was such that one encouraged changes that increased efficiency even though they might have had some detrimental effect on other goals. That is, the structure of the system was such that the gains from efficiency clearly outweighed any losses in other directions. Indeed, for most of the changes in the 1960s, the latter were very small or non-existent and one could thus focus on enhancing the efficiency of the system. In evaluating the recent suggestions for change it can be argued that the situation is quite different. First, the efficiency of the system is already rather high and further gains, although desirable, are perhaps not as valuable as they were when efficiency was lower. Second, for some of the changes it is not obvious how significant the gains on the efficiency side will be. Third, some of the recent and proposed changes have potential costs in terms of self-dealing, system stability, etc.

In any event, to the extent that two of the traditional means of dealing with self-dealing and financial conflicts of interest, namely widespread ownership and institutional separation of functions, are no longer as pervasive as they were in the past, different means will have to be found of dealing with these problems. Among the possibilities under consideration is a system which tries to prevent self-dealing by severely limiting or prohibiting non-arms-length transactions between affiliated financial and non-financial companies[8]. To deal with the problems of financial-financial conflicts of interest might require the establishment of so-called Chinese walls or a system of increased disclosure plus the enhancement of civil remedies. What is clear is that the regulatory system will have to adjust to cope with the current and prospective changes in the financial structure.

NOTES

1. See C. Freedman, 'Financial Innovations in Canada: Causes and Consequences', *American Economic Review*, May 1983, pp. 101–106 for a detailed discussion of the new instruments and the resulting abandonment of the monetary aggregate target in Canada.

2. There is the additional complication that once deposit insurance is introduced as a way of avoiding runs, regulations have to be introduced regarding the degree of portfolio risk that will be tolerated. Otherwise, the institution will tend to invest in an excessively risky portfolio since the potential gain from such an investment will accrue to shareholders and a substantial part of any loss that is incurred will be absorbed by the taxpayer or the customers of depository institutions through deposit insurance pay-outs. One might also argue that the financial institution has a fiduciary responsibility to the depositor which precludes excessively risky investments.

3. However, if there is widespread concern about abuses of conflict of interest, a loss of confidence in some parts of the financial system might result.

4. Networking is a term used to describe arrangements between financial institutions under which one of the institutions provides the public with access to an investment, contract or service issued by the other. This type of arrangement can exist between affiliated institutions or independent institutions.

5. Since the late 1960s residential mortgages in Canada have had a twenty-five or thirty year amortization period but a renewable term of one to five years. As interest rates became more volatile in the late 1970s and early 1980s there was gradual reduction of the typical term from five years to a much shorter period.

6. To the extent that the situation to which these institutions are responding arose in part from the inflationary surge of the 1970s, some reversal of the situation should accompany the gradual diminution of inflation in the 1980s.

7. It is clear that technical innovation has played some role in intensifying the pressures for change. Thus, for example, the ability to bring together all of a household's financial transactions in one computerized package might be considered by some to offer a considerable advantage to financial conglomerates in selling retail financial services to households. None-

theless, it would seem that the technical aspects of recent changes have not been the initiating or driving force behind the pressures for change but, rather, may have facilitated the changes deriving from the more basic economic factors.

8. This possibility is discussed in the Interim Report of the Ontario Task Force on Financial Institutions, December 1984.

Chapter XIX

SHIFTING FRONTIERS IN FINANCIAL MARKETS AND ADJUSTMENTS OF SUPERVISORY SYSTEMS

by *Morten Balling*

INTRODUCTION

Almost all countries have government agencies charged with responsibility for supervising financial institutions. The reason is that the proper functioning of financial markets has been a matter of political concern for many years. It is thus a common feature of the countries we are concerned with at this colloquium that they have supervisory systems. The systems differ, however, in many respects, and it is therefore likely that the needs to adjust them because of shifting frontiers in financial markets are somewhat different from country to country.

Discussions of national differences may be profitable. In the present context, however, it seems to be preferable to focus on trends and aspects, which are more or less common in most European countries. In accordance with this judgment, the author has decided to discuss adjustments of supervisory systems in a hypothetical institutional environment, which contains elements from a number of supervisory systems in Western Europe, without being identical with any existing system.

The selected environment has been inspired by a number of national reports and comparative studies of financial structure, supervisory systems and monetary policy[1].

THE ASSUMED ENVIRONMENT

The participants in the financial markets are in this paper the government, the central bank, a number of financial institutions owned by private investors, private companies, and consumers. Some, but not all, of the financial institutions operating in the financial markets are 'covered institutions', which means that they are supervised by a government agency. The most important covered institutions are commercial banks, savings

Fair, D.E., (ed.) Shifting Frontiers in Financial Markets.
© *1986, Martinus Nijhoff Publishers, Dordrecht/Boston/Lancaster. ISBN 90-247-3225-5.*
Printed in the Netherlands.

banks, bond issuing credit institutions, insurance companies, pension funds, mutual funds, a stock exchange with members, and a number of institutions-owned subsidiaries or joint venture companies which perform financial activities or operate computer-based communication and clearing systems etc.

Factoring and leasing companies, consumer finance companies and other finance companies may be owned by covered financial institutions as well as by other investors. Such companies are supposed to be outside the supervised area unless they are deposit takers, but it is evident that their operations in the border area of the field of the covered financial institutions may actualize the problem of equal treatment of supervised and non-supervised financial activities[2].

In the assumed environment there are five separate supervisory agencies outside the central bank. The paper assumes the existence of a supervisory agency for banks and savings banks, a supervisory agency for bond issuing institutions, an agency for insurance companies and pension funds, an agency for mutual funds, and a stock exchange supervisory agency. In other words the paper assumes a division of labor between five supervisory agencies, each of them being responsible for its own sector of the financial system.

A large number of non-financial private companies and consumers are assumed to be customers in the financial institutions mentioned. International transactions are important to non-financial companies as well as to many of the financial institutions. Some of the financial institutions are assumed to have branches and subsidiaries abroad, and some of the institutions and branches with residence in the country are assumed to be owned by foreign investors. When banks and other financial institutions belong to international groups there is an obvious need for cooperation between supervisory offices and central banks in different countries[3]. The supervisory and monetary authorities dealt with in this paper are assumed to participate in international cooperation through the Bank for International Settlements in Basle, the International Monetary Fund in Washington DC, the Organization for Economic Co-operation and Development in Paris and other organizations.

OUTLINE OF AN ILLUSTRATIVE SUPERVISORY SYSTEM

It is the task of a supervisory agency to exercise its powers in such a way that the financial system under its jurisdiction functions as well as possible in the public interest. In order to be able to analyse a supervisory system, an analytical framework with an explicit enumeration of policy goals and their relations to supervisory instruments is desirable, but it is very hard to develop such a framework[4].

Very critical observers may even contend that it is virtually impossible to determine what the various regulators are attempting to accomplish[5]. Another problem is that the structure of supervisory systems can differ markedly from sector to sector within the same country[6].

In spite of such difficulties, the author has decided to illustrate the assumed supervisory system in a framework with goals, instruments, structural relationships and information flows, and to structure the rest of the paper in accordance with that framework.

Figure 1 gives an outline of the assumed supervisory system in the paper's institutional environment. Each of the supervisory agencies mentioned above has been given the task of achieving a subset of the supervisory goals enumerated in Box A.

In order to enable the agencies to fulfil their tasks, the legislators have provided them with the supervisory instruments listed in Box B.

The development in the financial markets is not only affected by the supervisory authorities, but also by a number of factors beyond the control of the supervisory agencies (Box C).

The effects of a given combination of supervisory instruments depend on the reactions of the supervised financial institutions (Circle D). Supervisory agencies need in fact a theory of financial intermediaries. Firms and institutions outside the supervised sectors can also take initiatives because of factors beyond the control of supervisors or because of changes in the supervisory instruments (Circle E). Financial sophistication is increasing also outside the financial sectors, partly due to the rapid development in information and communication technology.

The supervisory agencies are supposed to have organized regular flows of information, which enables them to monitor the financial results and balance sheet developments etc. of the institutions covered by the supervisory systems (Box F).

The current achievement of the supervisory goals is also evaluated by means of official statistics and other sources (Box G). Finally, the supervisory agencies are supposed to have an eye on the financial activities outside the covered sectors, so that they will notice financial innovations close to the supervised activities (Box H).

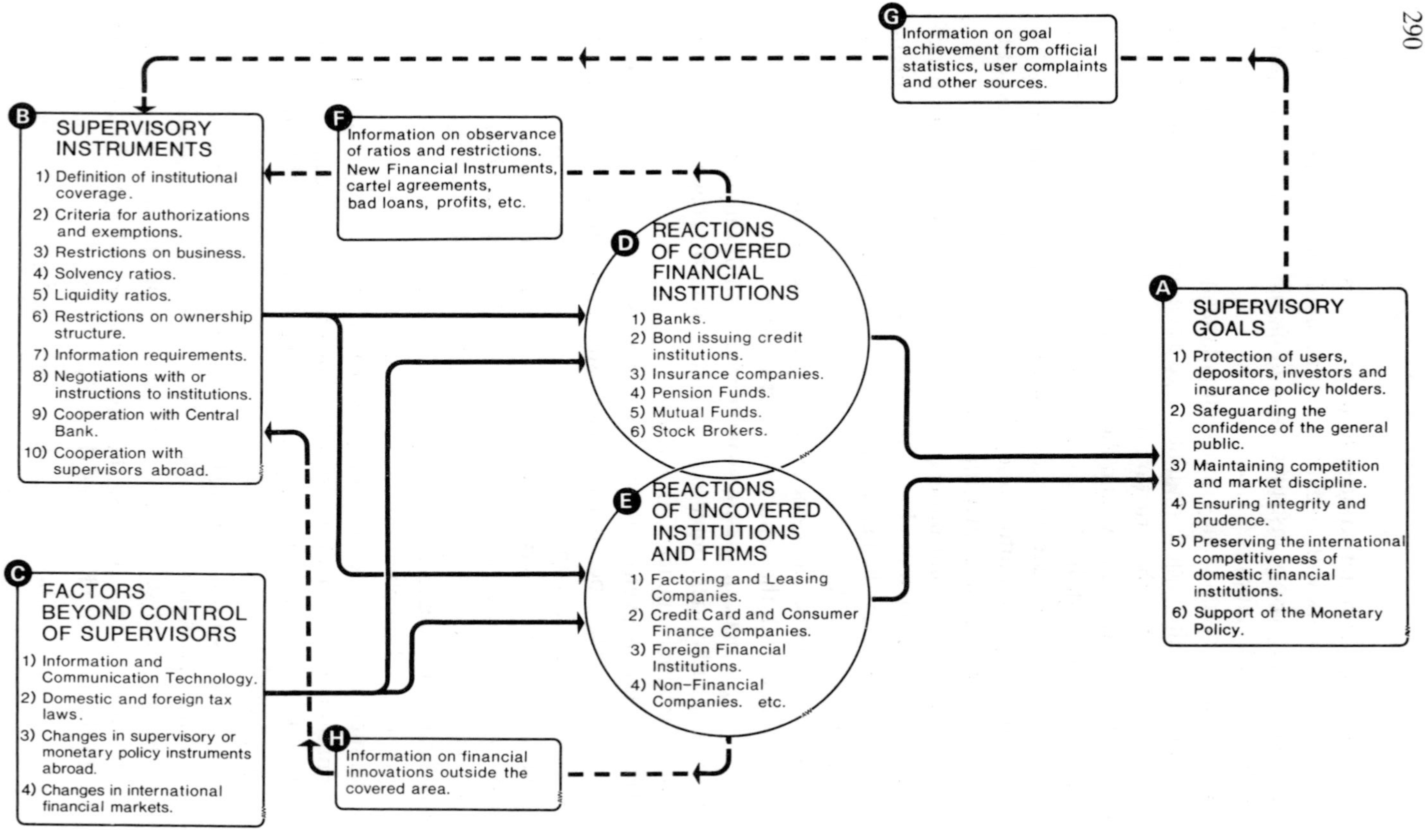

Figure 1. An illustrative supervisory system

A SUPERVISORY GOALS

1) Protection of users, depositors, investors and insurance policy holders.
2) Safeguarding the confidence of the general public.
3) Maintaining competition and market discipline.
4) Ensuring integrity and prudence.
5) Preserving the international competitiveness of domestic financial institutions.
6) Support of the Monetary Policy.

D REACTIONS OF COVERED FINANCIAL INSTITUTIONS

1) Banks.
2) Bond issuing credit institutions.
3) Insurance companies.
4) Pension Funds.
5) Mutual Funds.
6) Stock Brokers.

E REACTIONS OF UNCOVERED INSTITUTIONS AND FIRMS

1) Factoring and Leasing Companies.
2) Credit Card and Consumer Finance Companies.
3) Foreign Financial Institutions.
4) Non-Financial Companies. etc.

G Information on goal achievement from official statistics, user complaints and other sources.

F Information on observance of ratios and restrictions. New Financial Instruments, cartel agreements, bad loans, profits, etc.

H Information on financial innovations outside the covered area.

B SUPERVISORY INSTRUMENTS

1) Definition of institutional coverage.
2) Criteria for authorizations and exemptions.
3) Restrictions on business.
4) Solvency ratios.
5) Liquidity ratios.
6) Restrictions on ownership structure.
7) Information requirements.
8) Negotiations with or instructions to institutions.
9) Cooperation with Central Bank.
10) Cooperation with supervisors abroad.

C FACTORS BEYOND CONTROL OF SUPERVISORS

1) Information and Communication Technology.
2) Domestic and foreign tax laws.
3) Changes in supervisory or monetary policy instruments abroad.
4) Changes in international financial markets.

ADJUSTMENT OF SUPERVISORY GOALS

The appropriateness of a supervisory system depends of course on the political purposes it should serve. It is evident that there are very different political views with respect to the formulation and ranking of supervisory goals. This must be kept in mind when we look at Box A in Figure 1. We cannot expect politicians from different parties to agree on the list of goals. Some will stress the advantages of competition, others will express their scepticism with regard to the efficiency of the market mechanism. In the environment assumed here the supervisory system is supposed to be the result of a long series of compromises between parties with conflicting political views. In other words the list of goals is the result of a political process through a long period of time, and this may to some extent serve as an explanation for problems of inconsistency and overlapping between the goals in Box A. It is the task of parliament to adjust the supervisory goals, the structure of the supervisory agencies, and their jurisdictions. It is probably the rule rather than the exception that such adjustments are carried out at differing points in time for the different sectors of the financial system, and it is therefore not surprising that legislative actions reflected in the current supervisory system, have been taken for many differing purposes[7]. The literature on the objectives of supervisory systems is very extensive[8].

Most of the authors mentioned point out that the first goal – protection of users, depositors, investors and insurance policy holders – was introduced into the legislation primarily because of the distressing experiences in connection with failures of banks and other financial institutions in the 1930s or in earlier crisis periods. The majority of the voters felt that runs on banks and widespread losses on financial assets had demonstrated the need for risk reducing rules in the legislation. Capital adequacy rules, limitations on the exposure of financial institutions to risks on large individual customers and to movements of prices of stocks, bonds and real estate were introduced, and the supervisory agencies were provided with instruments to control the observance of these rules.

In more general terms, the electorate felt that the confidence of the general public in the institutions should be safeguarded (Goal No. 2). To some politicians it was acceptable to curb excessive competition among banks in order to promote the 'soundness' of banks and prevent bank failures.

Competition may however play an important part in promoting the interests of users, depositors, investors and insurance policy holders. Financial institutions operating in a competitive market are thus under permanent pressure to ensure that the instruments and services they offer, are priced properly and designed in accordance with their customers' needs. Maintaining competition and market discipline is therefore listed as goal number 3 in Box A. The recent trend towards deregulation in the US and liberalisation in the UK seems to reflect a recognition on the part of politicians and supervisors of the beneficial effects of more competition among different financial institutions[9].

The supervisory authorities must therefore try to strike a balance between maintaining competition and market discipline on the one side, and safeguarding the confidence of the general public on the other. There have been recent cases of bank failures, some of which could probably have been avoided through earlier intervention by the authorities, but it would in general be unwise to give managers of private financial institutions sure knowledge that the authorities would come to the rescue in the case of a failure. This brings us to goal number 4 in Box A. One of the most important tasks for managers of private financial institutions is to evaluate opportunities and risks in the market, and the incentive to perform that task in a competent and prudent way is enforced by the presence of risk of failure. Some doubt with regard to the intentions of the authorities under future crises may thus stimulate prudent management in the financial institutions.

Competition among financial institutions is increasingly becoming international. One consequence of this is that the achievement of the supervisory goals to an increasing extent depends on the behavior of financial institutions that are owned by foreigners. Another consequence is that the foreign exposure of the institutions within the covered area is growing, as they try to exploit the opportunities abroad. From a customer point of view, foreign competition is beneficial. From the point of view of domestic financial institutions, competition from large international banks and other foreign institutions may put a pressure on profitability. In the environment assumed here, the authorities are supposed to try to preserve the international competitiveness of domestic financial institutions (Goal No. 5). If the trend towards internationalization of financial markets continues, this goal may be expected to get more political attention.

As a whole, the tasks of the supervisory agencies can be summarized as protection of the functioning of the financial system. The efficient functioning of that system may be considered as a precondition for the conduct of the monetary policy of the central bank. We can therefore list support of the monetary policy as goal number 6 in Box A. This does not mean that the supervisory goals never are in conflict with monetary policy goals[10]. A goal conflict may for instance arise, when in order to improve the economy's macroeconomic performance the central bank contracts the money supply with the effect that some of the weaker banks get into liquidity troubles or have difficulties in observing capital adequacy ratios because of falling bond prices. The larger the interest rate and foreign exchange rate fluctuations in the financial markets are, the stronger is the impact on the supervised institutions. Therefore there is a connection between the needs to adjust the goals of the supervisory agencies and the attitude of central banks to intervention in the financial markets. The adjustment of the supervisory goals reflects to some extent gradual changes in the views of the supervisory agencies with regard to what are the most serious threats to the financial system. Failures of large financial institutions have historically induced changes in supervisory systems, because they revealed weaknesses in the systems, and this is also likely to happen from time to time in the future[11].

ADJUSTMENT OF SUPERVISORY INSTRUMENTS

Point 1 in Box B of Figure 1 – definition of institutional coverage– indicates that the legislation according to which each supervisory agency operates, is supposed to define or enumerate the financial institutions covered. The implication of the enumeration is that institutions which are not included in the list, fall outside the supervisory field of the agency in question. There are two types of border lines here. The first is drawn between the fields covered by different supervisory agencies. The second is drawn between covered and uncovered financial fields.

The name of the colloquium – shifting frontiers in financial markets – is presumably partly inspired by the impressive ingenuity of managers in the private sector with regard to creation of new types of institutions, some of which are multipurpose institutions offering financial instruments and services, which were earlier primarily supplied by specialized institutions[12]. Depending on the legal barriers the activity across the traditional borders may vary from looser forms of cooperation, in which different institutions act as agents for each other, to formation of groups comprising companies from several financial sectors, and further to genuine mergers, which bring together commercial banking, investment banking, securities dealing, stockbroking, trust business, administration of pension funds and insurance business under the same roof.

Thus in relation to the first type of border line shifting frontiers mean that the traditional division of labor between the institutions is gradually put to an end. In the paper's environment, the structure of the supervisory system reflects the specialization between the covered financial institutions. Therefore shifting frontiers in financial markets make it necessary to evaluate the appropriateness of the supervisory structure. If the trend away from specialized institutions and towards multiproduct financial institutions continues, it might be appropriate to merge the supervisory agencies into one[13].

The literature on the interaction between financial innovation and use of supervisory instruments has primarily been concerned with movements across the second type of border line[14].

New supervisory initiatives to some extent tend to be followed by innovative ways of avoidance, which inspire further regulations etc. There are two ways to reduce the problems of border line control. The first is to define the border line as clearly as possible. The second is to keep the incentives for crossing the border line small. It is thus likely that reliance on market determined rates and prices in the financial markets, makes it relatively easy for the authorities to police the border line around the supervised financial institutions.

In the paper's environment, it is assumed that establishing a new financial institution within a covered area requires approval by the supervisory agency, which is responsible for the sector in which the new institution intends to operate. The legislation is also supposed to give the agency the power to allow exemptions from rules under certain circumstances. The criteria for authorizations and exemptions are therefore listed as number 2 in Box B. Among the most important criteria may be mentioned requirements with regard to the legal form of financial institutions, a minimum paid-up equity capital, and management qualifications.

The criteria for authorization of new credit institutions are dealt with in the first directive on banking coordination, adopted by the EEC council in December 1977[15]. One of the most interesting features of the directive is that it abolishes the right of national supervisory agencies to let approval of new financial institutions depend on the outcome of an examination of the need for such institutions. Member countries with 'criteria of need' in their legislation will thus have to remove these criteria during a transition period.

As mentioned earlier, there is supposed to be a functional specialization among the various types of financial institutions in the paper's environment. It is assumed that the business of the supervised institutions is defined by law and that the institutions are restricted to that business. These restrictions are listed as instrument number 3 in Box B.

If we take bank business as an example, banks are thus prohibited from non-bank activities.

The first problem from a supervisory point of view is that the nature of banking is changing through time. Today the banks offer a wide range of services, which were virtually unknown ten or twenty years ago. Information service, electronic funds transfer, cash management service, options and financial futures, and portfolio management are illustrative examples. Restrictions on business must therefore be revised in order to be in accordance with the development of new financial services.

The second problem is to decide to what extent a prohibition against non-bank activities for supervisory reasons should be supported by restrictions with respect to the bank's equity participation in non-bank companies. This problem has been analysed for EEC member countries with restrictions on banking activity in their supervisory systems[16]. It is assumed in this paper that the banks are restricted from being 'Universal Banks' by limitations of their access to own stocks in companies outside the banking sector. They are permitted to have small holdings of stocks in manufacturing, trading, transportation and insurance companies, but they are not allowed to acquire controlling interests. The supervisory agency for banks may, however, permit temporary equity participation in cases where a customer is in trouble, and the banks are engaged in reconstruction efforts.

A third problem in connection with instrument number 3 is that financial institutions can create holding companies outside the supervised area. In the US, establishment of bank holding companies was used to an increasing extent in the 1970s to 'ease some of the economic rigidities created by banking regulation'[17].

In Western Europe, there seems to have been a similar trend in recent years. If the trend continues we may expect a political discussion of the implications for the achievement of the supervisory goals. Different adjustments of supervisory systems are conceivable. The Parliament could pass a law limiting the amount of guarantees a bank could undertake for its parent company, or it could place restrictions on the investments of the holding company in order to reduce the risks.

A third possibility might be an introduction of or a tightening of restrictions on the ownership structure of supervised financial institutions. (Instrument No. 6 in Box B.) In particular in the German literature such restrictions have been related to antitrust legislation and political desires to avoid concentration of corporate ownership and power[18].

Limits on individual large loans is an important example of restrictions on business. In this paper, the limits are supposed to be defined in relation to the institution's equity capital. The fraction may be called a 'large loan-capital ratio', and the result of a multiplication of this ratio by the equity capital may be called the institution's 'large loan capacity'.

When corporate customers grow due to increasing production activity, mergers or acquisitions, their needs for loans and guarantees will probably also grow. With a constant large loan-capital ratio, the severity of the limit depends on the growth of the institution's equity capital in relation to the large customers' financial needs.

It is necessary for supervisory reasons to define the items which should be included in the 'large loan' figure. It is assumed here that the figure includes loans and guarantees outstanding, loans and guarantees promised, and the financial institution's holdings of shares and convertible bonds issued by the large customer.

Solvency ratios (Instrument No. 4) relate the size of the equity capital of a financial institution to its volume of deposits, other liabilities or assets. For a given equity capital, the solvency ratio defines a limit on the volume of business, which may be called for instance the institution's portfolio capacity, credit capacity or deposit capacity. The basic function of equity capital is to serve as a buffer against unforeseen losses. Such losses may have their origin in the asset side as well as in the liability side of the balance sheet. The value of outstanding loans, stocks, bonds, and real estate owned by the institution or pledged as security for loans and guarantees, may fall unexpectedly, and the institution's liabilities may increase unexpectedly for instance because of exchange rate changes. The larger the equity capital is, the smaller is the risk of losses seen from the point of view of depositors, investors and insurance policy holders. It follows that the application of solvency ratios is a very appropriate supervisory instrument[19].

Supervisory agencies must deal with a number of border line cases in relation to the numerators in solvency ratios. In several countries, subordinated debt may to some extent be considered as equity capital for the purpose of calculating solvency ratios. In an increasing number of cases, banks have issued bonds, which are at the same time convertible and subordinated to the claims of depositors and other creditors.

The supervisory authorities must be aware that a financial institution with a given equity capital under certain circumstances can extend its volume of business through the establishment of subsidiaries abroad[20]. The reason for this 'Portfolio Capacity Multiplier Effect' is that the value of new subsidiary shares enters as an asset in the balance sheet of the parent institution, without reducing its equity capital and thus its solvency ratio, while the same shares constitute new equity capital from the subsidiary's point of view, which can be included in the numerator of the solvency ratio of the subsidiary institution.

Disregard of the increasing importance of international group relations among financial institutions, may thus undermine the observance of solvency ratios.

Concern about the 'Portfolio Capacity Multiplier Effect' seems to some extent to have encouraged the agreement, which has become known as the 'Basle Concordat'[21]. It is thus evident that supervisors in countries with multinational financial institutions should follow the principle that supervision of the institution's international business should be undertaken on a basis, which looks at their activity worldwide on a consolidated basis.

Liquidity ratios (Instrument No. 5 in Box B) relate the liquid assets of the financial institution to its liabilities or the most volatile part of the liabilities. The numerator as well as the denominator may be defined narrowly or broadly. The supervisory agencies may thus have to monitor several liquidity ratios for each of the covered financial institutions.

New types of financial instruments on the market must be evaluated by the supervisory agencies, and it must be decided whether they should be included in or excluded from the numerators and denominators in the prevailing liquidity ratios.

The supervisory implications of liquidity ratios may be diminishing compared with the implications for monetary policy[22]. Closer working relations between the central bank and the financial institutions in the money markets may thus weaken the concern of the supervisory agencies with respect to the liquidity of the covered institutions.

In the paper's environment the supervisory agencies have obliged the covered institutions to submit returns including balance sheets, income statements, and ratio observance forms to the agencies on a regular basis. The returns break down the balance sheet into its components, display the maturity structure of assets and liabilities, provide details of large loans and of bad loan provisions, and survey the institution's country exposure. These information requirements (Instrument No. 7) are intended to ensure that the supervisory agencies are provided with material, which can be used for evaluation of credit risks, liquidity risks, interest rate risks, political risks etc.

The move in the financial services industry towards computer records has opened up the possibility of conducting examinations of financial institutions partly by computer[23]. The computer and communication technology also supplies very efficient ways to control the observance of prescribed trading rules in stock exchanges. In the future, it must be decided to what extent the stock exchange supervisory agency should be provided with the power to demand computer records of volumes and prices of securities transactions[24]. In order to implement a partial computerization of supervisory systems, the agencies must cope with shortage of skilled manpower. One of the most serious implementation problems is perhaps that it may be difficult for the agencies to offer computer specialists competitive wages.

In addition to the obligation to provide recurrent information of this kind, the covered institutions have to inform the agency concerned, whenever changes are taking place in the composition of boards of directors, boards of management, the group of auditors, and in other organisational circumstances with obvious supervisory implications.

The supervisory agencies are supposed to have meetings with the management of the covered institutions regularly. During such meetings, the institutions must be prepared to explain and elaborate on the positions revealed in the returns and on other relevant information. Instrument No. 8 – negotiations with or instructions to institutions – is therefore closely related to No. 7; information requirements. It is also related to the distinction between statutory and non-statutory elements in supervisory systems.

The question of the proper combination of statutory and non-statutory elements has been discussed thoroughly in relation to the EEC Banking Directive from December 1977[25]. The British tradition has been to rely rather heavily on non-statutory elements, while statutory elements have been given a relatively larger weight in much of continental Europe. In this paper, it is assumed that the supervisory system is closer to the continental tradition than to the British tradition. The environment resembles, however, the British environment in some ways. Thus the supervisory agencies have a rather close contact with the management of the large covered institutions, and the agencies are supposed to use their frequent meetings with those managers to influence their operations, sometimes beyond their formal statutory powers. One aspect of a market structure, in which a few financial institutions have large market shares, is that it is practicable for the supervisory agencies and the central bank to maintain close contact with the managers and their lawyers. It is probably true that occasionally the supervisors can obtain ideas for adjustments of supervisory instruments through such contacts.

It belongs to the statutory powers of the agencies that they can arrange inspection of the institutions within their sectors. The covered institutions are obliged to assist the agencies during such inspections. The rules of inspection are included in the supervisory system for similar reasons as the information rules mentioned above. The idea is to ensure that problems are discovered in time[26].

In this paper the supervisory agencies are supposed to be obliged to support the monetary policy. At the same time they are administratively separated from the central bank. It follows that they must cooperate closely with the central bank (Instrument No. 9). It is the primary responsibility of the central bank to use its monetary policy instruments in order to improve the macroeconomic performance of the economy. The tasks of the supervisory agencies are primarily of a microeconomic nature. The closer working relations are between the central bank and the financial institutions in the money markets and the markets for foreign exchange, the more blurred becomes the border line between handling of macro- and micro-problems. The diminishing supervisory importance of liquidity ratios in a period, when the access of banks to loan facilities in the central bank is improved, is an obvious example, and it may be used to support proposals for incorporation of supervisory functions into the central bank[27]. The tendency towards closer contact between the central bank and the private financial institutions is likely to continue. Thus we can probably expect new proposals for incorporating supervisory agencies into the central bank.

The growth of international banking and other financial services has necessitated an intensification of the cooperation between supervisory agencies in different countries (Instrument No. 10). The financial institutions may use different organizational forms for their activities abroad. The distinction between branches, affiliates, and subsidiaries is important from a supervisory point of view. Branches are integral parts of their parent organizations, so that the responsibility for their supervision rests with the supervisory agency of the parent's country. The authorities of the host country will, however, often want to be informed about the activities of such branches, because they have implications for the achievement of the supervisory goals[28]. It follows that the information needs of supervisors of different nationalities overlap to some extent. Subsidiaries and affiliates are usually financial institutions with the same rights and obligations as similar institutions in the host country. Therefore they are in general subjected to the same supervisory system as institutions in the host country, which are not owned by foreign investors.

A subject, which has been discussed extensively in international meetings between supervisors, is to what extent a parent institution should take responsibility for the operations and liabilities of subsidiaries and affiliates in other countries. The supervisory agencies of a number of countries have been given the power to demand letters of comfort, letters of awareness or similar declarations of support from parent institutions abroad[29]. Obligations of that kind must, however, be included in the risk evaluation of the supervisors in the parent country. The implication is again that the super-

300

visory information needs overlap among countries.

A continued internationalization of the financial services industry seems to imply a continued internationalization of the supervisory systems.

SUMMARY

The responsibility for the appropriateness of supervisory systems rests partly with the legislators partly with the supervisors. Changes of laws are usually undertaken with long intervals, and the legal foundation of supervisory systems therefore tends to be slow to adapt to changing circumstances. The supervisors can adapt their procedures more rapidly if they have been provided by parliament with sufficient flexible instruments.

The needs to adjust supervisory systems may arise because of perceived weaknesses of old supervisory instruments, introduction of new financial instruments, formation of new multipurpose institutions or groups of institutions, financial innovations outside the supervised area, new information and communication technology, new control systems and reporting and auditing procedures, new tax systems, and because of changes in international financial markets.

The reactions of the legislators and supervisors to such challenges depend on the relative strength in parliament and the government of different political views on the supervisory goals. Most of the references in this paper indicate that the influence of politicians with confidence in the beneficial effects of competition has been increasing in recent years. The author wishes, however, to desist from forecasts with respect to the possible continuation of the ensuing deregulation trend.

NOTES

1. Jane Welch (ed.): *The Regulation of Banks in the Member States of the EEC*, 2. ed., Martinus Nijhoff Publishers, The Hague, Boston, London 1981. Philip Thorn and Jean M. Lach (eds.): *Banking and Sources of Finance in the European Community*, The Banker Research Unit, London 1977. Salvatore Mastropasqua: *The Banking System in the Countries of the EEC: Institutional and Structural Aspects*, Sijthoff and Noordhoff International Publishers, Alphen aan den Rijn 1978. Relations Between Government and Central Bank: A Survey of Twenty Countries, Appendix 8 to *Report from Committee to Review the Functioning of Financial Institutions*, Her Majesty's Stationery Office, London 1980. *Lov om Norges Bank og pengevesenet* (Law on the Norwegian Central Bank and the Monetary System), Norges Offentlige Utredninger, NOU 1983: 39, Oslo 1983. K. Bjørn Jensen og J. Nørgaard: *Bank- og*

Sparekasseloven (The law on Commercial Banks and Savings Banks), Copenhagen 1976. Hermann Delorme (Herausg.): *Kreditwesengesetz, Bundesbankgesetz*, 3. Aufl. Frankfurt 1977. The Amendment of the Banking Act, *Monthly Report of the Deutsche Bundesbank*, Vol. 28, No. 7, July 1976.

2. Christoph Schücking: Leasinggeschäfte der Banken nach der KWG-Novelle, *Zeitschrift für das Gesamte Kreditwesen*, Bd. 37, Heft 21, November 1984, p. 978ff.

3. Klaus Wagner: *Die internationale Tätigkeit der Banken als aufsichtsrechtliches Problem*, Nomos Verlagsgesellschaft, Baden-Baden 1982. Adrian E. Tschoegl: *The Regulation of Foreign Banks: Policy Formation in Countries Outside the United States*, Salomon Brothers Center for the Study of Financial Institutions, New York 1981.

4. Lester V. Chandler and Dwight M. Jaffee: Regulating the Regulators: A Review of the FINE Regulatory Reforms, *Journal of Money, Credit, and Banking* Vol. 9, 1977 p. 619ff. Johannes Welcker: *Neuordnung der Bankenaufsicht*, Fritz Knapp Verlag, Frankfurt 1978 p. 12ff.

5. James L. Pierce: The FINE Study, *Journal of Money, Credit, and Banking*, Vol. 9 1977 p. 610.

6. Regulation in the City and the Bank of England's role, *Bank of England Quarterly Bulletin*, Vol. 18, No. 3, September 1978 p. 379.

7. Lester V. Chandler and Dwight M. Jaffee: *op. cit.* p. 620.

8. The list of goals, which is presented in Box A, has been inspired by: Changing Boundaries in Financial Services, *Bank of England Quarterly Bulletin*, Vol. 24, No. 1. March 1984 p. 40ff. Allan H. Meltzer: Major Issues in the Regulation of Financial Institutions, *The Journal of Political Economy*, Vol. 75, No. 4, August 1976 p. 482ff. Lawrence G. Goldberg and Lawrence J. White: *The Deregulation of the Banking and Securities Industries*, Lexington Books, Lexington, Mass. 1979. Werner A. Müller: *Bankenaufsicht und Gläubigerschutz, Eine Analyse von Regulierungs- und Aufsichtsvorschriften für Kreditinstitute*, Nomos Verlagsgesellschaft, Baden-Baden 1981. H.J. Muller: *The Central Bank and Banking Supervision*, The Netherlands Bank, September 1983.

9. J.S. Fforde: Competition, Innovation and Regulation in British Banking, *Bank of England Quarterly Bulletin*, Vol. 23, No. 3, Sept. 1983, p. 365 and Robert Craig West: The Depository Institutions Deregulation Act of 1980: A Historical Perspective, in Thomas M. Havrilesky and Robert Schweitzer (eds.): *Contemporary Developments in Financial Institutions and Markets*, Harlan Davidson, Inc. Arlington Heights, Ill. 1983, p. 125ff.

10. Werner A. Müller: *op. cit.* p. 30.

11. A famous example is the closure of Bankhaus I.D. Herstatt KG in 1974, which induced a tightening of supervisory rules and procedures to reduce the foreign exchange risk exposure of banks in Germany as well as in other countries. See The Amendment of the Banking Act, *op. cit.* p. 17.

12. William A. Schreyer: The Future of the Financial Services Industry, *Financial Analysts Journal*, Vol. 38, No. 4, 1982 p. 51ff. Arnold W. Sametz: The New Financial Environment, in A.W. Sametz (ed.): *The Emerging Financial Industry, Implications for Insurance Products, Portfolios, and Planning*, Lexington Books, Lexington, Mass. 1984, p. 3ff. H. Felix Kloman: Insurance and Banking: How Good is the Fit? *ABA Banking Journal*, Oct. 1983 p. 33ff.

13. James L. Pierce: *op. cit.* p. 611.

14. Edward J. Kane: Policy Implications of Structural Changes in Financial Markets, *American Economic Review*, Papers and Proceedings, Vol. 73, No. 2, May 1983 p. 96ff., and Thomas Mayer: Financial Innovation – The Conflict Between Micro and Macro Optimality,

American Economic Review, Papers and Proceedings, Vol. 72, No. 2, May 1982 p. 29ff. William L. Silber: The Process of Financial Innovation, *American Economic Review,* Papers and Proceedings, Vol. 73, No. 2. May 1983 p. 89ff.

15. Peter Troberg: *Europäische Aufsicht über das Kreditwesen, Eine Analyse der ersten EG-Koordinierungsrichtlinie, ihrer Hintergründe und der Aussichten auf weitere Harmonisierung,* Fritz Knapp Verlag, Frankfurt 1979. p. 24ff.

16. Ulrich Immenga: *Beteiligungen von Banken in anderen Wirtschaftszweigen,* Nomos Verlagsgesellschaft, Baden-Baden 1978.

17. Merton H. Miller and Richard A. Posner: An Approach to the Regulation of Bank Holding Companies, *Journal of Business,* Vol. 51, No. 3, 1978 p. 379ff.

18. Ulrich Immenga: *op. cit.* p. 112ff. Peter Liepmann:*Bankenverhalten und Bankenregulierung,* Duncker und Humblot, Berlin 1980 p. 53ff.

19. George Emir Morgan: On the Adequace of Bank Capital Regulation, *Journal of Financial and Quantitative Analysis,* Vol. 19, No. 2, June 1984 p. 141ff. Robert A. Taggart and Stuart I. Greenbaum: Bank Capital and Public Regulation, *Journal of Money, Credit, and Banking,* Vol. 10, 1978 p. 158ff. B. Short: Capital Requirements for Commercial Banks: A Survey of the Issues, *IMF Staff Papers,* Vol. 25, No. 3. 1978 p. 528ff.

20. Klaus Wagner: *op. cit.* p. 67ff.

21. W.P. Cooke: *Address to the SUERF-Colloquium in Vienna:* International Lending in a Fragile World Economy, April 1982 p. 10 and H.I. Muller: The Concordat: A Model for international cooperation, *International Conference of Banking Supervisors,* London, July 1979 p. 6ff. *Principles for the Supervision of Banks' Foreign Establishments,* Committee on Banking Regulations and Supervisory Practices Basle, May 1983. Directive from the EEC Council of June 13, 1983 on *Supervision of Financial Institutions on a Consolidated Basis.*

22. Donald D. Hester: On the Adequacy of Policy Instruments and Information when the Meaning of Money is Changing, *American Economic Review,* Papers and Proceedings, Vol. 72, No. 2, May 1982 p. 40ff. M.A. Akhtar: Financial Innovations and their Implications for Monetary Policy: An International Perspective, *BIS Economic Papers* No 9, Basle, December 1983.

23. J.R.S. Revell: *Banking and Electronic Fund Transfers,* OECD, Paris 1983 p. 178.

24. Robert Winder: The final days of the trading floor, *Euromoney,* Oct. 1984 p. 81.

25. Regulation in the City and the Bank of England's rôle, *op. cit.* p. 382.

26. Joseph F. Sinkey: Identifying 'Problem' Banks, How Do the Banking Authorities Measure A Bank's Risk Exposure? *Journal of Money, Credit, and Banking,* Vol. 10, No. 2, May 1978 p. 184ff. Joseph F. Sinkey: *Problem and Failed Institutions in the Commercial Banking Industry,* JAI Press, Inc. Greenwich, Conn. 1979.

27. *Overføring av Bankinspeksjonen til Norges Bank* (Transfer of Banking supervision to the Norwegian Central Bank), Norges Offentlige Utredninger, NOU 1974: 23, Oslo 1974 p. 24.

28. Supervision of Banks and Other Deposit-taking Institutions, *Bank of England Quarterly Bulletin,* Vol. 18, No. 3, Sept. 1978 p. 385. Charles Freedman: The FINE Proposals on Foreign Banks in the United States and American Banks Abroad, *Journal of Money, Credit, and Banking,* Vol. 9, 1977 p. 648.

29. Klaus Wagner: *op. cit.* p. 30ff.

Chapter XX

THE IMPLICATIONS OF SHIFTING FRONTIERS IN FINANCIAL MARKETS FOR MONETARY CONTROL

by *Charles A.E. Goodhart*

INTRODUCTION

The purpose of this paper is to try to weave the theoretical work of that emerging school of monetary economists who have espoused the 'Legal Restrictions' theory of the demand for money and monetary policy together with practical observations taken from the experience of the UK in recent years. Professor Neil Wallace, Professor of Economics at the University of Minnesota, coined this term, 'The Legal Restrictions Theory of Money', in a paper in the *Federal Reserve Bank of Minneapolis Quarterly Review* (Winter 1983), in his paper, 'A Legal Restrictions Theory of the Demand for 'Money' and the Role of Monetary Policy' (31). There had been forerunners of this approach in the literature much earlier, for example the article on 'Problems of Efficiency in Monetary Management' by Harry Johnson in 1968 (14), and in an extraordinarily prescient article by Fischer Black on 'Banking and Interest Rates in a World Without Money', in the *Journal of Bank Research*, (Autumn 1970) (2). More recently, this theoretical approach has been taken further by economists such as Fama (6), Robert Hall (12), Kareken (16), Sargent (24, 25), Wallace (16, 24, 25, 31), and other economists, with a centre in Minneapolis: the arguments and analysis of this developing school have been summarised and pooled together in a brilliant survey paper, 'A Libertarian Approach to Monetary Theory and Policy', by Professor Y.C. Jao of the Department of Economics, University of Hong Kong (13). This new school, which also has strong links with the 'new view' of money creation put forward by James Tobin in 1963 (28), ascribes both the particular characteristics of bank deposits, and also some special features of currency, together with the observed regularities between such money holdings and nominal incomes, to legal restrictions placed upon the banking system; they go on to suggest that such regularities will collapse as, and when, the restrictions are lifted, or eroded by innovation.

Fair, D.E., (ed.) Shifting Frontiers in Financial Markets.
© *1986, Martinus Nijhoff Publishers, Dordrecht/Boston/Lancaster. ISBN 90-247-3225-5.*
Printed in the Netherlands.

Let me provide some examples of their approach. First, Robert Hall, in his review of Friedman and Schwartz, in the *Journal of Economic Literature* (12), writes, 'The new monetary economics views the quantity theory as nothing more than an artifact of government regulation. An economy organised along free-market principles could function without money at all (Fischer Black, 1970). It is true that the kinds of monetary regulations imposed by the American and British Governments of the past century create a more-or-less stable relation between a certain class of assets called money and nominal spending (Eugene Fama, 1980), but different regulations would alter that relation'.

Again, Jao (13) writes, 'To sum up then, the libertarians' theoretical case against mainstream monetarism rests on the latter's uncritical acceptance of the various legal restrictions and regulations on money and finance. Without such restrictions and regulations, the distinctions between banks and other non-bank intermediaries would vanish, and the conceptual differences between various monetary aggregates would also become meaningless. With these foundations gone, the major components of the monetarist upper structure, such as a stable demand function for money, and a constant money growth rule, also fall to the ground' (page 14). Later (page 17), Jao writes, 'There is nothing unique about bank deposits. In an unregulated setting, competitive yields have to be offered on deposits; in principle, they can be issued by any other financial intermediary and acquired as portfolio assets by wealth-holders. Full competition will force banks to offer more portfolio management services, and non-bank intermediaries to offer more transactions services. The blurring of the distinction between banks and other intermediaries has already been mentioned. Thus, the term 'deposits' is now a rubric for all the different forms of wealth that have access to the accounting system of exchange provided by 'banks' defined in the widest sense'.

BANK DEPOSITS

In this section we will examine how far the erosion of legal, and conventional, restrictions on the banking system in the UK has already tended to disturb previous statistical regularities, and also ask whether that same process is still continuing. During the 1950s and 1960s, interest rates offered on bank deposits in the UK were, for the most part, determined in a conventional manner. Thus no interest was offered on sight deposits; the interest rate offered by the clearing banks on time deposits was related, by a cartel arrangement, to the administratively-determined Bank rate. Certain other non-clearing banks were offering more market-related interest rates on time deposits, but, although such banks were growing considerably more rapidly than the clearing banks, the proportion of time deposits held with them still represented a small proportion of total time deposits. Thus the own rate on sight deposits was fixed at zero, while the own rate on time deposits was relatively sticky, since conventionally related to an administratively-fixed Bank rate. The demand-for-money functions estimated around that time (see (8) and the references in that paper to contemporary econometric work), indicated that both M1 and broader money, M3, were significantly related, inversely, to the level of competing interest rates. Own rates were rarely included in such equations: yet, despite that omission, the equations generally demonstrated stability.

Then in 1971, partly at the prompting of earlier academic and official studies, (1, 22), the cartel was ended, with the intention of generating greater competition and efficiency, as one element of the package of reforms, described as 'Competition and Credit Control' introduced in 1971. The abolition of the cartel did, indeed, induce both the clearing and the non-clearing banks to compete much more strongly between, and among, themselves for deposits, by offering more market-related interest rates on a wider range of instruments, including Certificates of Deposits (CDs), following the practice and example of liability management developed by US banks during the preceding decade. It is difficult to be certain whether the previous stable relationship between the broad money aggregate (M3) and nominal incomes and interest rates broke down at that time because of the adoption of liability management, or for a range of other reasons. Nevertheless, following the adoption of such liability management, this relationship did collapse; in particular, with the banks now offering market-related interest rates on a wide range of wholesale deposits, the prior (inverse) relationship between the general level of interest rates in the economy and the growth of broad money totally disappeared (11). Nevertheless, there did still seem to be a relationship between the growth of broad money and the *subsequent* development of nominal incomes, with broad money leading nominal incomes by about 8 quarters, or nearly two years. This relationship, shown in Figure 1, was, of course, particularly marked over the period 1972–75 but did appear to hold even outside that time period, up until the end of the 1970s (see 21). One strand of thought ascribed this relationship to the effect of 'supply shocks' (e.g. resulting from surges in extending bank loans, notably following Competition and Credit Control; and/or as a consequence of large fiscal deficits), inducing temporary 'excessive' holdings of broad money, which subsequently, and more slowly, became absorbed into higher nominal incomes through additional expenditures. This 'buffer stock' analysis has been examined by Laidler (19), Goodhart (8), Davidson (5), Knoester (18), and others. Whatever the cognitive attractions of the 'buffer stock' analysis may be, this latter 'lead' relationship between £M3 and subsequent nominal incomes also broke down comprehensively in the early 1980s, when a sharp rise in the growth rate of £M3 during 1980 and 1981 preceded quite rapid declines in the growth rate of nominal incomes over the two or three years, as can also be seen clearly in Figure 1. This latter experience is considered further below.

Meanwhile, during the course of the 1970s the convention that interest would not be paid on sight deposits remained generally in force. Perhaps as a result, the demand-for-money function for M1 remained stable, with a significant and well-behaved interest elasticity (although the fit was never close and the predictive ability of the equation was rather weak). Nevertheless, in this area also competitive pressures, both from building societies, who have been increasingly offering transaction services on their interest-bearing deposits (and who have remained open on Saturdays for the convenience of their customers whereas the banks have (mostly) shut), and also competition from within the banking system itself, were inducing the banks to pay market-related interest rates first on wholesale sight deposits and more recently and increasingly on a wider range of available retail-type chequable sight deposits. The growth of such interest-bearing sight deposits has been remarkably fast over the last four years, and such deposits now represent an increasing proportion of total M1 (see Table 1). Under these circumstances what has remained surprising has been the relative *success* of the standard M1 demand-for-money equations in continuing to fit the path of M1, despite its growing share of interest-bearing deposits. Nevertheless we believe that an important structural change in the characteristics of retail-type sight deposits is in process, and we regularly expect the imminent break-down of the stability of its demand function – even though it has not yet happened.

As already mentioned, building societies in the UK are increasingly providing a range of transaction services for their depositors. Nevertheless, legal restrictions, notably on their ability to provide overdrafts, or even to lend on any security other than mortgages, have restricted their capacity to provide a full range of transactions and other financial services to their depositors. The recent Green Paper on building societies (29) proposes to relax sufficient of these restrictions to make it prospectively possible for building societies to offer a wider range of financial services, including

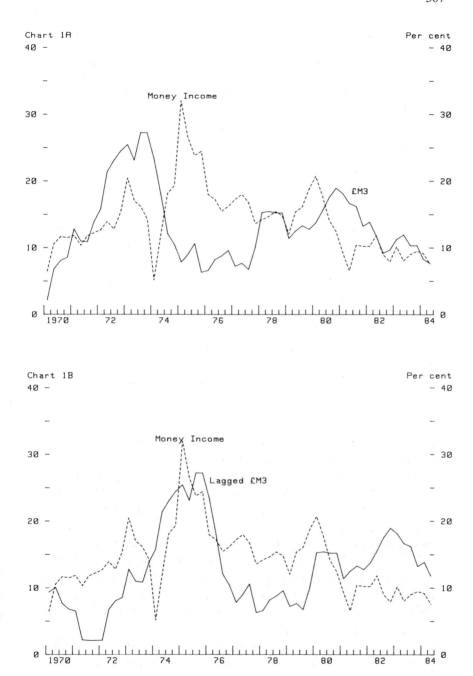

Figure 1. £M3 and money income (% changes on a year earlier – seasonally adjusted).

Table 1. Interest bearing sight deposits and M1. £ millions unadjusted

		Interest-bearing sight deposits	M1	IB sight deposits as a percentage of M1
1980	1	4,332	28,979	14.95
	2	4,521	29,513	15.32
	3	4,263	29,567	14.42
	4	4,587	31,044	14.78
1981	1	4,678	31,441	14.88
	2	5,007	32,539	15.39
	3	5,516	33,090	16.67
	4	7,985	36,533	21.86
1982	1	8,279	36,341	22.78
	2	8,458	37,261	22.70
	3	8,659	38,205	22.66
	4	9,998	40,664	24.59
1983	1	10,320	41,723	24.73
	2	11,247	42,825	26.26
	3	11,186	43,269	25.85
	4	11,700	45,201	25.88
1984	1	13,309	46,835	28.42
	2	14,332	48,927	29.29
	3	15,544	50,394	30.84

transaction services, notably via ATMs, to their personal depositors. Moreover, the transaction services that they already provide allow their depositors to choose among quite a wide range of alternative options of instruments with varying withdrawal facilities and interest rates. If the proposals in the Green Paper are promulgated as suggested, it will further blur the distinction between banks and building societies, at least for macro-economic purposes. Together with the foreshadowed changes in the form and structure of the capital market, previous clear lines of distinction between separate types of financial intermediary are disappearing, as is also the distinction between transactions balances, e.g. M1, and savings balances.

Not only, therefore, are these distinctions between financial intermediaries, and between chequable and non-chequable instruments becoming blurred, but also an increasing proportion of monetary assets, with the exception of currency, discussed further below, is bearing a market-related interest rate (though several of the facilities now being offered by the clearing banks which provide interest on chequable facilities do not incorporate any automatic adjustment of that interest rate in line with market variations). Under these circumstances, the choice of the asset-holder to shift between one asset and another depends on interest-rate *relativities,* where the relative own rate offered by each individual financial intermediary is *not* subject to the direct influence of the authorities, and cannot be easily made greater, or less, by the authorities seeking to influence the *general* level of interest rates, which latter they still remain capable of doing. Under such circumstances, and with the increasing financial sophistication of wealth holders, the elasticity of substitution, i.e. the speed and responsiveness of shifting between different assets in response to changing interest-rate relativities may well increase, but the authorities may equally find it increasingly difficult to exert much influence over such relativities. It is not moreover just the alternative interest rates on different *assets* that matters for the disposition of wealth holders' funds. The 'spread' between deposit and lending rates is at the same time a particularly important relativity, measuring, as it does, the actual cost of financial intermediation.

When the cost of providing a service is relatively low, then one would expect that more use would be made of such services. A theoretical analysis demonstrating that additional use will be made of intermediation, with both bank lending and bank deposits increasing, when the cost of intermediation falls, has been provided by Sprenkle and Miller (26). Effectively when the 'spread', or cost of intermediation is low, the cost of acquiring liquidity services, through borrowing, also declines to a point at which (large) wealth holders may find it desirable to increase borrowing for the purpose of adding to their wholly-owned deposit holdings. Various additional features, such as the tendency of banks to withdraw, or at least to query, overdraft facilities that remain unused, and fees on unused facilities, also serve to encourage large wealth holders to expand their borrowings and deposits simultaneously, as the spread narrows. The importance of the spread in this respect has been demonstrated by Johnston for the Euro-markets (15), and, although there is no direct evidence domestically, it is also believed to have played some, possibly important, role in explaining the large-scale build up of both company sector advances and deposits by UK companies during the 1980s. Thus, the cost of intermediation to large borrowers, such as sovereign countries and large companies, has probably already fallen to a point at which the choice of whether to obtain funds by borrowing, or by running down deposits, or even under certain occasions to expand both borrowing and deposits simultaneously, may depend rather finely on apparently small changes in interest rate relativities.

Fischer Black (1970) (2) considers the circumstances that would allow a

310

world 'in which money does not exist'. A major requirement is that, 'Each
bank is allowed to accept deposits under any conditions that it chooses to
specify, and to pay any rate of interest on these deposits. In particular, the
bank can allow transfers of credit by check between two interest-bearing
accounts. Demand deposits will pay interest, and depositors are likely to be
charged the full cost of transferring credit from one account to another.
Almost all deposits will be in the form of demand deposits' (page 10). In this
world, 'An individual, business or government will simply have an account
at a bank; there will be no need to distinguish between accounts with
positive balances (deposits) and accounts with negative balances (loans).
An individual may write a check that converts his deposit into a loan, or he
may receive a salary payment that converts his loan into a deposit. So long
as his loan does not come to exceed the maximum permitted by the bank,
there is no need to make special note of these transactions' (page 11).
Abstracting from currency holdings, then '... there is nothing in this
simpler world that can meaningfully be called a quantity of money. Some
might say that the total value of all positive bank accounts is the quantity of
money. But this makes a completely arbitrary distinction between positive
and negative bank accounts. And it means that the quantity of money will
change every time an individual transfers credit from his negative bank
account to another individual's positive bank account. Others might say
that the net value of all bank accounts, both positive and negative, is the
quantity of money. But the net value of all the accounts in a bank is simply
the capital of that bank. It is equal to the assets of the bank (its loans) minus
the liabilities of the bank (its deposits). Thus, the net value of all bank
accounts is equal to the aggregate value of all bank securities. We would
hardly want to call this the quantity of money'.

Along similar lines, Wallace (1983) (31) asks 'But what is so special about
deposits subject to check and private bank notes? They are particular
private credit instruments. If it makes sense to control their quantities, why
not those of other credit instruments? For example, most economists would
not favor a proposal to constrain the dollar volume of mortgages on single
family residences to grow at a prescribed rate. Almost certainly, most
would say that it is a necessary feature of a well-functioning credit system
that the number of mortgages be determined in the market and not be set
administratively. But if this is right for one set of private credit instruments,
why is it not right for all? No satisfactory answer has ever been given' (page
6).

Have we then reached the point in the UK at which the legal restrictions
surrounding banking have been eroded so far that not only is it hardly

feasible to give an unambiguous answer to the question 'What is money?', but also at which the econometric relationships that applied earlier are now comprehensively breaking down? The conditions described by Fischer Black as consistent with such a world do increasingly seem to hold for the UK at least. Such arguments would seem to have some considerable validity when considering the behaviour of the *wealthier* asset-holders at least. In particular, given the sensitivity of, for example, sovereign countries and large corporate treasurers in deciding on their disposition of their liquid financial assets and liabilities to the 'spread', or cost of intermediation, it becomes difficult to believe that their behaviour will be affected in a stable and systematic manner by their access to bank *deposits* only; instead such wealthy asset holders may be more responsive to changes in their *net liquidity* position. As James Davidson has pointed out (8) (page 265), however, the same is not necessarily true of persons. The imperfections of financial and capital markets are still such that the spread between the cost of borrowing and the return on deposits facing an ordinary individual can still be extremely large, and the abcence of collateral may mean that a person in many circumstances is unable to borrow al all. When subject to financial constraints of this kind, an individual's expenditure may well be strongly influenced, indeed constrained, by his access to liquid assets, or even to more narrowly defined monetary balances. Thus the buffer-stock approach may be applicable to persons, but less so to the company or public sectors: indeed, that is why public sector (government) deposits are generally excluded from definitions of the aggregate money stock, precisely because they are thought to bear virtually no relation to the public sector's other general economic activities e.g. their expenditure.

If this is so, then an accurate sectoral analysis of incomes, and expenditures, together with sectoral holdings of money-like liquid assets (and short-term liabilities and facilities), would be important for macro-economic analytical purposes. Unfortunately, in the UK at least, the financial data on sectoral accounts exhibit very little coherence with the national income accounts for those same sectors. Thus, the quarterly data on the company sector surplus, or deficit, obtained from the national income accounts, shows little coherence or correlation with the estimated data on net financial borrowing, as obtained from financial sources (largely from the banks). As can be seen from Table 2, the unidentified residual between these two has been huge and extremely variable over the course of recent quarters. The available quarterly sectoral national income data base is unfortunately poor, at least in the UK. If we are to make much headway in developing our understanding of behavioural responses to monetary stim-

Table 2. Reconciliation of ICCs' surplus/deficit and net borrowing requirement (£ millions seasonally adjusted)

		Financial surplus/deficit (1)	Identifiable financial transactions* (2)	Balancing item (3)	Net borrowing requirement (4)
1982	1	−458	−443	−2,458	3,359
	2	234	−2,011	−456	2,233
	3	1,765	−1,111	−1,270	616
	4	2,880	−1,947	122	−1,055
1983	1	2,021	408	−1,418	−1,011
	2	1,497	−1,184	−1,175	862
	3	2,527	−1,764	−1,756	993
	4	1,827	−1,487	2,236	−2,576
1984	1	3,016	−698	−4,219	1,901
	2	2,396	−2,779	−1,894	2,277

* Including: Net unremitted profits, net identified trade and other credit, investment in UK company securities and investment abroad.

Columns (1) + (2) + (3) + (4) sum to zero.

Source: Economic Trends Table 62.

uli, we may instead have to do much more work at the micro level, perhaps trying to develop additional sources of data. I continually hope to be able to persuade commercial bank economists to make more use of the micro data available within their own banks, despite problems of confidentiality. For ourselves, we are seeking also to push ahead with trying to develop understanding at the micro level by the use of an additional data source, in this case the annual balance sheet returns from a wide sample of companies as collected by Datastream. The nature of such data, obtained from annual balance sheets, will, however, condition and limit the general applicability of such research. It may be that economists from other countries would be able to obtain better data sources.

CURRENCY

Wallace (31) argues that legal restrictions are also responsible for the peculiar nature of currency, notably its non-interest-bearing form. He notes that large-value, riskless, government-issued Treasury bills and bonds exist. Why cannot a financial intermediary issue much lower valued currency assets, bearing interest, against the backing of such riskless government debt, with a small interest margin to remunerate the intermediary for 'breaking bulk'? Wallace's answer is that such financial intermediaries would, indeed, develop but for legal constraints, (such as the 1844 Bank of England Act) which restrict other commercial banks, and other intermediaries from competing with the Central Bank in the production of small notes. It is, Wallace claims, such institutional constraints that explain the continuation of the monopoly, non-interest-bearing currency issue by Central Banks.

Two minor qualifications should, perhaps, be made at this stage. First, there are, on occasions, overtones from the 'legal restrictions' school that such restrictions were imposed on an unwilling public by governments keen to raise revenue from seigniorage. This is far from wholly true, as a study of 19th century monetary history would indicate. First, the unification of the currency via the Central Bank in countries such as Germany, Italy and Switzerland was regarded not only as a welcome symbol of national unification, but ended years of inconvenience and public disaffection with often badly-working systems of pluralist note emission. Second, the centralisation of note issue in the Central Bank was regarded as a valuable prudential measure; as Leslie Pressnell has reminded me, in 19th century Britain there was a clear distinction, comparable with that between the external creditor

314

and the equity holder in ordinary business, between notes and deposits. The acceptor, and then holder, of notes had less choice, often facing a local, or regional, monopolist (or oligopolist), whereas the depositor acted virtually by free choice. The depositor was not normally protected in the case of a bank run, when, by contrast, local worthies would proclaim support for note holders. Restricting note issue to the Central Bank was widely seen as improving the security and general acceptability of the public's currency, and as such was generally popular, except among private note issuers facing a loss of property rights.

The second qualification is that there do remain some examples of 'competitive' private bank note issues, e.g. in Scotland and Hong Kong. In these cases, however, the banks, though benefiting from a small fiduciary issue, have to back any incremental issue, one for one, with non-interest-bearing legal tender (Bank of England notes in Scotland; US dollars now in Hong Kong). Nevertheless the banks obtain a benefit in that their till money becomes costless, and they obtain some extra public recognition. Indeed, following on the recent notification of the withdrawal of the £1 note in England, there was a query whether English banks could follow the Scottish example. However, note issue under such severe constraints, is not what Wallace, and others, have in mind for freely competitive note issue.

Anyhow, Wallace (31) (page 4) predicts that 'the effects of imposing laissez-faire (would take) the form of an either/or statement: either nominal rates go to zero or existing government currency becomes worthless'. That statement can be explained, and partly qualified, as follows. Any holder of non-interest-bearing (nib) currency, issued by the Central Bank, could take such notes to his (her) own commercial bank, and exchange non-interest-bearing for interest-bearing (ib) private notes. The commercial bank, in turn, could use the Central Bank currency to buy Treasury bills. The Central Bank could force its own nib notes back into circulation, e.g. by open market purchases, since these are legal tender, but they would only stay in circulation if the return to the holder in going to exchange such notes for private ib notes was low enough to make the exercise not worthwhile (i.e. interest rates on privately issued notes would have to fall to low levels). Alternatively the Central Bank's nib notes would be forced out of circulation, (which is not quite the same as becoming worthless), and would be replaced by privately issued ib notes.

That analysis is based on the assumption, however, that privately issued notes would provide equivalent transactions' services to existing Central Bank currency. As already noted, there must remain a presumption that private bank notes would, at least under certain circumstances, be perceived as carrying more risk. In addition, it is possible that currency enjoys such economies of scale and economies of information that it becomes a form of 'public good'. The wider the range over which a currency is used, and the greater the trust attributed to the ability of the currency issuer to maintain the value of that currency, the greater will be the usefulness, and use, of that particular currency. Thus it may be that currency issue approximates to a 'natural monopoly', and, as a monopolist, the issuer is not then under competitive pressure to offer an interest rate. Claassen (4) argues that the objective of monetary integration, and the convenience of monetary union, would seem to require a single currency, a 'natural monopoly', which then conflicts with the objectives of achieving a greater degree of competition in the provision of currencies. Others, Vaubel (30), Salin (23), agree that economies of scale and information would restrict the number of potential competitive issuers, but claim that the result of competition would be oligopoly, rather than (governmental) monopoly, a state of affairs which they view as preferable. Also see Klein (17).

Nevertheless, in a sense, there already exist competitive issues of privately-produced currencies by commercial entities in the form of Travellers Cheques. For most practical purposes, a Travellers Cheque, such as an American Express Check, is a form of currency. Interestingly enough, these also do not offer interest[1]: perhaps when a bank has reached a size and reputation to make its Travellers Cheques widely acceptable, such issuers have already obtained a sufficient degree of monopoly to enable them to make their 'currencies' acceptable *without* having to offer an interest rate.

Another feature which is sometimes advanced as an explanation of the absence of payment of interest on currency is the technical difficulties that would be involved in doing so. In particular, if the currency issue included a coupon payable at a certain moment, or if the holder of the currency receives interest on a particular date, then the return to holding that currency would rise sharply as the date of interest payment neared. At the limit such currency issues, particularly of a higher face value, would be withdrawn entirely from circulation, as the date of payment drew near (an example of Gresham's Law). Nevertheless such technical difficulties could be circumvented, or at least mitigated, in certain respects. Thus, for example, the issuer of a Travellers Cheque could provide a randomised prize for the holders of such cheques based on the number on the cheque, akin to a premium bond in the UK, which would make the mathematical expectation of interest receipt the same as a regular interest payment, but would reduce somewhat the resultant disincentive to using such cheques as currency. Again, the arrival of 'smart' plastic cards might allow the funds represented by the remaining value of that card to be continuously (and slowly) augmented electronically at the going rate of interest. In the meantime, the spread of the ability of bank customers to draw, and redeposit, cash via ATMs from (to) interest-bearing deposit accounts, and the possible further step of making the ATM card usable in an EFTPOS system, will enhance the ability of customers to earn interest on all their liquid asset holdings for a larger proportion of the time.

Be that as it may, one can certainly imagine ways in which the technical difficulties of providing a yield, or interest, on currency instruments could be overcome. In that case, absent legal restrictions, could we expect commercial financial intermediaries to compete in making such instruments available, and what might be the consequences?

CONTROL

Wallace (31), and Jao (13), argue further that, not only does the stable relationship between certain forms of monetary deposit and nominal incomes and interest rates depend upon a particular set of legal restrictions, but that so also does the ability of the authorities to control the money stock. Wallace and Jao consider the case in which both government and private sector issue notes competitively side-by-side.

Thus Jao (13) writes (pages 18 and 19), 'Now suppose that government monopoly of currency issue and reserve requirement no longer exist, and a common constant-cost technology for the production and distribution of small-denomination bearer notes is available to the government as well as private intermediaries. Consider the same open market operation again, whereby the purchase of Treasury bills is made by issue of currency notes. This time, however, there is no increase in the money stock. For the private intermediaries simply scale down their note-issue operations, offsetting one-for-one the government issue in the open market operation. The resources thus released from private intermediaries are employed by the government to produce and maintain a larger stock of government currency. The said open market operation merely changes the location of a particular economic activity. Otherwise, nothing else is affected: neither interest rates, nor the price level, nor the level of economic activity . . . The re-interpretation and extension of the Modigliani-Miller theorem undermines the monetarist case in two ways. First, the theorem demonstrates that it is neither necessary nor possible to control bank intermediation and hence bank deposits. Second, government exogenous control of the money stock is an illusion, an illusion made possible only by an uncritical acceptance of a host of binding legal restrictions'.

This claim, that the provision of privately issued (ib) notes in conditions of laissez-faire would undermine the authorities' monetary control, in my view goes too far, and is based on the implicit assumption that the authorities, in those circumstances, would peg the interest rate on their own notes at a *fixed* level. But it is already well established that, if the authorities fix the interest rate(s) on their own liabilities (e.g. Treasury bills), they cannot simultaneously fix the monetary quantities outstanding. Thus I argued earlier that, if the authorities offered only nib currency while private financial institutions offered ib notes, the two sets of notes would only co-exist when the interest rate was driven low enough to make the utility of holding both at the same time equal at the margin. If the Central Bank then forced more nib currency into the system, it would tend to drive down real rates of interest by forcing up inflation or driving down nominal interest rates. That would induce private sector note issuers to reduce their own issues. If this process of substitution was virtually perfect, as Jao implies, there need be little change in the total volume of currency outstanding, etc.

But the authorities could, in these circumstances, restore their own grip simply enough. All that they would need to do would be to vary the interest rate that they themselves offered on their own currency. This would then provide the basis for the *general* level of rates, while the various costs of intermediation, maturity preferences, etc, would determine the *relativities* between rates. The authorities' control over the general level of rates would, in turn, influence the demand for credit and saving, and the general rate of expansion of nominal incomes and monetary expansion. Under the legal restrictions of the present regime the general level of rates is determined by the rate charged for *access* to cash. If such legal restrictions were removed (and the technical problems of offering interest on cash overcome), the general rate of interest would be determined by the rate offered *on cash* by the Central Bank. If the Central Bank issued notes providing the bearer with a risk-less return of $X\%$, then that would provide the base-line from which all other rates would be determined. If technical means of providing and varying interest yields on cash could be developed, it might even offer an administratively-easier system of control for the authorities to operate than the present.

The above analysis assumes, however, not only that all legal restrictions, and technical obstacles, to the provision of ib currency by private intermediaries are removed, but also that the Central Bank competes in the provision of currency, the yield on which could, *and would,* be varied by administrative fiat. But what would happen in the (even more extreme) case in which, for one reason or another, the Central Bank in the country should cease to issue notes at all and passed over that function entirely to commercial banks? In such a circumstance, in which the note issuing function became entirely the responsibility of commercial banks, could the authorities subsequently maintain control over either interest rates or the money stock? In order to answer that question, it is necessary first to consider on what basis – or policy regime – banking would then be organised.

The first question is whether the bank deposits, and private note issues, would be convertible into a more 'fundamental' store of value, or would simply represent a proportionate share to the market value of the underlying assets held by the banks. The latter alternative would involve the commercial banks shifting towards a 'unit trust' approach. One of the major differences between banks and unit trusts, in their roles as financial intermediaries, relates to the nature of the valuation of their assets. The assets held by unit trusts are, for the most part, marketable; in the case of banks, the assets held by them are, for the most part, non-marketable (or, at least, are not marketed), and there is no market mechanism for establishing in a competitive and open fashion their true expected value. One of the more interesting questions about banking (to which no answer will be attempted here), is why any sizeable (secondary) market in bank loans, or at least loans of certain specific kinds, has not already developed; though there are currently some signs of developments in that direction.

So long as such markets in loans do not develop (and may in general perhaps not be possible to develop), thereby allowing a market price to be placed on the assets on the commercial banks, considerable uncertainty about the underlying asset values of the banks will persist (even after taking account of the effect of supervision, accounting, etc). There would, therefore, in a world in which banks faced similar market and accounting practices as now, remain considerable uncertainty as to what the true value of a proportionate share in such assets would amount to. This would complicate the development of 'unit trust' banking. Furthermore, it would remain to be seen how popular such an institution would be; White (33) expresses certain reservations on this score. Nevertheless, certain institutions along such lines are beginning to emerge, which offer transactions services against a deposit holding which is, or can be, revalued continuously in line with the value of the institutions' own portfolio. For example, some of the fund management arrangements in the US, and also some aspects of Islamic banking – a neglected topic among Western monetary economists –

have similarities with the concept of 'unit trust' banking. Such an institution, with deposits which were *not* nominally capital certain, could not, however, qualify as a 'bank' in the UK, under the definition as set out in the 1979 Banking Act. Some recent analysts have further envisaged a hypothetical future system in which both the note and deposit liabilities of such 'unit trust' banks are valued in terms of a numeraire consisting, perhaps, of (an indexed combination of) commodities, which no note/deposit holder would have any incentive to hold directly (see Greenfield and Yeager (10)). There are various problems about the feasibility of such a world, e.g. how would the relative prices of the commodities entering the numeraire be set themselves, or the practical likelihood of its development (see White (33)).

Nevertheless if we should accept the hypothetical possibility of such a system, what role would then be left for a Central Bank, with no outside currency in existence and, thus, no shifts between inside and outside money? One important role that now exists is as banker to the government, and, as we shall later again pick up, that function nowadays provides an even more important reason for commercial banks to hold bankers' balances than the need for access to notes: but that function could, in theory, also be transferred to, and among, competitive private banks. One major problem would, however, remain within this commercial banking system. So long as deposits are much more easily transferable between banks than are bank loans – because arranging the latter requires specialised information and confidential arrangements – any large scale shifts of funds from one bank to another could cause major difficulties for the borrowers of banks losing deposits, and would require recycling. This will be discussed at greater length in a forthcoming longer paper on 'The Evolution of Central Banks: A Natural Development?' (9). So a supervisory, recycling function would remain, but whether, in such a world, the authorities would either wish, or be able, to maintain any control functions, i.e. whether they would need, or be able, to influence interest rates, seems obscure.

Let us assume, instead, that banks retain the particular feature of offering liabilities which are fixed in value, i.e. convertible, against some other asset (i.e. that they do not simply represent a proportionate share of the value of the bank's asset book). Again we could imagine banks choosing to make their liabilities convertible into differing stores of value, e.g. gold, a foreign currency, another commodity, a basket of commodities, or perhaps an index such as the RPI. If banks independently chose a whole set of differing stores of value, into which to make their liabilities convertible, that would add considerably to the inconvenience of the public. Thus the current values of the banks' individual liabilities, would be continually shifting re the numeraire, as the spot prices of the more 'fundamental' assets into which their liabilities were convertible fluctuated, and the interest rates offered by each of the independent banks would have to adjust as expectations of the relative future prices of their particular fundamental assets altered. So, there would be considerable advantages, economies of scale and information, of a public good nature, to encouraging all the various banks to adhere to the same brand of convertibility.

The present form of convertibility requires the banks to make their deposits convertible into the legal tender non-interest-bearing notes issued by the Central Bank. Let us consider instead a convertible system, in which the banks make their liabilities, both deposits and notes, both of which bear a competitive interest rate, convertible into a commodity, say gold. If there was to be such a return to the gold standard, would there be any need for a Central Bank. Would it have a function? If such a Central Bank was established in a gold standard world, could it influence interest rates and the money stock?

As a factual matter of historical record, Central Banks in the main industrialized countries of Europe and Japan became established, and evolved a role, during the gold standard period. Although their influence over interest rates and monetary developments was subject to the constraints involved in maintaining the gold standard regime, they undoubtedly played a considerable role in influencing the timing and extent of interest rate changes in their country, and also a role in fostering the development of financial intermediation in their countries. It is, however, the argument of a number of monetary historians, who have adopted, in some large part, the legal restrictions approach, that central banks were established primarily as a result of governmental legislative intervention, which unnecessarily and undesirably restricted the freedom of the financial systems. They claim that there was no necessary function for central banks within such a gold standard system, and, indeed, that such systems, as in Scotland, would have functioned better without them (see 3, 27, 32).

In my longer, forthcoming paper (9), I shall challenge this latest historical interpretation of the evolution of Central Banks. In this paper, I argue that there *are* natural reasons why a central bank would develop within such a convertible commodity system. Let me here give three reasons for this view.

First, the commodity, into which the deposits and the notes are to be made convertible, itself is barren, in the sense of being non-interest-bearing. There are, therefore, economies of reserve centralisation to be obtained by the individual banks, particularly in a unit-banking system, centralising their own reserves with a strong and trust-worthy bank at the centre: then the remaining banks can hold their own reserves in this central bank in the form of interest-bearing correspondent balances. Particularly if this central bank has the support of the government behind it, so that it need not be profit-maximising, such centralisation would allow the banks as a whole to maintain convertibility into the chosen commodity at a higher rate of profit than would otherwise be feasible.

Secondly, given the difficulty of observing the true value of each bank's assets, which has already been mentioned, the value attached by the depositor, and note holder, to a commercial bank's liabilities, will depend as much on confidence and trust in the bank's reputation, as on the available valuation (for what it is worth) of the bank's assets. There is a public good aspect to such reputation, in the sense that the failure, and/or revealed bad behaviour, of one bank, will throw doubt and distrust over the reputation of a wider range of other banks. Given this public good nature of reputation, there will be a felt need among banks for rules of good conduct to be followed. Owing to conflicts of interest, it would be difficult for commercial banks to act together to set such rules, e.g. for the criteria required to become a bank, or to monitor the adherence of each other to such rules, since that would involve at least some degree of opening of books, and exchange of confidentiality, with competitors. A solution to this latter problem is to shift such supervisory and control functions to an outside institution, such as a central bank, particularly since its lender of last resort function would seem to entail its close involvement in such matters.

Finally, the combination of the convertibility promise, together with the uncertainty about each bank's underlying asset value, allows, as history has shown only too clearly, the possibility of contagion of distrust to occur, in which the failure of one bank can trigger off doubts about other banks, leading to a crisis of illiquidity, and associated insolvency. So, there would seem to be a need for an institution, which would be capable of stemming such panics by acting as lender of last resort in the traditional Bagehot manner.

For all such reasons, a Central Bank is likely to emerge, even when the liabilities of the private commercial banks are convertible into a commodity, rather than into fiat money, and even when the note issue within the country is provided entirely, or in the main, by the same private commercial banks. The essential functions of a Central Bank, as a central (efficient) repository of barren reserves and as a lender of last resort, bring in their train a (reasonably stable) behavioural demand among the commercial banks for balances with the central bank. This latter is the key to the influence of the Central Bank over the level of interest rates and the rate of growth of the monetary aggregates. Given this (stable) demand function for Central Bank balances, the authorities can undertake open market operations, to affect at the same time both the quantities of such balances and the rate of interest at which banks can obtain access to such balances. The question of whether the Central Bank should aim primarily to influence the quantity of balances held with it, or the level of interest rates at which the banks can obtain access to such balances, is, for this purpose, a secondary issue.

Nevertheless, within a regime of convertibility into a commodity, such as the gold standard, the Central Bank's influence on interest rates is both more direct, and more directly influential in affecting the inward and outward flow of gold into the country, than is its influence via control over the quantity of bank reserves: the relationship of bankers' balances at the Central Bank with the various wider monetary aggregates, is, in a free system, subject to the changing behaviour of the individual commercial banks. Variations in such reserve ratios, however, can be limited by making them mandatory. But if such required ratios then act as an effective constraint on bank behaviour, they must represent, to a greater or lesser extent, a burden, and therefore involve a tax on banking, which in turn the banks will try to avoid by innovation or disintermediation.

To conclude and summarise, the question of whether the Central Bank, or the commercial banks, provide the notes which are used as hand-to-hand currency is actually irrelevant to the question of whether the Central Bank can establish control. What is needed, and essential, is a relatively stable demand function by the banking system for the liabilities of the Central Bank. Wallace and Jao examined a case in which no such stable demand function existed, because Central Bank and commercial bank notes co-existed and were (perfectly) substitutable. Even then, I have argued, the Central Bank can simply restore its control over the general level of interest rates, and thence over monetary developments, by varying the rate of interest that it was itself prepared to offer on cash instruments. Moreover, even if the Central Bank completely abandoned the note-issuing function to the commercial banks, there would still be a stable demand for balances to be held with a Central Bank.

This latter was argued in the context of a system with deposits, and private notes, convertible into a commodity. The same would obviously be true within a fiat money system of the kind now generally existing. Indeed the need of the commercial banks to obtain notes and currency from the

Table 3.

(£mns)		Exchequer transactions	Maturing assistance	Notes[1]	Other[2]	Total shortage
Monday	19.11.84	−55	−685	+279	+216	−245
Tuesday	20.11.84	+203	−349	+41	+23	−82
Wednesday	21.11.84	−221	−326	−102	+39	−610
Thursday	22.11.84	+269	−686	−36	+204	−249
Friday	23.11.84	+186	−707	−232	−243	−996
Total for week		+382	−2,753	−50	+239	−2,182

1. No figures available for coin but the sums involved are minute on a daily basis.
2. Includes bankers balances brought forward, net gilt transactions, take-up of Treasury Bills, Foreign Exchange and miscellaneous.

Central Bank currently represents a relatively small proportion of the cash flows influencing the commercial banks' overall reserve position on a day-to-day basis. A much larger proportion of the daily cash flows, affecting banks' reserve positions, is the result of transactions with the public sector. Indeed, as can-be seen from Table 3 above, which reports the main cash flows in the UK in a recent, reasonably representative, week, the flows resulting from transactions with the government were very much larger than those arising from changes in the outstanding note issue. So long as the Central Bank is the government's bank[2], and the government, therefore requires payment in the form of a claim on its own bank, i.e. on the Central Bank, there will be another important reason for the commercial banks to maintain reserve balances with the Central Bank. It is such bankers' balances at the Central Bank, and not the note issue, which serves as the main fulcrum for establishing a Central Bank's control.

CONCLUSION

The ability of a Central Bank to maintain its influence over interest rates, and a generalised pressure on the rate of monetary expansion, depends ultimately on commercial banks needing to retain balances with itself. That need would appear likely to continue so long as the banks themselves need to maintain the convertibility of their own liabilities, whether deposits or notes, into a more 'fundamental' store of value, whether that be (a basket of) commodities, or into fiat money. It does *not,* I have argued, depend to any important extent on the note-issuing function of the Central Bank, and, in the perhaps improbable circumstances that that latter function were to pass, in part or in whole, to the commercial banks, the Central Bank's power would not be seriously diminished. So, I do not myself believe that any of the many, far-reaching structural changes now underway (or indeed even if some of the more visionary changes were to take place in future), would seriously erode the present power of Central Banks to influence interest rates and the pace of monetary expansion.

The problems that the structural changes do bring are not that they diminish the Central Bank's power to control, but rather that the blurring of instruments and institutions make it more difficult to assess and to interpret financial developments, and thence to judge how to apply monetary controls. I have quoted assertions by others, and presented arguments that suggest that, in these circumstances, there can be no single, continuously reliable, unambiguous, and unchanging definition of money; and also that there are likely to be sizeable shifts between different forms of liquid assets by wealth holders in response to interest-rate *relativities,* which the authorities cannot control, although they can still influence the general level of short-term interest rates.

In such circumstances, if these are indeed a proper reflection of today's reality, it would hardly be possible, nor sensible, for the authorities to commit themselves *rigidly* to achieving a specified numerical growth rate for any particular definition of money over any period much longer than a year, or two. Nevertheless, in a fiat system world, there is an understandable fear that the growth of the money stock, and thence inflation, is driven by the short-term expedients of the authorities, which may not only have a bias to inflation, but also gives no basis for confidence about longer-term price stability, nor even what rate of inflation might be reasonably expected. As Leijonhufvud has shown, for example in (20), such general uncertainty can have most adverse economic effects. Against that background, there is an understandable and justifiable demand for the authorities to adopt a degree of pre-commitment, to submit themselves to certain clearly-defined rules, sufficient to allay fears about future uncertain inflation, and to provide the necessary basis of financial stability for the economic system to work effectively. It is the counter-balance between the shifting structure of the financial system on the one hand, and the need for rules and pre-commitment on the part of the authorities on the other, that makes it so hard to select an optimal form of monetary targetry, one that could retain underlying discipline, while at the same time allowing a sensible and flexible response to the rapidly changing form of the financial system.

NOTES

1. Issuers of such cheques do provide a service, to wit refund in the case of loss, which is not available from holding currency; on the other hand most purchasers pay a commission to the selling agent when buying Travellers Cheques. I am indebted to Mr L.D.D. Price for this, and other helpful comments.

2. It might be argued that, in a laissez-faire world, the government need not necessarily place the handling of its financial affairs with the Central Bank, but with whichever bank offered it the best competitive terms. There would, however, be problems with this course. The government would be such a large customer that it might – or it might be feared that it might – use its market power to exert direct influence on the commercial banks with which it was dealing. Furthermore, switching banking operations from one bank to another, or dividing the operations between several banks, could well be less efficient than the present course: the Bank of England prides itself on the efficiency with which it handles the government's

326

financial affairs. Again, the role of the government as the fiscal authority, and in some cases as the supervisory authority, might cause it to face conflicts of interest in the course of any direct commercial dealings with the privately-owned banks.

REFERENCES

1. Artis, M.J. 'The Monopolies Commission Report', *Bankers' Magazine*, Vol. 206, No. 1494 (September 1968), pages 128–135: also see Section IV, 'Efficiency', ed. M.J. Artis, pages 281–338 in *Readings in British Monetary Economies*, ed. H.G. Johnson (Clarendon Press: Oxford, 1972).
2. Black, Fischer 'Banking and Interest Rates in a World Without Money', *Journal of Bank Research*, Vol. 1, No. 3 (Autumn 1970), pages 8–28.
3. Cameron, R. *Banking in the Early Stages of Industrialization* (Oxford University Press: New York, 1967).
4. Claassen, E.M. 'Monetary Integration and Monetary Stability: The Economic Criteria of the Monetary Constitution', Chapter I.3 in *Currency Competition and Monetary Union*, ed. P. Salin (Martinus Nijhoff: The Hague, 1984).
5. Davidson, J.E.H. 'Money Disequilibrium: An Approach to Modelling Monetary Phenomena in the UK', London School of Economics, mimeo, 1984.
6. Fama, E.F. 'Banking in the Theory of Finance', *Journal of Monetary Economics* (No. 6, 1980), pages 39–57.
7. Goodhart, C.A.E. 'The Importance of Money', *Bank of England Quarterly Bulletin*, Vol. 10, No. 2 (June 1970), pages 159–198; reprinted in *Monetary Theory and Practice* (Macmillan: London, 1984), pages 21–66.
8. Goodhart, C.A.E. 'Disequilibrium Money – A Note', Chapter 10, pages 254–276, in *Monetary Theory and Practice* (Macmillan: London, 1984).
9. Goodhart, C.A.E. *The Evolution of Central Banks: A Natural Development?* London School of Economics Monographs; London, 1985.
10. Greenfield, R.L. and Yeager, L.B. 'A Laissez-Faire Approach to Monetary Stability', *Journal of Money, Credit, and Banking*, Vol. 15, No. 3 (August 1983).
11. Hacche, G. 'The Demand for Money in the United Kingdom: Experience Since 1971', *Bank of England Quarterly Bulletin*, Vol. 14, No. 3 (September 1974), pages 284–305.
12. Hall, R.E. 'A Review of Monetary Trends in the United States and the United Kingdom from the Perspective of New Developments in Monetary Economics', *Journal of Economic Literature*, Vol. 20 (December 1982), pages 1552–1556.
13. Jao, Y.C. 'A Libertarian Approach to Monetary Theory and Policy', University of Hong Kong, Department of Economics Discussion Paper, No. 23 (November 1983).
14. Johnson, H.G. 'Problems of Efficiency in Monetary Management', *Journal of Political Economy*, Vol. 76, No. 5 (September/October 1968), pages 971–90; reprinted in *Readings in British Monetary Economics*, ed. H.G. Johnson (Clarendon Press: Oxford, 1972), pages 285–308.
15. Johnston, R.B. *The Economics of the Euro-Market* (Macmillan: London, 1983).
16. Kareken, J. and Wallace, N. 'On the Indeterminancy of Equilibrium Exchange Rates', *Quarterly Journal of Economics*, Vol. 96 (May 1981), pages 207–222.
17. Klein, B. 'The Competitive Supply of Money', *Journal of Money, Credit and Banking*, Vol. 6, No. 4 (November 1974), pages 423–453.

18. Knoester, A. 'Theoretical Principles of the Buffer Mechanism, Monetary Quasi-Equilibrium and its Spillover Effects', Institute for Economic Research, Discussion Paper Series (7908/G/M), Erasmus University, Rotterdam, 1979.

19. Laidler, D.E.W. 'The 'Buffer Stock' Notion in Monetary Economics', *Economic Journal Supplement*, Vol. 94 – Selected Papers from the 1983 AUTE Conference at Oxford University (1984), pages 17–34.

20. Leijonhufvud, A. 'Costs and Consequences of Inflation', Chapter 9 in *The Microeconomic Foundations of Macroeconomics* (Macmillan: London, 1977), pages 265–312.

21. Mills, T.C. 'The Information Content of the UK Monetary Aggregates', Bank of England, mimeo, presented at the AUTE Conference, University of Surrey, April 1982, see the 1983 Conference Supplement of the *Economic Journal*, page 142.

22. National board for prices and incomes Report No. 34, *Bank Charges*, Cmnd. 3292 (HMSO: London, 1967).

23. Salin, P. (ed.) *Currency Competition and Monetary Union* (Martinus Nijhoff: The Hague, 1984), especially the Introduction and Chapters I–III.

24. Sargent, T.J. and Wallace, N. 'The Real-Bills Doctrine Versus the Quantity Theory: A Reconsideration', *Journal of Political Economy*, Vol. 90 (December 1982), pages 1212–1236.

25. Sargent, T.J. and Wallace, N. 'A Model of Commodity Money', Federal Reserve Bank of Minneapolis, Research Department Staff Report, No. 85 (1983).

26. Sprenkle, C.M. and Miller, M.H. 'The Precautionary Demand for Narrow and Broad Money', *Economica*, Vol. 47 (November 1980), pages 407–421.

27. Timberlake, R.H., Jr. *The Origins of Central Banking in the United States* (Harvard University Press: Cambridge, Mass., 1978).

28. Tobin, J. 'Commercial Banks as Creators of 'Money', in *Banking and Monetary Studies*, ed. Deane Carson (Irwin, Homewood, Ill., 1963), pages 408–419.

29. Treasury, Her Majesty's *Building Societies: A New Framework*, Cmnd. 9316 (HMSO: London, July 1984).

30. Vaubel, R. 'The Government's Money Monopoly: Externalities or Natural Monopoly', *Kyklos*, Vol. 37, No. 1 (1984), pages 27–58.

31. Wallace, N. 'A Legal Restrictions Theory of the Demand for 'Money' and the Role of Monetary Policy', *Federal Reserve Bank of Minneapolis Quarterly Review* (Winter 1983), pages 1–7.

32. White, L.H. 'Competitive Payments Systems and the Unit of Account', *American Economic Review*, Vol. 74, No. 4 (September 1984).

33. White, L.H. *Free Banking in Britain* (Cambridge University Press: Cambridge, 1984).

Chapter XXI

FINANCIAL INNOVATION AND MONETARY AGGREGATE
TARGETING

by *Jan H. Koning**

INTRODUCTION

Monetary policy is used by the monetary authorities to achieve certain macro economic goals, usually summarized as GNP and the rate of inflation. The influence of monetary policy on these ultimate goals of economic policy is not direct, but indirect, working through what are usually called intermediate targets. Neither the final goals of monetary policy, nor the intermediate targets are under the complete control of the central bank. Therefore, the structure of the intermediate target strategy suggests three important criteria for choosing a suitable target. First, and most obviously, the intermediate target must be sufficiently closely and stably linked to the final goals of policy so that a policy which makes the intermediate target reach certain levels will also mean that the ultimate targets reach certain associated levels. The second criterion concerns the controllability of the intermediate target. The problem of controlling the intermediate target gives rise to an operational target. In this respect it is important to distinguish between these two targets. The operating target plays an important role in the day-to-day conduct of monetary policy. This variable is closely associated with the instruments of monetary policy. By altering the policy instruments, the central bank has significant influence on the operational target, which in turn must be closely linked to the intermediate target. The final criterion for the choice of an intermediate target concerns the quality of measurement of this variable. It is quite obvious that it should provide frequent and accurate information, so that it can be monitored easily.

Intermediate targets fall into two groups, namely long-term interest rates on the one hand and monetary aggregates on the other. Until the mid-1970's the long-term interest rate was the most popular intermediate target.

* The present paper reflects the opinions of the author and does not purport to represent those of the institute (Netherlands Central Bureau of Statistics) of which he is an official.

Fair, D.E., (ed.) Shifting Frontiers in Financial Markets.
© *1986, Martinus Nijhoff Publishers, Dordrecht/Boston/Lancaster. ISBN 90-247-3225-5.*
Printed in the Netherlands.

However, in recent years the central banks of many developed countries have shifted to a monetary aggregate.[1] One of the greatest problems central bankers are faced with is that the financial environment in which they decide on and execute monetary policy is changing continuously. In this paper we analyse some important implications of financial innovation for the role of monetary aggregates as intermediate targets in the formulation and implementation of monetary policy.

In the second section, the salient features of financial innovation observed in a large number of countries are surveyed briefly. The subsequent section focuses on the extent to which financial innovation complicates the current conduct of monetary policy. The fourth and final section provides a summary and some tentative conclusions. Our main conclusion is that monetary aggregate targeting remains a useful strategy of monetary policy. However, there is a danger that financial innovations, on occasion, alter the degree of restraint desired by the central bank and intended by its choice of monetary growth targets. Therefore, it might be useful to supplement monetary growth rate targets with interest rates as a monetary indicator.

FINANCIAL CHANGES

The nature of financial institutions as well as the structure of the entire financial system has changed drastically during the past two decades. One of the most important changes concerns the fact that the liability side of the balance sheet of financial institutions is becoming increasingly dominated by 'managed liabilities', that is liabilities actively sought by their suppliers, the financial institutions themselves. Traditionally, banks passively accepted whatever funds depositors made available and then decided how to invest these funds. For the most part, banks have taken the liability side of the balance sheet as given and concerned themselves with asset management. Nowadays banks engage much more in liability management. They use the liability side of the balance sheet much more activily to obtain funds needed to meet reserve losses or to accommodate new loan demands. Because of greater competition, the emergence of liability management has produced a new financial environment in which the prevalent liabilities of the banks pay market-determined interest rates.

As a consequence of the process of financial innovation, fostered by liability management, a myriad of new financial instruments has appeared in the last ten years. According to Hadjimichalakis, these new liability instruments can be grouped into two categories.[2]

The first category refers to instruments which were designed to compete with the traditional demand deposits. These innovations concern the evolution of interest-bearing transaction accounts. These funds provide private households as well as corporations with new assets offering market-related interest rates and at the same time have the quality of a medium of exchange. The second category consists of instruments that were designed to compete with savings and time deposits. These innovations involve the introduction of remunerative assets which, although generally not directly used in transactions, can easily be converted into demand deposits or currency. As is well-known, recent financial innovations have been governed by a number of interrelated factors. Undoubtedly the major cause has been the rising, high, and highly variable nominal interest rates and the corresponding increase in the level of uncertainty about future rates. A second important influence has been the rapid technological advances applicable to the financial sector. Finally, the attempt by managers of financial institutions to avoid regulatory restrictions has induced substantial financial innovations.[3] An important result of the various innovations has been the creation of a financial structure with a growing number of instruments with both investment and transaction characteristics. Further, the transaction costs resulting from the substitution between different assets, have been substantially reduced.

The 'marketisation' of banking and finance – a term that refers to financial intermediation on conditions that are mainly determined by market forces – has not been restricted to the liability side of the balance sheet.[4] In general, financial institutions provide the service of intermediation across maturities; this means that they raise funds from investors who desire to lend their funds with a short maturity, and lend those funds on to borrowers who desire a long maturity. By maturity intermediation, financial intermediaries bear the risk of fluctuations in short-term interest rates. The risk borne by a financial institution which borrows short and lends long is the risk that short-term interest rates may rise and that the institution may have to increase its own short-term rates in order to retain its funds. Within the context of more volatile interest rates, financial institutions therefore are faced with a considerable interest rate risk. This risk is not a risk that can be diversified. In order to offset the higher interest rate risk, financial institutions attempt to match the conditions on their assets and liabilities by extending variable rate loans and by shortening the effective maturity of their fixed-rate earning assets. These matching activities explain the appearance on the asset side of the balance sheet of mostly assets earning marked-determined interest rates. It is clear that in this way borrowers are forced to share much of the risk that was formerly borne almost entirely by the financial institutions.

As has been mentioned above, the financial sector of the economy is currently in a state of very rapid change. One aspect of this change is that the old compartmentalization of financial institutions is breaking down. Therefore we finally pay attention to a third significant change in the financial system, namely the blurring and overlap in the functions of specific financial institutions. In recent past, financial institutions have been acting on the belief that they serve their customers best by offering them many different services. Consequently, an important reason for the increasing homogeneity of financial institutions has been the more intensive competition for all kinds of financial services among depository institutions and that between depository and non-depository institutions. With regard to the depository institutions, it can be said that these institutions have broadened their deposit and loan services, and in doing this they have overlapped considerably. The non-depository institutions have also diversified their financial activities and in some cases offer nowadays quasi-transactions services.

Summarizing it may be stated that, within a more homogeneous financial system, both the liabilities and the assets of financial institutions pay and earn, respectively, market-determined interest rates. In this financial environment interest rate adjustment has become faster and more important.

IMPLICATIONS FOR MONETARY AGGREGATE TARGETING

In this section first the implications of the marketisation of the financial sector for the transmission mechanism of monetary policy will be briefly indicated. The second sub-section is devoted to the analysis of the ways in which innovation-induced disturbances tend to undermine the monetary targeting approach.

The monetary transmission mechanism

In this sub-section we want to outline that the changes in the structure of the financial system as described in the previous section have important implications for the modus operandi of monetary policy. As is well-known from economic literature, four monetary transmission channels have always received special attention: the credit cost channel, the relative price mechanism, the wealth mechanism and the credit rationing channel.

In the first-mentioned transmission mechanism the effect of money on income operates through the cost of credit. The yields on short- and long-term debt instruments represent costs of borrowed funds to business firms and households. Consequently, the decrease in the yields that follows upon an increase in the quantity of money stimulates spending as a result of the lower costs of external finance. The higher the interest elasticity of spending, the higher will be the change in spending for a given change in the rate of interest. In the relative price mechanism a rise in the price of existing physical assets relative to the costs of reproducing them constitutes the crucial incentive for corporations to increase their investment activity. In this second transmission channel the fact is stressed that all assets, including money, have one common characteristic, namely they all involve costs and returns from holding them. This means that all assets in a portfolio can be treated as potential substitutes for each other. An increase in the quantity of money – brought about through open-market purchases by the central bank – results in a rise of the public's stock of cash balances relative to other assets. In consequence a portfolio adjustment process will come about. A complicated process of financial-asset substitution, induced by differences in relative yields, brings about a decline in the yields on financial assets. If the yields on these assets decline, then physical assets become relatively more attractive, resulting in an increase of spending on existing physical assets. This causes a rise in the price of existing physical assets relative to the price of newly produced capital goods. This ultimate price differential gives rise to an increased investment activity. The third transmission mechanism concentrates on the wealth effect. The operation of the wealth effect comes about in two ways. Firstly, a general decline in market interest rates, induced by an expansive monetary impulse, raises the current market value of assets with income streams of constant nominal value. The predicted effect of this indirect, interest-induced, wealth effect is an increase in consumer expenditures. Secondly, it is also possible that an increase in consumption is induced by a direct wealth effect. This effect operates through an increase in net wealth generated by a monetary expansion or through a fall in the general price level.

The effects that are based on the credit rationing channel are due to the absence of a market clearing price on the market for loans in general, and for bank loans in particular. Credit rationing exists when there is an unsatisfied demand for credit at the existing vector of credit conditions.[5] This excess demand for credit is not eliminated immediately by an increase of the price of credit. According to this mechanism the question is not so much what one has to pay for borrowed funds, but whether one can get funds at all. The crucial transmission-element of this availability channel refers to the spill-over effect which links up the credit market with the commodity market. If there exists an unsatisfied demand for credit the availability effect comes into operation, which generates a negative effect on expenditures. The impact of the credit rationing mechanism *cet. par.* will be greater according to a lesser flexibility of the price of credit. In this respect this channel differs basically from the three transmission channels which we have briefly discussed above. For the impact of these transmission channels – the credit cost mechanism, the relative price mechanism and the interest-induced wealth mechanism – is even stronger according to a greater flexibility of interest rates and prices of financial assets respectively. Therefore we can basically distinguish between two channels by which monetary policy is transmitted to the real sector of the economy, namely interest rates and credit availability.

The marketisation of the financial sector has significantly altered the transmission mechanism of monetary policy. The tendency for banks increasingly to buy funds at market-related interest rates and to relend them at rates related to the cost of interest-sensitive funds has diminished substantially the degree to which monetary policy works through the availability of credit. Before the marketisation of banking, restrictive monetary policy measures raising short-term interest rates tended to reduce bank profits. This decrease in profitability induced banks to reduce their lending at least in the short run. In terms of modern disequilibrium theory banks adjusted quantities rather than prices. The conventional demand functions for goods which assume market-clearing are no longer relevant in this sticky-interest rate world and must be replaced by 'effective' demand functions which take account of the quantity constraint in the credit market. In the flexible-rate financial markets fostered by the growth of marketisation monetary policy actions affecting bank funding costs are reflected quickly in the price of credit and to a much lower degree in the supply of credit. This means that in the present financial system, with its increased variability of interest rates as a result of stricter monetary targeting, interest rates have become the main monetary transmission variables.

An important question is whether the switch in the transmission mechanism has modified the strength of monetary policy. In this respect it is important to emphasize that under a credit rationing regime restrictive policy measures operate through credit *supply* constraints. Therefore the strength of monetary policy through the credit rationing channel is very dependent on the lack of alternative sources of finance or imperfect substitutability of these sources with bank loans. However, in the present flexible rate environment these measures work through reduction in the *demand* for credit. For this reason, the interest elasticity of aggregate expenditures is an important determinant of the present strength of monetary policy. If this elasticity is low, interest rates must rise higher to achieve significant restraint than was true in the period before the marketisation of the financial sector took place. It is quite possible that the interest elasticity of expenditures has risen over time because of the fact that more loans have been on a variable rate basis. For, in a world with fixed rate banking, when rates rise only the prospective borrower is affected, whereas with variable rate loans the cash flow of all borrowers, not just new borrowers, is affected. However, Wenninger points out quite rightly that, if variable-rate borrowers expect to pay some average rate and not the initial rate, then the transition to floating rates would not have to affect the interest responsiveness of final demand.[6] It is clear that, on a priori grounds, the effect of financial innovation on the strength of monetary policy is difficult to spell out and that the subject should be studied on an empirical basis.

Financial shocks

This sub-section is primarily concerned with the question whether the marketisation of the financial sector has decreased the usefulness of monetary aggregates as intermediary targets. In order to analyse this question we formulate a simple model of a stylized financial system.[7] We shall assume that the financial sector consists of only one kind of financial institution, which we shall call banks. This construction reflects the increasing homogeneity among financial institutions. The balance sheet of this typical financial institution resembles the following:

Balance sheet of typical financial institution

Assets			Liabilities
Reserves	R	Deposits	D
Earning assets	A	Borrowed reserves	RB

We shall examine a situation in which banks supply only one type of deposit to the non-financial sector. The banks pay a flexible, market-determined, interest rate, r_D, on the deposits they issue. These deposits – collectively called demand deposits – are managed actively by banks. The assumption of a single category of deposit liabilities is an expression of the characteristic that deposits nowadays are largely 'managed liabilities'. In order to attract these liabilities banks have to raise the deposit rate. On the asset side of the balance sheet banks held reserves and a single kind of earning asset, A. The variable A, is a portmanteau variable designed for simplicity to include all earning assets held by banks. The rate of return on earning assets is the flexible, market-determined, interest rate, r_A; since no interest is paid by the central bank on bank-reserves these assets have a zero yield.

The model of the financial sector consists of three markets: the market for reserves, the market for earning assets and the market for demand deposits. By Walras' law we only need examine two of these markets. We shall solve the market for demand deposits and the market for reserves for the two unknown variables, r_D and r_A. With regard to the market for demand deposits we first specify the demand for deposits, D_d:

$$D_d = a_0 + a_1 (r_D - r_A) + s_d \qquad a_1 > 0 \qquad (1)$$

The demand for deposits is an increasing function of the interest differential $r_D - r_A$. The shift parameter s_d reflects a positive shift in the demand function. The supply of demand deposits, D_s, is specified as follows:

$$D_s = b_0 + b_1 [(1 - k)r_A - r_D] + s_s \qquad b_1 > 0 \qquad (2)$$

The supply of deposits is an increasing function of the net profit margin, $(1 - k) r_A - r_D$; the coefficient k represents the reserve requirement ratio. Further, the supply function depicts a shift parameter, s_s, which reflects a positive shift in the supply of demand deposits. Clearance of the deposit market requires that

$$D_d = D_s \qquad (3)$$

Substituting (1) and (2) into (3) results in the following expression for the deposit rate:

$$r_D = \frac{1}{(a_1 + b_1)} [(b_0 - a_0) + \{a_1 + b_1 (1 - k)\} r_A + b_2 s_s - a_2 s_d] \qquad (3a)$$

Substitution of (3a) in (1) or (2) gives the following expression for the amount of demand deposits:

$$D = \frac{1}{(a_1 + b_1)} [(a_0 b_1 + a_1 b_0) + (a_1 b_2 s_s + a_2 b_1 s_d) - a_1 b_1 k r_A] \qquad (3b)$$

The equation for clearance of the reserves market is:

$$RR + RE - RB - RNB = 0 \tag{4}$$

The first component of the demand for reserves – required reserves, RR – is equal to the ratio k multiplied by the amount of demand deposits:

$$RR = kD \tag{5}$$

For simplicity, we assume that the second component of the demand for reserves – excess reserves, RE – is constant:

$$RE = \overline{RE} \tag{6}$$

The supply of reserves also has two components, namely nonborrowed reserves, RNB, and borrowed reserves, RB. The former component is an instrument of monetary policy:

$$RNB = \overline{RNB} \tag{7}$$

The amount of borrowed reserves depends positively on the spread between the interest rate on earning assets, r_A, and the discount rate, d:

$$RB = c_0 + c_1(r_A - \bar{d}) \qquad c_1 > 0 \tag{8}$$

Substitution of (5) through (8) into (4) gives:

$$kD + \overline{RE} - c_0 - c_1(r_A - \bar{d}) - \overline{RNB} = 0 \tag{4a}$$

Applying Cramer's rule to equations (3a), (3b) and (4a), we can solve the full financial equilibrium values of the three endogenous variables, r_D^*, r_A^* and D^*:

$$r_D^* = \frac{(a_0 - b_0 + b_2 s_s - a_2 s_d)\,\{a_1 b_1 k^2 + c_1(a_1 + b_1)\} + N_2\{kN_1 - (a_1 + b_1)N_3\}}{(a_1 + b_1)N} \tag{9a}$$

$$r_A^* = \frac{kN_1 - (a_1 + c_1)N_3}{N} \tag{9b}$$

$$D^* = \frac{c_1 N_1 + a_1 b_1 k N_3}{N} \tag{9c}$$

with:
$$N_1 = \{(a_0 b_1 + a_1 b_0) + (a_1 b_2 s_s + a_2 b_1 s_d)\} > 0$$
$$N_2 = \{a_1 + b_1(1-k)\} > 0$$
$$N_3 = \overline{RNB} - \overline{RE} + c_0 - c_1 \bar{d}$$
$$N = \{a_1 b_1 k^2 + c_1(a_1 + b_1)\} > 0$$

With regard to equation (9c) it is important to notice that shifts in either the demand function or the supply function of demand deposits will result in a change in the quantity of demand deposits, D^*, and consequently in a change in the quantity of money.

The effects of a change in the shift parameters s_d and s_s, taken one at a time, on the three endogenous variables r_D^*, r_A^* and D^* can be determined by the respective derivatives of (9a), (9b) and (9c). Table 1 summarizes these qualitative effects. In addition this table presents the effects of the instrument variables $\overline{RNB}$ and $\bar{d}$.

On the basis of Table 1 we successively discuss the implications of shocks in the demand for and the supply of demand deposits. Within the framework of our model, the analysis of demand and supply shocks is restricted to the issue of financial innovation.

The demand shock can be applied to cases in which a negative shift in the demand for deposits and, hence, a fall in s_d is the consequence of cash-management techniques. By reducing money demand directly or by inducing the non-financial sector to economize on cash, these techniques cause an inward shift in the demand for deposits. Although demand shocks were considered prevalent in the pre-marketisation era, these shocks may occur in the present flexible-rate world as well. Next we discuss a positive shift in the supply of deposits, caused by cost-reducing financial innovations. This shock is unique with the new flexible-rate environment.

For, in the fixed-rate constellation that existed before the introduction of liability management, the supply of deposits did not play any active role in the determination of either the quantity of money or of interest rates. Therefore we give more attention to the case of the supply shock. Supply shocks reflect financial innovations on the production side of banking activities. Because of technological advances in data processing the marginal costs of servicing the demand deposits of banks and/or of managing their

Table 1. Effects of shift parameters and instrument variables on interest rates and deposits

Change in	Effect on		
	r_D^*	r_A^*	D^*
s_d	?	+	+
s_s	+	+	+
$\overline{RNB}$	−	−	+
$\bar{d}$	+	+	−

assets fall. Lower marginal costs induce banks to offer a greater quantity of deposits at the same interest rate r_D, which means that the supply curve of deposits shifts to the right. The increased supply of deposits causes a higher deposit rate, with the result that funds are attracted away from other assets. Therefore the rise in the deposit rate will force up the interest rate of earning assets, r_A. Inspection of equations (9a) through (9c) shows that the ultimate effect of a rise in s_s will be a greater quantity of money and higher interest rates.

It is important to emphasize that cost-reducing, supply-augmenting financial innovations are contractionary rather than expansionary. For, if nowadays interest rates – as was demonstrated in the preceding subsection – are the main transmission variables between the monetary and the real sector of the economy, a rise in the interest rate r_A will have a negative effect on economic activity and, hence, on nominal income. However, the increase in the quantity of money indicates an expansive effect on the economy. So we can conclude that monetary aggregates give a wrong signal to the central bank. This means that an increase in the quantity of money caused by an outward shift in the supply curve, may be interpreted as expansionary rather than contractionary, and vice versa. A very crucial qualification is that the wrong signal associated with a supply shock may be intensified by the practice of targeting monetary aggregates. This follows from the fact that, to the extent that the true source of the shift is not detected by the monetary authorities, they will try to eliminate the observed increase in the quantity of money.[8]

This induces the central bank to pursue a restrictive monetary policy, which will result in a further rise in interest rates. Thus, strict targeting of monetary aggregates may bring about unintentional damage to the economy. Because the actual target path has become more contractionary than originally intended, a flexible targeting policy should aim at an upward revision of the monetary target. Of course, this option is possible only if the central bank recognizes the true source of the shock. In this respect things have become more complicated for the monetary authorities, because nowadays the financial sector – as a result of the marketisation phenomenon – is exposed to more financial shocks than before. As previously noted, in the flexible rate environment, financial innovations can exert influence through the demand as well as through the supply side of the deposit market. Demand shocks also give a wrong signal to the central bank. Inspection of Table 1 shows that a negative shift in the demand for deposits results in a decrease in the quantity of money and a fall in the interest rate r_A. If the monetary authorities do not recognize the true source of the shock, they will wrongly interpret a reduction in the quantity of money as too contractionary. In that case the central bank will follow an expansionary monetary policy, generating a further fall in interest rates. So it can be stated that in case of financial shocks the correct monetary policy is the opposite of that suggested by targeting monetary aggregates.

It is evident that as a result of the marketisation of the financial sector there is an increased uncertainty about the meaning of the signals emitted by changes in the monetary aggregates. Furthermore, targeting monetary aggregates may cause additional damage to the economy.

SUMMARY AND CONCLUSIONS

This paper has shown that liability management and the concomitant introduction of variable rate lending have effectuated a transition to a new financial environment in which the interest rate is the dominant monetary transmission variable. In this flexible-rate world financial innovations can affect not only the demand side but also the supply side of the deposit market. These financial shocks emit wrong signals about changes in monetary aggregates to the central bank. In this respect the fundamental question which may be raised is to what extent financial innovations impair the effectiveness of money aggregate targeting. It has generally been accepted that the usefulness of monetary aggregates as an intermediate target depends largely on the stability and predictability of the velocity of money. In quantity-theory terminology financial shocks represent unpredicted changes in velocity. Therefore, shocks generated by financial innovations may seriously complicate the use of monetary targets. However, in our opinion these targets still can play a vital role in monetary policy, provided that the extent and frequency of financial shocks remain within reasonable bounds. We should like to stress that in a dynamic, innovative financial system, monetary targets have to be operated pragmatically. We do not believe in fixed, mechanistic, monetary rules. In addition to monetary target aggregates, the central bank should also pay attention to other monetary indicators, especially interest rates. We hasten to warn that we do not want to return to a regime of virtual interest pegging. In our view monetary growth rate targets have to be regarded as long-term targets. However financial shocks cause prediction errors with regard to the velocity of money and then interest rates can serve as indicators of these velocity shifts. Therefore, it may be advisable to supplement monetary growth targets with interest rates as a monetary indicator.

NOTES

1. For an extensive discussion of the theoretical foundations of monetary policy see J.J. Sijben, *Rational Expectations and Monetary Policy,* Alphen aan den Rijn, 1980, pp. 5–34.

2. M.G. Hadjimichalakis, *The Federal Reserve, Money, and Interest Rates,* New York, 1984, p. 153.

3. See also J.H. Koning, Financiële Innovatie en Monetaire Politiek, in J.H. Koning, G.P.L. van Roy, J.J. Sijben, *Zicht op Bancaire en Monetaire Wereld,* Liber Amicorum for Prof.Dr. H.W.J. Bosman, Leiden, 1984, pp. 187–206.

4. The term 'marketisation' has been introduced recently by T. Bingham in his interesting OECD-study: Banking and Monetary Policy (to be published). For a summary of this study see *Financial Market Trends,* October 1984, p. 16.

5. An extensive analysis of the micro-economic foundation, the macro-economic modeling and the empirical relevance of credit rationing is presented in J.H. Koning, *Kredietrantsoenering en onevenwichtigheid,* Tilburg, 1982.

6. J. Wenninger, Financial Innovation – A Complex Problem Even in a Simple Framework, *Quarterly Review Federal Reserve Bank of New York,* Summer 1984, p. 2. For more on this topic, see M. Akthar, Financial Innovations and their Implications for Monetary Policy: An International Perspective, *Bank for International Settlements,* December 1983, *Economic Papers* nr. 9, pp. 39–44.

7. Our analysis is mainly based on M. Hadjimichalakis, op. cit., especially chapters 6 and 7, and M. Hadjimichalakis, *Monetary Policy and Modern Money Markets,* Lexington, 1982, chapter 7.

8. Of course it is also possible that the monetary authorities do not recognize any shift in the supply curve at all.

Part F

REPORT ON THE COLLOQUIUM

Chapter XXII

GENERAL REPORT

by *Christopher Johnson*

THE EXTERNAL FRONTIERS

I begin by exploring the concept of the frontier on which the conference theme is based. Here I found Rybczynski's distinction between the external and the internal frontiers quite thought-provoking.

To look first at the external frontier, we can interpret this word in the sense well known to students of American history, the frontier, the Wild West. We think here of the conquest of new territory by some of the outlaws of the financial services industry, the loan sharks, the bucket shops, the slick operators, who open up the markets. They are followed in due course by the established order, the large commercial banks and so on. One could describe the start-up of new markets as something akin to the law of the gun. (In this context GUN stands for Grantor Underwritten Notes.)

Then we can look at the frontier in the sense in which the empire builders understood it, the great powers who set up colonies in distant parts, often disputing territory with each other. Here they found the kind of conflict which banks and indeed host countries often find when they are moving across frontiers. There is a choice when operating in foreign territory between going native – trying to follow the local customs – or expecting the foreign country to conform to what one does at home, which is usually called reciprocity. Somewhere between these two a compromise is found between the guest and the host. This serves to remind us that what is routine financial practice in one country is a rather upsetting form of innovation when it is exported to another.

Finally one could conceive of one world in which there were no frontiers any more. I gather from our Chairman that he expects this to be in about eighteen months time. Perhaps this is an example to the politicians of the speed with which they should move to set up one world. If this is happening it is more true of wholesale corporate banking and capital markets than it is of domestic retail banking, where countries' markets are still only mar-

Fair, D.E., (ed.) Shifting Frontiers in Financial Markets.
© *1986, Martinus Nijhoff Publishers, Dordrecht/Boston/Lancaster. ISBN 90-247-3225-5.*
Printed in the Netherlands.

ginally penetrable by each other and non-tariff barriers to trade are still very considerable. One must issue a warning about a world in which there are supposedly no frontiers. It was once the objective of the Organization of African Unity to have an Africa where all the old colonial frontiers were abolished. Alas, in these circumstances tribal warfare is apt to break out. People do not know where the frontier is, but that does not mean that they can live in amity with each other. In this kind of jungle warfare, the practice of head-hunting becomes increasingly common.

THE INTERNAL FRONTIERS

Now let us turn to the internal frontiers. One of these frontiers has been caricatured by being called the Chinese wall. As you all know if you have been to China, the Great Wall of China is now something internal which separates two bits of Chinese territory. There are two things you can observe about the Great Wall in China. One is that it is always falling down; many bits are in bad repair and always having to be reconstructed. The other is that the bit which is open to inspection to outsiders is in a most beautiful state of repair and looks quite impossible to get through.

The Chinese wall is one justification of specialization. If you specialize you do not need a Chinese wall because you are separate in the first place. Some of what is happening now seems to impose the obligation to build Chinese walls where none were necessary before, when you bring together different activities between which there are conflicts of interest under one corporate roof.

Another kind of internal frontier exists in the political organisation of a federal State. Some conglomerates are like federations. You have the central governing body, which may be a one bank holding company with interests in many other fields, in United States terms. There is a large degree of autonomy for the separate States of the Federation. This indeed is regarded as being operationally desirable. It gives each of them more initiative to do its own thing. From the supervisory point of view it may encourage the separability of capital resources, and responsibility to different supervisors.

Then we have the antithetic model of the unitary state, in which everything is being done by one large organization, and where the benefits of synergy are being reaped, in distinction to the Chinese wall model, where you are more worried about conflicts of interest. The universal bank from German practice, and many other banks in other countries, are now behaving like universal banks in a unitary State model. We must expect that in other parts of the financial services world we shall have a kind of Balkanization, where we have a lot of small concerns existing together, sometimes happily, sometimes not. That does seem to be an equally valid model for some parts of the financial industry in the future.

SCOPE OF FRONTIERS

Let us see what kind of concepts these frontiers apply to. Are we talking about frontiers between financial institutions? I suspect that this is mainly what is in our minds. Here we need to remind ourselves of all the different types of institutions which are involved. There are the major commercial banks, investment or merchant banks, which are often separate, savings institutions, the central banks themselves, insurance companies, pension funds, brokers, jobbers and so one could go on, including organizations such as retailers, which fall outside the conventional boundaries of the financial services industry.

We could also look at frontiers between different financial instruments, the degree to which finance is done in one form or in another. We can think of bank loans which may be at fixed or variable interest rates, or bonds which may again be at fixed or variable rates. We can think of equities. We can think of different currency assets and liabilities, and how the frontiers are changing between all these different financial instruments. It is also relevant to think in terms of financial functions, irrespective of the institution which carries them out or the instrument through which they are carried out. We have the functions for example of money transmission, money changing, deposit taking, investment management, lending, underwriting, guaranteeing, syndicating, placing, swapping, broking, and so one could go on.

Finally, as long time addicts of the flow of funds, still trying to explain the residual errors, we can look at this in terms of the way all the assets and liabilities in a country or in the world are broken down between the different flow of funds sectors, the public, personal, business and overseas sectors, and the changing frontiers between these sectors in the issuing of liabilities or the holding of assets.

In the simplest kind of system we have a one to one correspondence between the institution, the instrument, the function and the sector which is lending or borrowing. The paradigm of this is the old style UK building society. You have a particular specialized institution which creates a specialized instrument, the home mortgage, for a particular purpose – financing house building – and both the assets and liabilities are nearly all vis-a-vis the household sector. In a complex system you have as it were a blank which you can fill in by anything you like at each stage of the description. For example you may have a stockbroker who arranges a note issuance facility, which is a claim on a government by a corporation. But any other institution could have arranged it, the stockbroker could have carried out many other functions with regard to it, it could have been one of many different instruments other than a note issuance facility, it could have been a claim on any suitably rated borrower, and the holding of the asset can shift around in the secondary market. Those are two extreme cases, between which we could classify all of our different financial processes.

REASONS FOR CHANGE

I want to list what seem to be the reasons for the changes in financial frontiers. First of all we have the changing *economic climate,* the high variability of variables such as inflation, economic growth, fixed investment, interest rates, and exchange rates, and the wish to avoid risk which this uncertainty creates. The Governor of the Bank of England reminded us that it is all very well to talk about shifting risk or laying off risk, but you do not necessarily reduce the total amount of risk in the system. The risk is going to end up somewhere, maybe with governments, maybe with large banks. It is a good question to ask where the risk has ended up.

Then we have changes in *regulation.* These may be monetary controls or supervisory regimes. Many financial innovations, or frontier changes, have been due to the desire to evade what seemed like irksome regulations. It is possible that regulation will once again shift the frontier back. If a practice in response to regulation was thought to be undesirable in the first place, then the fact that somebody has managed to do it is not necessarily an argument for legitimizing it by fresh regulation. It may be an argument for tightening up.

Then we have increasing *competition* in financial services. This may lead to greater concentration, which in its turn will diminish the competition. Even in an oligopolistic regime, according to many standard economic models, competition can be quite severe. It is worth remembering the recent model presented by Baumol of what he calls contestation, which is a new kind of competition. If entry into a certain industry is easy and fixed costs are low, then even if there are very few firms in an industry, as long as it is possible for new entrants to make raids on that industry, we have many of the characteristics of competition.

There is new *technology*. We are talking not only about computers but about telecommunications technology. There are many debates over what the advantages are. Does new technology give the advantage of scale, does it make this essential, or does it on the other hand permit quite small units to compete if they have access to it?

We have the search to increase *profits*. Some of the uncertainties have tended to depress profits in the financial services industry. There has therefore been a stimulus to seek new sources of profit to make up for some of the provisions, some of the risks incurred in old types of business. The way in which commercial banks have tried to move into investment banking or merchant banking to find non-asset based sources of income is an example of this.

Finally financial *innovation* itself has caused a lot of changes in frontiers. It is not identical with the shifting of frontiers. Innovation is conceivable within a totally unchanging structure, but it is probably less likely. For example, in Germany, where you have the universal bank structure, it is arguable that the innovation in terms of financial instruments has been less than where you had changing structures.

COMMISSION I. CAUSES OF CHANGE AND INNOVATION IN THE MIX OF FINANCIAL INSTRUMENTS

The main trends which seemed to emerge from our discussions were first the tendency for corporate borrowers to borrow more at the short than at the long end of the market. This has been the trend in the United States, as Lawler showed us with his figures for the diminution in the number of twenty-year corporate bonds, corresponding to an increase in the issue of commercial paper, even more than short bank lending.

In the UK we have seen a similar trend, as Bain reminded us in his paper. Corporations have borrowed more from banks, and the medium to long term corporate bond market has become inactive. There has also been some increase in borrowing in commercial bills in the UK. This is attributed to very high nominal interest rates and to uncertainty about both inflation and real interest rates. The borrower fears that if inflation falls, as indeed it has been doing, rather unexpectedly, the real rate of interest on a fixed loan will be too onerous.

The second tendency is that governments have increasingly, in contrast to corporations, been borrowing at the longer end of the market rather than at the shorter end. This again was shown in the papers by Lawler and Bain. In the UK there is a demand for risk-free long term assets by insurance funds justifying the government's policy. In the US it seems to be due rather more to the rising federal deficit and the desire to avoid having to re-finance debt in the short to medium term. The contrast between the two countries is one between over-funding by the government at the long end of the market in the UK in excess of its borrowing requirement, while in the US if anything the tendency has been to under-funding, to try to catch up with the rising deficit. In both cases the effect has been the same. There has been crowding out of the corporate sector at the long end of the bond market, and in the US at any rate quite a sharp rise in the yield curve.

The third trend is the preference for variable rather than fixed interest rates by corporations. This is a point independent of the maturity of the debt. It is possible for example to have a system in which there is an increase in medium-term bond finance but at variable rates. This seems to have been the case in France recently. As Bruneel showed in his paper, the bond market for both the public sector and the corporate sector has taken off just in the last year, but there has been a particular increase in variable rate bonds as a form of finance. The banks themselves are involved in both issuing and holding bonds, so it is not necessarily a form of disintermediation.

Finally the other trend related to all these is that in certain sectors there has been a substitution of bond for bank loan finance much more on the part of the public sector as issuer than the corporate sector. This clearly helps monetary control. It keeps down bank deposits in the system and it helps to finance deficits, whether public or corporate, in a non-inflationary manner. One may wonder in the case of the UK whether this has not been carried too far by the practice of over-funding, which has tended to raise interest rates at the long end of the market. In the UK there is a new measure in the Budget permitting the issue of one to five year corporate bonds. This may well prove to be a more beneficial form of monetary control, if corporations resort to a relatively short bond instead of bank loan finance.

Another trend has been innovation in the type of instrument issued. We were given a good example by Lawler of something known as 'STRIPS'. This may sound like something from a Wild West saloon. It does in fact stand for Separate Trading of Interest and Principal of Securities. We have a whole menagerie of new instruments which is being issued by the smart New York investment firms such as CATS, COUGARS, LIONS AND

TIGERS. We also have an alphabet soup of BONUSES, GUNS, RUFS AND SNIFS. I hope some of you know what some of those are. This illustrates the degree to which banks are prepared to go in suiting the preference of the customer. That at least is the story of the banks. Sometimes I think they are trying too to justify the very high fees which they pay people on the investment banking side to devise ever more weird and wonderful new instruments. I am tempted to say: 'I do not know if it confuses the customer, but it certainly confuses me.'

We have a trend towards new equity instruments in the small to medium sized company sector. This may be wishful thinking. I was not sure in reading Schmidt's paper about small company equities how much of this was actually going on in Germany, but there are markets, such as the London Unlisted Securities Market, where at least a start is being made in following the US tradition, a much more vigorous tradition of equity issuing and holding. Here the tax treatment may be a very important factor. One is reminded of schemes such as the UK Business Expansion Scheme, which give perhaps an excessive tax incentive to set up and hold shares in small companies. If it is being done mainly for the sake of the tax saving rather than for the ultimate objective, then one might regard it as being a distortion in what is otherwise a desirable direction.

We can also see, looking at financial instruments, the extent to which some countries are catching up and telescoping twenty years of progress into two or three years. They have the model of the United States and the international markets. Wissén's paper showed how much had happened in Sweden since CD's were allowed in 1980. We are all very much aware of the way in which Japan is in a very measured way introducing many of the financial instruments which have long been well known in other parts of the world. The Governor did say that he found the Japanese caution understandable in not wishing too suddenly to open their markets to too many unfamiliar and uncontrollable practices.

Finally, something which is so familiar that we hardly need reminding of it is the extent to which international instruments are being used in preference to those available in domestic markets. Lawler showed us how US corporations had been using the Eurobond market since the repeal of withholding tax, which some people thought would have the opposite effect. This ties in with the earlier point about the response to regulation. International instruments and markets have developed as a way round national regulations. This in its turn acts as a stimulus to domestic markets to deregulate if they are not to lose business to international markets. One of these markets which is extremely interesting at the moment is that in the

ECU, the European Currency Unit. I have quite seriously put forward to one of the commissions here the idea that if the dollar goes on falling, and US interest rates rise, the US Treasury might even be tempted to finance some of its foreign debt in ECU's.

COMMISSION II. THE COST OF CAPITAL FUNDS AND THE FINANCING OF GROWTH

Commission II in some ways seemed to be a bit of an outlier. Some people, including members of the commission, were not sure what it had to do with the rest of the conference. They nevertheless became involved in the most fascinating academic debates, parts of which were conducted in French and parts of which relied on a very deep knowledge of Swedish economic thought. There is some fascinating material there on the interest theories of Fisher, Keynes and Wicksell. The justification for Commission II is that it is the high real interest rates we have had in recent years which have triggered off many of the changes in the financial markets. Therefore some explanation is called for as to why real interest rates are so high.

One explanation that was put forward by Adam and Farber in their paper was that you really could not explain real interest rates thanks to unanticipated inflation, but they vary randomly, because unanticipated inflation is a white noise process. If we could anticipate inflation correctly, then real interest rates would be remarkably constant. It is the fact that we cannot do so which makes them vary. The problem was raised of what happens if expectations are asymmetrical as between lenders and borrowers. One should not assume that lenders and borrowers all use the same forecasting bureaus. Sometimes they pick forecasting bureaus which correspond to their own prejudices.

There is another explanation put forward by Gebauer, basing himself on Irving Fisher, that real interest rates tend to fluctuate inversely with the inflation rate. Usually one finds that the elasticity of nominal interest rates with regard to inflation is very much less than one; it might be about one half. The story appears to be that when inflation rises very sharply people fail to anticipate the full extent of the rise. But by the time the rise has occurred they are then already expecting inflation to fall again because of action that has been taken by the authorities to control it. There may well be a parallel process when inflation is falling. People fail to forecast how rapidly and low inflation is going to fall and they therefore ex ante demand what turn out to be rather high ex post real interest rates. Once inflation has fallen it is very difficult to make people expect that it will remain as low or that it will go on falling. The expectation may well be that inflation, having bottomed out, will rise again. There are many reasons why this might happen, particularly in the United States. On the basis of future expectations about inflation at this moment, one might say that ex ante real rates are not all that high.

There is another phenomenon at work here. This is the effect of lower inflation on the savings ratio, which is generally, at least in Europe, to lower it, tending to make savings more scarce. Therefore depositors are in a position to demand higher interest rates, which in their turn may cause saving to rise slightly again.

The other explanation which Develle put forward, among those which he touched on, were the very high and rising levels of debt, both public and corporate, and the fact that the debt:income ratio has been rising in countries such as the United States and Japan. When this happens the markets see the vicious spiral. The authorities need to finance ever rising debt interest by borrowing more and more. Markets therefore expect that the debt will be partly monetized in future, and that this will lead to inflation. Their inflation expectations rise and again real rates ex ante are not as high as ex post.

Finally, the process of deregulation itself has done something to raise interest rates, simply by letting them move up to market clearing levels, notably in US banking.

COMMISSION III. IMPLICATIONS FOR FINANCIAL
INSTITUTIONS

This is the most topical part of the discussion, particularly as regards the changing scene in the City of London. There are several different processes going on. One is that of outright takeover of one institution or one type of institution by another. In Aspinwall's paper he suggested that the economies of scale, among conglomerates especially, were so far unproven. The ability of management trained in one department of financial services to cope successfully with quite different kinds of financial service has yet to be fully tested. The adequacy of capital is another problem in conglomerates. If they have to be capitalized separately with regard to each of their activities, then the financial advantages of conglomeration seem rather thin. Indeed there may be disadvantages taking the form of a kind of contagion of one part of the conglomerate if the other fails, I would remind you of the sad story of Johnson Matthey Bankers. A perfectly good gold trading subsidiary in the group was instantly contaminated by the failure of the bank in the group. This led to the rescue operation, which might otherwise not have been necessary.

We also get frontier raids by institutions into each other's territory, not takeovers but simply doing each other's kind of business. In this way in the UK, banks have moved into the home mortgage business, and building societies have reacted by moving into money transmission. They would indeed, as Gilchrist showed in his paper, like to move into many other areas such as have been described in the recent Green Paper; unsecured consumer loans, second mortgages, agency services. Freedman in his paper on Canada showed how the trust companies, which are similar to building societies or American thrifts, are moving into the consumer loan business. There interestingly the growth of mortgage assets has proved inadequate, because there is not the same tax discrimination in favour of mortgage loans as against consumer loans that we have in the UK.

The other main kind of frontier raid is that which goes on between commercial banking and investment banking. You have the frontier set up by the Glass/Steagall Act, which has been outflanked in all sorts of ways. This process is also taking place in London. The major clearing banks all have some kind of merchant banking activity. They are now moving further into this field by taking over stockbrokers and stockjobbers. One of the problems is that, even if there is not a total merger or takeover, if two firms exist within the same group which have enormous differences of culture and remuneration level, it can be very difficult to co-exist. One implication of all this additional competition for institutions is that their products are tending to become more and more alike. There is no longer what you might call the dedication of interest terms to particular purposes or institutions which Cotula cited in his paper about Italian banking. There is a tendency now for bank deposits to take on the same characteristics as building society savings deposits with similar interest rates and for current accounts to be remunerated on the same sort of terms as deposit accounts.

I would hope that we might move towards a system like the Swedish universal account where there is just one structure of deposit rates and the remuneration of the account depends on the size of the deposit and the number of transactions carried out. This might well simplify matters for the consumer faced with a bewildering array of products.

The effect of new technology on institutions was described by Revell in his paper. He opened up the interesting possibility that because of the need to share technology, which is sometimes imposed by the public authorities, it would be possible for quite small firms to take advantage of it. The indivisibility of the large capital cost which can only be incurred by the large institution could be overcome in this way.

Technology also opens up the possibility that institutions can franchise new forms of technology, and thus in a different way allow smaller institutions to participate. It may be that in future the main scarce resource in banking will not be money, which often seems to be very plentiful and to attract a very low spread, but technology. Whoever has access to an exclusive form of new technology and can exploit it may well make the principal profit.

Revell, in his paper, opened up the interesting possibility that the CHAPS system of same day settlement in the London market, made possible by new technology, might have been called the Financial Institutions Settlement House. Taken together with its equivalent, CHIPS, in New York, we could have had FISH and CHIPS. But alas it was not to be, it is CHIPS and CHAPS.

The other trend is the marketization of financial instruments. This was described in Rybczynski's Three Ages of Financial Markets, rather a Toynbeean general theory of the evolution of financial institutions. He pointed out that many financial market services now consist not just in holding the asset but in creating the asset in the first place, the issuing function, and in trading it, the broking or secondary market function. This explains the desire of banks to move into this field. It goes with the move from liability management, when the growth of assets was unbounded, to asset management, when banks are trying to achieve desired capital ratios by selling or trading assets and putting them on the books of other institutions.

To sum up on Commission III, we have twin processes; at the same time concentration in some areas, and fragmentation or unbundling of services and functions in others. We also have a withdrawal from certain types of cross-border lending, one could call this a ·frontier too far – and the rediscovery of the home market; of retail banking, investment banking, and treasury operations by large international banks which have decided to reduce their international exposure.

COMMISSION IV. IMPLICATIONS FOR MONETARY CONTROL AND THE SUPERVISION OF FINANCIAL INSTITUTIONS

These turned out to be two rather separate topics. Thygesen, in his introductory paper, reminded us of some of the possible targets which monetary control might use. He was in favour of targeting monetary base and the exchange rate. In a paper by Koning the idea of an interest rate indicator – rather out of fashion but one to which governments do tend to subscribe whether or not they admit it – was also outlined. Thygesen's idea for a broader target was that of total credit. I myself, being more of a Radcliffian, might have preferred something like broad private sector liquidity, a liability target. The point of these broad targets is that they should abstract from shifts in the composition of the monetary aggregate to which any intermediate aggregate such as our sterling M3 is subject. Liabilities cross the frontier between different definitions of money supply with bewildering rapidity.

Goodhart pointed out in what we should call Goodhart's Second Law that innovation does not make money impossible to control, but makes it very difficult to define what it is that you are controlling. I would add to this that innovation, if it can be roughly predicted, can be accommodated within the scope of monetary targetry. This was the problem which the Federal Reserve had. They dealt with it with remarkably few failures. If you can predict the growth rate of money market funds, if you can define which aggregate they are counted in and which they are excluded from, then, if you can have a good shot at predicting them, you can set a target on the basis of your predictions which you can attempt to control. There is still the problem of prediction, not only of the growth of new instruments, but of the actual origination of them within a target period. The main difficulty for monetary control has been the conceptual one that so many bank liabilities now combine savings characteristics with transactions characteristics. There is an economy, in that the depositor does not have to have two separate kinds of account; one will fulfil his purpose. This means that the velocity of many broad aggregates is tending to fall as people increase their savings with income. On the other hand the velocity of the narrower aggregates will tend to rise as the cashless society comes in. In so far as these narrower aggregates consist mainly of banknotes and coins their velocity will rise, which makes them the dream of every monetary regulator. He can then have a target which is growing more slowly than almost anything else in the economy, and will be easy to control.

Monetary control has a philosophical objection posed to it by the growth of competition in financial markets. There is the paradox that while freeing everything else in financial markets you are trying to control one key variable, which is money. I have always thought that this was a flaw at the heart of the Thatcherite approach to monetary control, as it is in fact at the deepest level incompatible with total freedom in financial markets.

To turn to supervision, this was one of the main themes of the Governor. Therefore one can consider what he said together with Commission IV. The Governor was concerned about the 'big bang' in the London markets, which will be triggered off by the ending of minimum commissions in the Stock Exchange. Having quoted last week from Beatrix Potter, this week he quoted from Gilbert and Sullivan and said: 'The policeman's lot is not a happy one'. He described his task as 'trying to get the right balance between safety on the one hand and experimental growth in development on the other' and he said that this was 'never easy'. He quoted as an example the way in which banks are responding to the call by supervisors to improve their capital ratios by getting their assets off the balance sheet in the way that I described. Here there are dangers that there will still be contingent liabilities even where items are off the balance sheet. One of the themes which I would have hoped to see discussed more here was that of transferring some bank assets or at least the risk attaching to them to the insurance sector, which on the whole is more plentifully endowed with capital than the banking sector. An attempt by Citibank to insure its loans with Cigna came to nothing. There is the alternative option being pursued in some areas of packaging loans and selling them to insurance companies or pension funds.

The Governor called for self-imposed prudential restraint and he then wondered whether that would make the supervisors superfluous if everybody was prepared to supervise themselves. The answer is: 'No, it would not', because the presence of a supervisor is always a deterrent. As is the case with all deterrents, one hopes that it will seldom if ever need to be used. The presence of the deterrent is an important spur to self-regulation.

The other points which came out of Commission IV on supervision were, first of all, what is going on in the supervisory industry, which in some ways parallels what is going on in the financial services industry. Supervisors are having to work together more closely. One might wonder whether, if there are going to be large conglomerates, the supervision process itself should not be united under one management. The UK has already got off to a false start by creating both the Securities and Investments Board and the Marketing of Investments Board, with related but separate responsibilities.

When this proposal was originally made the government wondered whether it would not have been better to have one board. They have nevertheless created two, and there potential conflicts can arise.

One can discuss what the supervisor's stance should be towards change. Is he going to have an incentive to play safe to avoid being charged with bank collapses? This, as the Governor pointed out, may now well be the trend in the United States. Or is the supervisor going to allow financial companies to make their own mistakes and learn by trial and error, with all the attendant risks to the stability of the system if fairly large organizations make fairly large mistakes? Or do we have the third possibility that, as has happened in many areas of utility regulation in the United States, the supervisor is captured by his customers and simply acts as a kind of voice within the government for acceding to customers' requests for ever greater freedom of operation?

One unintended function of supervision has been to stimulate innovation with the purpose of circumventing the supervision. One remembers the secondary banks in the UK, and loan production offices, which are a form of branching across State lines, in the United States. The authorities have the difficult choice between either sanctioning the breach of the original regulations by deregulating and making it above board or, if they think the practice was undesirable in the first place, they have the option of reregulating and terminating something which they never intended to happen. In the UK the 1979 Banking Act is an example of reregulation – tightening up on the licensed or previously unlicensed deposit takers – after the deregulation of Competition and Credit Control.

COSTS AND BENEFITS

In concluding, I want to look more broadly at some of the costs and benefits of this whole process. Akhtar's paper was an extremely helpful survey of some of the arguments. The extension of credit facilities and money transmission facilities to wider sections of the population is one clear benefit from the extension of financial frontiers. The countries which have been rather backward in this area, such as France and Japan, may expect to show the most benefit from the process. Even in the UK the extension of bank accounts to people who hold only building societies accounts may have some benefit attached to it, although the building societies are trying hard to improve their service so that there is no longer a benefit.

We have the questionable advantage of higher interest rates. They are good for savers and bad for borrowers. One might say that these two balance each other out, but there are credit risks attached to industry which may have much wider consequences for society as a whole, including the depositors. They may be savers getting high rates of interest, but they are also employees dependent on the financial health of the corporate sector or the public sector for their jobs.

We also have a tendency, together with higher interest rates, to lower spreads. Spreads are being competed away in many areas. Bank margins are at risk. They are sometimes being raised by asset growth and by the addition of non-interest income or the lowering of non-interest costs. There is nevertheless a threat to the financial stability of the system if some of the larger institutions are not able to withstand the competition.

We have the advantages of new technology which is cutting transactions costs. As Akhtar pointed out it does also cut the float in the system, which has been a great advantage to individuals. Similarly point of sale technology may mean that people have to pay immediately for their purchases in shops instead of getting an interest-free grace period attaching to their credit cards.

Undoubtedly, the wider choice of instruments and institutions available to the customer for financial services offers some advantages. It may also carry with it the risk of confusion and inability to distinguish clearly between the characteristics of competing products. In some ways the fixed price *table d'hote* menu is a lot simpler than the elaborate *à la carte* with a separate price for every dish, particularly if the menus are in a foreign language. There is a danger that financial institutions, by trying to keep up with the competition, are entering into what one might call by medical analogy 'a hyper-active syndrome'. This is not necessarily a sign of good health. One is reminded of the poor foreign exchange dealers who have to stay up all night, maybe by a screen, maybe by a phone, dealing with trades in every market all over the world. Ultimately there must be some bound to this process.

Finally, we should all question ourselves about the human capital, to say nothing of the other resources which are being invested in the financial services industry. We must think of the opportunity cost of these resources and what they would bring in the way of a return if they were invested elsewhere in the economy, in industry particularly. Enormous resources of ingenuity are being put into the financial services industry for what may turn out to be rather a marginal return, in many cases at very high salaries. Perhaps the ultimate objective of a good financial system, after all the upheavals and changes, should be that it would rather unobtrusively, using fairly low grade bank clerks or even robots, serve the needs of the growth of the rest of the economy, rather than the needs of its own self-aggrandize-ment. I end with a Latin tag which I think many people in financial services need to be reminded of: 'Ars est celare artem'. We do not often hide what we are doing quite enough. We make a big song and dance about it. Perhaps we should, like Keynes, think what a nice world it would be if economists and financiers would just be reduced to the role of humble technicians like dentists.

FINANCIAL AND MONETARY POLICY STUDIES

1. Multinational Enterprises – Financial and Monetary Aspects.
   Editors: J.S.G. Wilson and C.F. Scheffer, with 16 contributors.
   1974. ISBN 90-286-0124-4
   (SUERF Colloquium Nottingham University, England, April 1973)
2. Floating Exchange Rates – The Lessons of Recent Experience.
   Editors: H. Fournier and J.E. Wadsworth, with 14 contributors.
   1976. ISBN 90-286-0565-7
   (SUERF Colloquium Venice, October 1974)
3. The Development of Financial Institutions in Europe, 1956–76.
   Editors: J.E. Wadsworth, J.S.G. Wilson and F. Fournier, with 26 contributors.
   1977. ISBN 90-286-0337-9
   (SUERF Colloquium Brussels, April 1976)
4. New Approaches in Monetary Policy.
   Editors: J.E. Wadsworth and F. Léonard de Juvigny, with 29 contributors.
   1979. ISBN 90-286-0848-6
   (SUERF Colloquium Wiesbaden, September 1977)
5. Europe and the Dollar in the World-wide Disequilibrium.
   Editor: J.R. Sargent, with 17 contributors.
   1981. ISBN 90-286-0700-5
   (SUERF Colloquium Basel, Switzerland, May 1979)
6. Bank Management in a Changing Domestic and International Environment: The Challenges of the Eighties.
   Editors: Donald E. Fair and F. Léonard de Juvigny, with 25 contributors.
   1982. ISBN 90-247-2606-9
   (SUERF Colloquium Helsingør, Denmark, October 1980)
7. International Lending in a Fragile World Economy.
   Editors: Donald E. Fair in co-operation with Raymond Bertrand, with 25 contributors.
   1983. ISBN 90-247-2809-6
   (SUERF Colloquium Vienna, April 1982)
8. Currency Competition and Monetary Union.
   Editor: Pascal Salin.
   1984. ISBN 90-247-2817-7
9. Government Policies and the Working of Financial Systems in Industrialized Countries.
   Editors: Donald E. Fair in co-operation with F. Léonard de Juvigny, with 24 contributors.
   1984. ISBN 90-247-3076-7
10. Jelle Zijlstra, A Central Banker's View.
    Editors: C. Goedhart, G.A. Kessler, J. Kymmell and F. de Roos.
    1985. ISBN 90-247-3184-4
11. Monetary Conditions for Economic Recovery.
    Editors: C. van Ewijk and J.J. Klant.
    1985. ISBN 90-247-3219-0
12. Shifting Frontiers in Financial Markets.
    Editor: D.E. Fair.
    1986. ISBN 90-247-3225-5.